kimi ni todoke

From Me to You

Vol. 11

Story & Art by
Karuho Shiina

Volume 11

Contents

Story Thus Far

Sawako Kuronuma has always been a loner. Though not by choice, this optimistic 16-year-old girl can't seem to make any friends. Stuck with the unfortunate nickname "Sadako" after the haunting movie character, rumors about her summoning spirits have been greatly exaggerated. With her shy personality and scary looks, most of her classmates will barely talk to her, much less look into her eyes for more than three seconds lest they be cursed. Thanks to Kazehaya, who always treats her nicely, Sawako makes her first friends at school, Ayane and Chizu.

Since Sawako is not used to people being nice to her, she has trouble understanding Kazehaya's feelings toward her and tells him she's afraid their classmates will misunderstand their relationship. Kazehaya thinks his confession is making her stressed out. However, Ayane and Chizu encourage Sawako to tell Kazehaya about her feelings for him and she does. The two finally express their feelings for each other and start a relationship. While Sawako feels a dreamy happiness, Chizu tells her some girls are upset about it. That reminds Sawako about Kurumi. She goes to Kurumi to make things clear between the two of them...

Kimi ni todoke
From Me to You

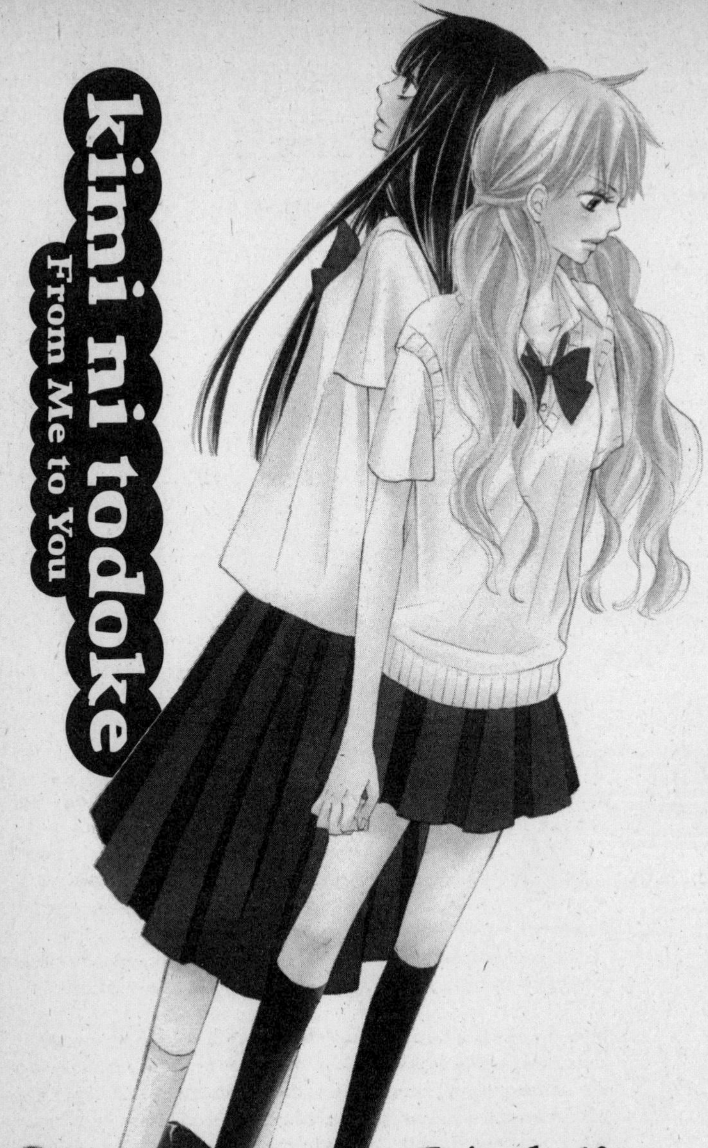

Episode 43: Because of You

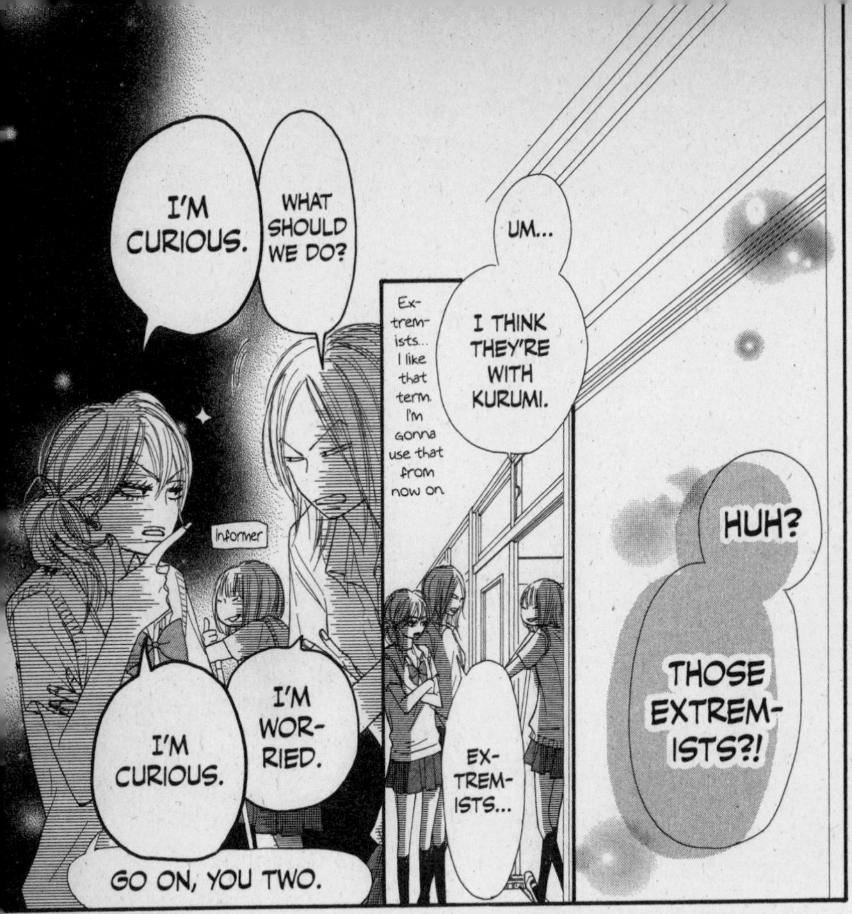
HUH?
THOSE EXTREM-ISTS?!
UM...
I THINK THEY'RE WITH KURUMI.
Ex-trem-ists... I like that term. I'm gonna use that from now on.
EX-TREM-ISTS...
WHAT SHOULD WE DO?
I'M CURIOUS.
I'M WOR-RIED.
I'M CURIOUS.
Informer
GO ON, YOU TWO.

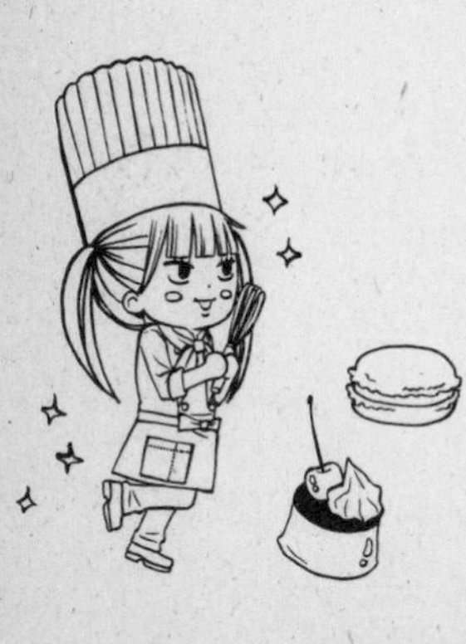

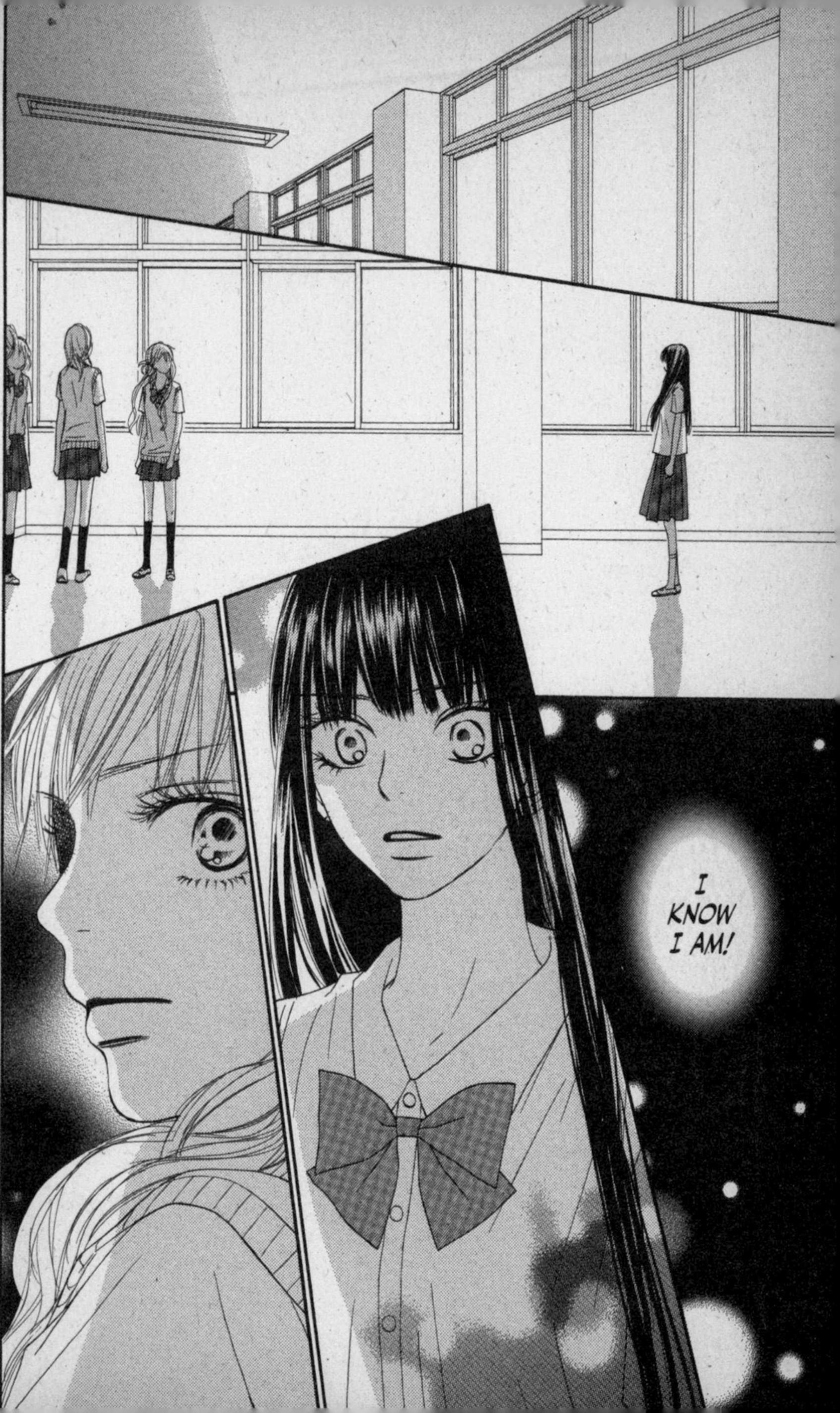
I KNOW I AM!

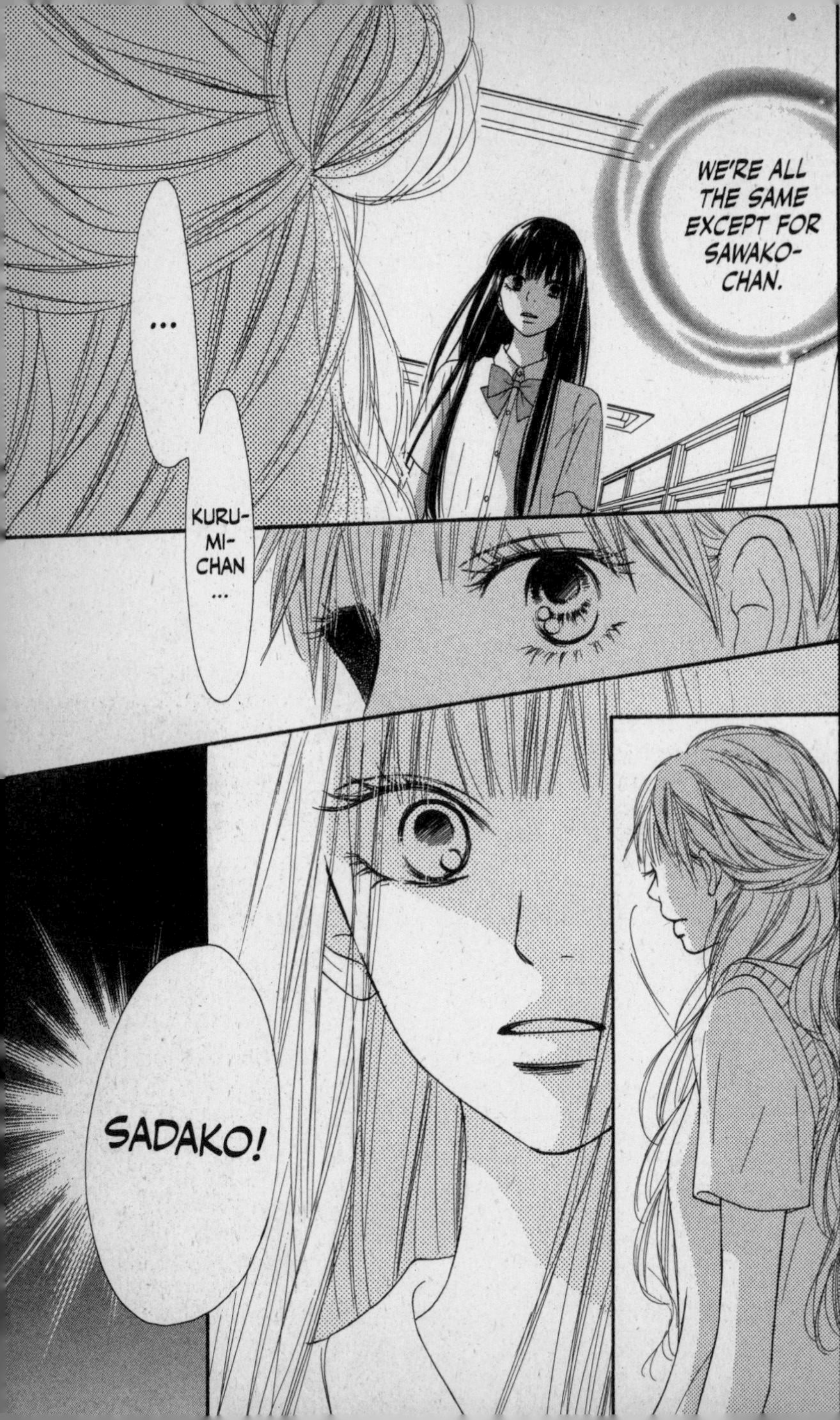
WE'RE ALL THE SAME EXCEPT FOR SAWAKO-CHAN.
...
KURUMI-CHAN...
SADAKO!

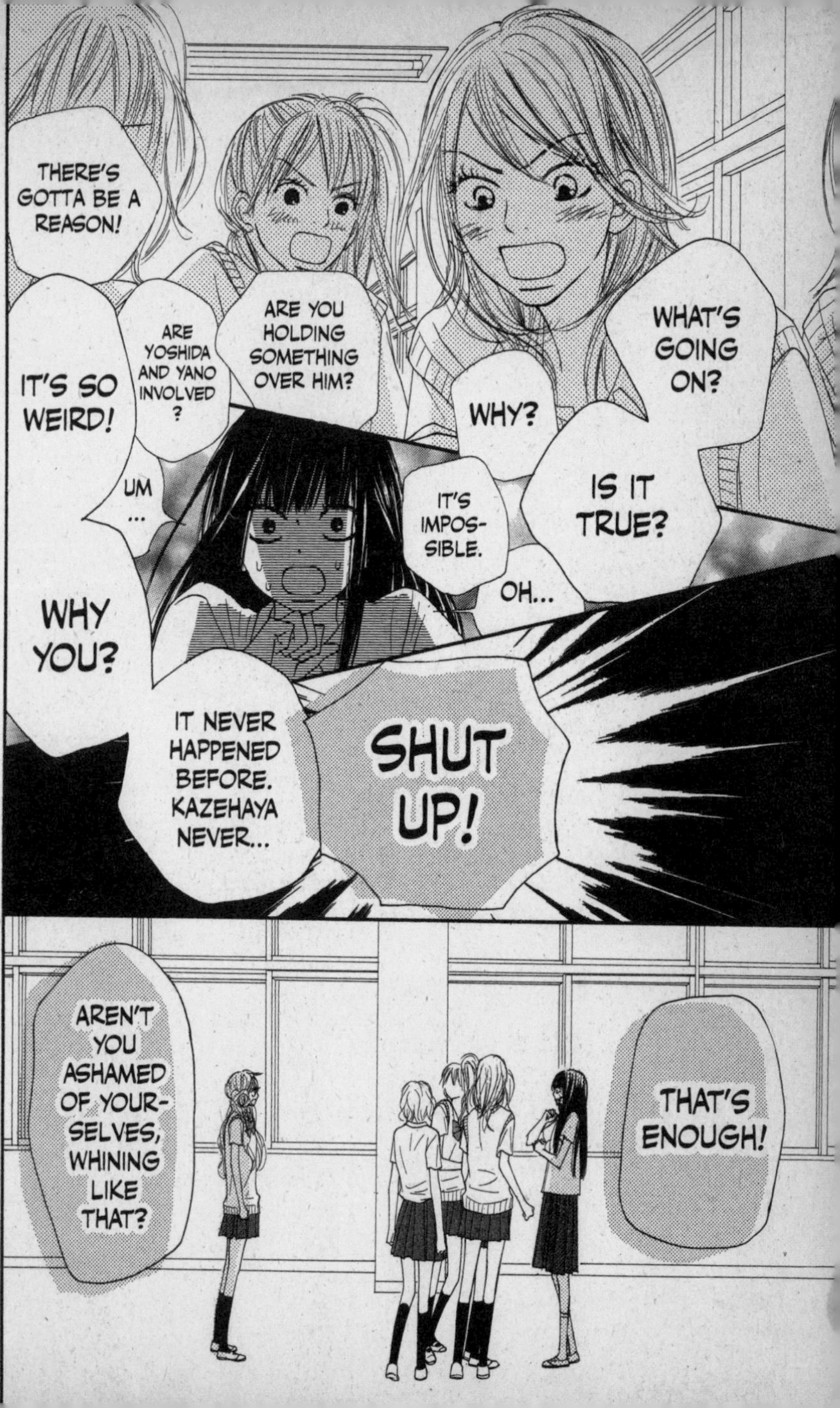
WHAT'S GOING ON?
THERE'S GOTTA BE A REASON!
ARE YOU HOLDING SOMETHING OVER HIM?
ARE YOSHIDA AND YANO INVOLVED?
WHY?
IS IT TRUE?
IT'S SO WEIRD!
IT'S IMPOSSIBLE.
UM...
OH...
WHY YOU?
IT NEVER HAPPENED BEFORE. KAZEHAYA NEVER...
SHUT UP!
THAT'S ENOUGH!
AREN'T YOU ASHAMED OF YOURSELVES, WHINING LIKE THAT?

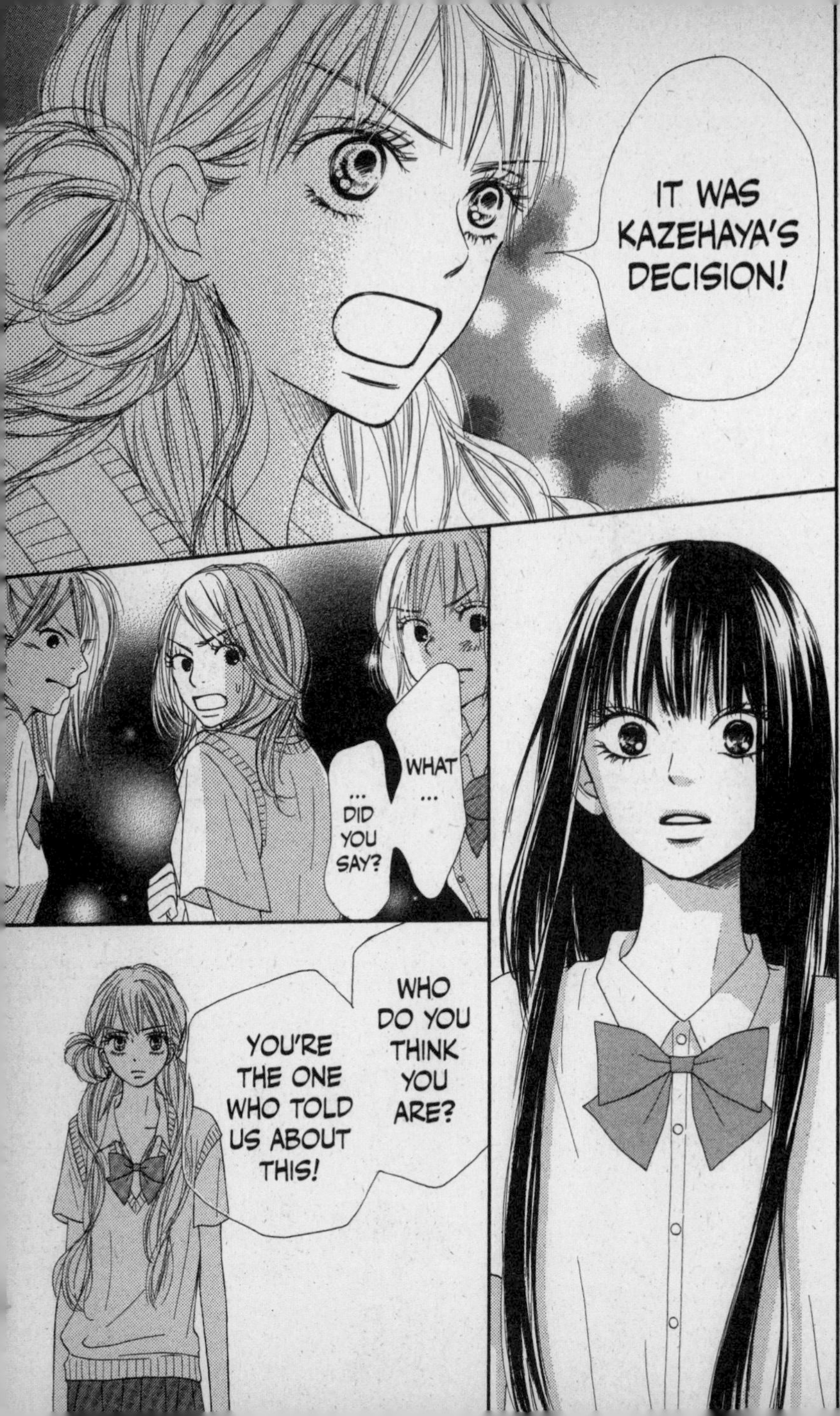
IT WAS KAZEHAYA'S DECISION!
WHAT ...
... DID YOU SAY?
WHO DO YOU THINK YOU ARE?
YOU'RE THE ONE WHO TOLD US ABOUT THIS!

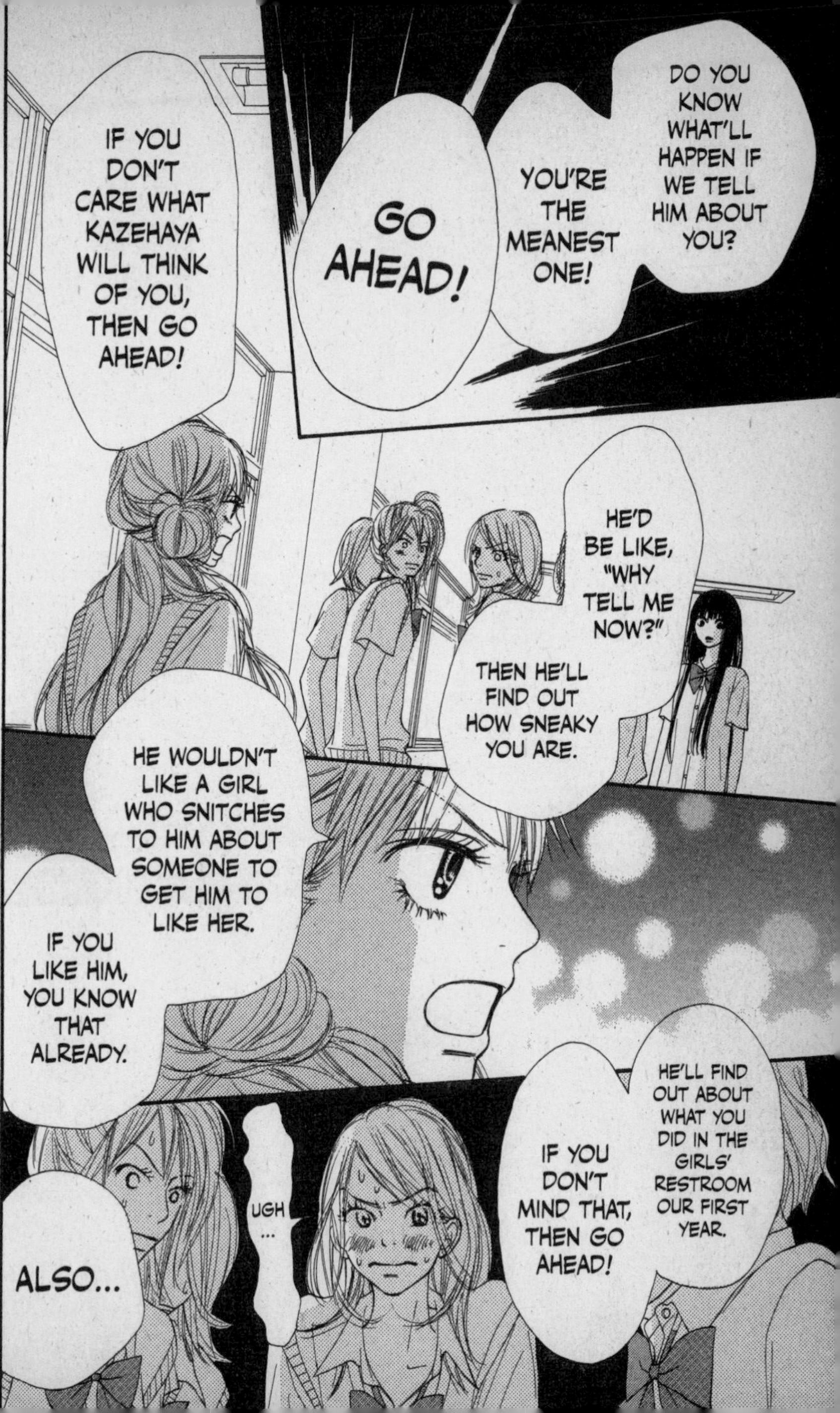
DO YOU KNOW WHAT'LL HAPPEN IF WE TELL HIM ABOUT YOU?
YOU'RE THE MEANEST ONE!
GO AHEAD!
IF YOU DON'T CARE WHAT KAZEHAYA WILL THINK OF YOU, THEN GO AHEAD!
HE'D BE LIKE, "WHY TELL ME NOW?"
THEN HE'LL FIND OUT HOW SNEAKY YOU ARE.
HE WOULDN'T LIKE A GIRL WHO SNITCHES TO HIM ABOUT SOMEONE TO GET HIM TO LIKE HER.
IF YOU LIKE HIM, YOU KNOW THAT ALREADY.
ALSO...
HE'LL FIND OUT ABOUT WHAT YOU DID IN THE GIRLS' RESTROOM OUR FIRST YEAR.
IF YOU DON'T MIND THAT, THEN GO AHEAD!
UGH ...

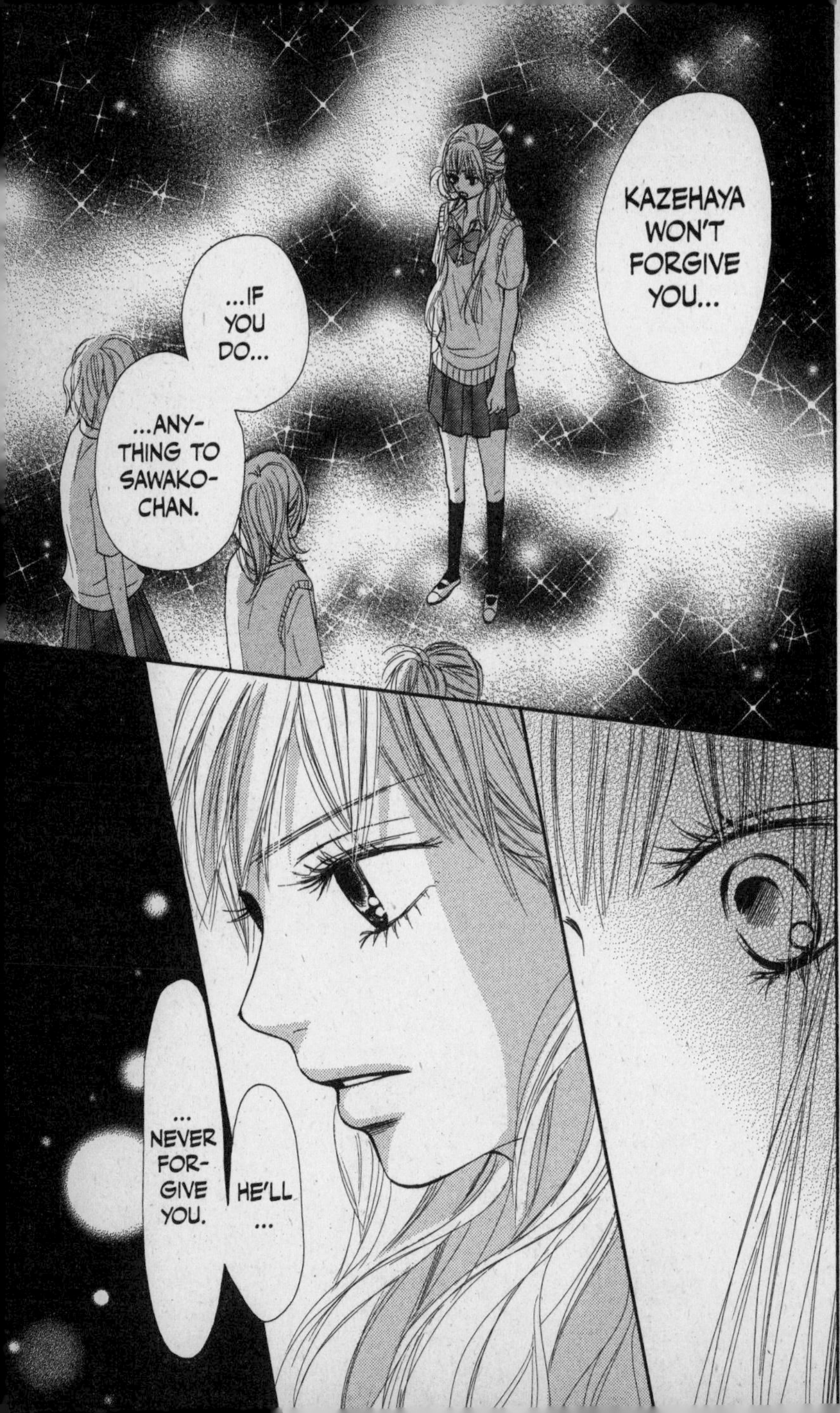
KAZEHAYA WON'T FORGIVE YOU...
...IF YOU DO...
...ANY-THING TO SAWAKO-CHAN.
HE'LL ...
... NEVER FOR-GIVE YOU.

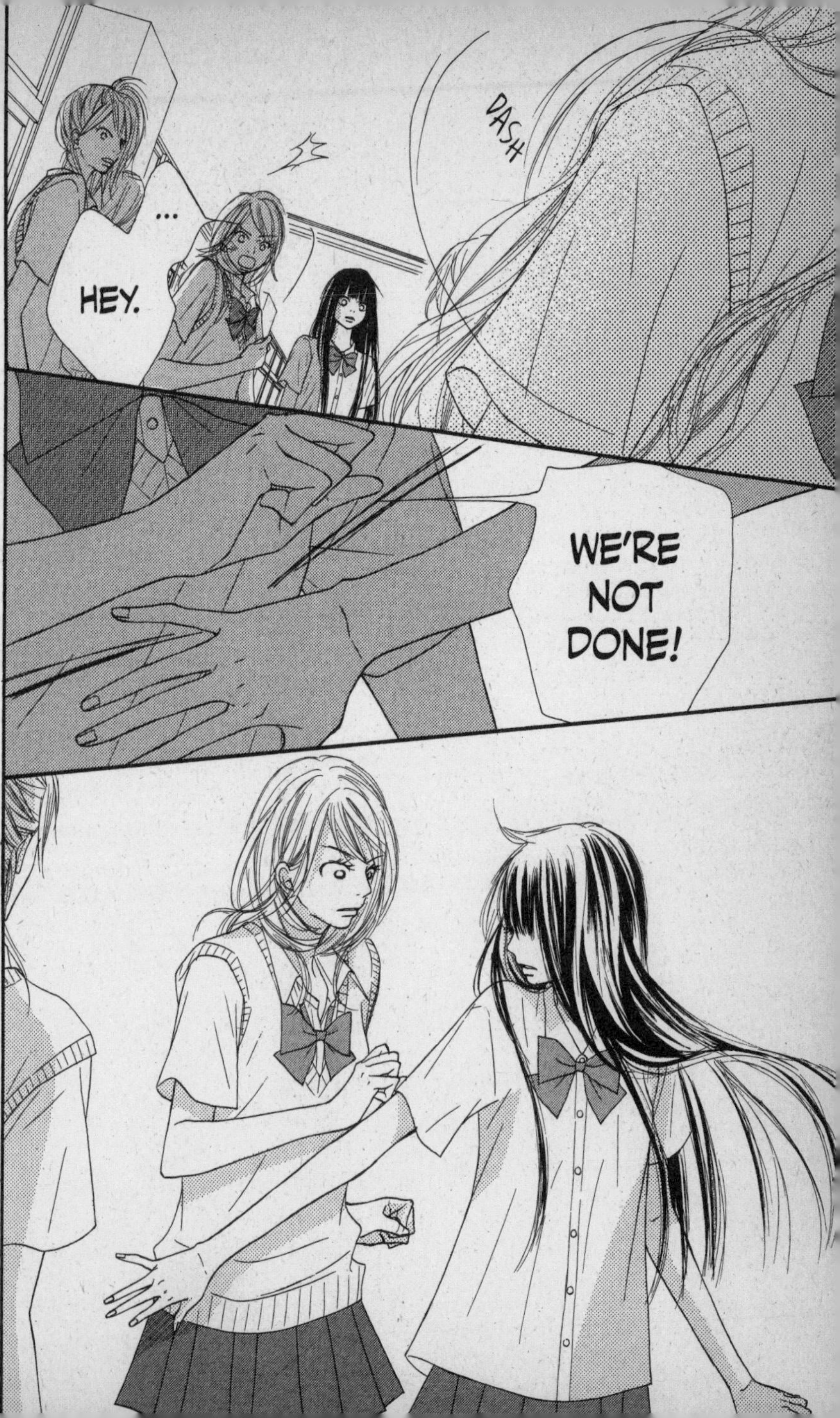
DASH
...
HEY.
WE'RE NOT DONE!

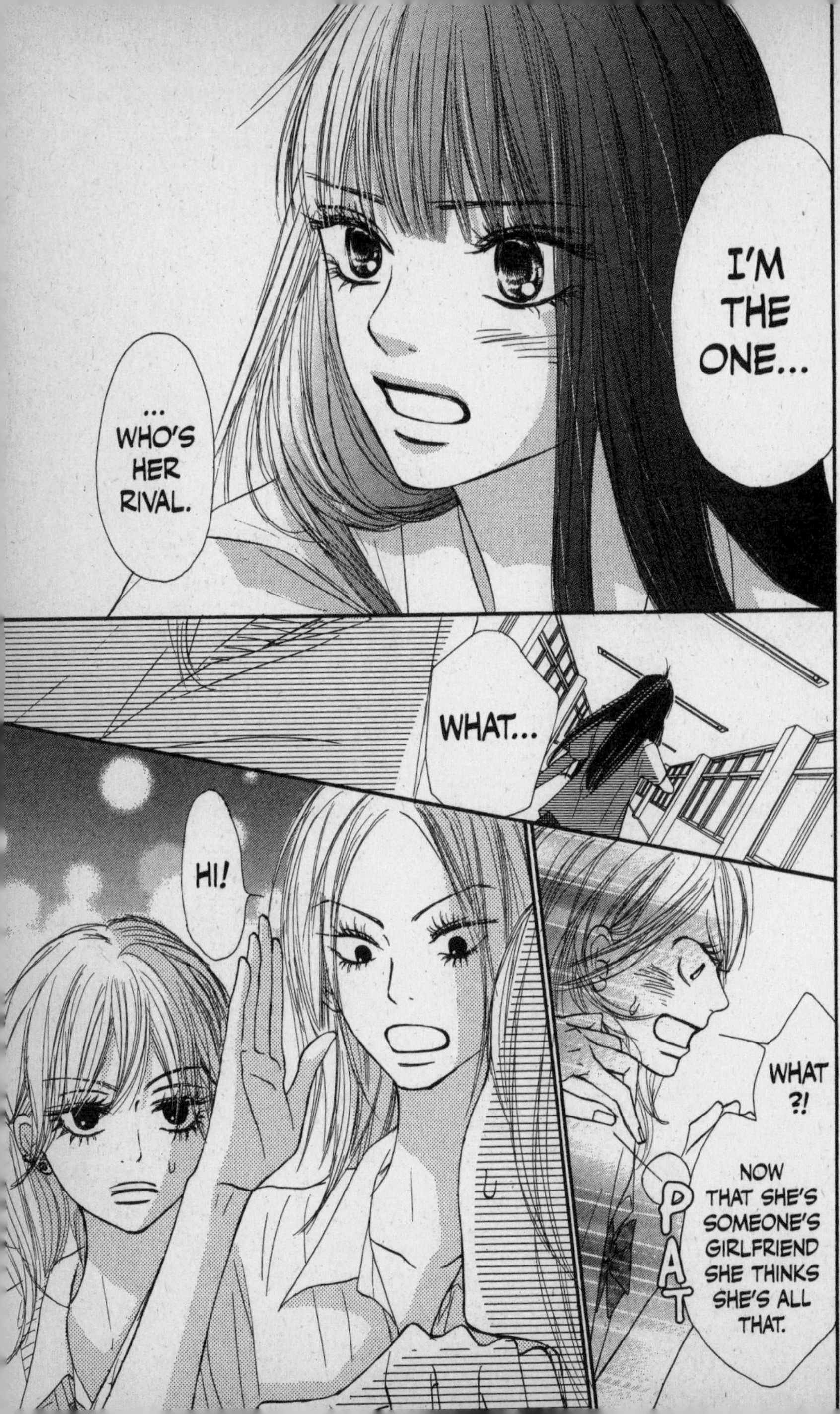
I'M THE ONE...
... WHO'S HER RIVAL.
WHAT...
WHAT?!
PAT
NOW THAT SHE'S SOMEONE'S GIRLFRIEND SHE THINKS SHE'S ALL THAT.
HI!

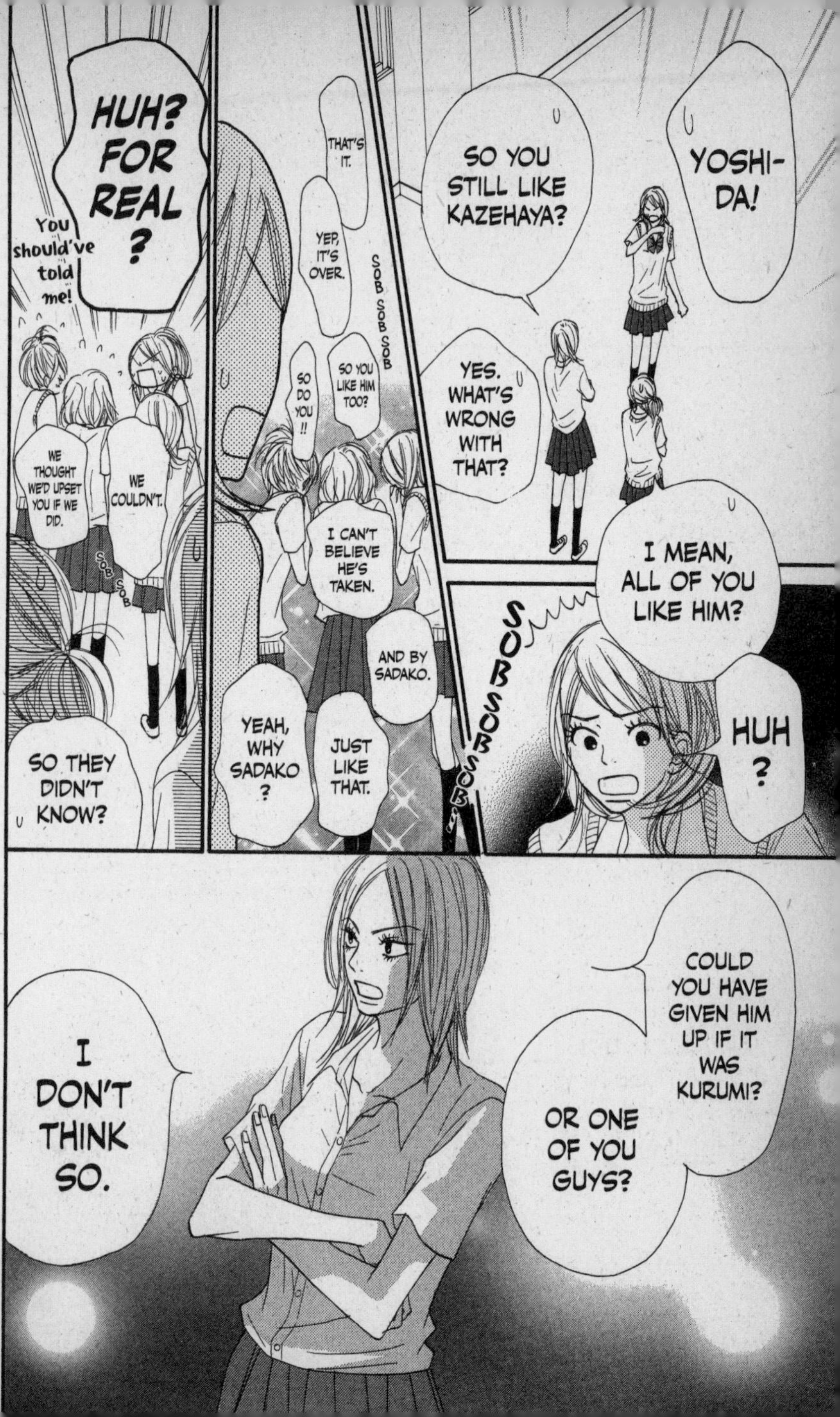
YOSHIDA!
SO YOU STILL LIKE KAZEHAYA?
YES. WHAT'S WRONG WITH THAT?
I MEAN, ALL OF YOU LIKE HIM?
HUH?
SOB SOB SOB
THAT'S IT.
YEP, IT'S OVER.
SOB SOB SOB SOB
SO YOU LIKE HIM TOO?
SO DO YOU!!
I CAN'T BELIEVE HE'S TAKEN.
AND BY SADAKO.
JUST LIKE THAT.
YEAH, WHY SADAKO?
HUH? FOR REAL?
You should've told me!
WE COULDN'T.
WE THOUGHT WE'D UPSET YOU IF WE DID.
SOB SOB
SO THEY DIDN'T KNOW?
COULD YOU HAVE GIVEN HIM UP IF IT WAS KURUMI?
OR ONE OF YOU GUYS?
I DON'T THINK SO.

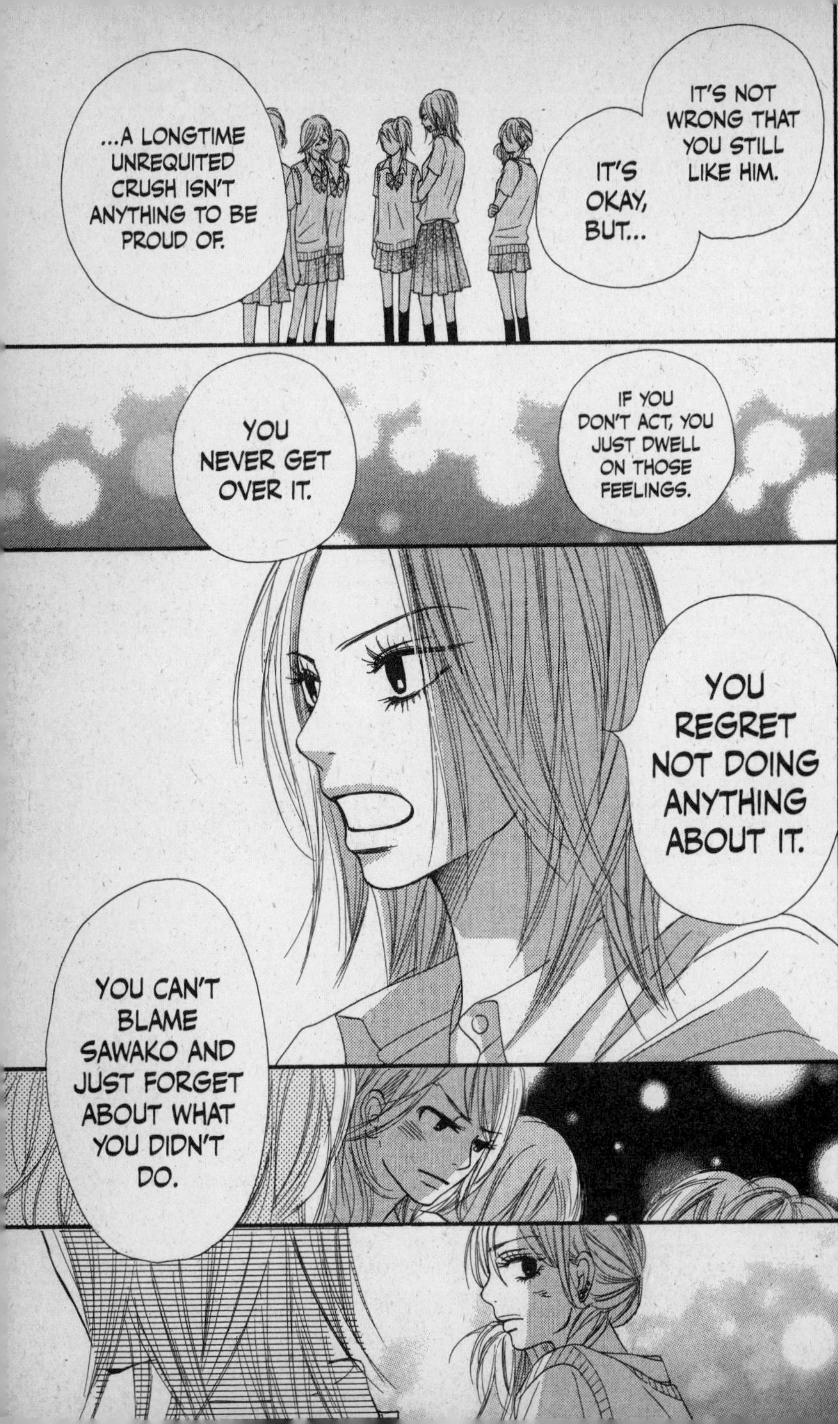
IT'S NOT WRONG THAT YOU STILL LIKE HIM.
IT'S OKAY, BUT...
...A LONGTIME UNREQUITED CRUSH ISN'T ANYTHING TO BE PROUD OF.
IF YOU DON'T ACT, YOU JUST DWELL ON THOSE FEELINGS.
YOU NEVER GET OVER IT.
YOU REGRET NOT DOING ANYTHING ABOUT IT.
YOU CAN'T BLAME SAWAKO AND JUST FORGET ABOUT WHAT YOU DIDN'T DO.

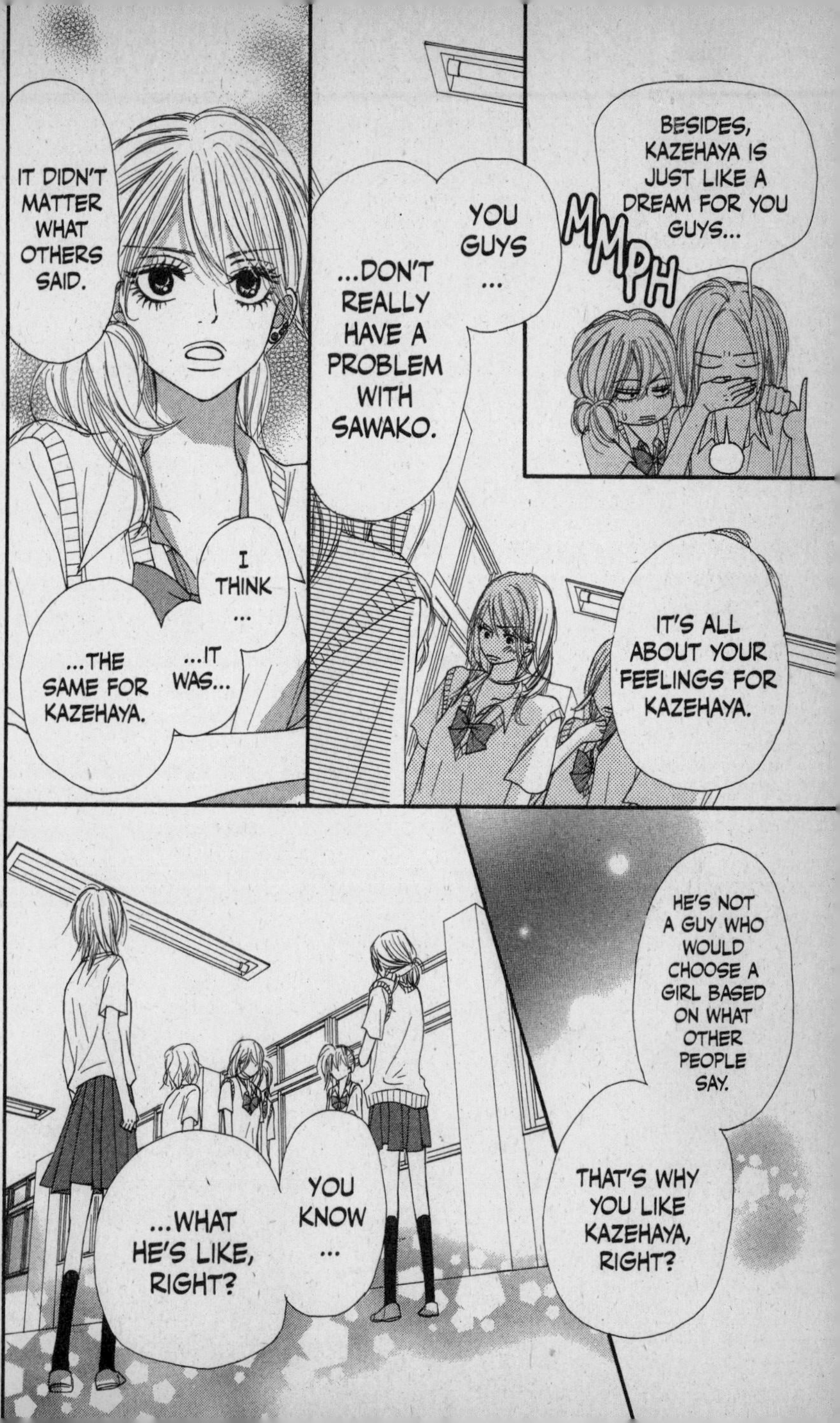
YOU GUYS ...
...DON'T REALLY HAVE A PROBLEM WITH SAWAKO.
IT'S ALL ABOUT YOUR FEELINGS FOR KAZEHAYA.
BESIDES, KAZEHAYA IS JUST LIKE A DREAM FOR YOU GUYS...
MMPH
IT DIDN'T MATTER WHAT OTHERS SAID.
I THINK ...
...IT WAS...
...THE SAME FOR KAZEHAYA.
HE'S NOT A GUY WHO WOULD CHOOSE A GIRL BASED ON WHAT OTHER PEOPLE SAY.
THAT'S WHY YOU LIKE KAZEHAYA, RIGHT?
YOU KNOW ...
...WHAT HE'S LIKE, RIGHT?

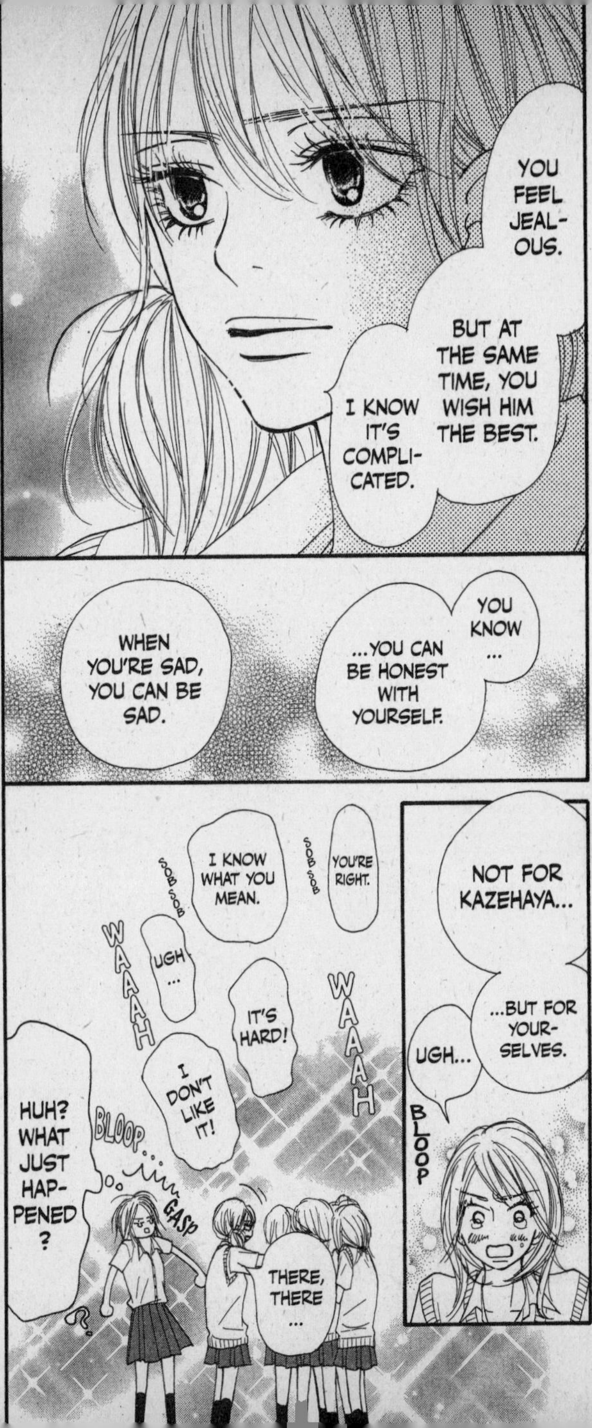
YOU FEEL JEAL-OUS.
BUT AT THE SAME TIME, YOU WISH HIM THE BEST.
I KNOW IT'S COMPLI-CATED.
YOU KNOW ...
...YOU CAN BE HONEST WITH YOURSELF.
WHEN YOU'RE SAD, YOU CAN BE SAD.
NOT FOR KAZEHAYA...
...BUT FOR YOUR-SELVES.
UGH...
BLOOP
YOU'RE RIGHT.
SOB SOB
I KNOW WHAT YOU MEAN.
SOB SOB
WAAAAH
IT'S HARD!
UGH ...
WAAAAH
I DON'T LIKE IT!
HUH? WHAT JUST HAP-PENED ?
BLOOP...
GASP
THERE, THERE ...

KARUPIN on JAPAN 1

Hello. This is volume 11. I'm Shiina. How are you?

Right now, as I'm writing these comments, it's the last day of Golden Week, 2010. I've been informed about the shoot for the movie and I feel happy.

It will be a wonderful movie, so please look forward to it and go watch it! The editor sent me photos (videos?), and Mikako Tabe-chan and Haruma Miura-kun surprisingly look like Sawako and Kazehaya. The other cast members also resemble the characters they portray. They are all young and cute!

This manga is lucky in that everyone involved with the anime, movie, video game and novel care about it.

PLIP PLIP

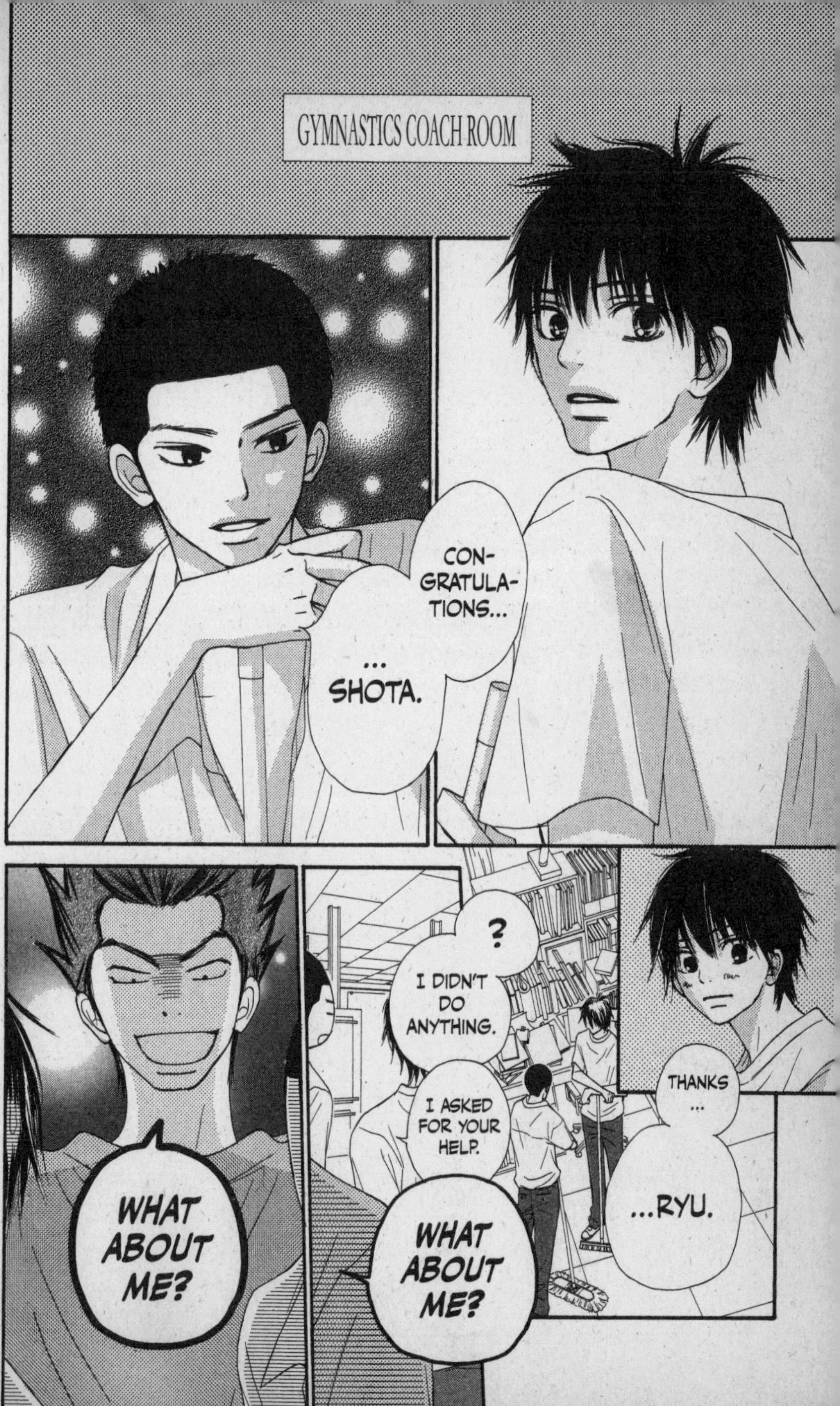
GYMNASTICS COACH ROOM
CON-GRATULATIONS...
... SHOTA.
THANKS ...
...RYU.
?
I DIDN'T DO ANYTHING.
I ASKED FOR YOUR HELP.
WHAT ABOUT ME?
WHAT ABOUT ME?

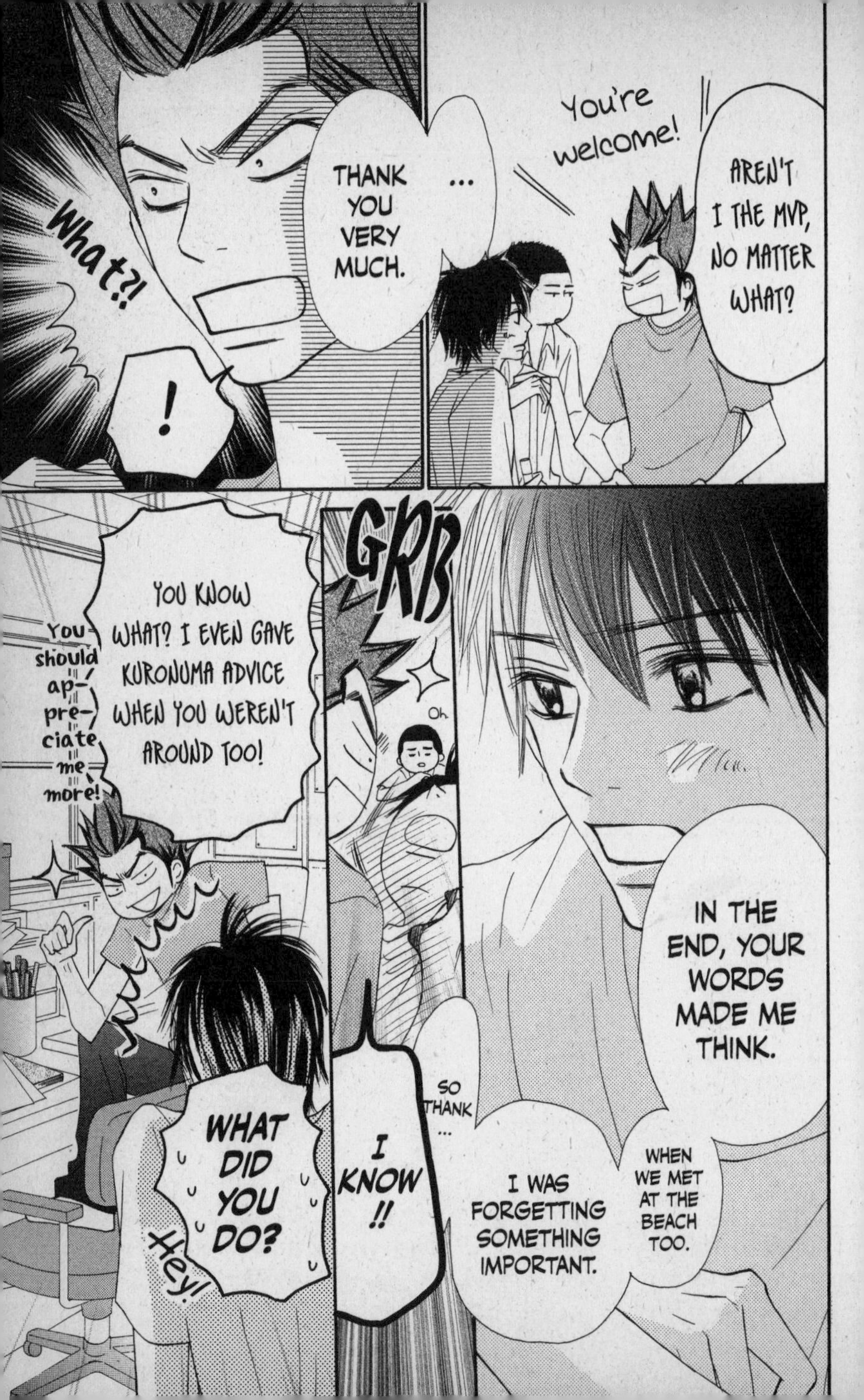
AREN'T I THE MVP, NO MATTER WHAT?
You're welcome!
...
THANK YOU VERY MUCH.
What?!
!
IN THE END, YOUR WORDS MADE ME THINK.
WHEN WE MET AT THE BEACH TOO.
I WAS FORGETTING SOMETHING IMPORTANT.
SO THANK...
GRB
Oh.
I KNOW!!
YOU KNOW WHAT? I EVEN GAVE KURONUMA ADVICE WHEN YOU WEREN'T AROUND TOO!
You should appreciate me more!
WHAT DID YOU DO?
Hey!

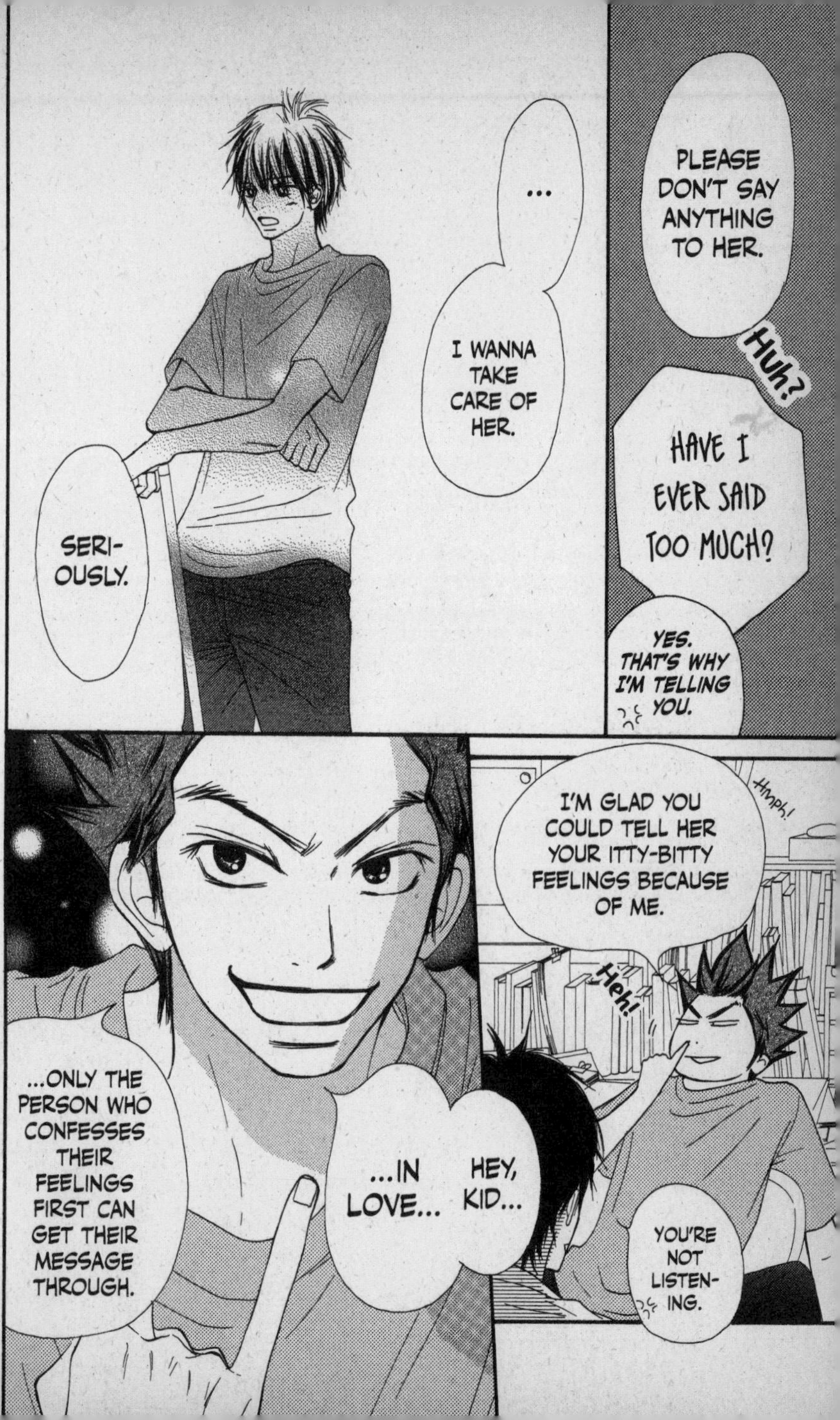
PLEASE DON'T SAY ANYTHING TO HER.
Huh?
HAVE I EVER SAID TOO MUCH?
YES. THAT'S WHY I'M TELLING YOU.
...
I WANNA TAKE CARE OF HER.
SERI-OUSLY.
Hmph!
I'M GLAD YOU COULD TELL HER YOUR ITTY-BITTY FEELINGS BECAUSE OF ME.
Heh!
YOU'RE NOT LISTEN-ING.
HEY, KID...
...IN LOVE...
...ONLY THE PERSON WHO CONFESSES THEIR FEELINGS FIRST CAN GET THEIR MESSAGE THROUGH.

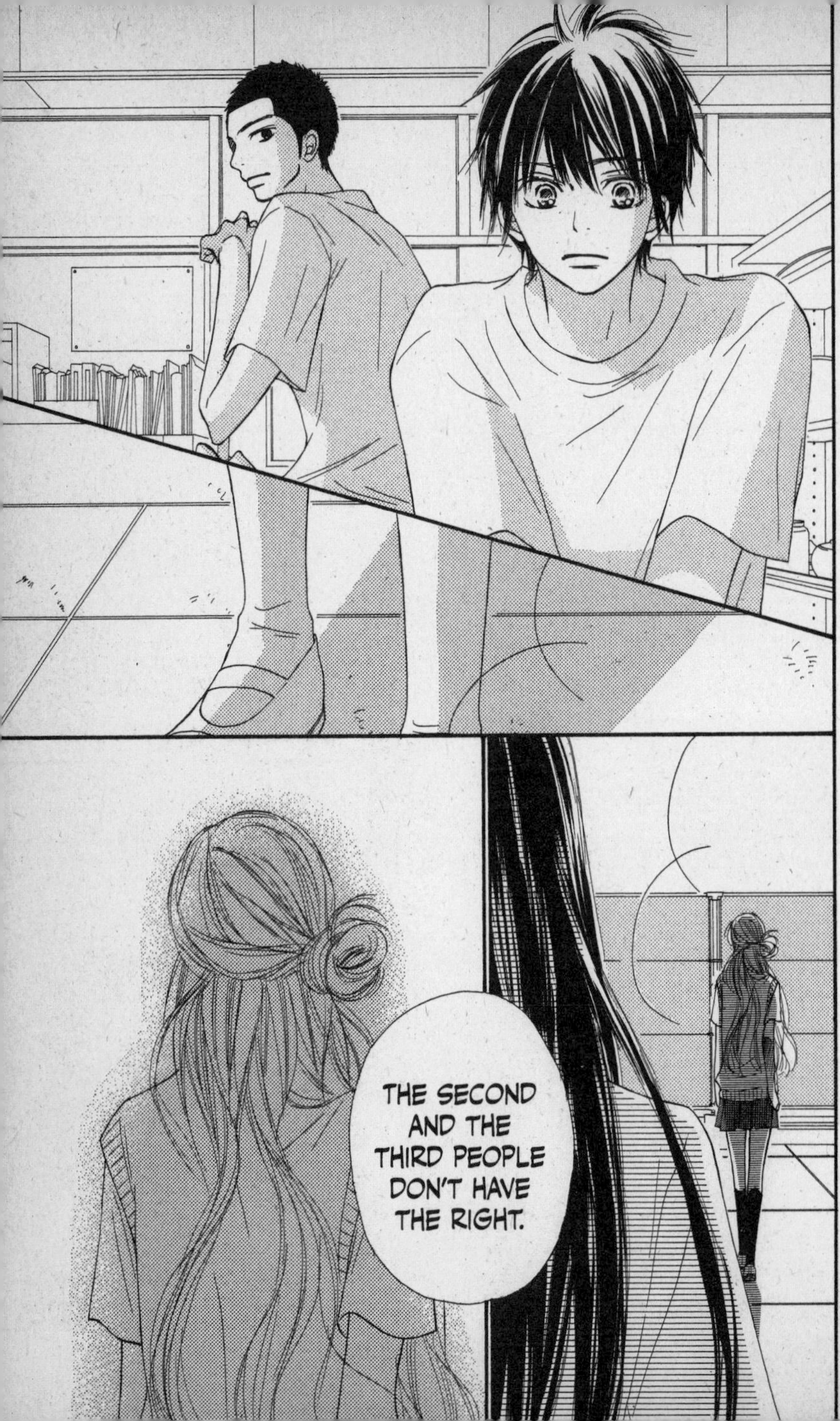
THE SECOND AND THE THIRD PEOPLE DON'T HAVE THE RIGHT.

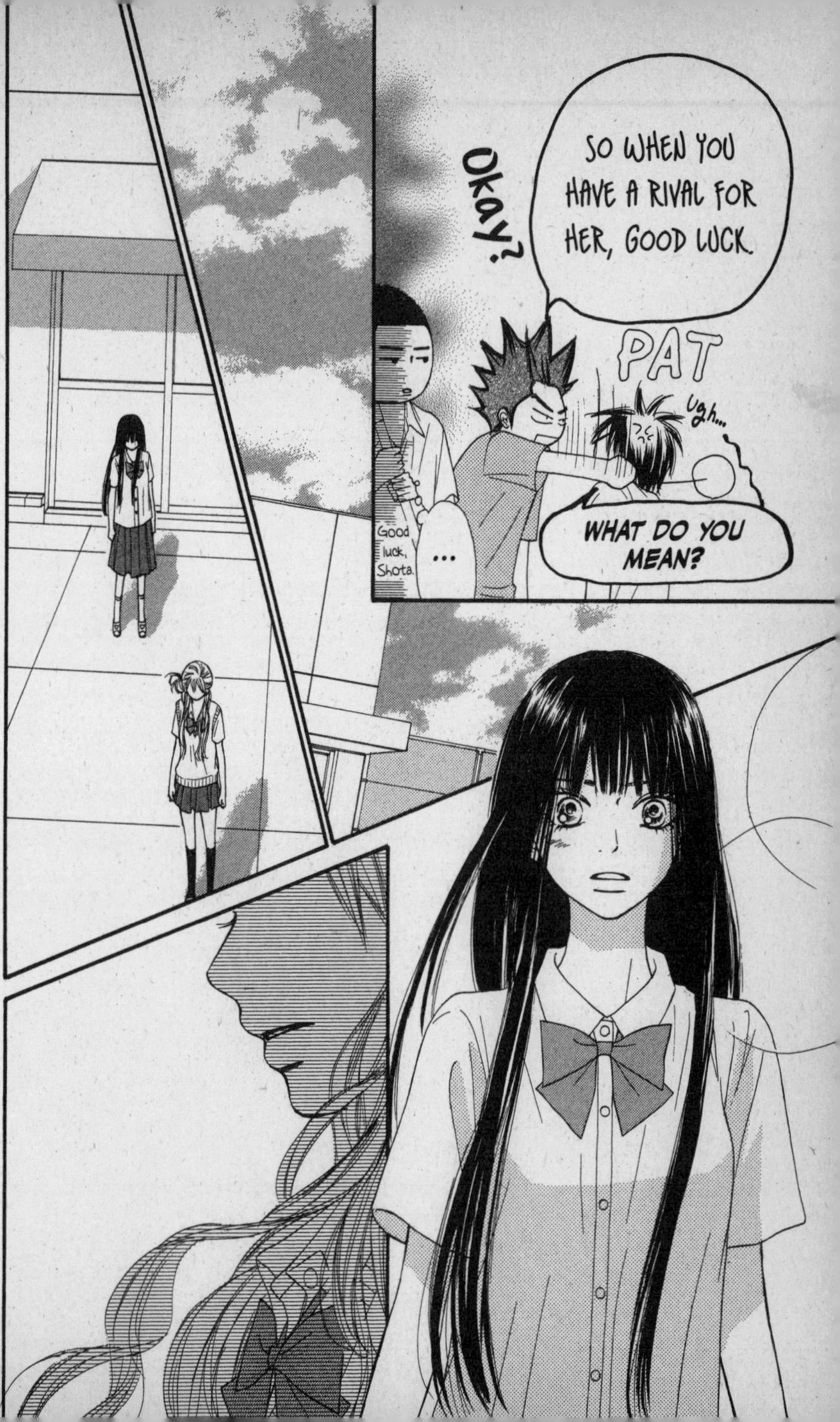
SO WHEN YOU HAVE A RIVAL FOR HER, GOOD LUCK.
Okay?
PAT
Ugh...
WHAT DO YOU MEAN?
...
Good luck, Shota.

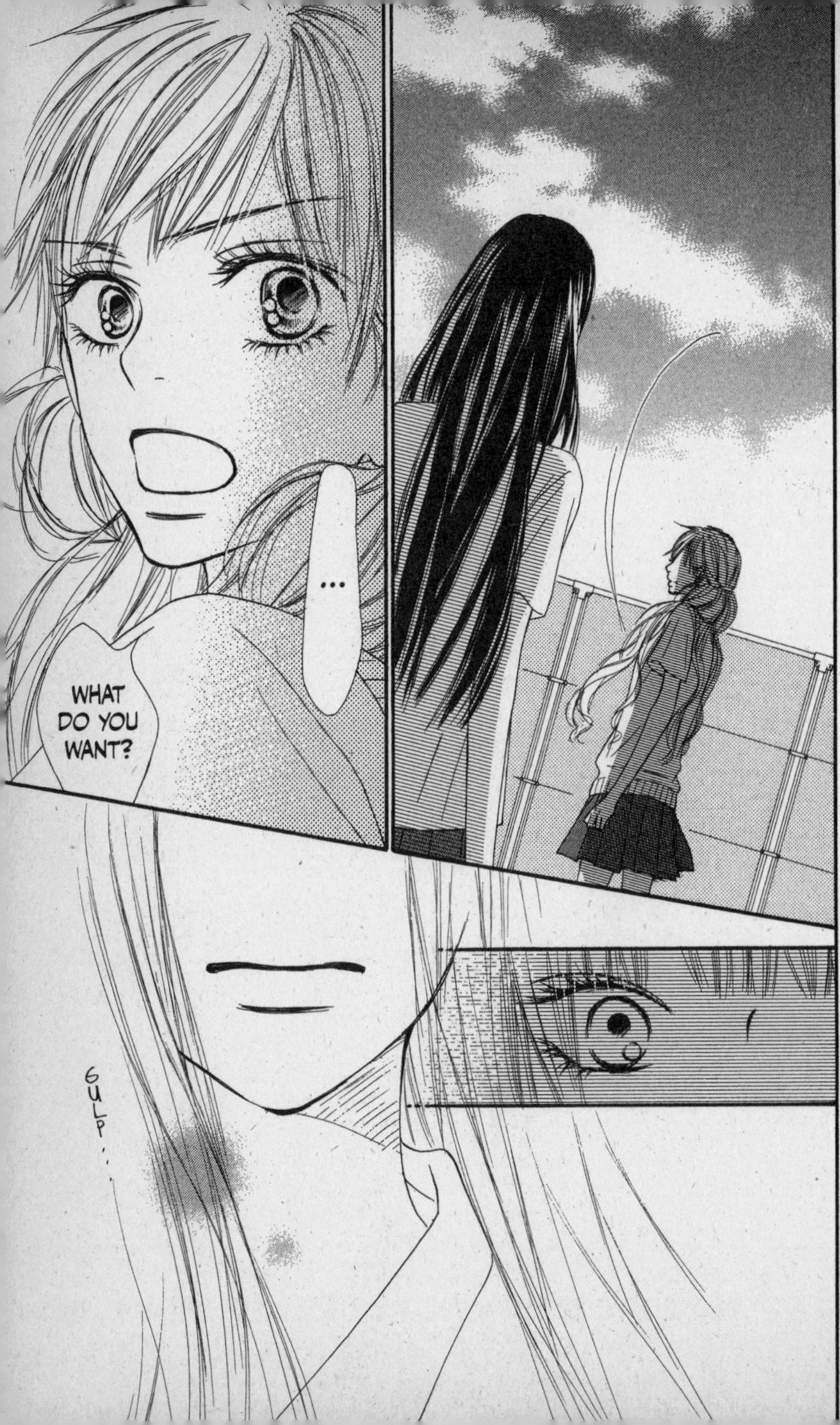
...
WHAT DO YOU WANT?
GULP..

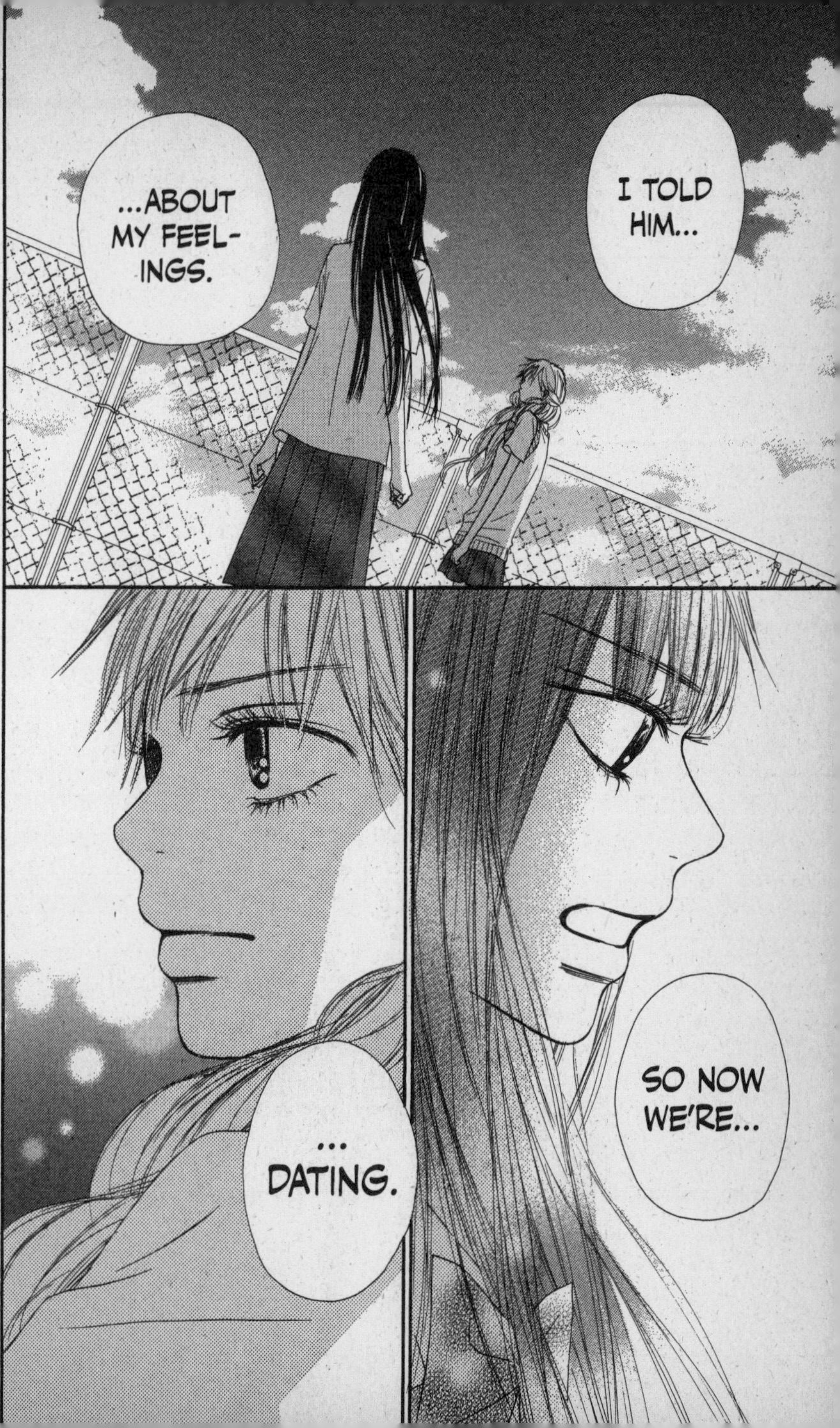
I TOLD HIM...
...ABOUT MY FEEL-INGS.
SO NOW WE'RE...
... DATING.

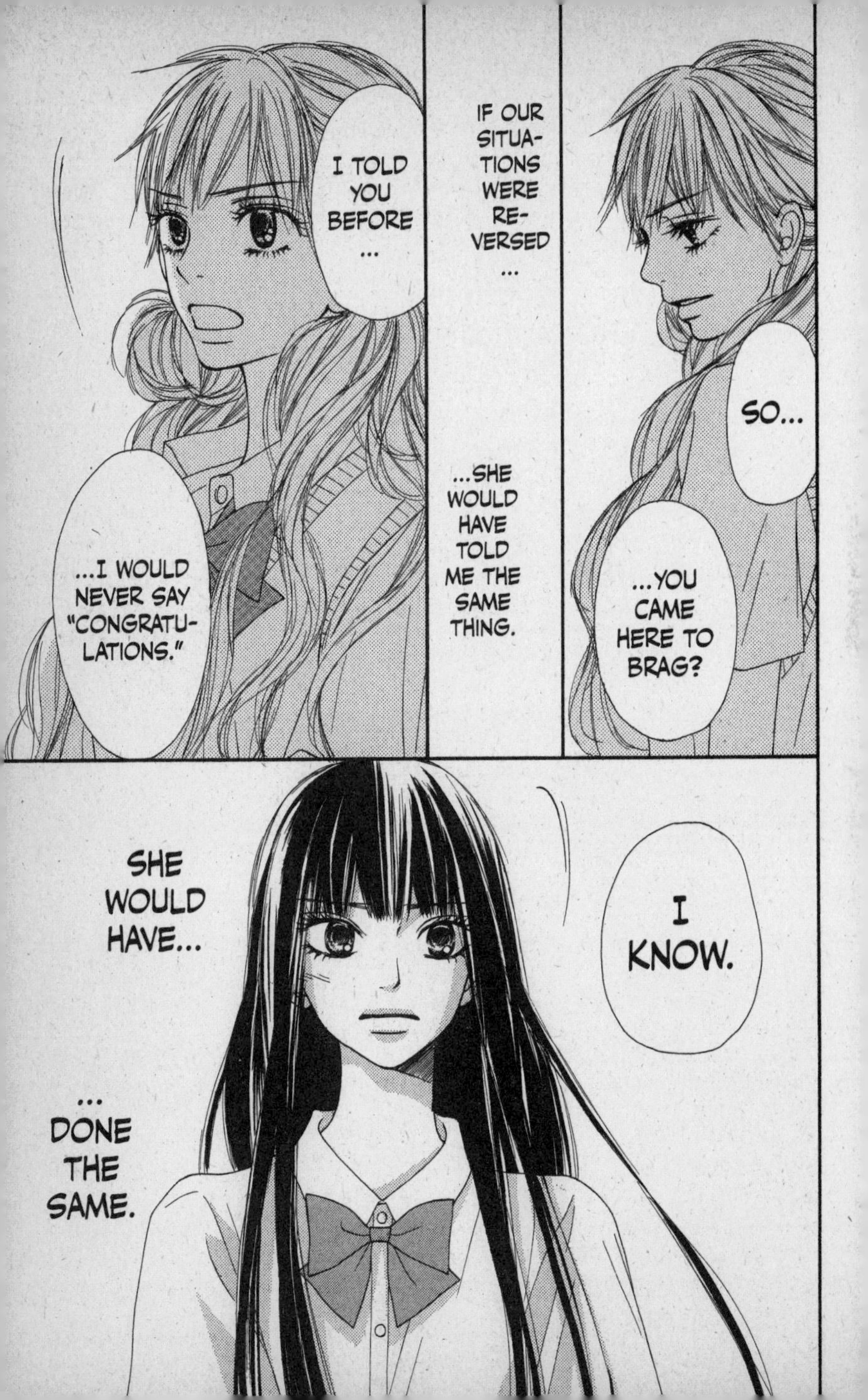
SO...
...YOU CAME HERE TO BRAG?
IF OUR SITUATIONS WERE REVERSED...
...SHE WOULD HAVE TOLD ME THE SAME THING.
I TOLD YOU BEFORE...
...I WOULD NEVER SAY "CONGRATULATIONS."
I KNOW.
SHE WOULD HAVE...
...DONE THE SAME.

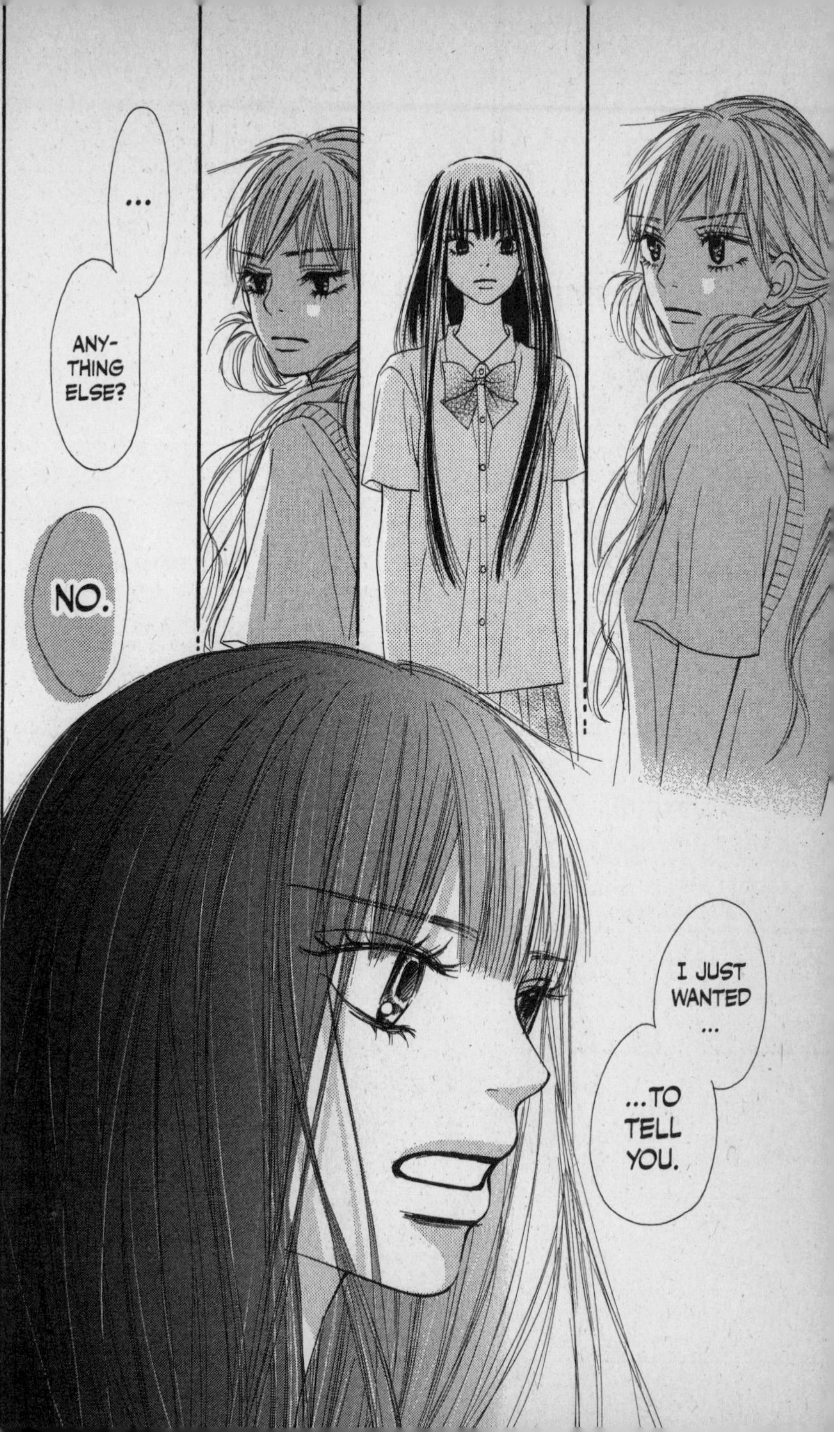
...
ANY-THING ELSE?
NO.
I JUST WANTED ...
...TO TELL YOU.

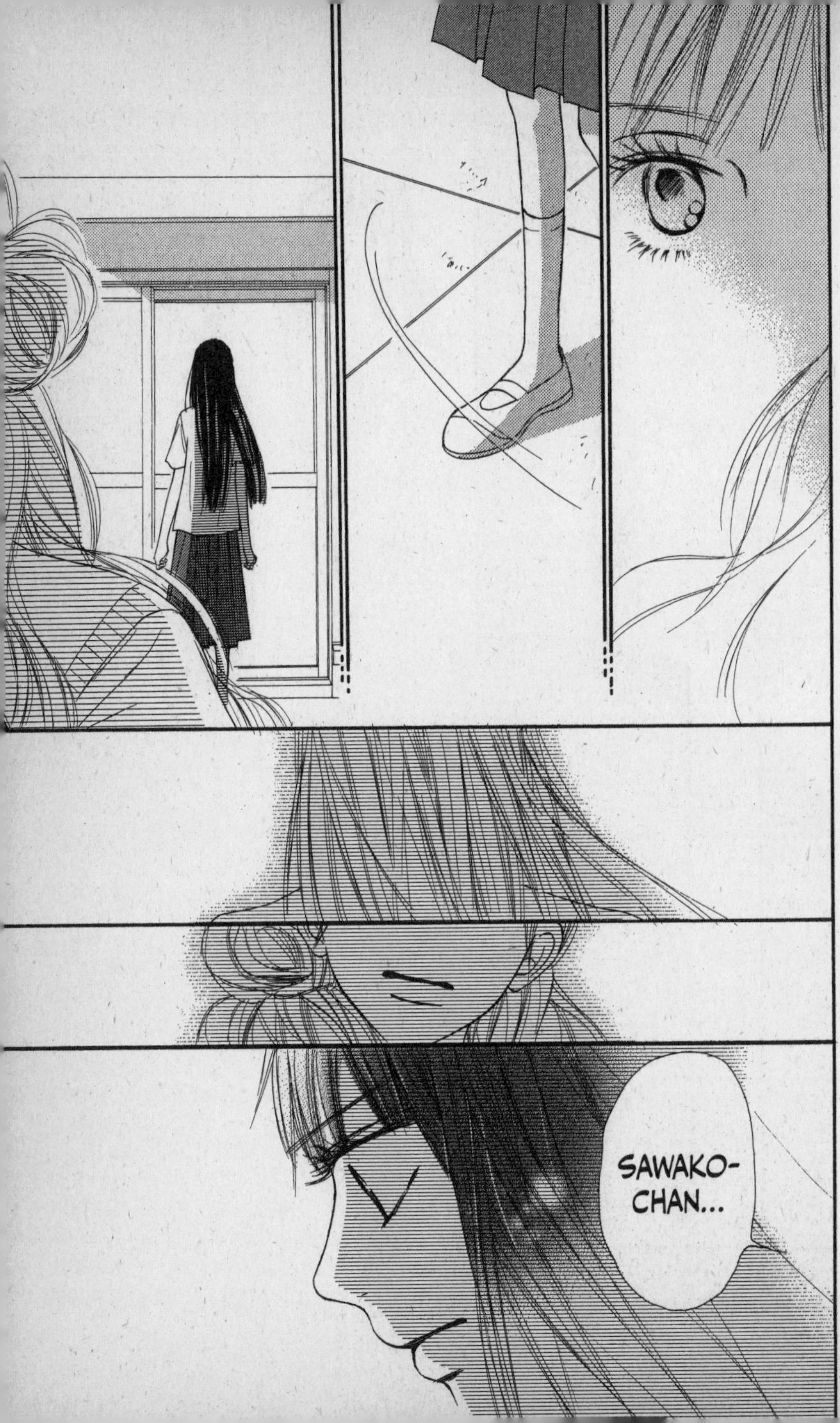
SAWAKO-CHAN...

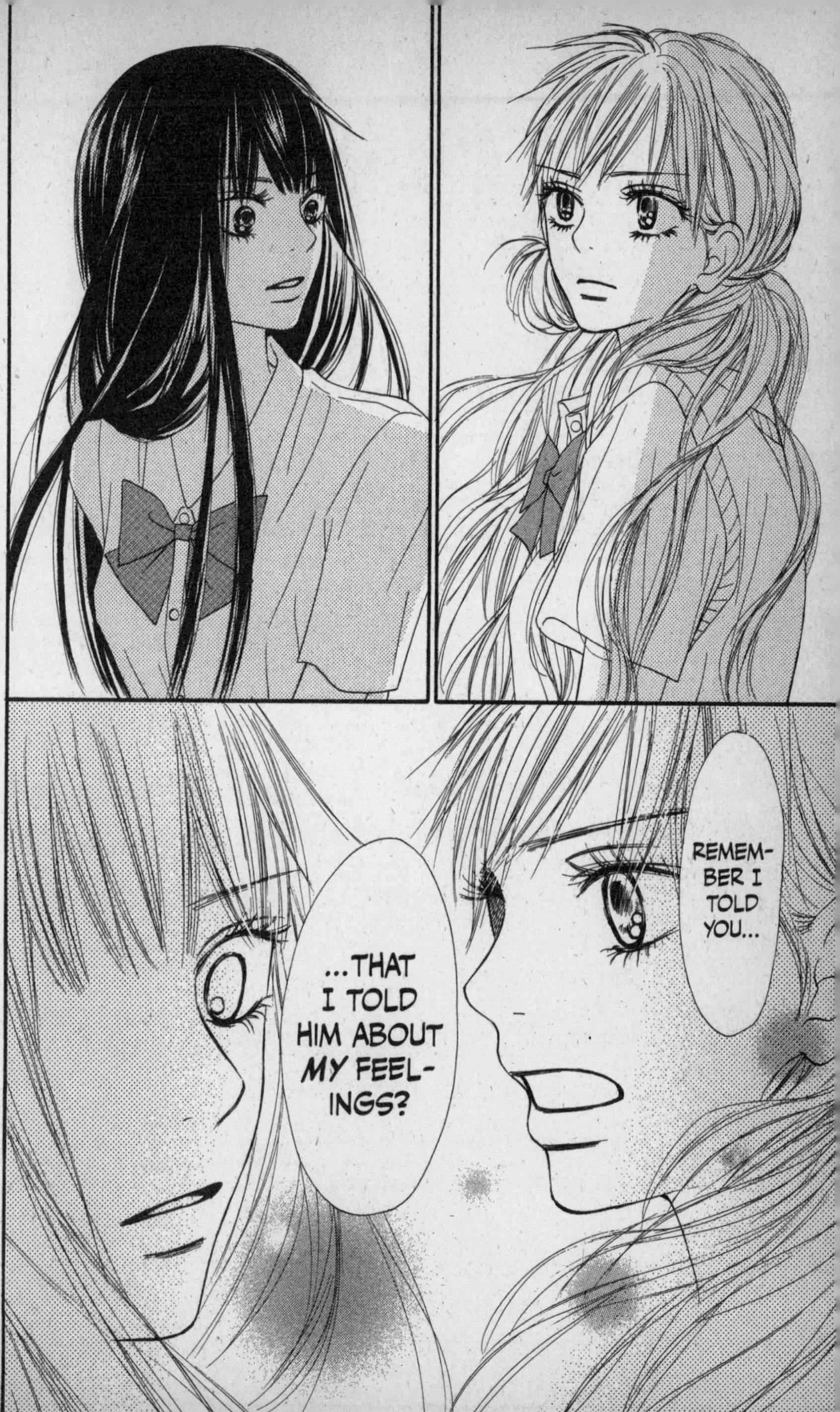
REMEM-BER I TOLD YOU...
...THAT I TOLD HIM ABOUT MY FEEL-INGS?

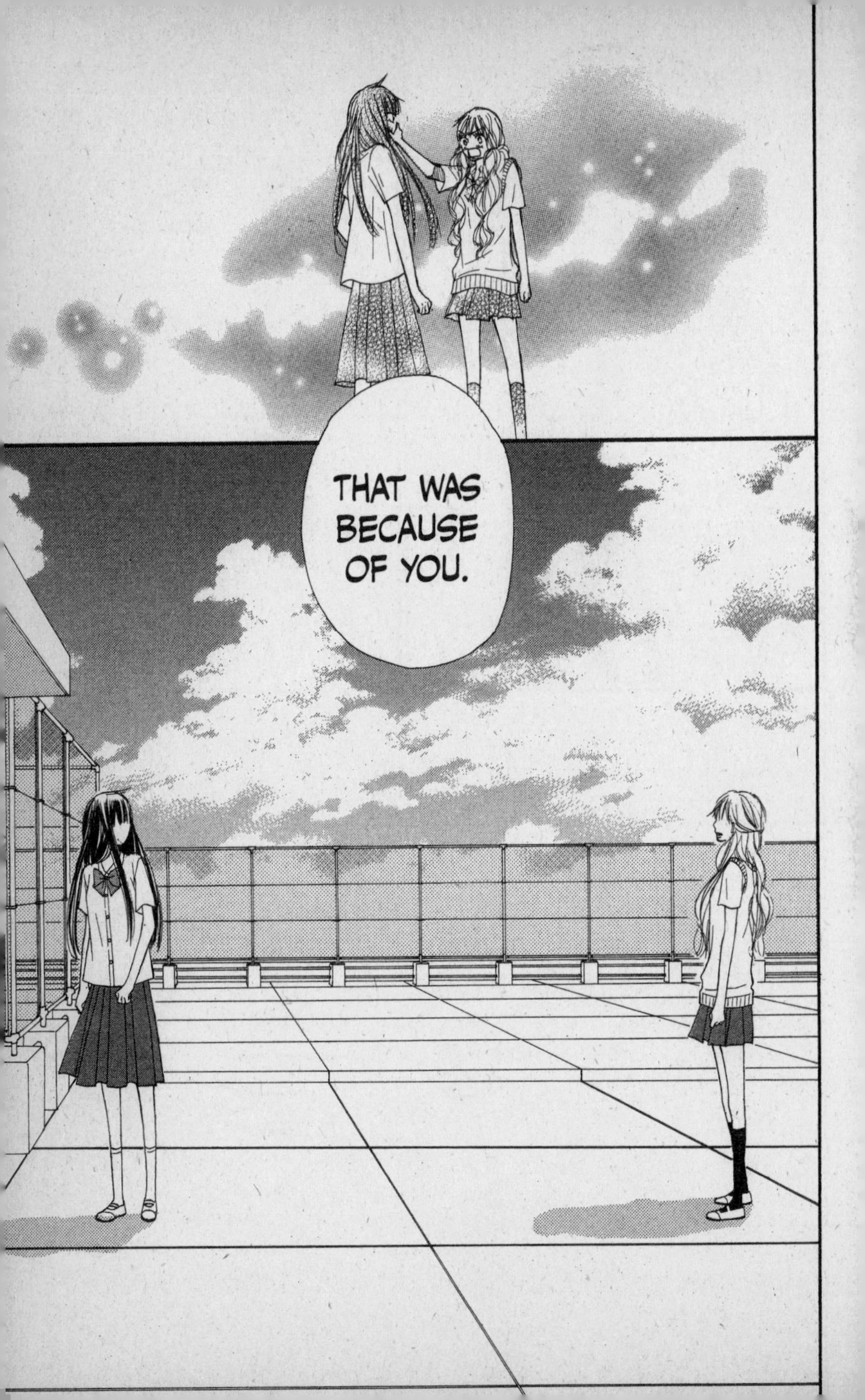
THAT WAS BECAUSE OF YOU.

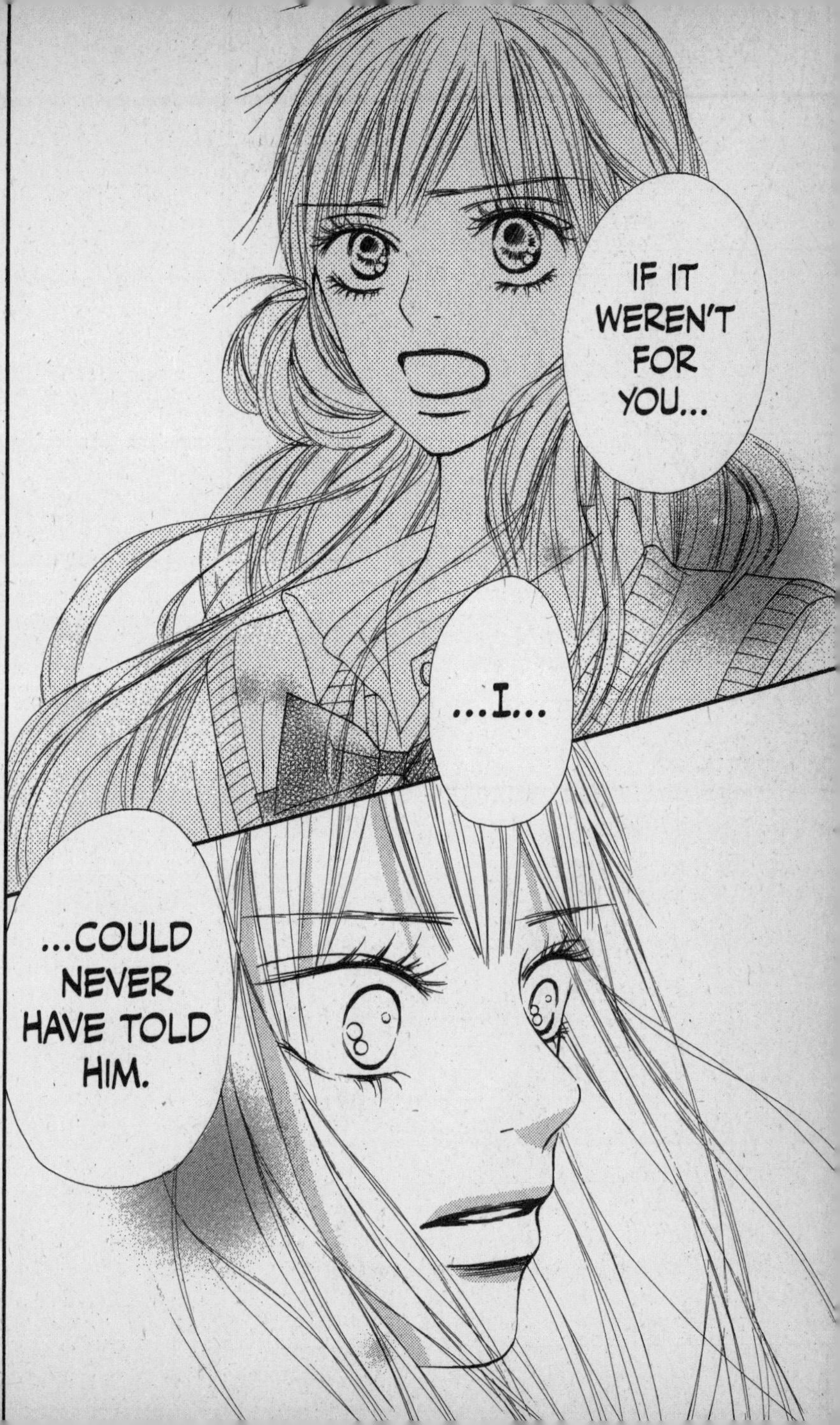
IF IT WEREN'T FOR YOU...
...I...
...COULD NEVER HAVE TOLD HIM.

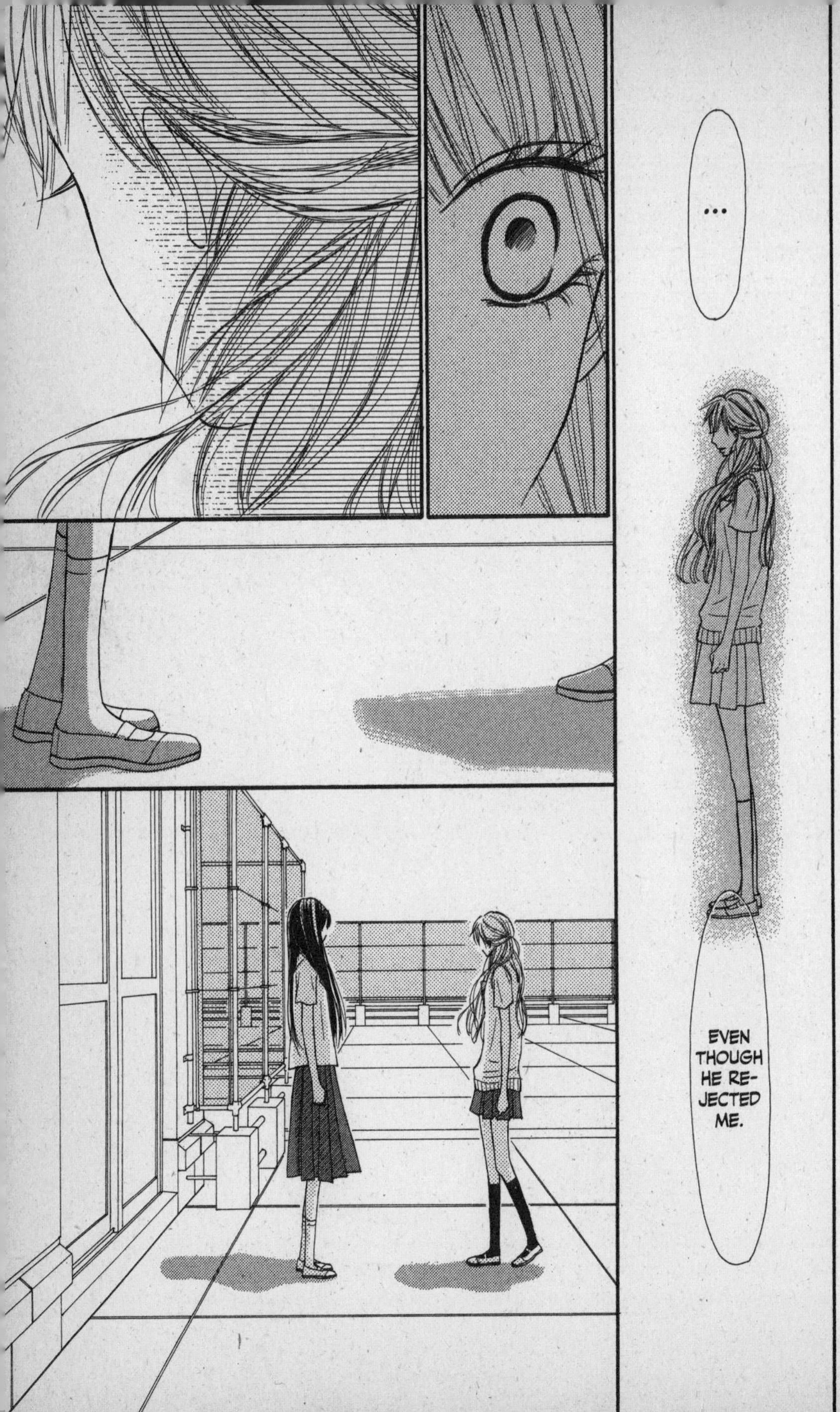
...
EVEN THOUGH HE RE-JECTED ME.

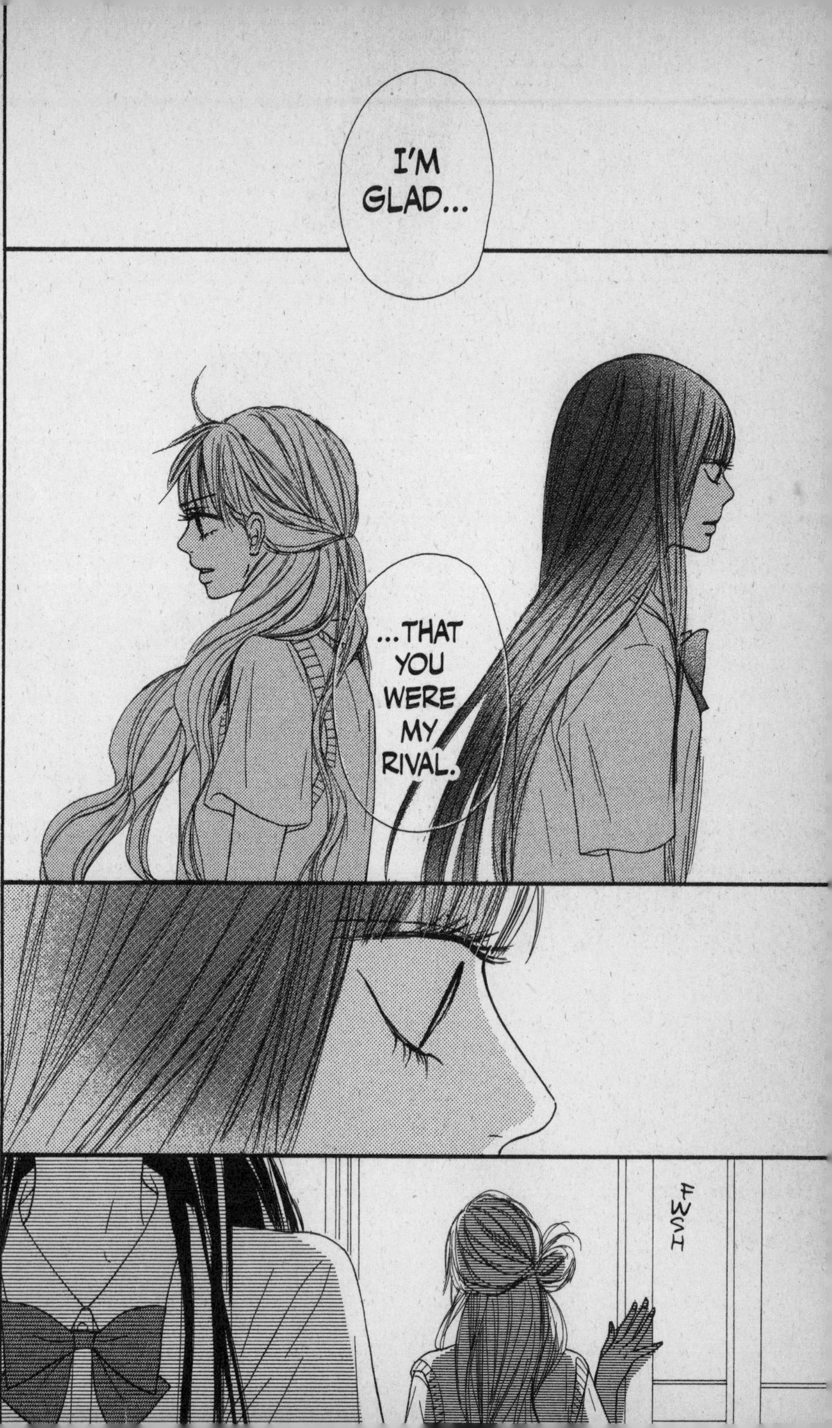
I'M GLAD...
...THAT YOU WERE MY RIVAL.
FWSH

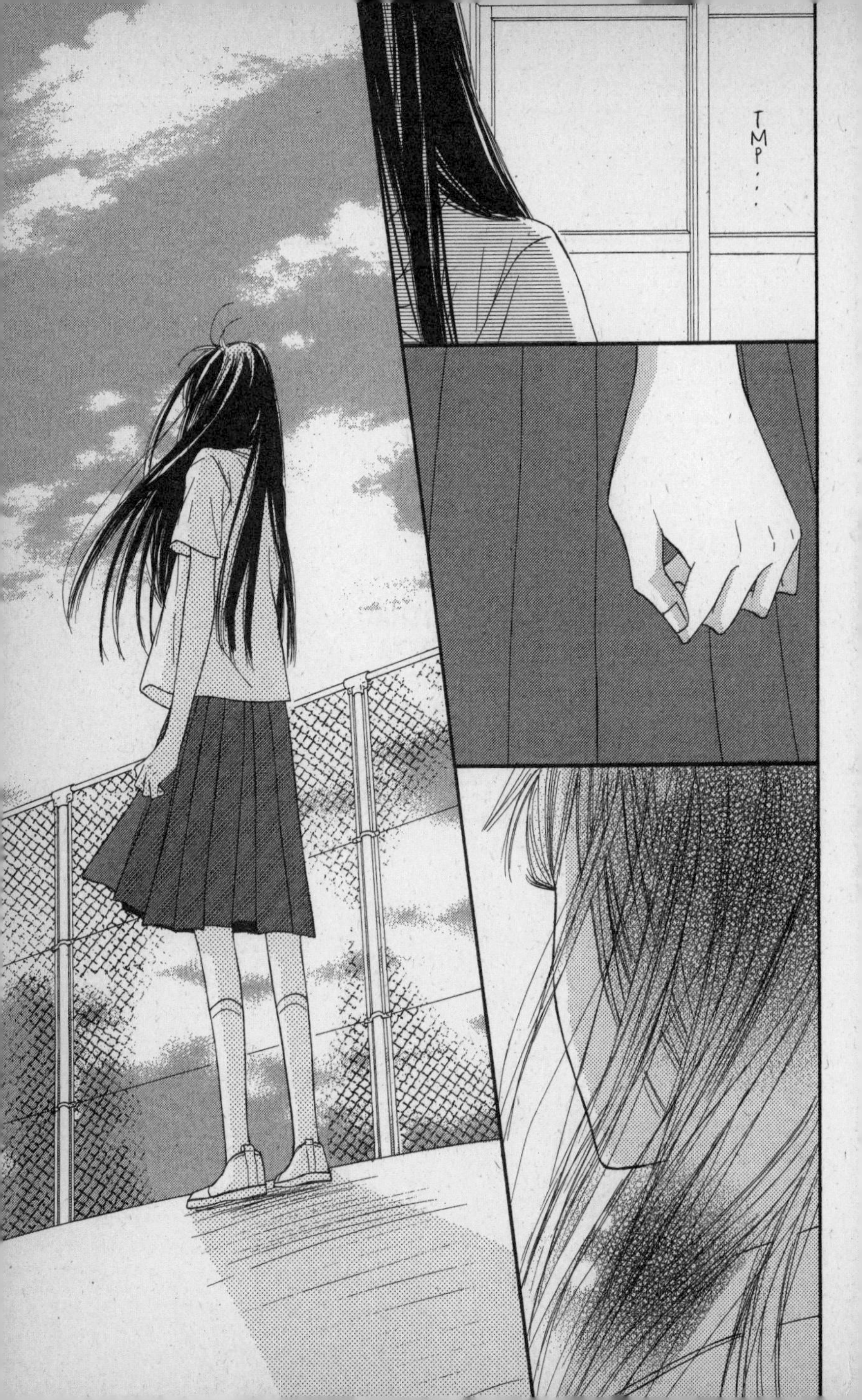
TMP...

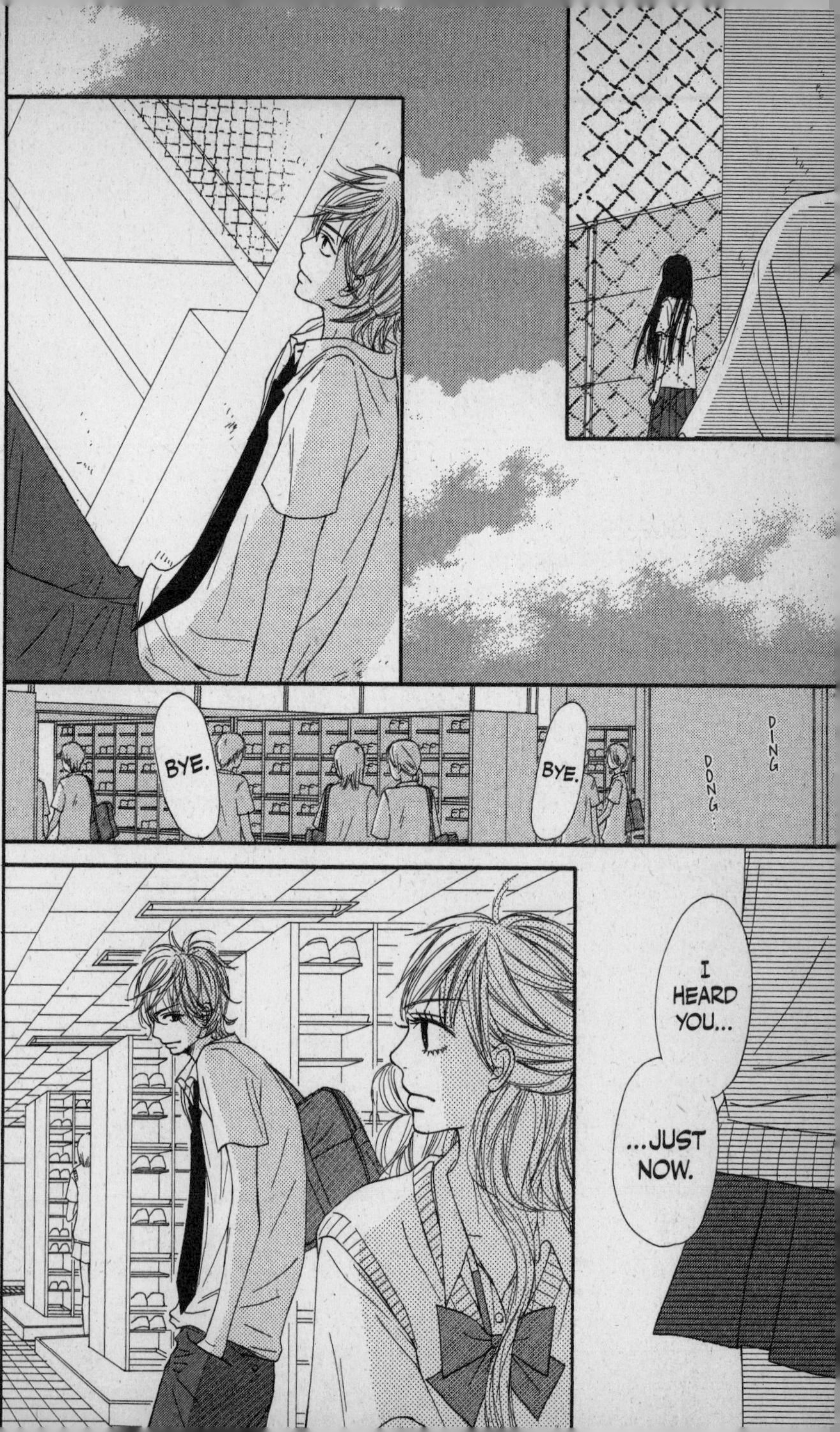
DING
DONG...
BYE.
BYE.
I HEARD YOU...
...JUST NOW.

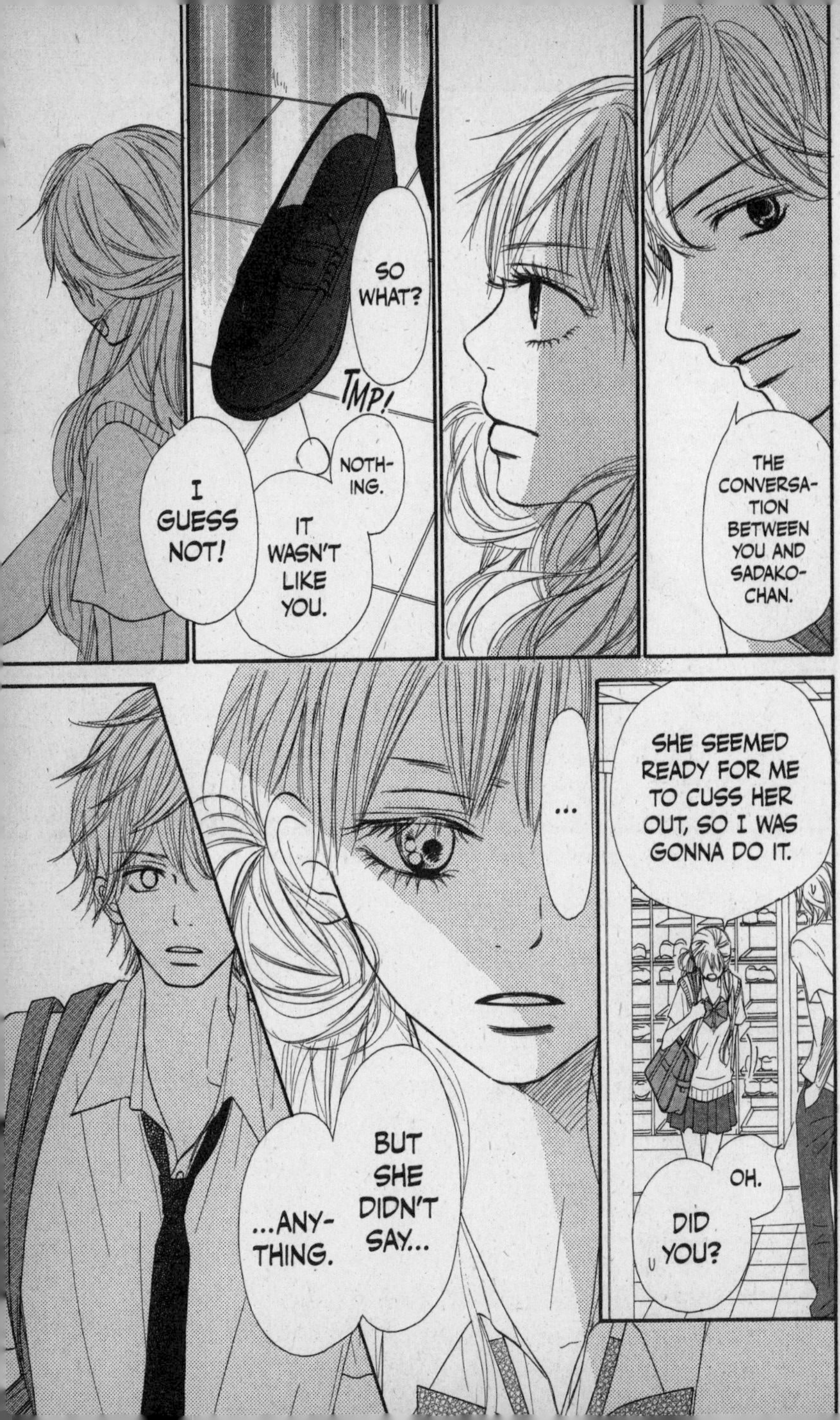
THE CONVERSATION BETWEEN YOU AND SADAKO-CHAN.
SO WHAT?
TMP!
NOTHING.
IT WASN'T LIKE YOU.
I GUESS NOT!
SHE SEEMED READY FOR ME TO CUSS HER OUT, SO I WAS GONNA DO IT.
OH.
DID YOU?
...
BUT SHE DIDN'T SAY...
...ANYTHING.

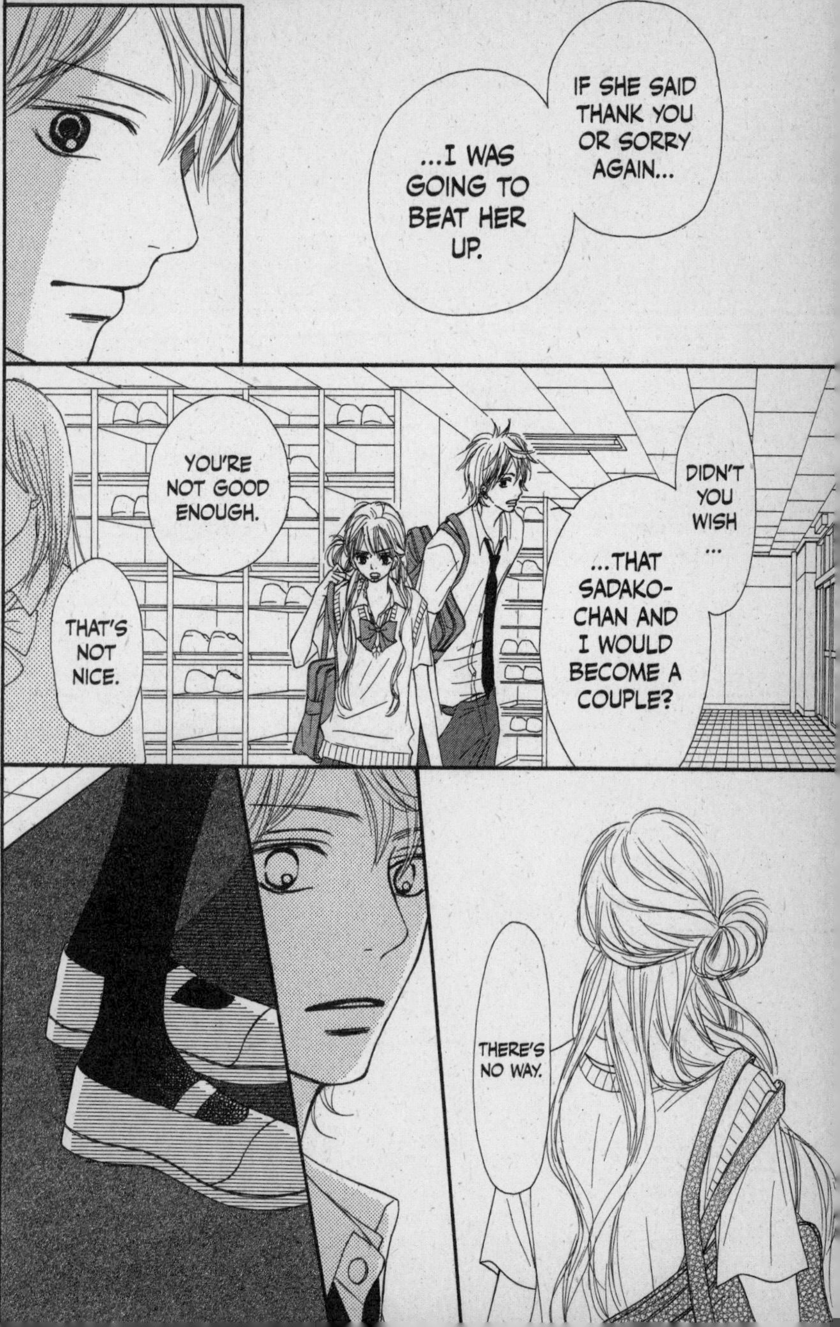
IF SHE SAID THANK YOU OR SORRY AGAIN...
...I WAS GOING TO BEAT HER UP.
DIDN'T YOU WISH ...
...THAT SADAKO-CHAN AND I WOULD BECOME A COUPLE?
YOU'RE NOT GOOD ENOUGH.
THAT'S NOT NICE.
THERE'S NO WAY.

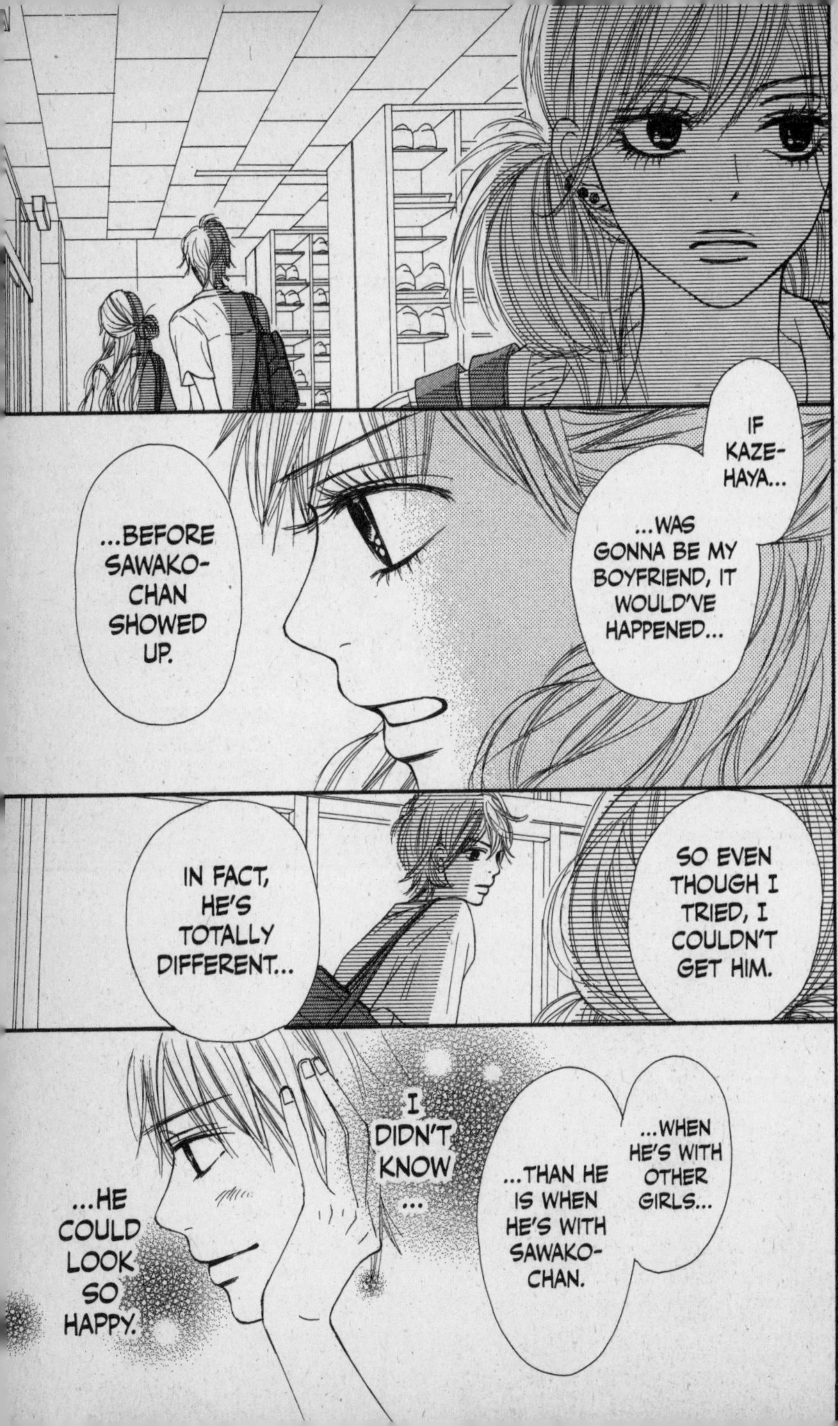
IF KAZE-HAYA...
...WAS GONNA BE MY BOYFRIEND, IT WOULD'VE HAPPENED...
...BEFORE SAWAKO-CHAN SHOWED UP.
SO EVEN THOUGH I TRIED, I COULDN'T GET HIM.
IN FACT, HE'S TOTALLY DIFFERENT...
...WHEN HE'S WITH OTHER GIRLS...
...THAN HE IS WHEN HE'S WITH SAWAKO-CHAN.
I DIDN'T KNOW ...
...HE COULD LOOK SO HAPPY.

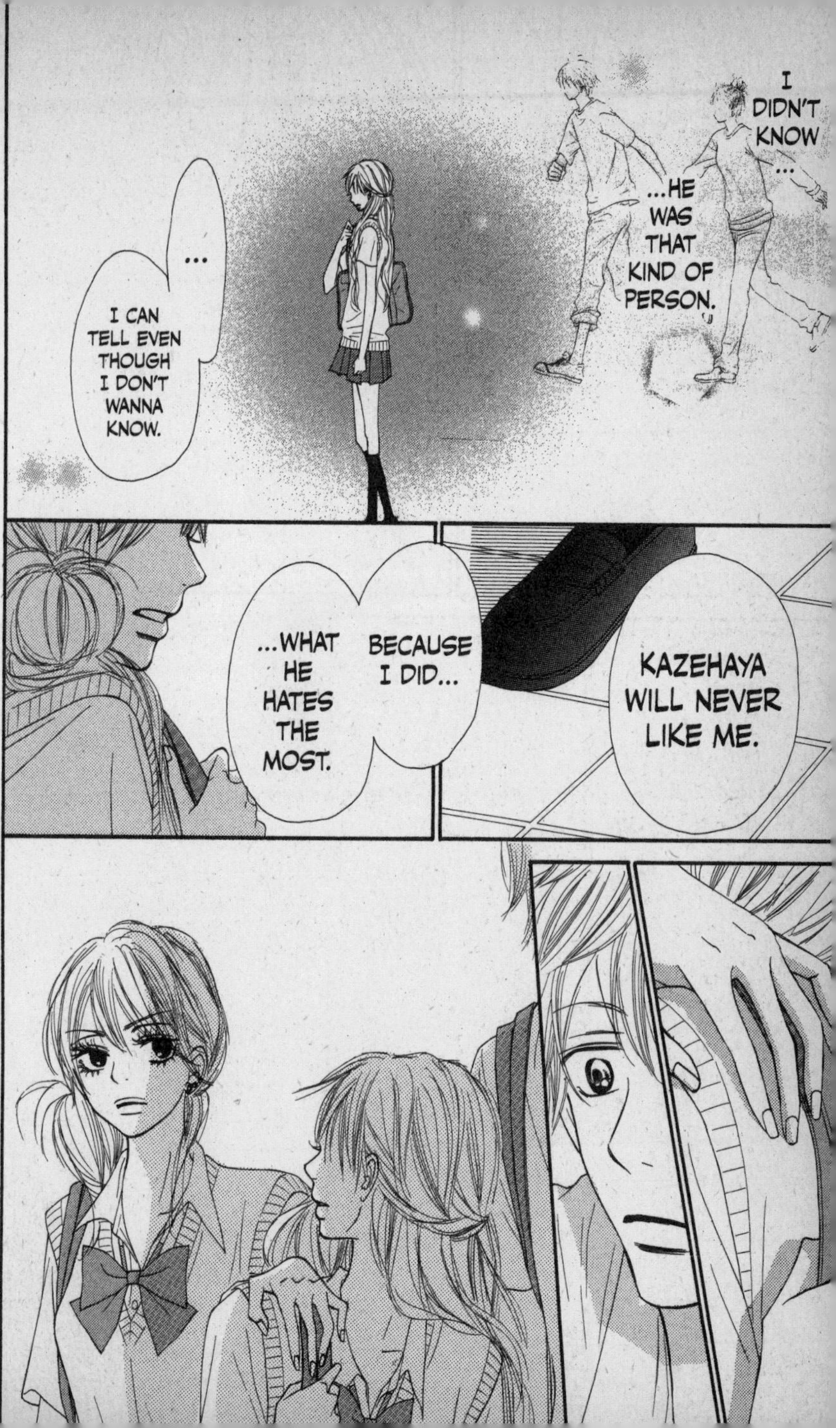
I DIDN'T KNOW...
...HE WAS THAT KIND OF PERSON.
... I CAN TELL EVEN THOUGH I DON'T WANNA KNOW.
KAZEHAYA WILL NEVER LIKE ME.
BECAUSE I DID...
...WHAT HE HATES THE MOST.

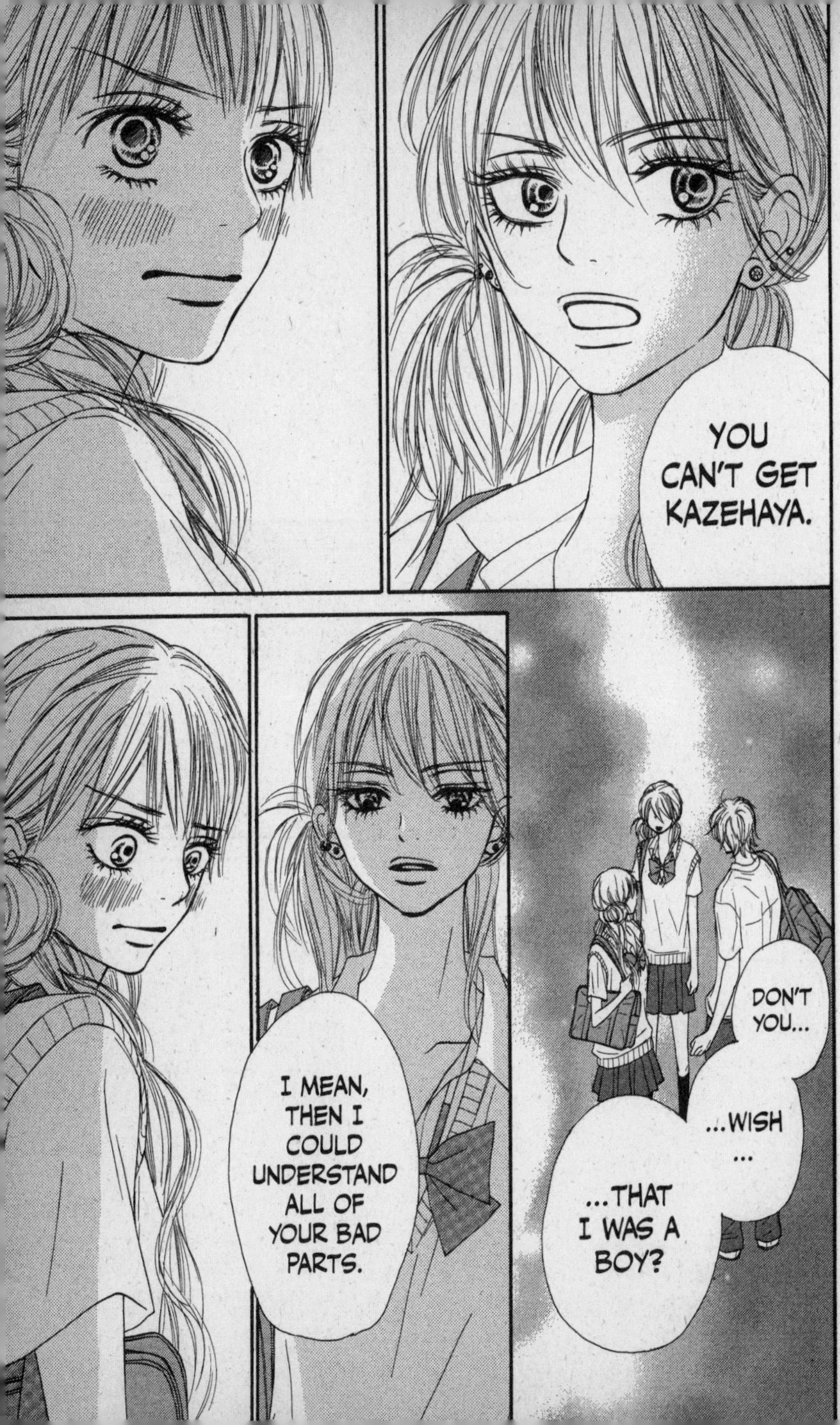
YOU CAN'T GET KAZEHAYA.
DON'T YOU...
...WISH ...
...THAT I WAS A BOY?
I MEAN, THEN I COULD UNDERSTAND ALL OF YOUR BAD PARTS.

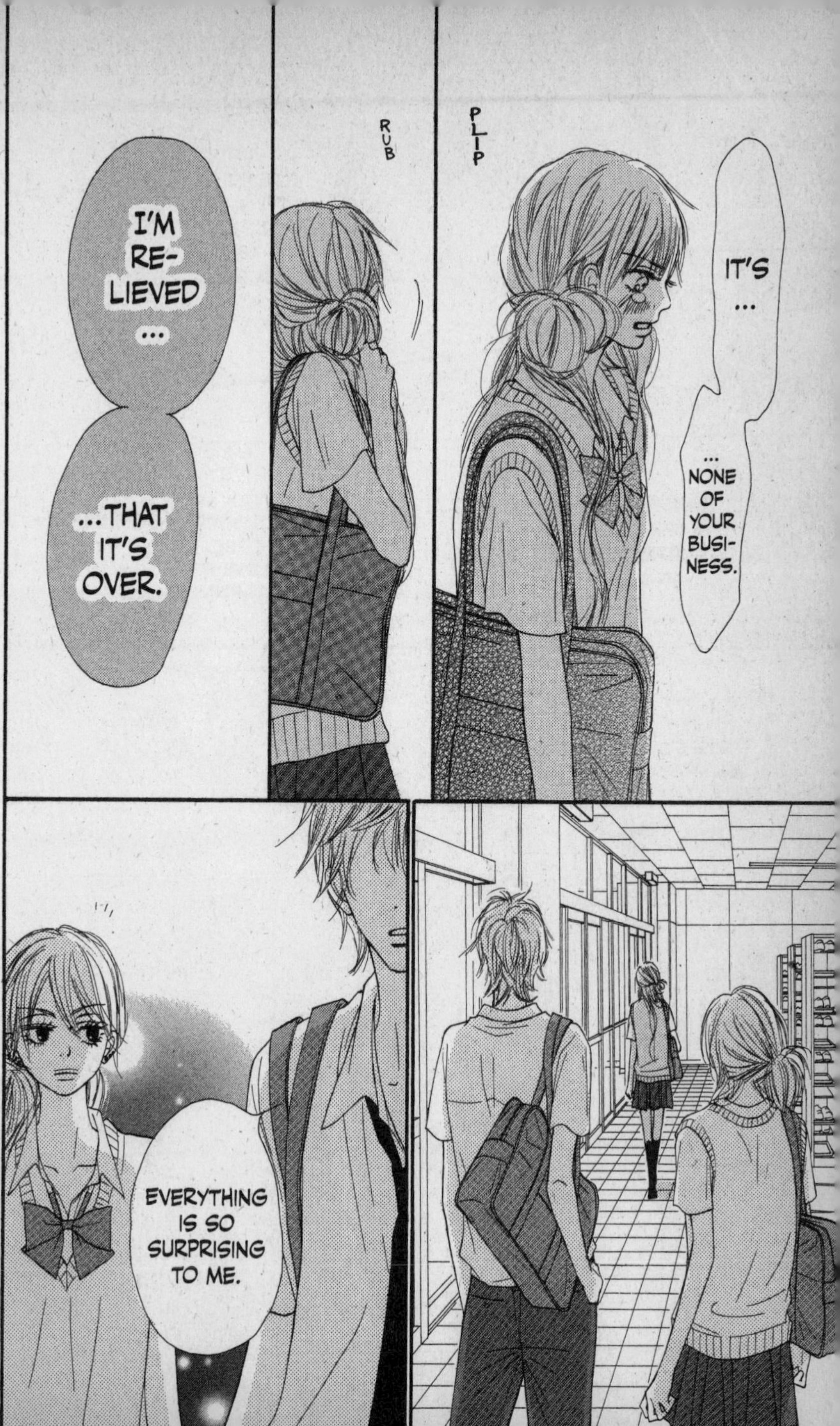
IT'S ...
... NONE OF YOUR BUSINESS.
PLIP
RUB
I'M RELIEVED ...
...THAT IT'S OVER.
EVERYTHING IS SO SURPRISING TO ME.

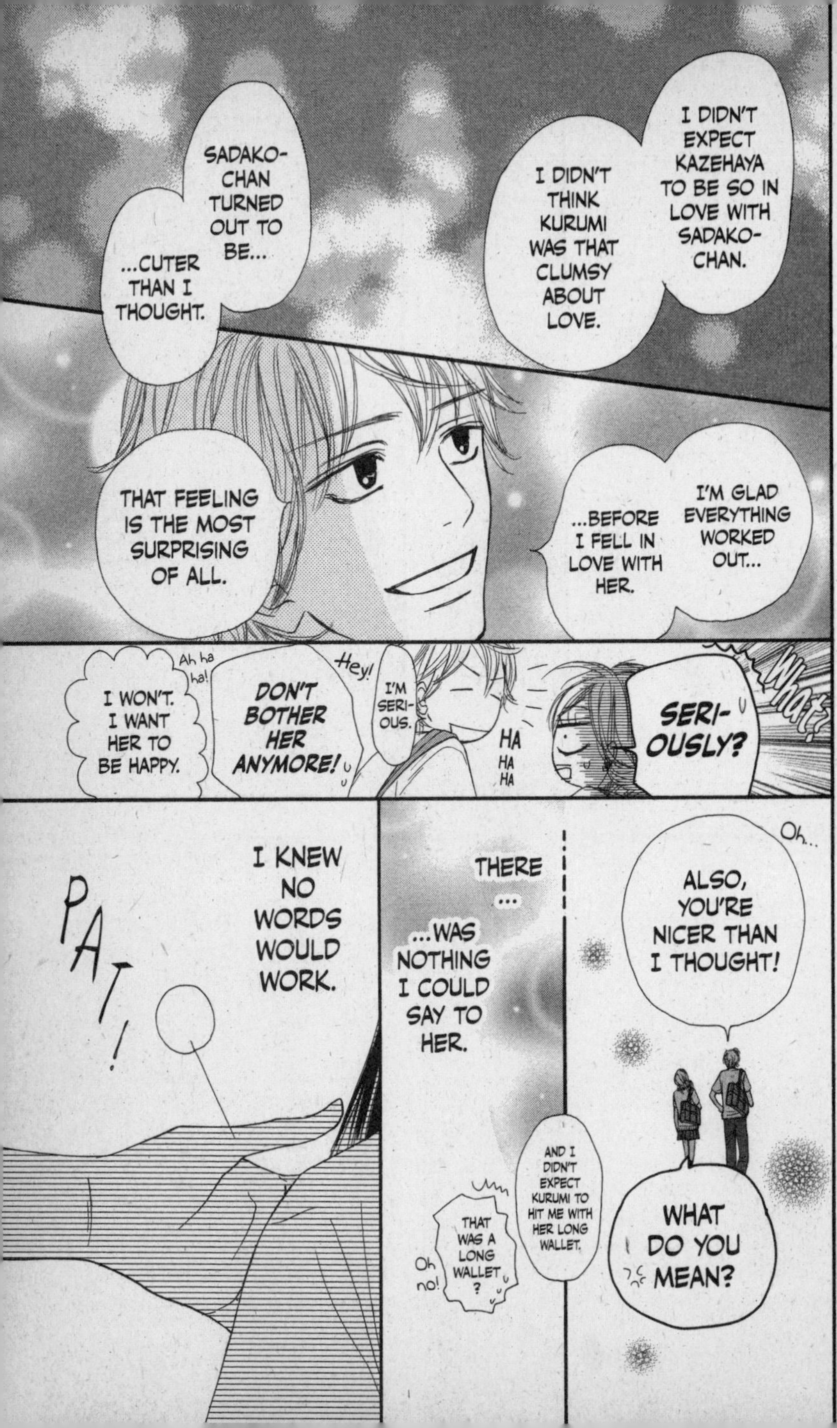
I DIDN'T EXPECT KAZEHAYA TO BE SO IN LOVE WITH SADAKO-CHAN.
I DIDN'T THINK KURUMI WAS THAT CLUMSY ABOUT LOVE.
SADAKO-CHAN TURNED OUT TO BE...
...CUTER THAN I THOUGHT.
I'M GLAD EVERYTHING WORKED OUT...
...BEFORE I FELL IN LOVE WITH HER.
THAT FEELING IS THE MOST SURPRISING OF ALL.
What?!
SERI-OUSLY?
HA HA HA HA
I'M SERI-OUS.
Hey!
DON'T BOTHER HER ANYMORE!
Ah ha ha!
I WON'T. I WANT HER TO BE HAPPY.
Oh...
ALSO, YOU'RE NICER THAN I THOUGHT!
WHAT DO YOU MEAN?
AND I DIDN'T EXPECT KURUMI TO HIT ME WITH HER LONG WALLET.
THAT WAS A LONG WALLET?
Oh no!
THERE...
...WAS NOTHING I COULD SAY TO HER.
I KNEW NO WORDS WOULD WORK.
PAT!

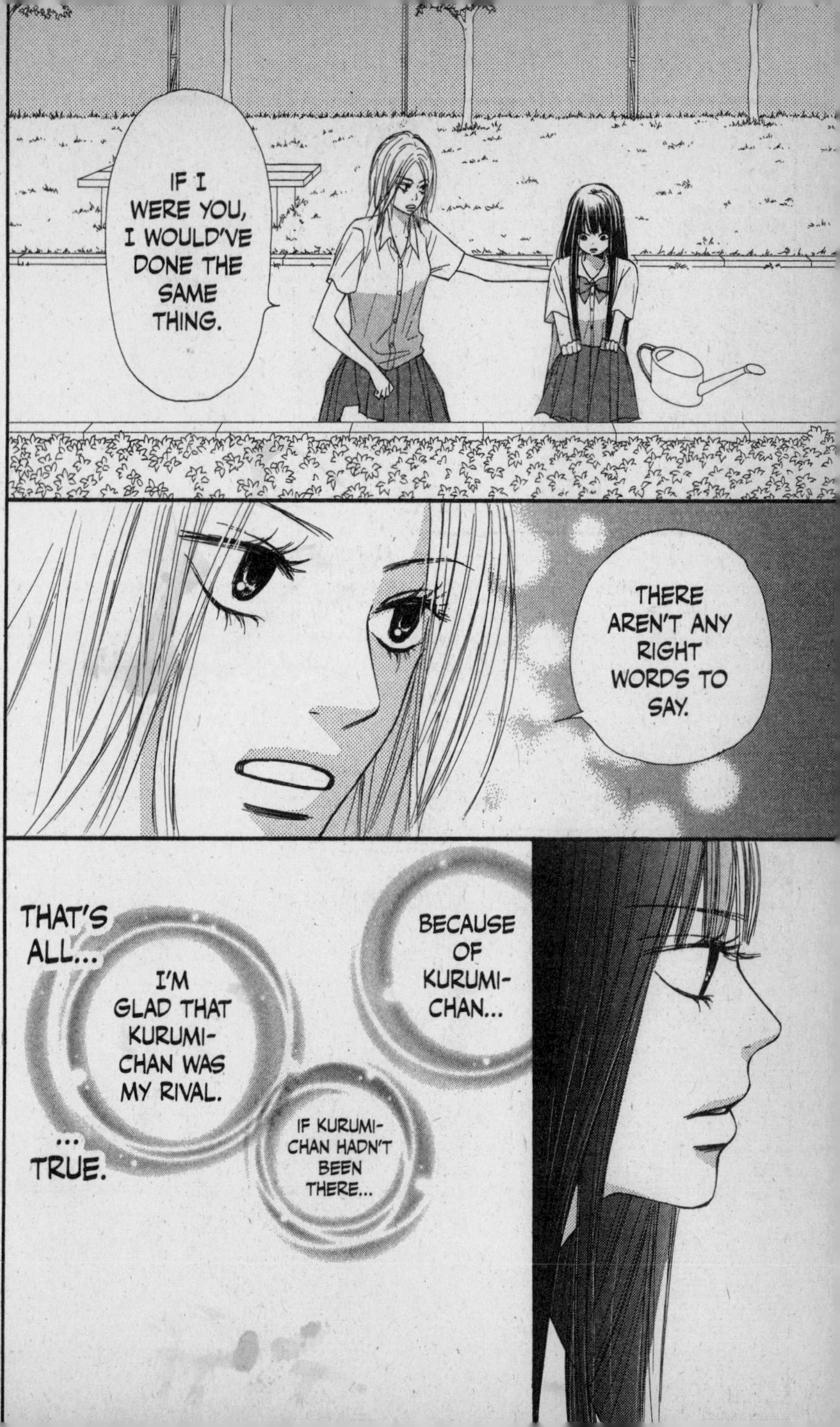
IF I WERE YOU, I WOULD'VE DONE THE SAME THING.
THERE AREN'T ANY RIGHT WORDS TO SAY.
BECAUSE OF KURUMI-CHAN...
IF KURUMI-CHAN HADN'T BEEN THERE...
I'M GLAD THAT KURUMI-CHAN WAS MY RIVAL.
THAT'S ALL...
... TRUE.

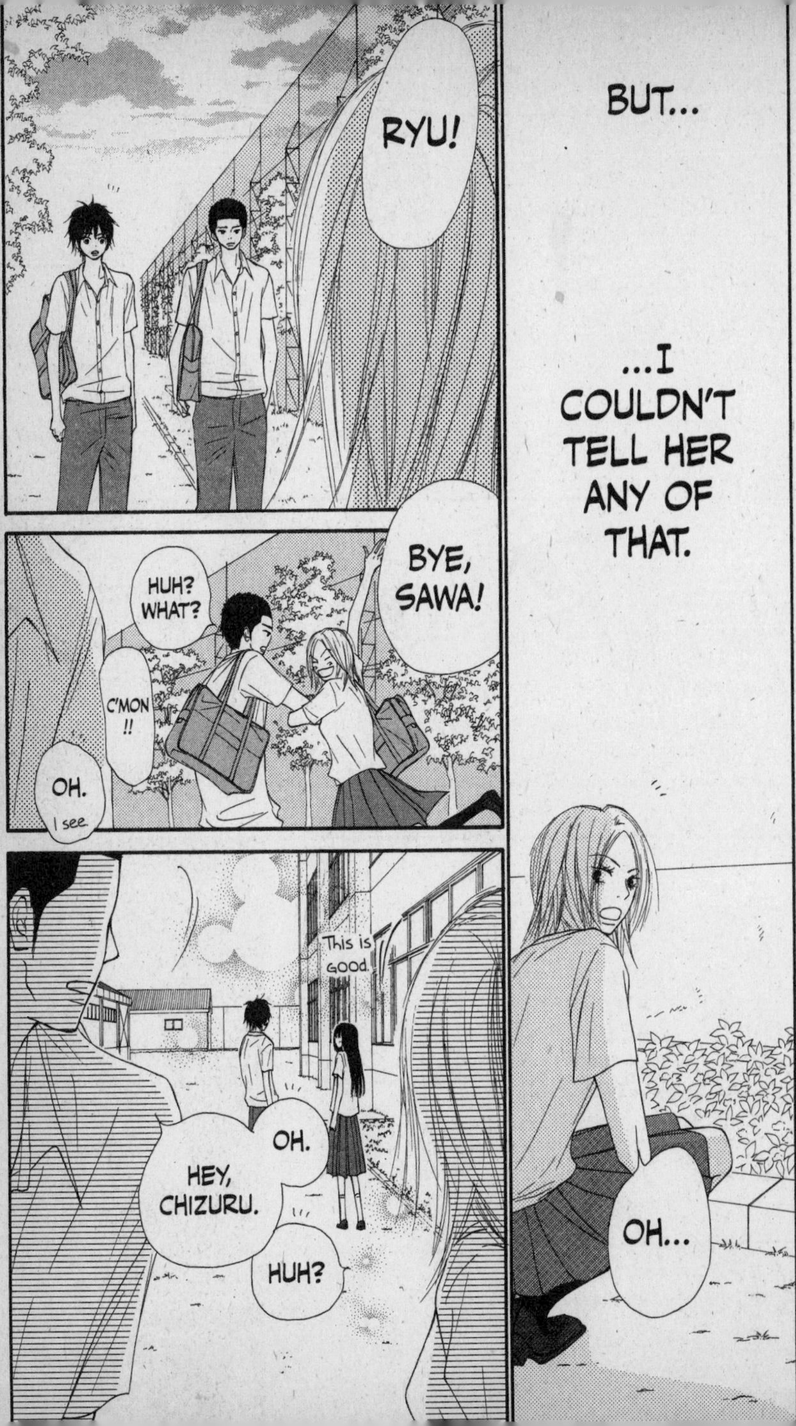
BUT...
...I COULDN'T TELL HER ANY OF THAT.
OH...
RYU!
BYE, SAWA!
HUH? WHAT?
C'MON!!
OH.
I see.
OH.
HEY, CHIZURU.
This is good.
HUH?

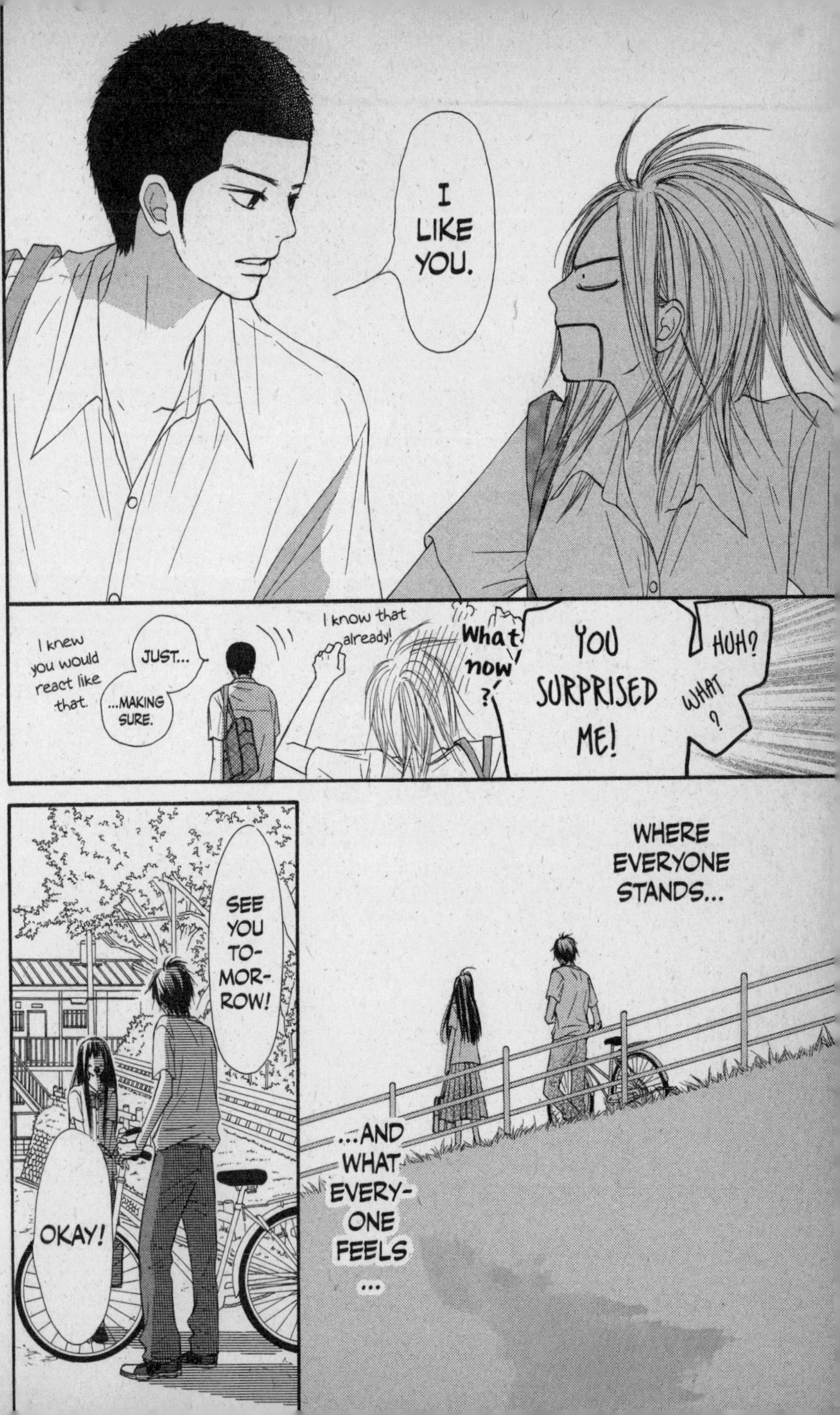
I LIKE YOU.
HUH? WHAT?
YOU SURPRISED ME!
What now?
I know that already!
JUST... ...MAKING SURE.
I knew you would react like that.
WHERE EVERYONE STANDS...
...AND WHAT EVERY-ONE FEELS...
SEE YOU TO-MOR-ROW!
OKAY!

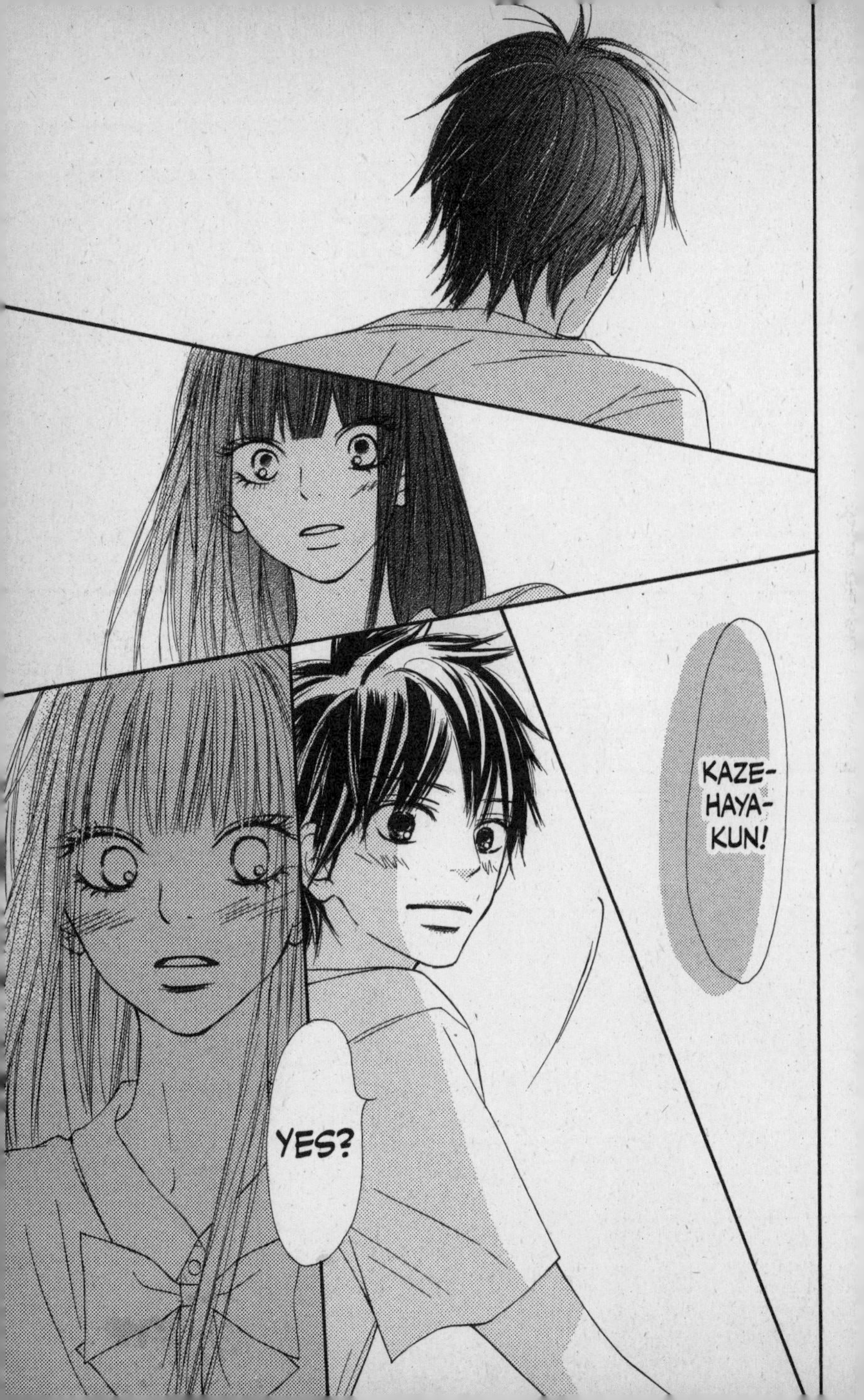
KAZE-HAYA-KUN!
YES?

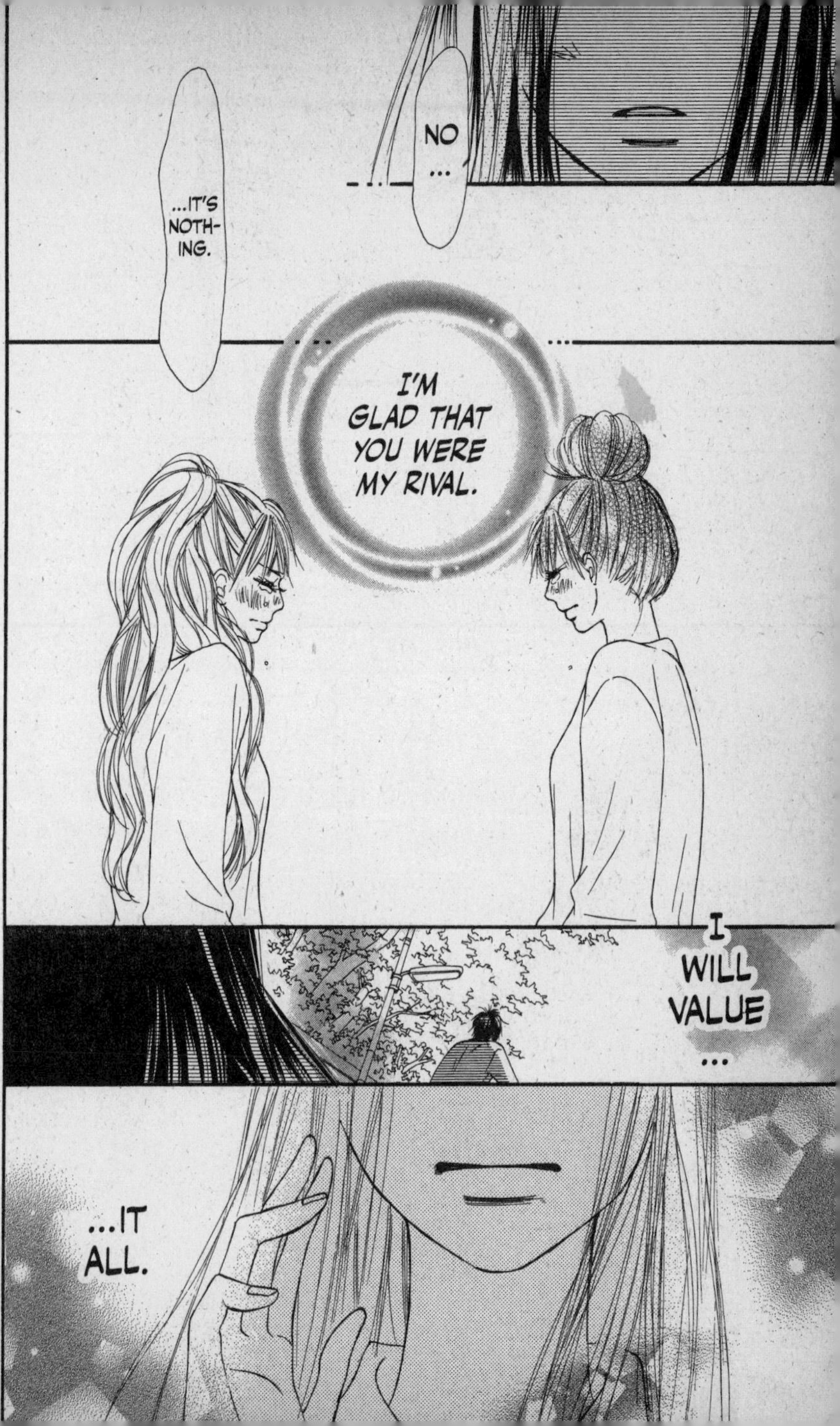
NO ...
...IT'S NOTHING.
I'M GLAD THAT YOU WERE MY RIVAL.
I WILL VALUE ...
...IT ALL.

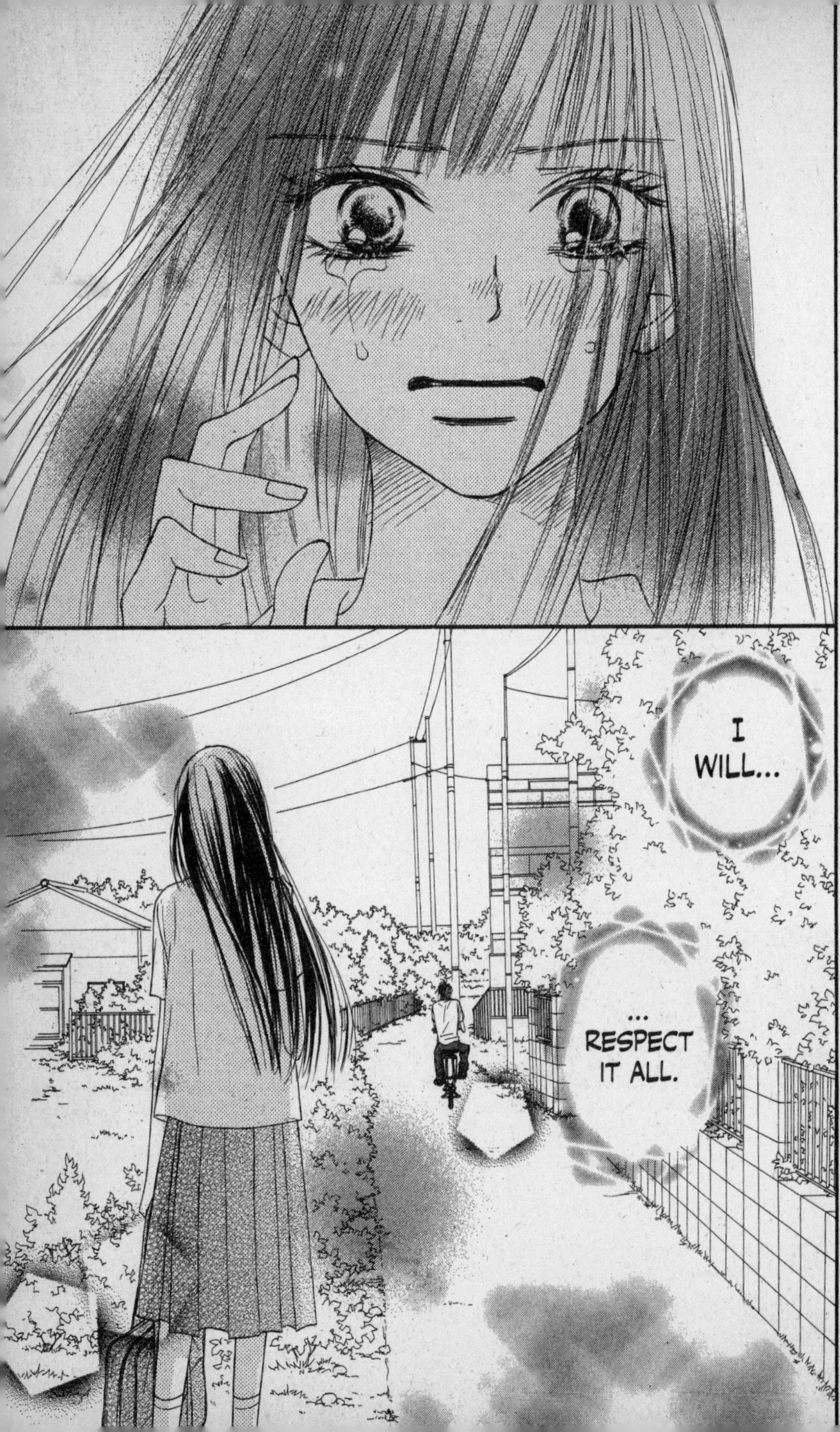
I WILL...
... RESPECT IT ALL.

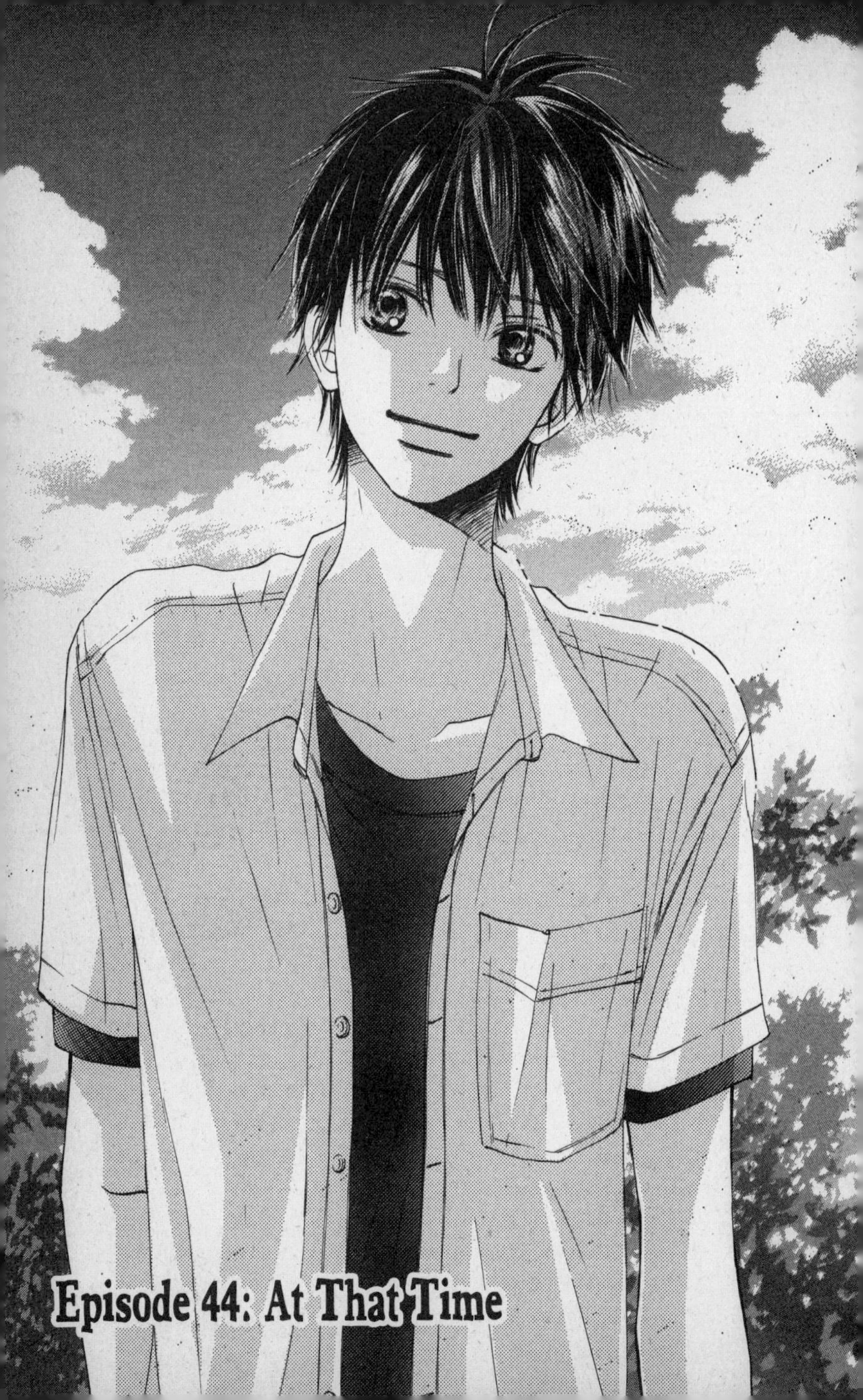

Episode 44: At That Time

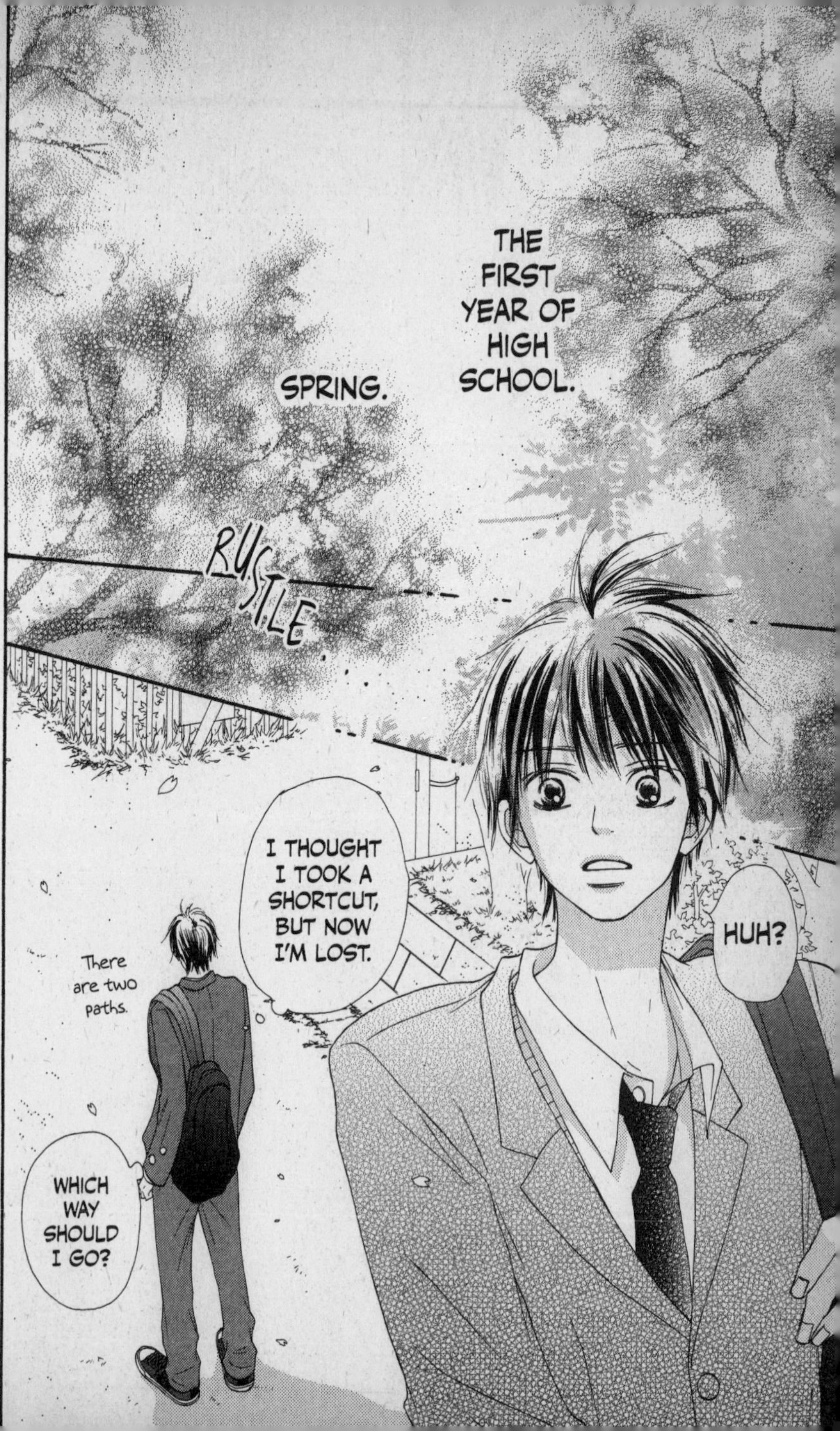
THE FIRST YEAR OF HIGH SCHOOL.
SPRING.
RUSTLE
HUH?
I THOUGHT I TOOK A SHORTCUT, BUT NOW I'M LOST.
There are two paths.
WHICH WAY SHOULD I GO?

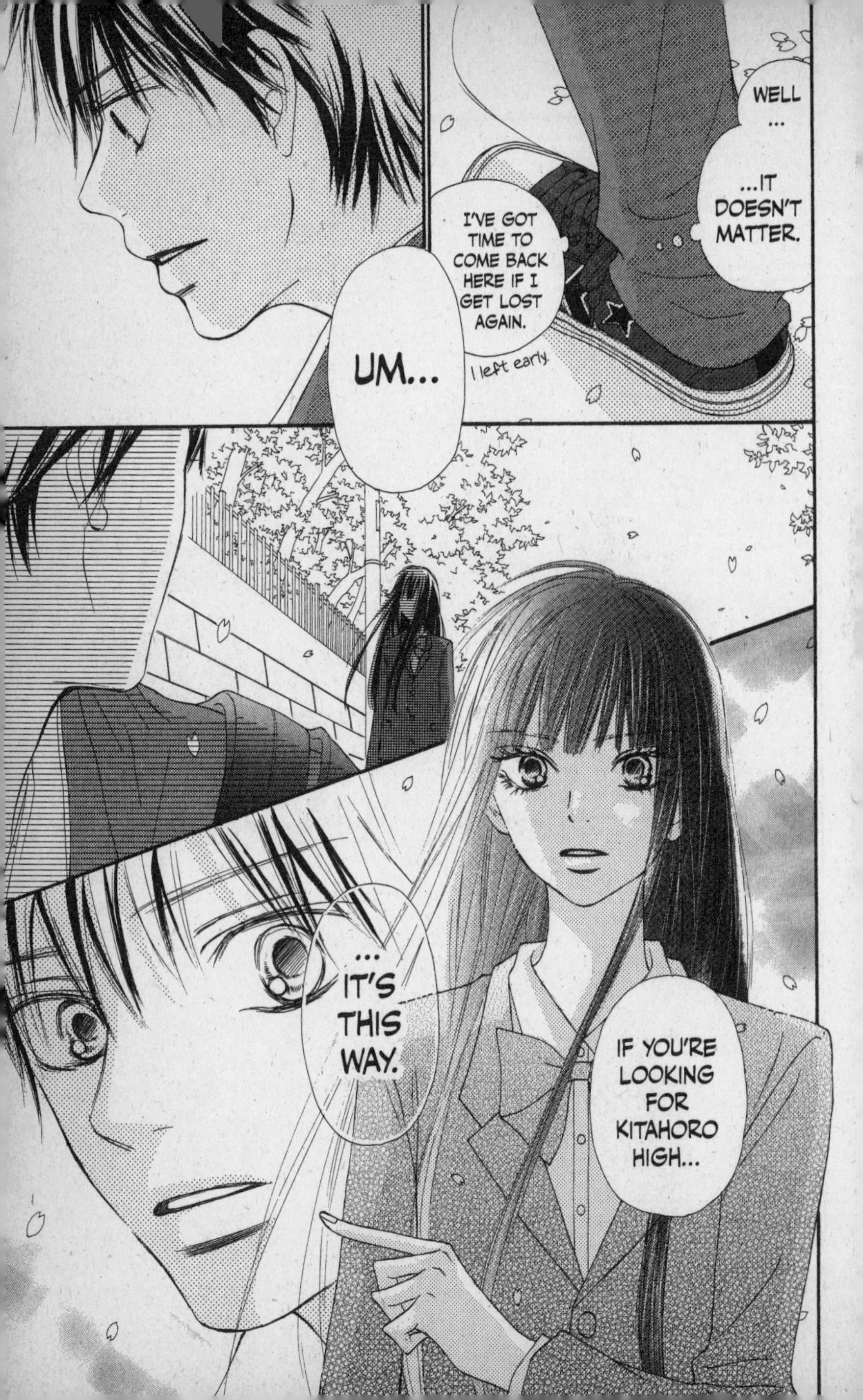
WELL ...
...IT DOESN'T MATTER.
I'VE GOT TIME TO COME BACK HERE IF I GET LOST AGAIN.
I left early.
UM...
IF YOU'RE LOOKING FOR KITAHORO HIGH...
...IT'S THIS WAY.

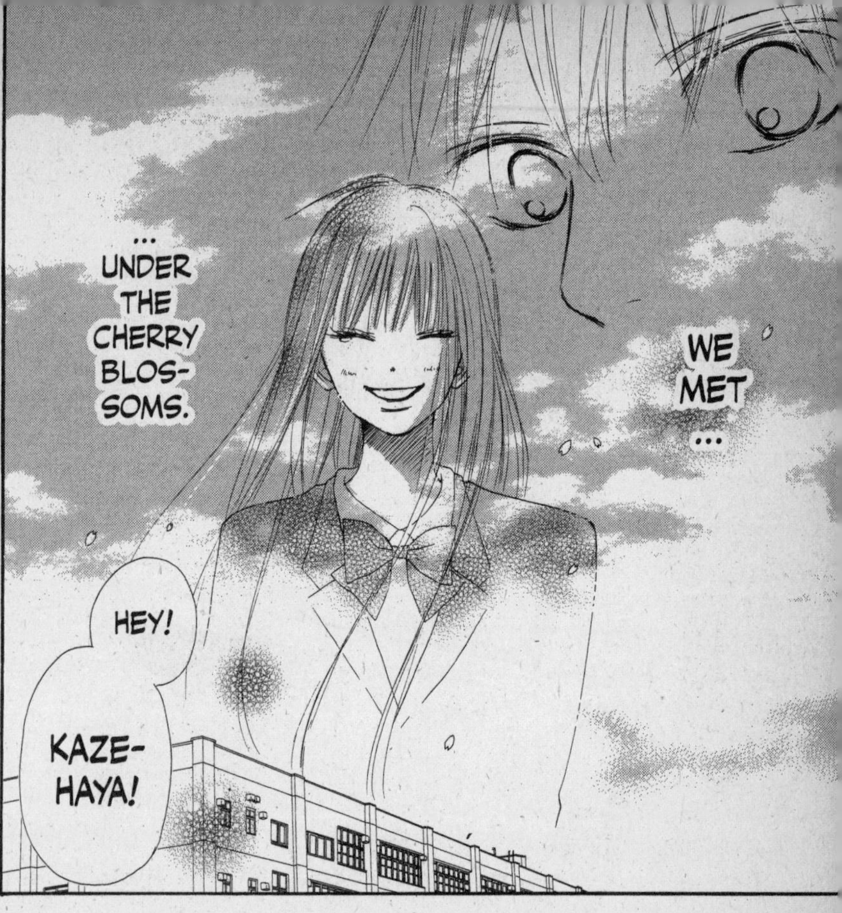
WE MET ...
... UNDER THE CHERRY BLOS-SOMS.
HEY!
KAZE-HAYA!

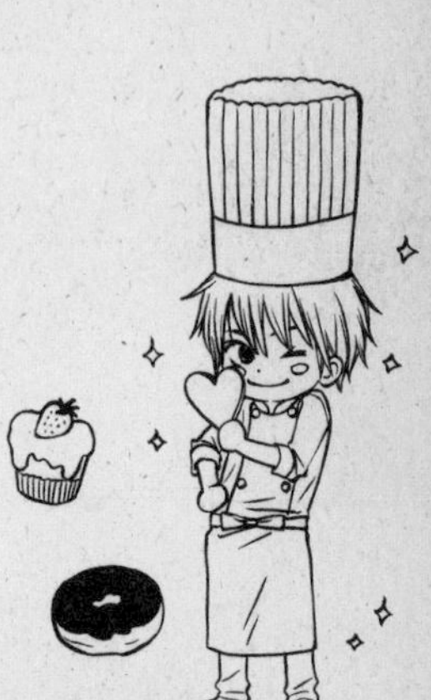

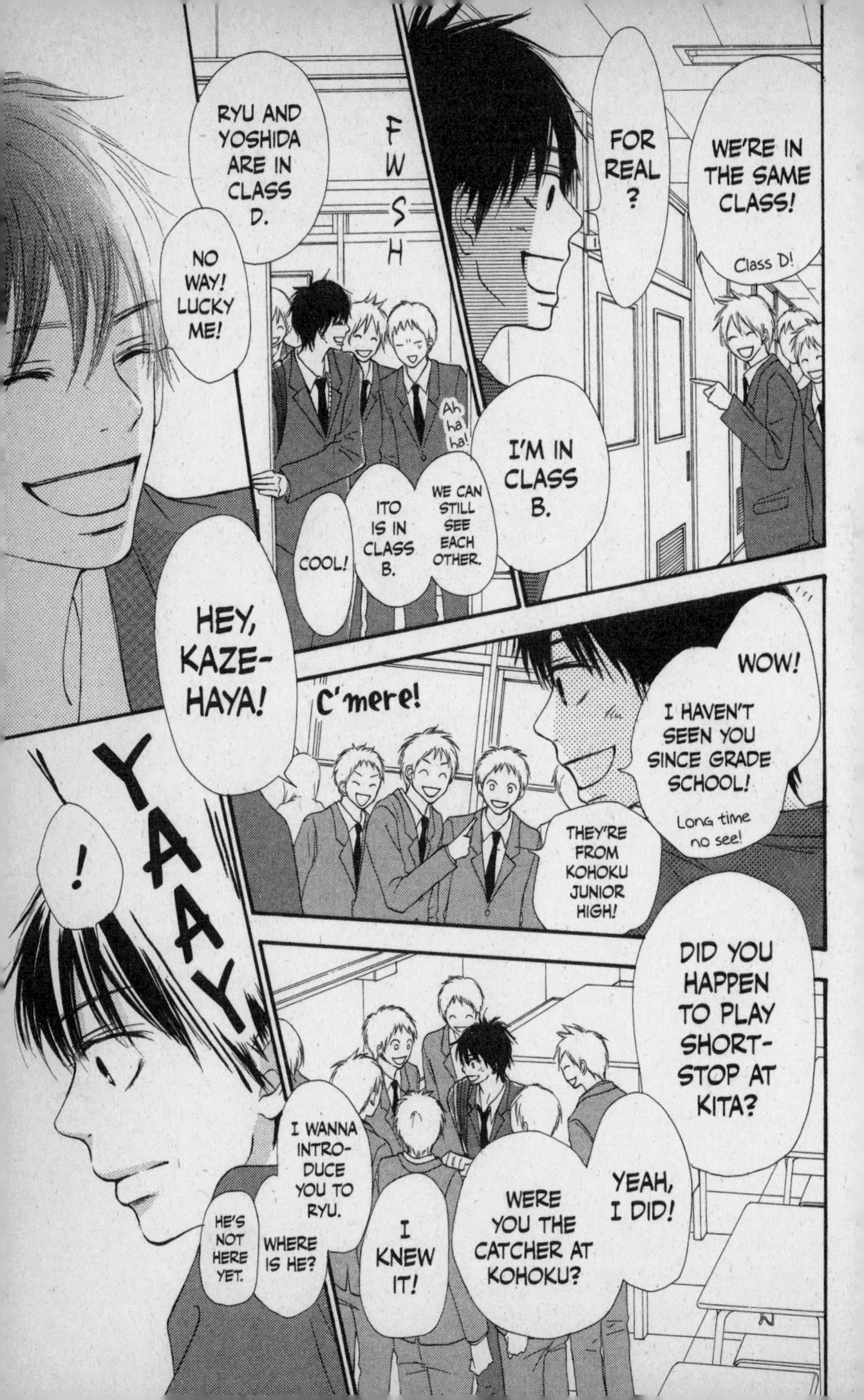
WE'RE IN THE SAME CLASS!
Class D!
FOR REAL?
I'M IN CLASS B.
RYU AND YOSHIDA ARE IN CLASS D.
FWSH
NO WAY! LUCKY ME!
Ah ha ha!
WE CAN STILL SEE EACH OTHER.
ITO IS IN CLASS B.
COOL!
HEY, KAZE-HAYA!
WOW!
I HAVEN'T SEEN YOU SINCE GRADE SCHOOL!
Long time no see!
THEY'RE FROM KOHOKU JUNIOR HIGH!
C'mere!
YAAY!
!
DID YOU HAPPEN TO PLAY SHORT-STOP AT KITA?
YEAH, I DID!
WERE YOU THE CATCHER AT KOHOKU?
I KNEW IT!
I WANNA INTRO-DUCE YOU TO RYU.
WHERE IS HE?
HE'S NOT HERE YET.

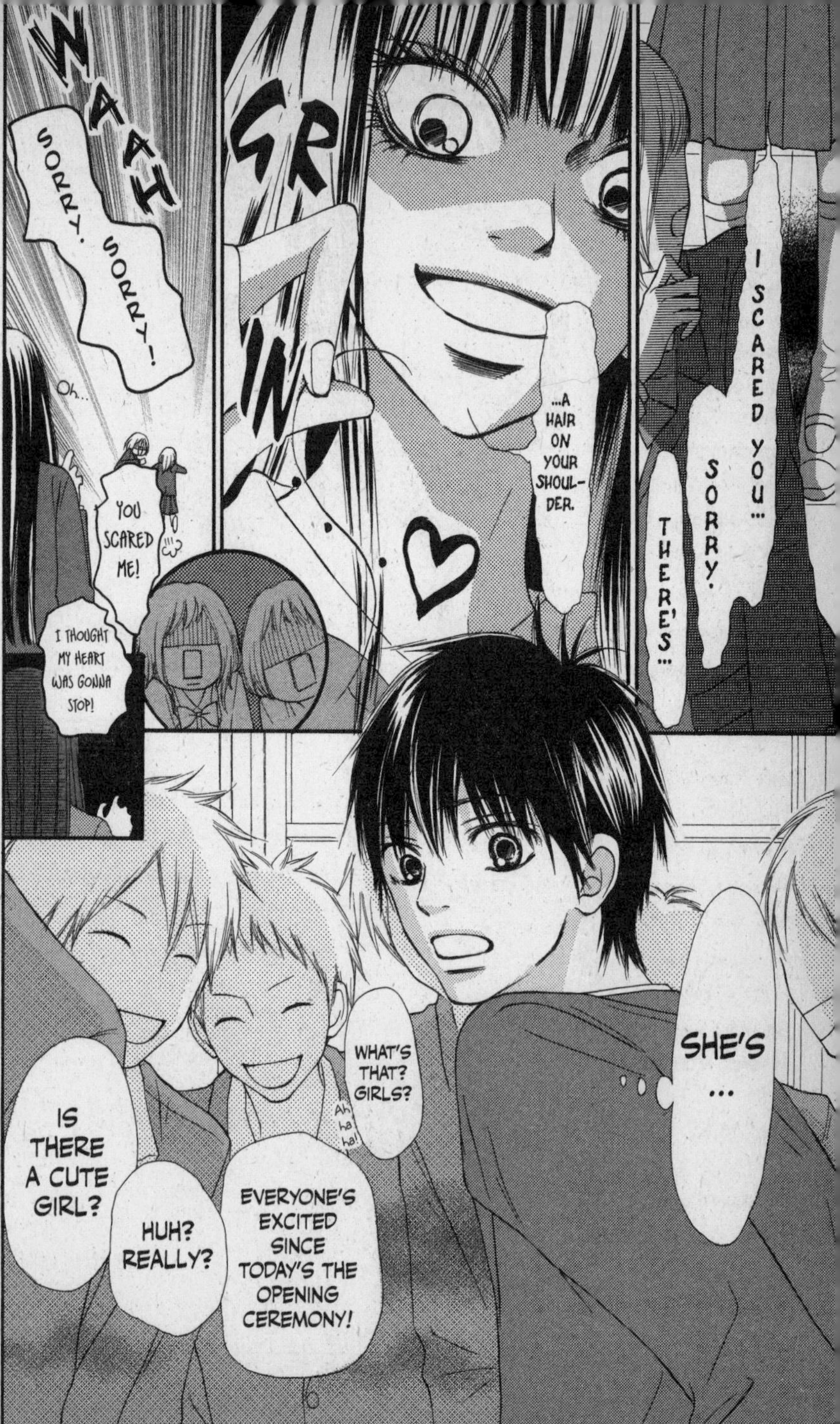
I SCARED YOU...
SORRY.
THERE'S...
SRN
...A HAIR ON YOUR SHOULDER.
WAAAH
SORRY! SORRY! SORRY!
Oh...
YOU SCARED ME!
I THOUGHT MY HEART WAS GONNA STOP!
SHE'S ...
WHAT'S THAT? GIRLS?
Ah ha ha!
EVERYONE'S EXCITED SINCE TODAY'S THE OPENING CEREMONY!
IS THERE A CUTE GIRL?
HUH? REALLY?

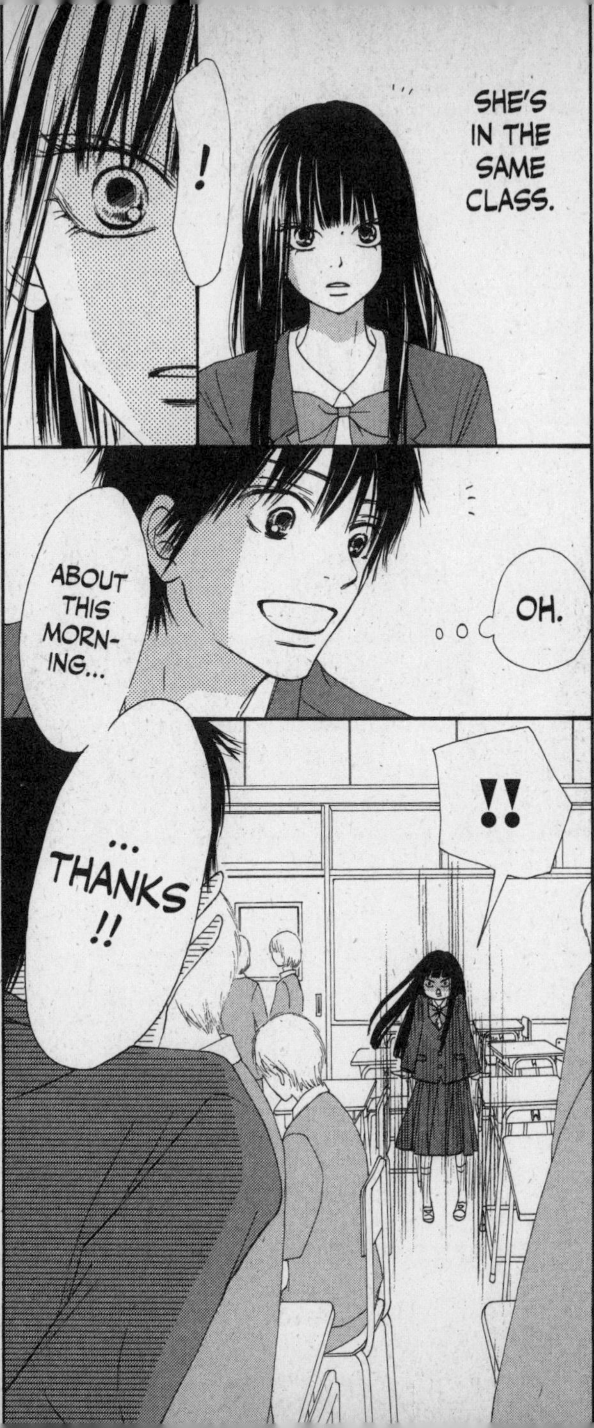
SHE'S IN THE SAME CLASS.
!
OH.
ABOUT THIS MORNING...
!!
...THANKS!!

KARUPIN on JAPAN 2

By the way, a fan book will be released at the same time as this volume! How nice that sounds! Fan book! To celebrate, I'll be signing autographs in Sapporo!

An autograph session...

Isn't it amazing?

I get so nervous just thinking about it.

We might see each other there!

I'll probably sign copies of volume 11.

Sorry if I have "an accident" when we meet.

PSSS PSSS

No, I didn't do what you think! I really didn't!

Waaah!

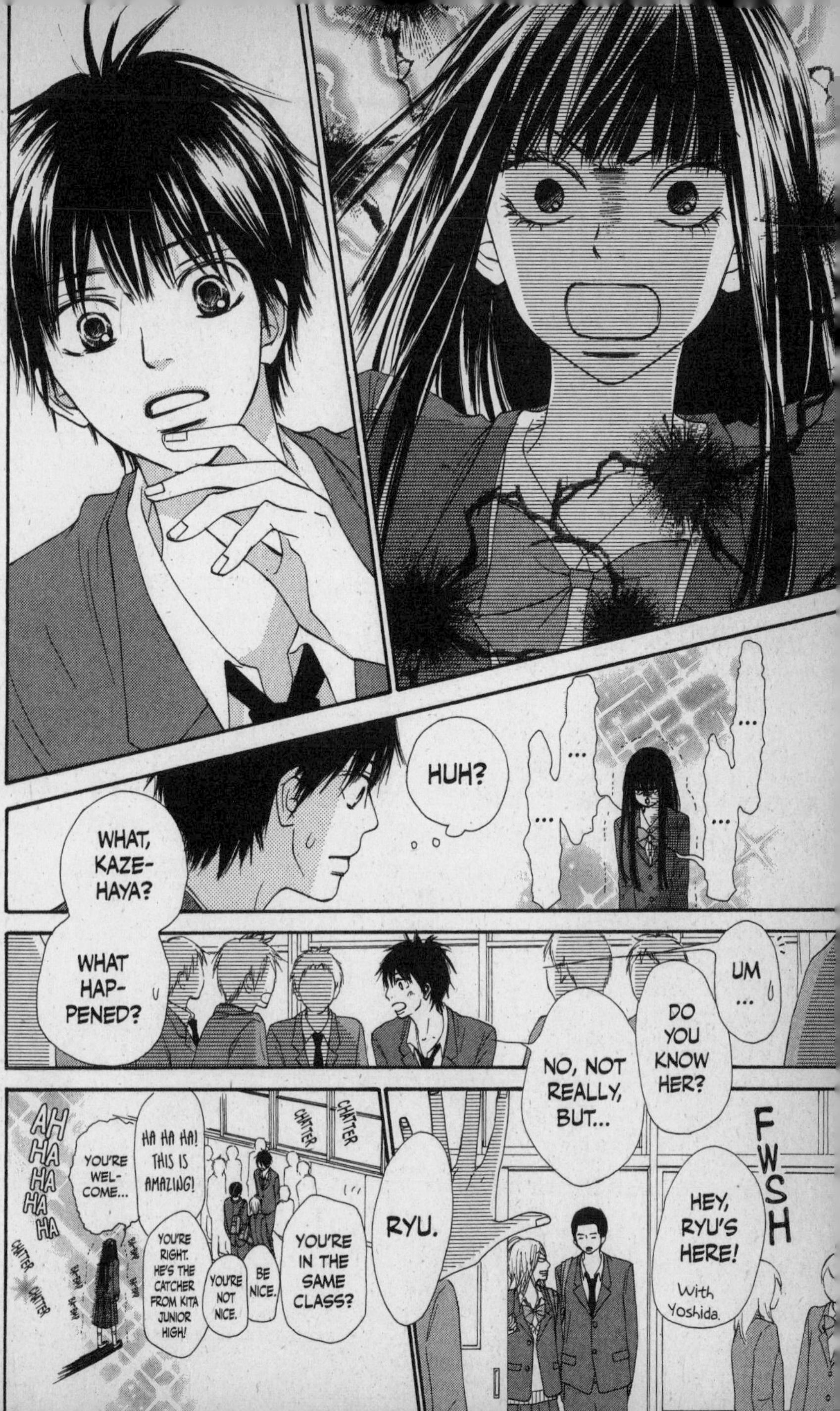
...
...
...
...
HUH?
WHAT, KAZE-HAYA?
WHAT HAP-PENED?
UM ...
DO YOU KNOW HER?
NO, NOT REALLY, BUT...
FWSH
HEY, RYU'S HERE!
With Yoshida.
RYU.
YOU'RE IN THE SAME CLASS?
CHATTER
CHATTER
HA HA HA! THIS IS AMAZING!
YOU'RE WEL-COME...
AH HA HA HA HA HA
BE NICE.
YOU'RE NOT NICE.
YOU'RE RIGHT. HE'S THE CATCHER FROM KITA JUNIOR HIGH!
CHATTER
CHATTER

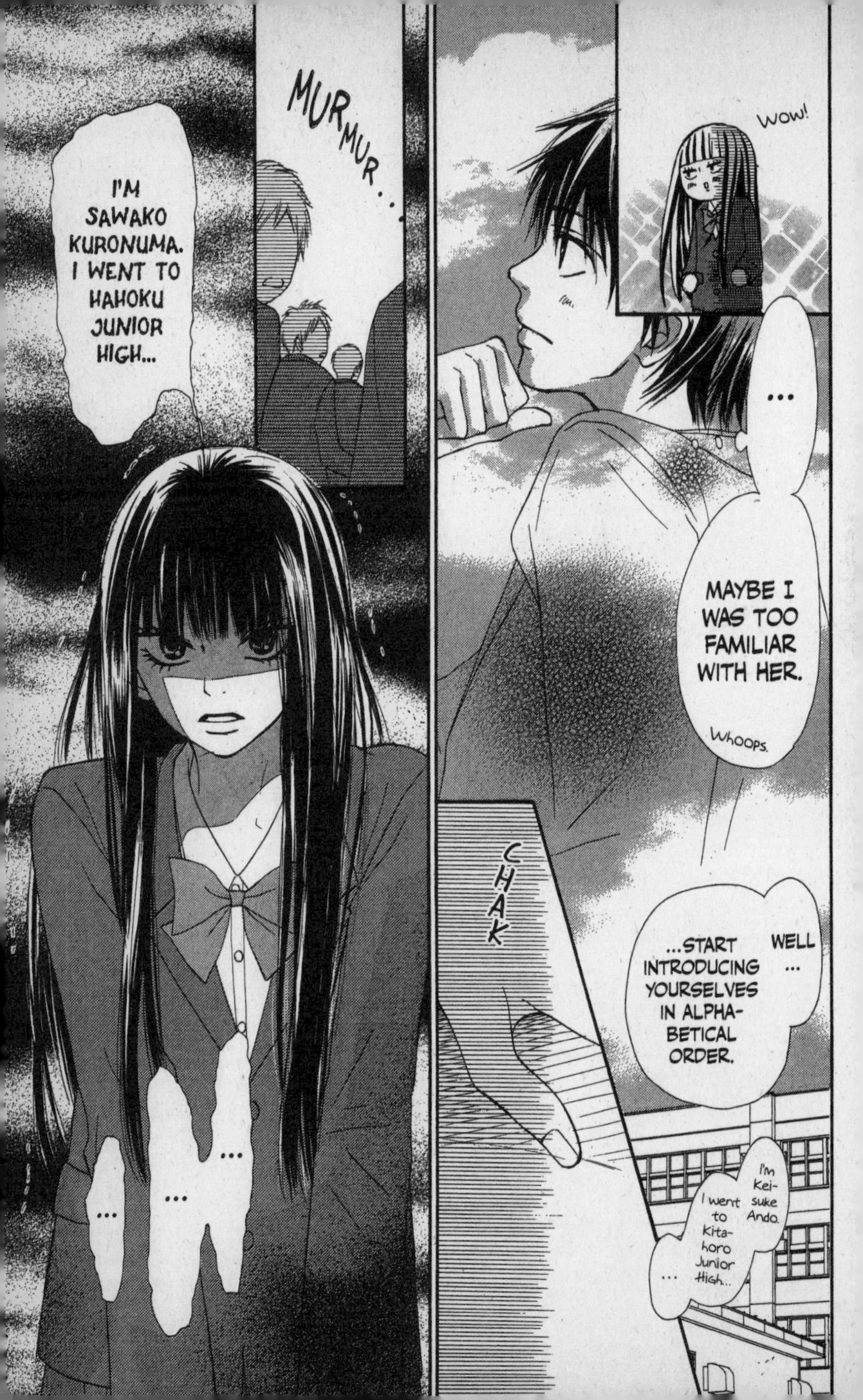
WOW!
...
MAYBE I WAS TOO FAMILIAR WITH HER.
Whoops.
WELL ...
...START INTRODUCING YOURSELVES IN ALPHABETICAL ORDER.
CHAK
I'm Keisuke Ando. I went to Kitahoro Junior High...
...
MURMUR...
I'M SAWAKO KURONUMA. I WENT TO HAHOKU JUNIOR HIGH...
...
...
...

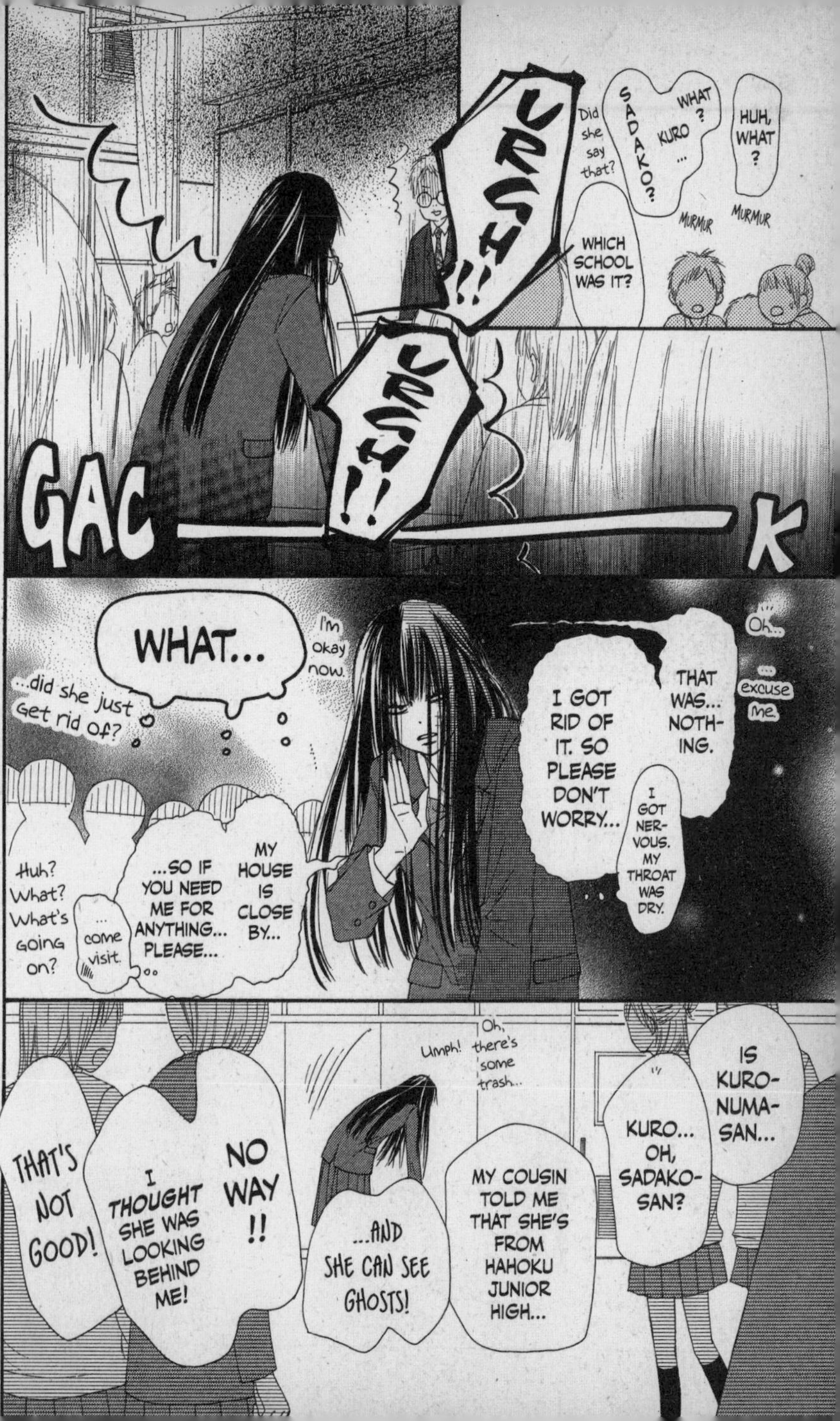
HUH, WHAT?
MURMUR
WHAT? KURO... SADAKO?
MURMUR
Did she say that?
WHICH SCHOOL WAS IT?
URSH!!
URSH!!
GAC—K
Oh...
...excuse me.
THAT WAS... NOTHING.
I GOT RID OF IT. SO PLEASE DON'T WORRY...
I GOT NERVOUS. MY THROAT WAS DRY.
I'm okay now.
WHAT...
...did she just get rid of?
MY HOUSE IS CLOSE BY...
...SO IF YOU NEED ME FOR ANYTHING... PLEASE...
...come visit.
Huh? What? What's going on?
IS KURONUMA-SAN...
KURO... OH, SADAKO-SAN?
Oh, there's some trash...
Umph!
MY COUSIN TOLD ME THAT SHE'S FROM HAHOKU JUNIOR HIGH...
...AND SHE CAN SEE GHOSTS!
NO WAY!!
I THOUGHT SHE WAS LOOKING BEHIND ME!
THAT'S NOT GOOD!

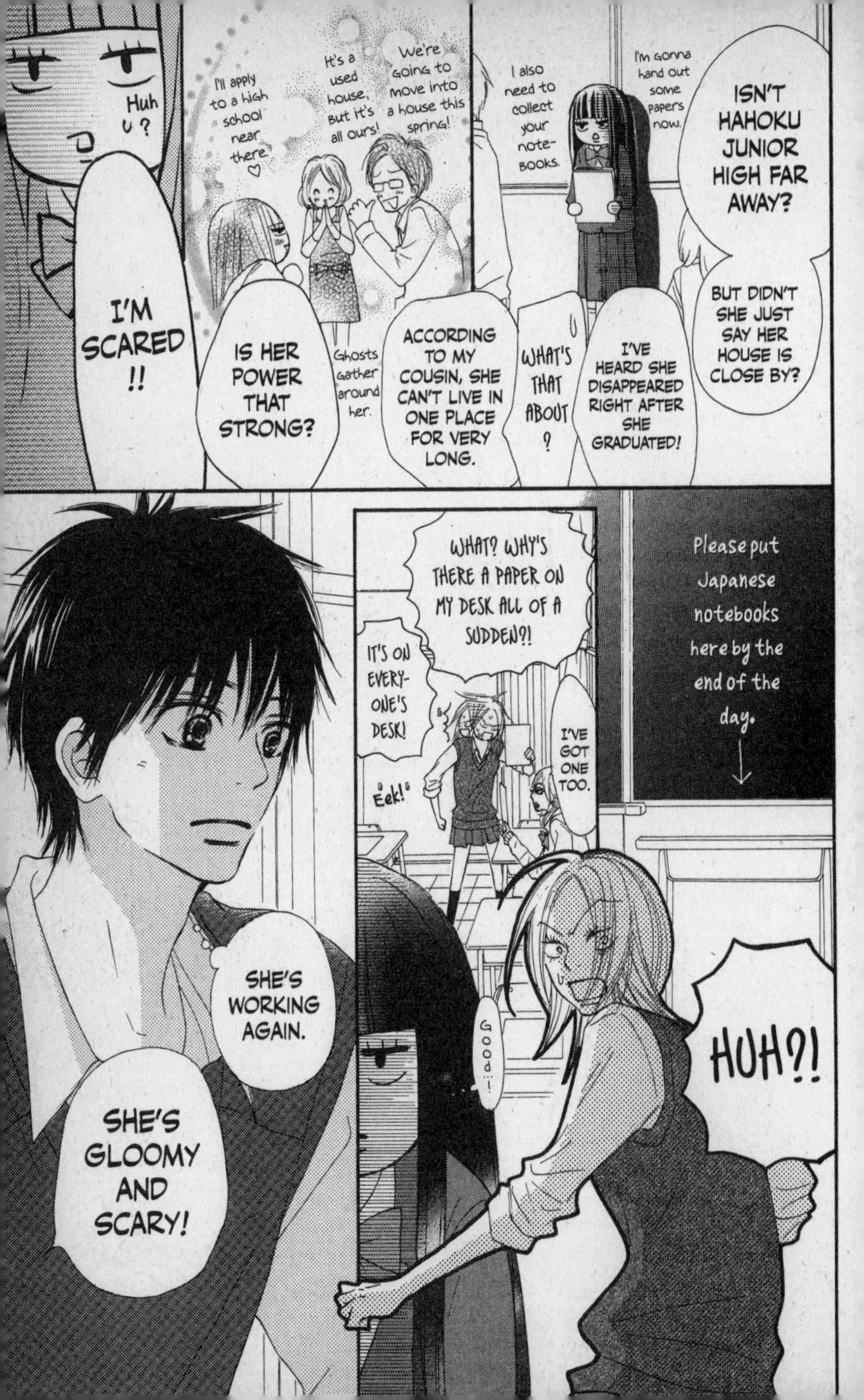
I'm gonna hand out some papers now.
I also need to collect your notebooks.
ISN'T HAHOKU JUNIOR HIGH FAR AWAY?
BUT DIDN'T SHE JUST SAY HER HOUSE IS CLOSE BY?
I'VE HEARD SHE DISAPPEARED RIGHT AFTER SHE GRADUATED!
WHAT'S THAT ABOUT?
We're going to move into a house this spring!
It's a used house, but it's all ours!
I'll apply to a high school near there ♡
ACCORDING TO MY COUSIN, SHE CAN'T LIVE IN ONE PLACE FOR VERY LONG.
Ghosts gather around her.
IS HER POWER THAT STRONG?
Huh?
I'M SCARED!!
Please put Japanese notebooks here by the end of the day.
WHAT? WHY'S THERE A PAPER ON MY DESK ALL OF A SUDDEN?!
I'VE GOT ONE TOO.
IT'S ON EVERYONE'S DESK!
Eek!
HUH?!
Good...!
SHE'S WORKING AGAIN.
SHE'S GLOOMY AND SCARY!

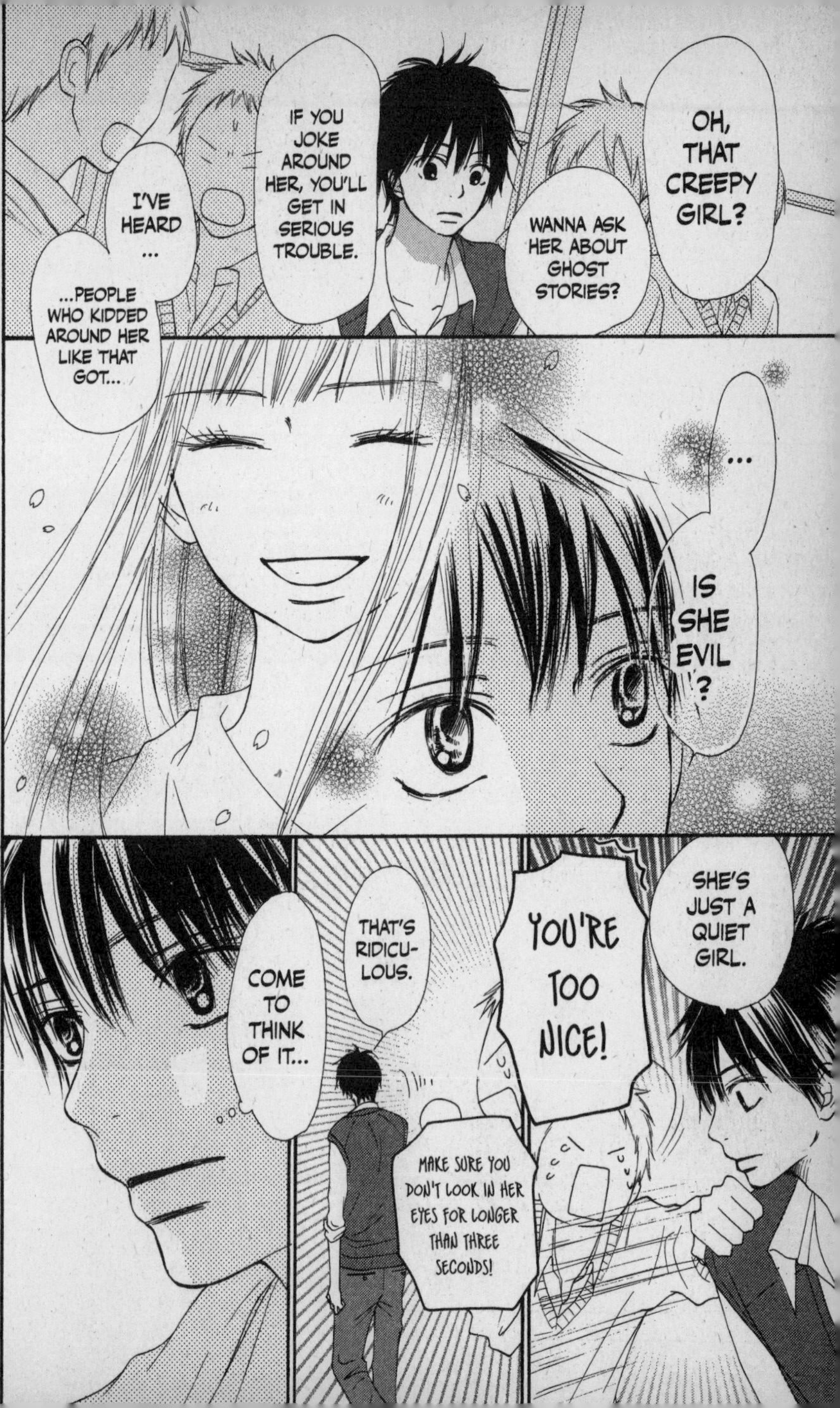
OH, THAT CREEPY GIRL?
WANNA ASK HER ABOUT GHOST STORIES?
IF YOU JOKE AROUND HER, YOU'LL GET IN SERIOUS TROUBLE.
I'VE HEARD ...
...PEOPLE WHO KIDDED AROUND HER LIKE THAT GOT...
...
IS SHE EVIL ?
SHE'S JUST A QUIET GIRL.
YOU'RE TOO NICE!
MAKE SURE YOU DON'T LOOK IN HER EYES FOR LONGER THAN THREE SECONDS!
THAT'S RIDICU-LOUS.
COME TO THINK OF IT...

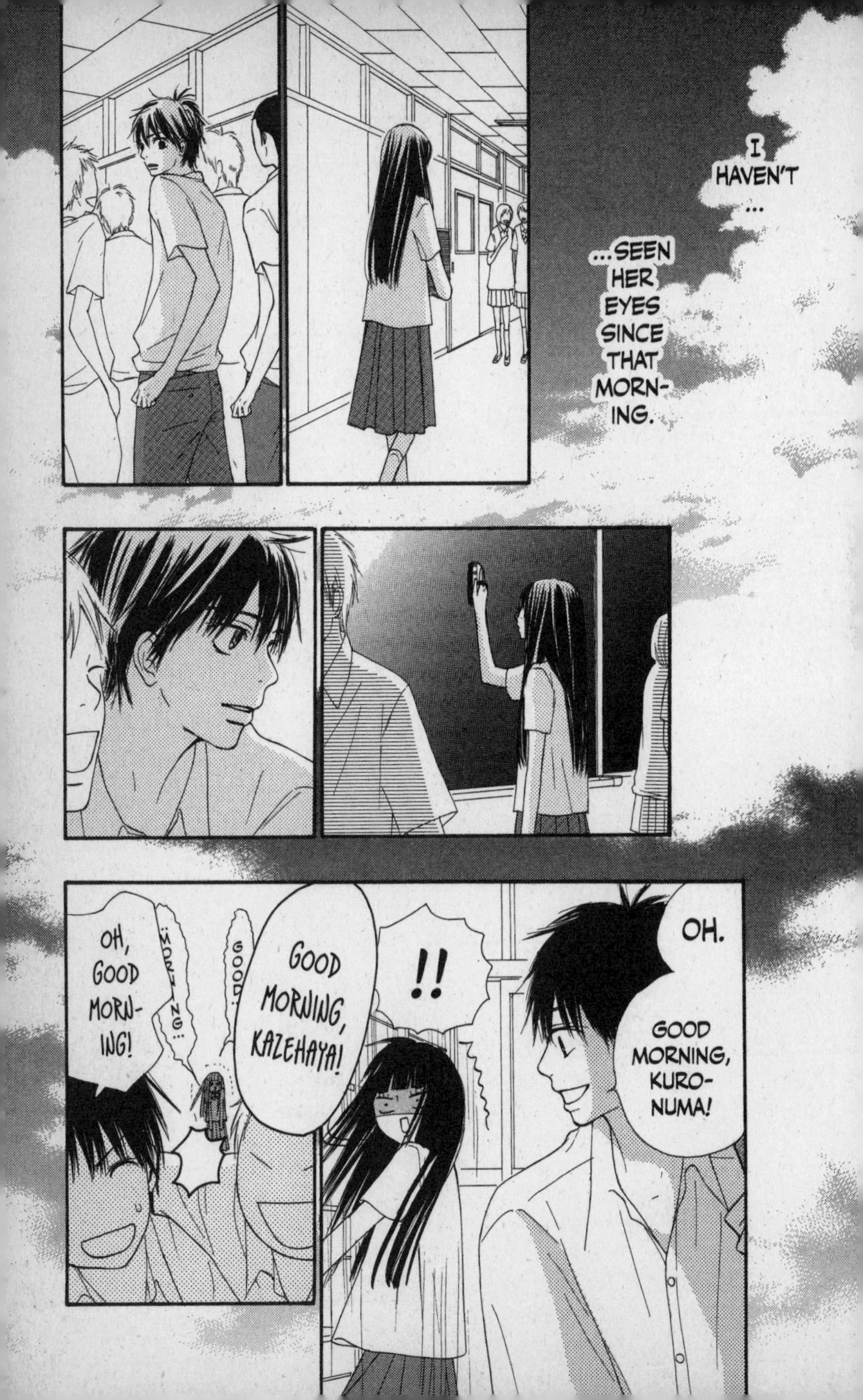
I HAVEN'T ...
...SEEN HER EYES SINCE THAT MORNING.
OH.
GOOD MORNING, KURONUMA!
!!
GOOD MORNING, KAZEHAYA!
GOOD...
MORNING...
OH, GOOD MORNING!

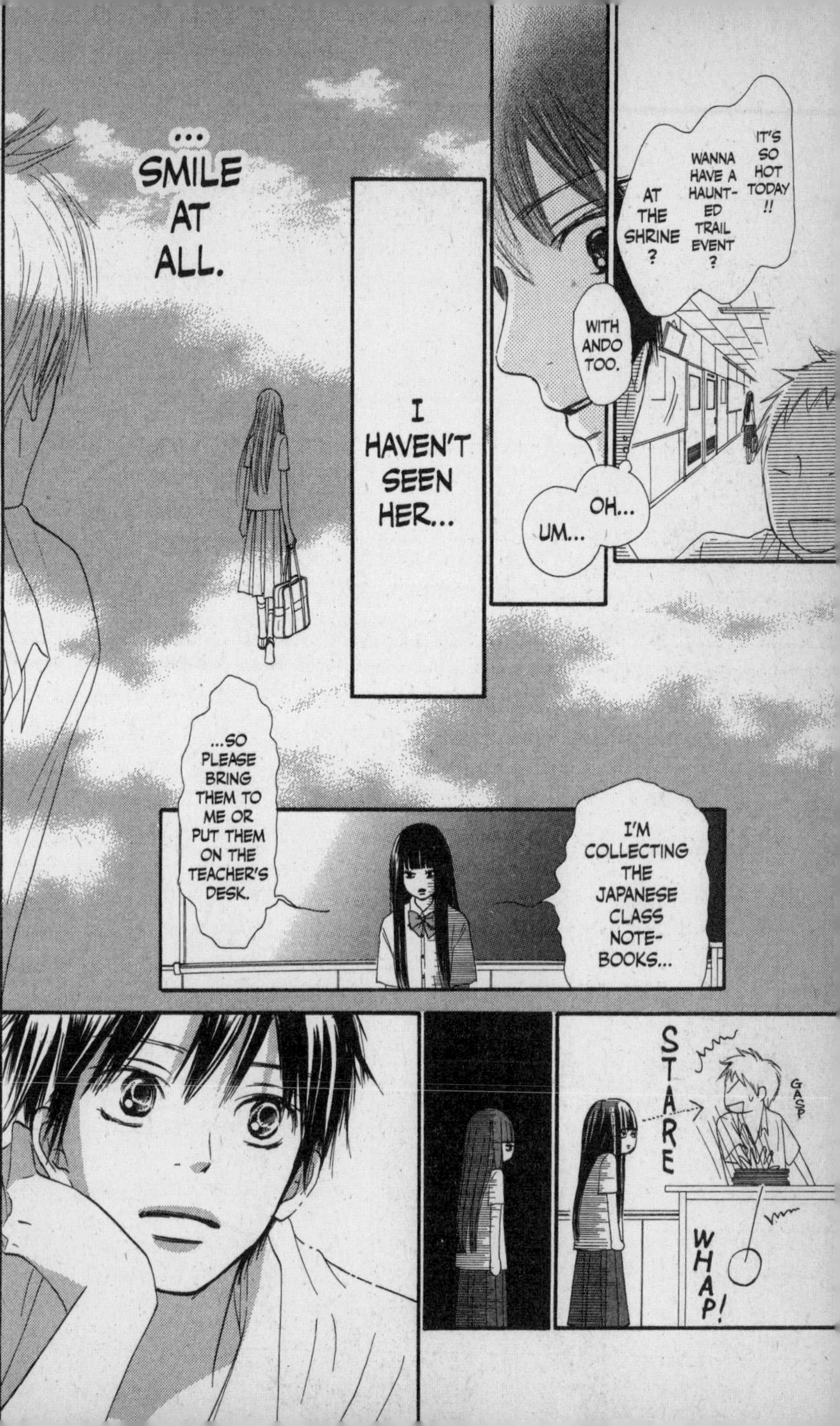
IT'S SO HOT TODAY!!
WANNA HAVE A HAUNT-ED TRAIL EVENT?
AT THE SHRINE?
WITH ANDO TOO.
OH... UM...
I HAVEN'T SEEN HER...
...SMILE AT ALL.
I'M COLLECTING THE JAPANESE CLASS NOTE-BOOKS...
...SO PLEASE BRING THEM TO ME OR PUT THEM ON THE TEACHER'S DESK.
STARE
GASP
WHAP!

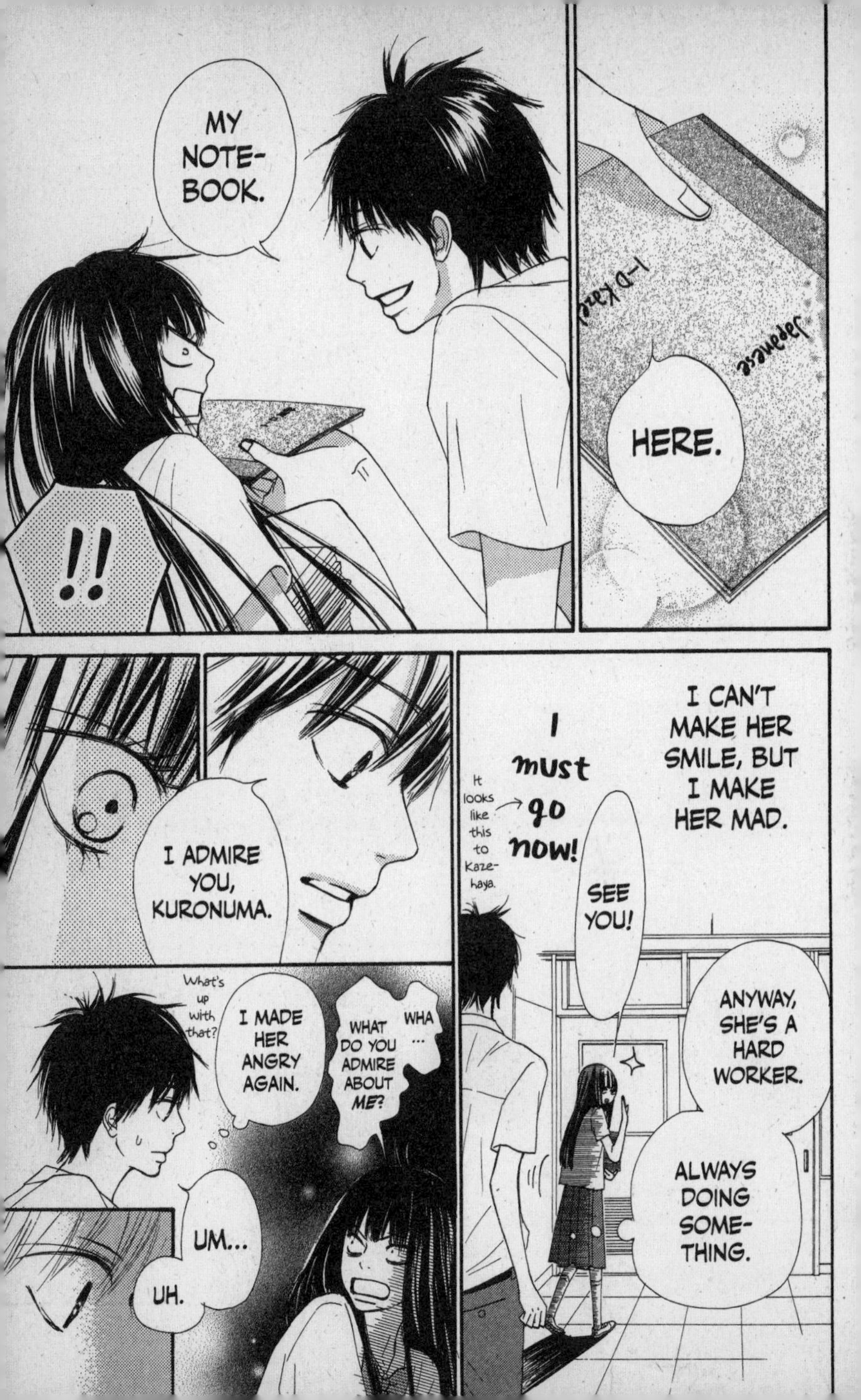
HERE.
MY NOTE-BOOK.
!!
I CAN'T MAKE HER SMILE, BUT I MAKE HER MAD.
I must go now!
It looks like this to Kaze-haya.
SEE YOU!
ANYWAY, SHE'S A HARD WORKER.
ALWAYS DOING SOME-THING.
I ADMIRE YOU, KURONUMA.
WHA...
WHAT DO YOU ADMIRE ABOUT *ME*?
I MADE HER ANGRY AGAIN.
What's up with that?
UM...
UH.

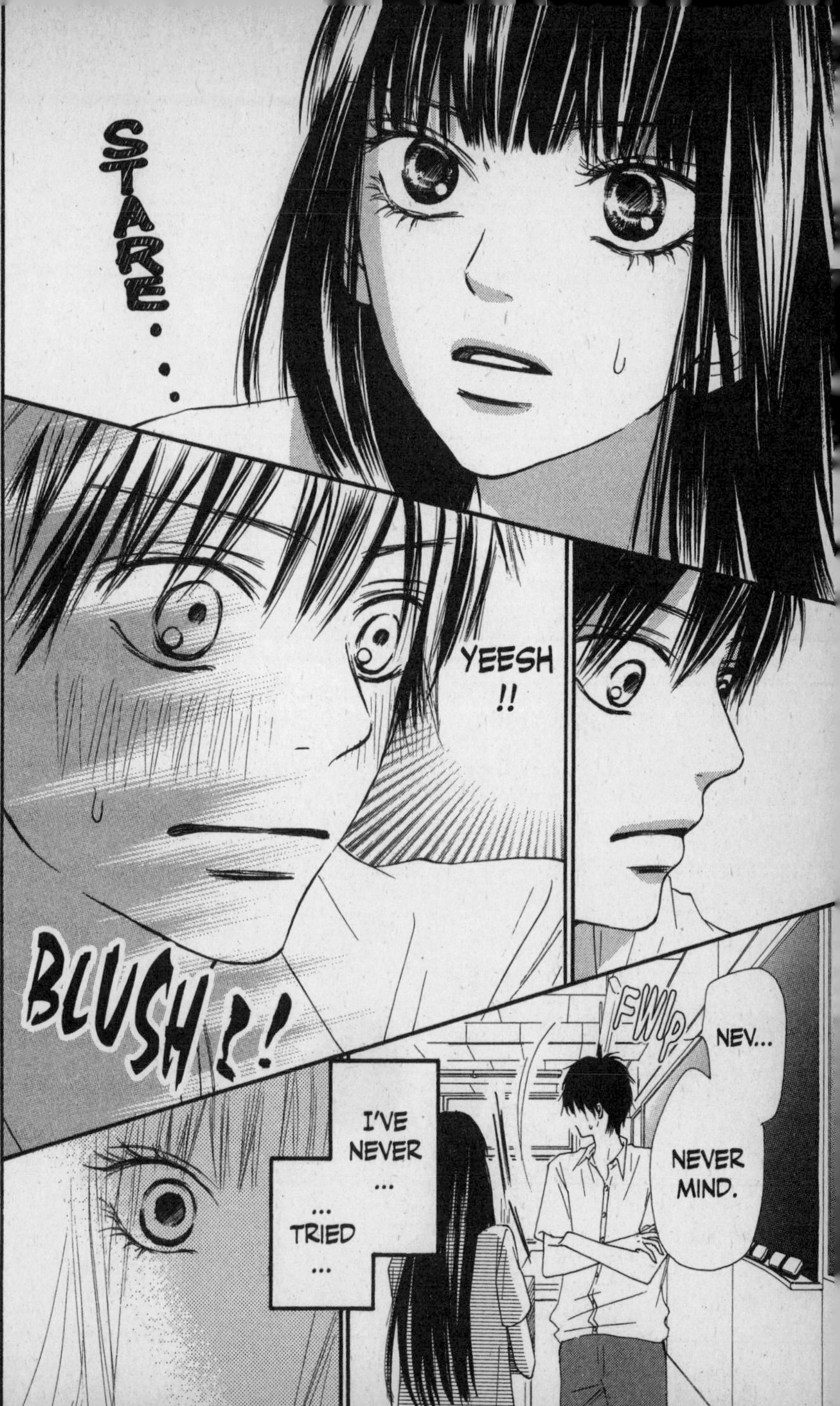
STARE...
YEESH!!
BLUSH?!
FWIP
NEV...
NEVER MIND.
I'VE NEVER ...
... TRIED ...

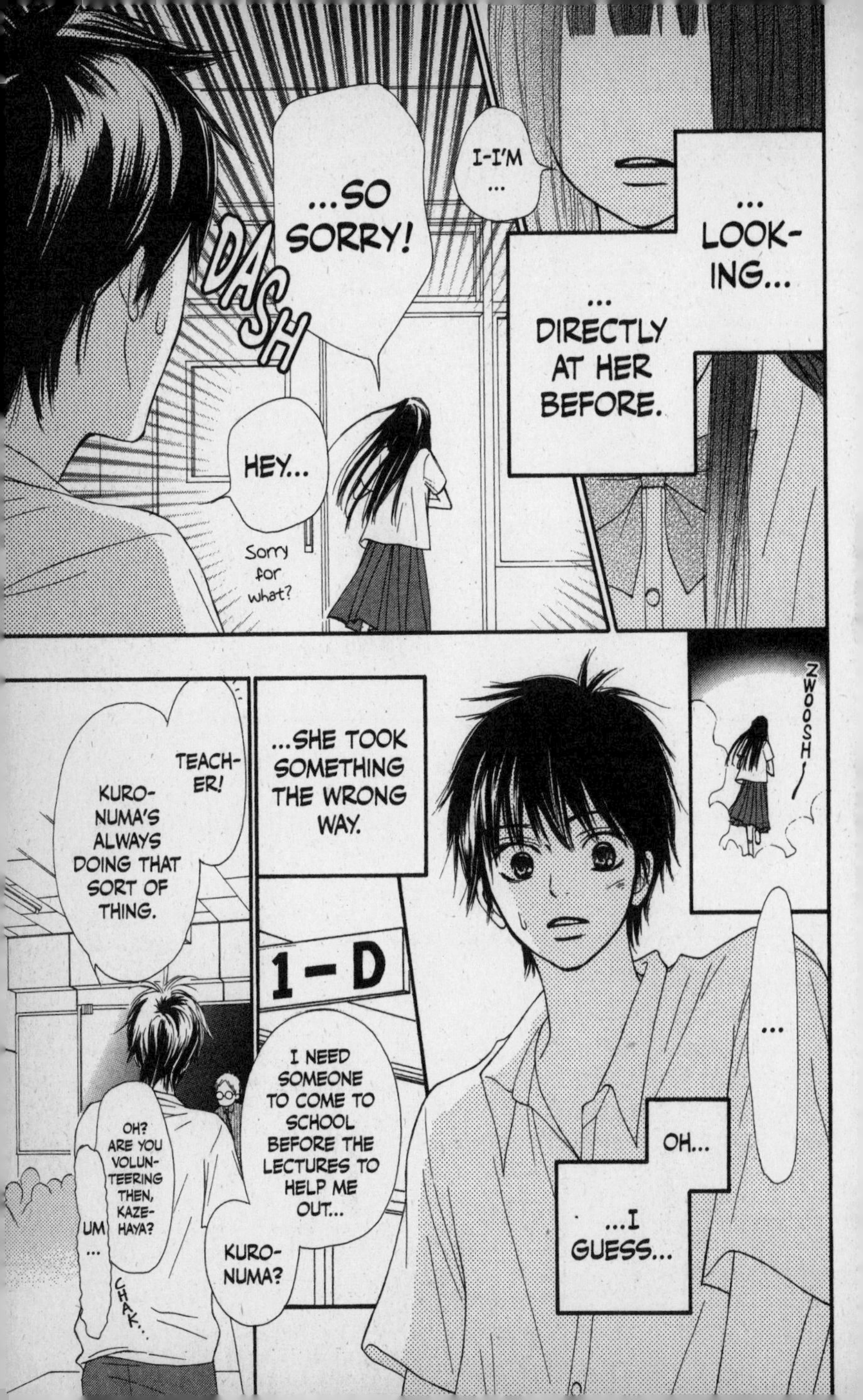
... LOOKING...
... DIRECTLY AT HER BEFORE.
I-I'M ...
...SO SORRY!
DASH
HEY...
Sorry for what?
ZWOOSH!
...
OH...
...I GUESS...
...SHE TOOK SOMETHING THE WRONG WAY.
TEACHER!
KURO-NUMA'S ALWAYS DOING THAT SORT OF THING.
1-D
I NEED SOMEONE TO COME TO SCHOOL BEFORE THE LECTURES TO HELP ME OUT...
KURO-NUMA?
OH? ARE YOU VOLUN-TEERING THEN, KAZE-HAYA?
UM ...
CHAK...

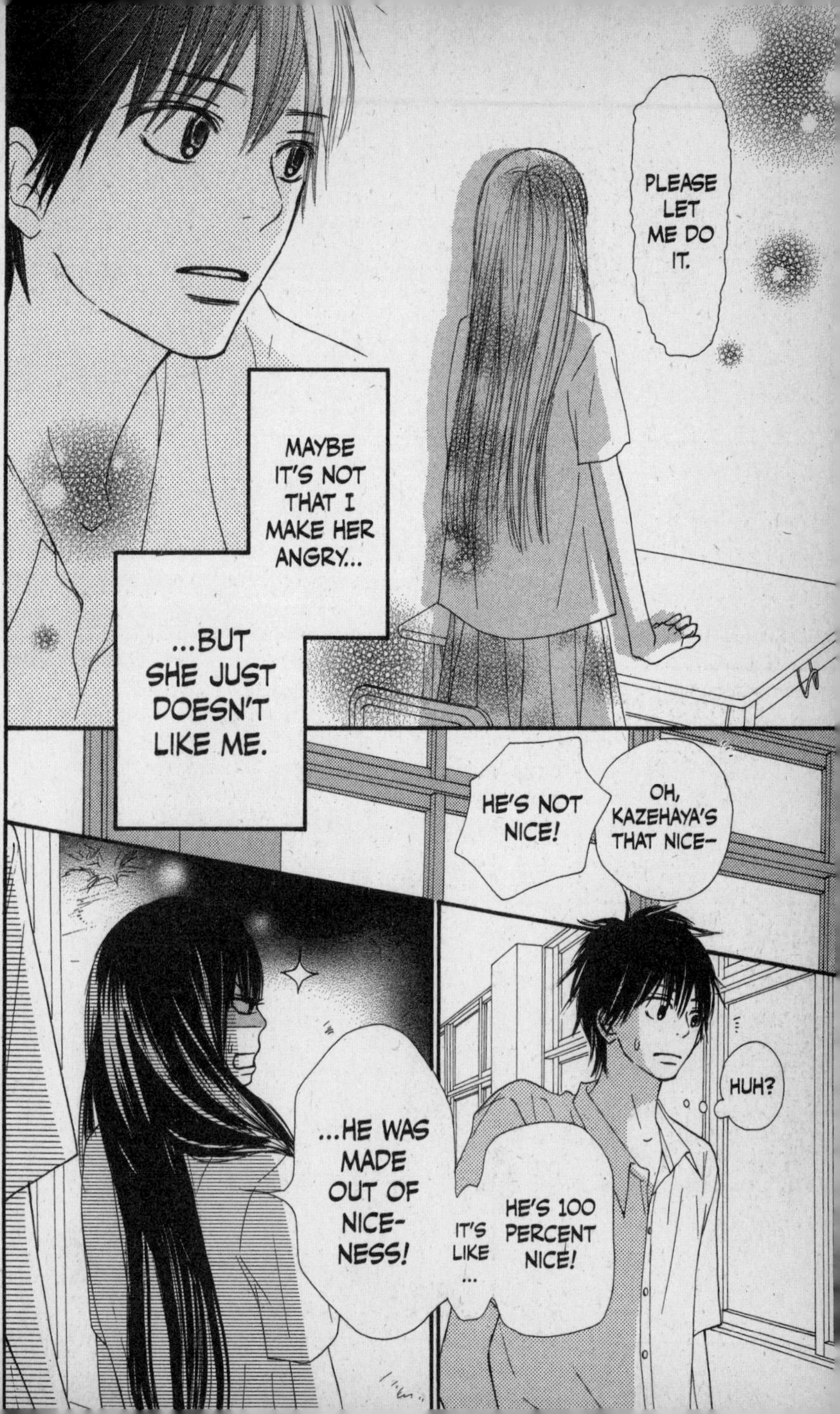
PLEASE LET ME DO IT.
MAYBE IT'S NOT THAT I MAKE HER ANGRY...
...BUT SHE JUST DOESN'T LIKE ME.
OH, KAZEHAYA'S THAT NICE-
HE'S NOT NICE!
HUH?
HE'S 100 PERCENT NICE!
IT'S LIKE ...
...HE WAS MADE OUT OF NICE-NESS!

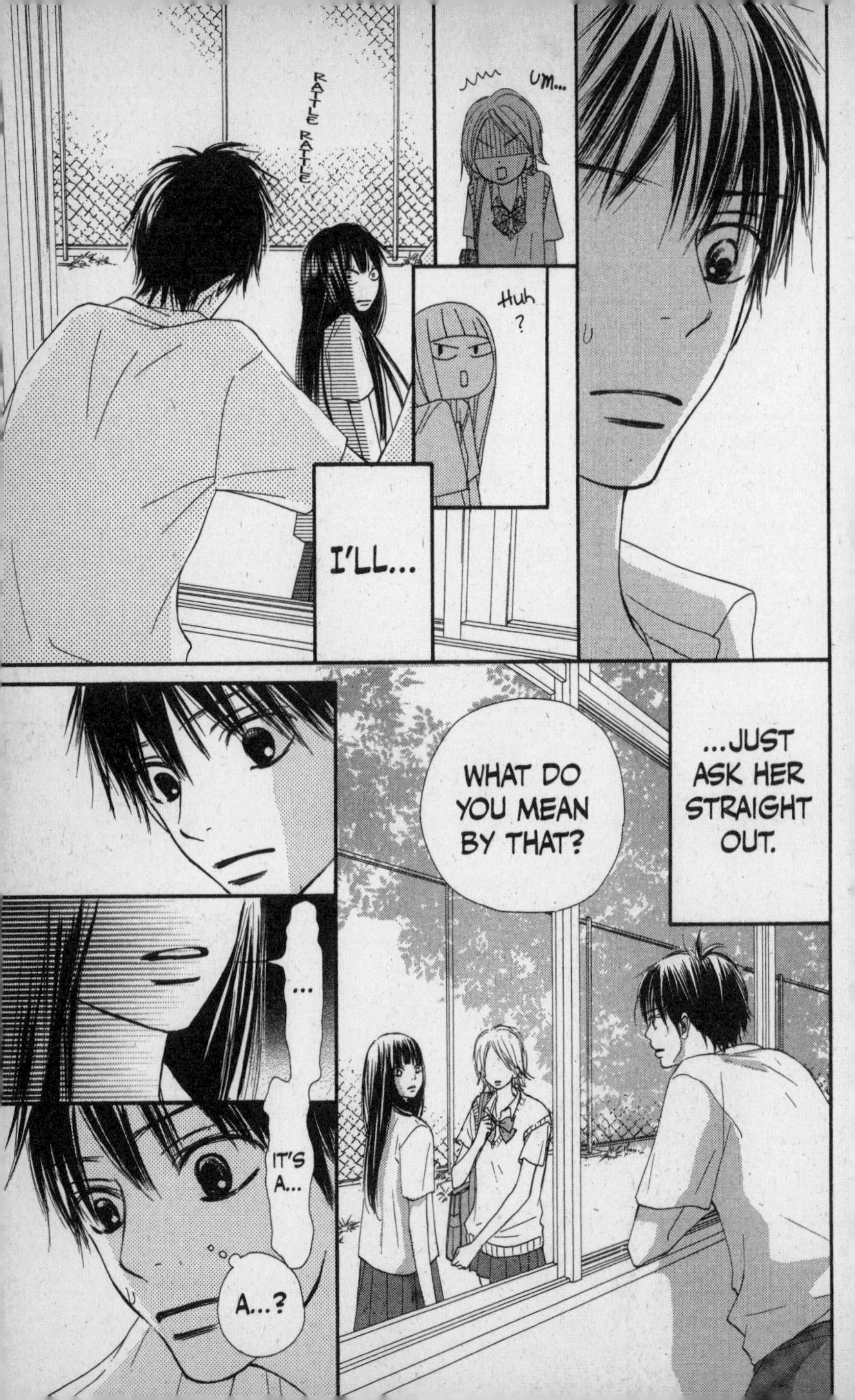
UM...
RATTLE RATTLE
Huh?
I'LL...
...JUST ASK HER STRAIGHT OUT.
WHAT DO YOU MEAN BY THAT?
...
IT'S A...
A...?

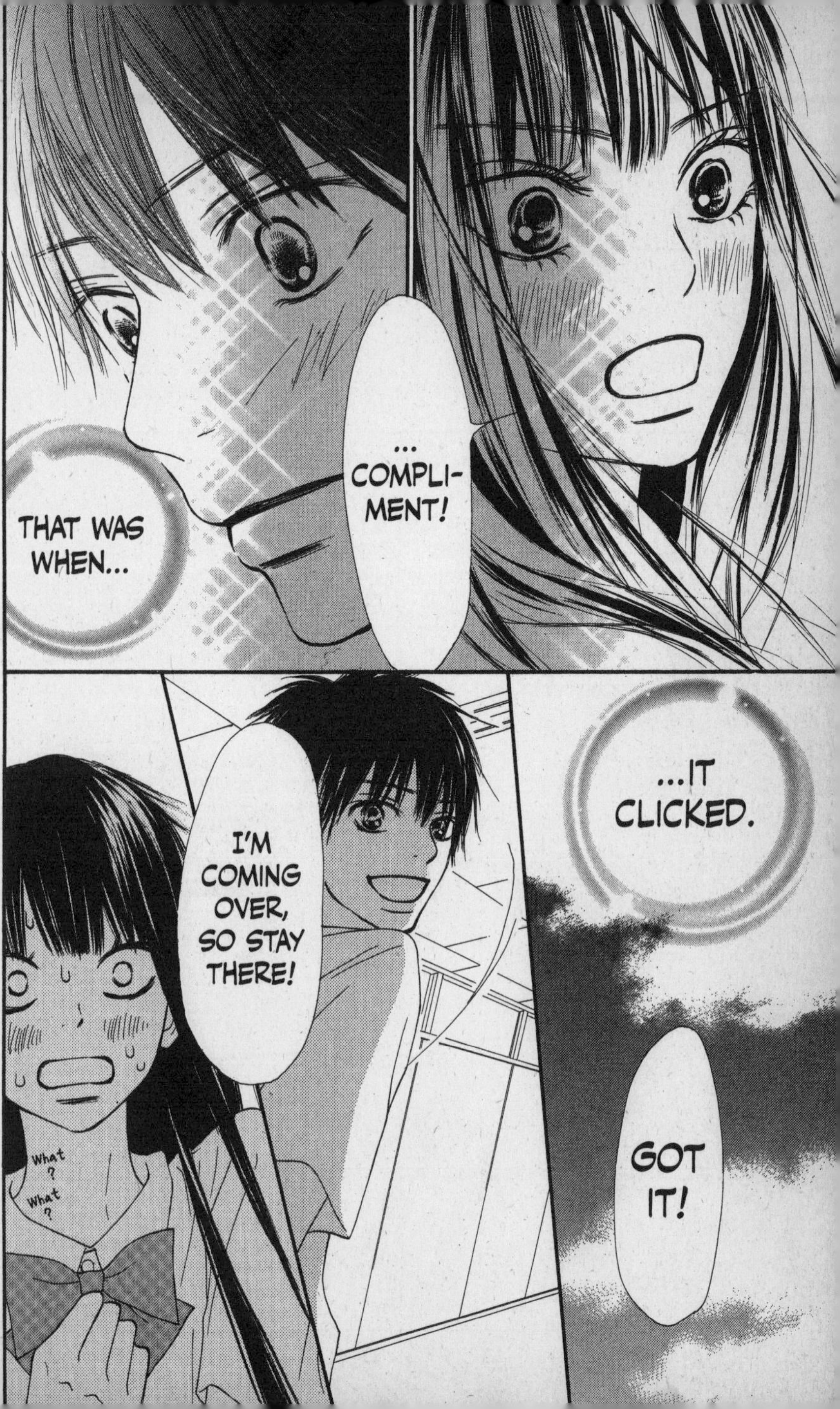
...COMPLIMENT!
THAT WAS WHEN...
...IT CLICKED.
GOT IT!
I'M COMING OVER, SO STAY THERE!
What? What?

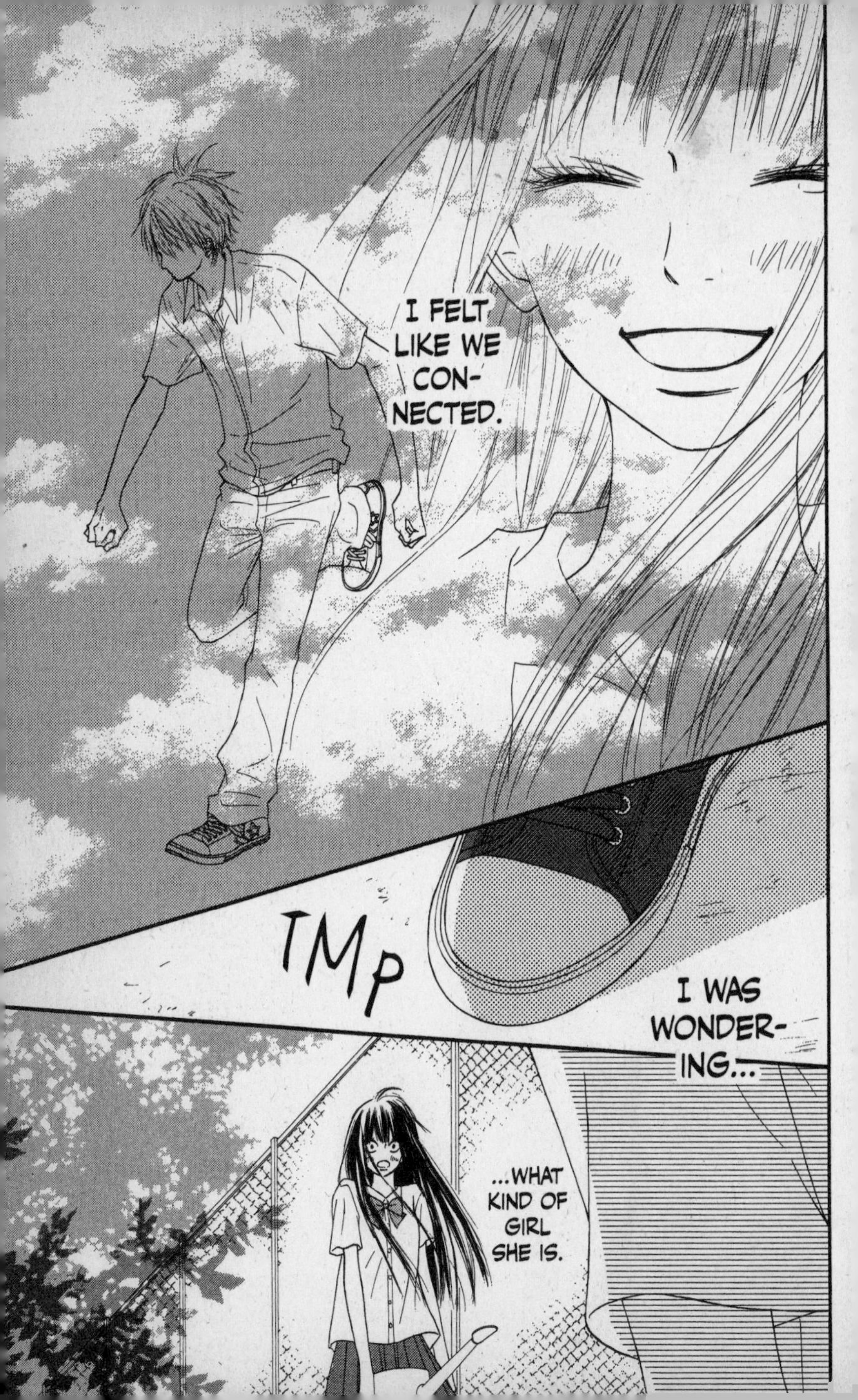
I FELT LIKE WE CON-NECTED.
TMP
I WAS WONDER-ING...
...WHAT KIND OF GIRL SHE IS.

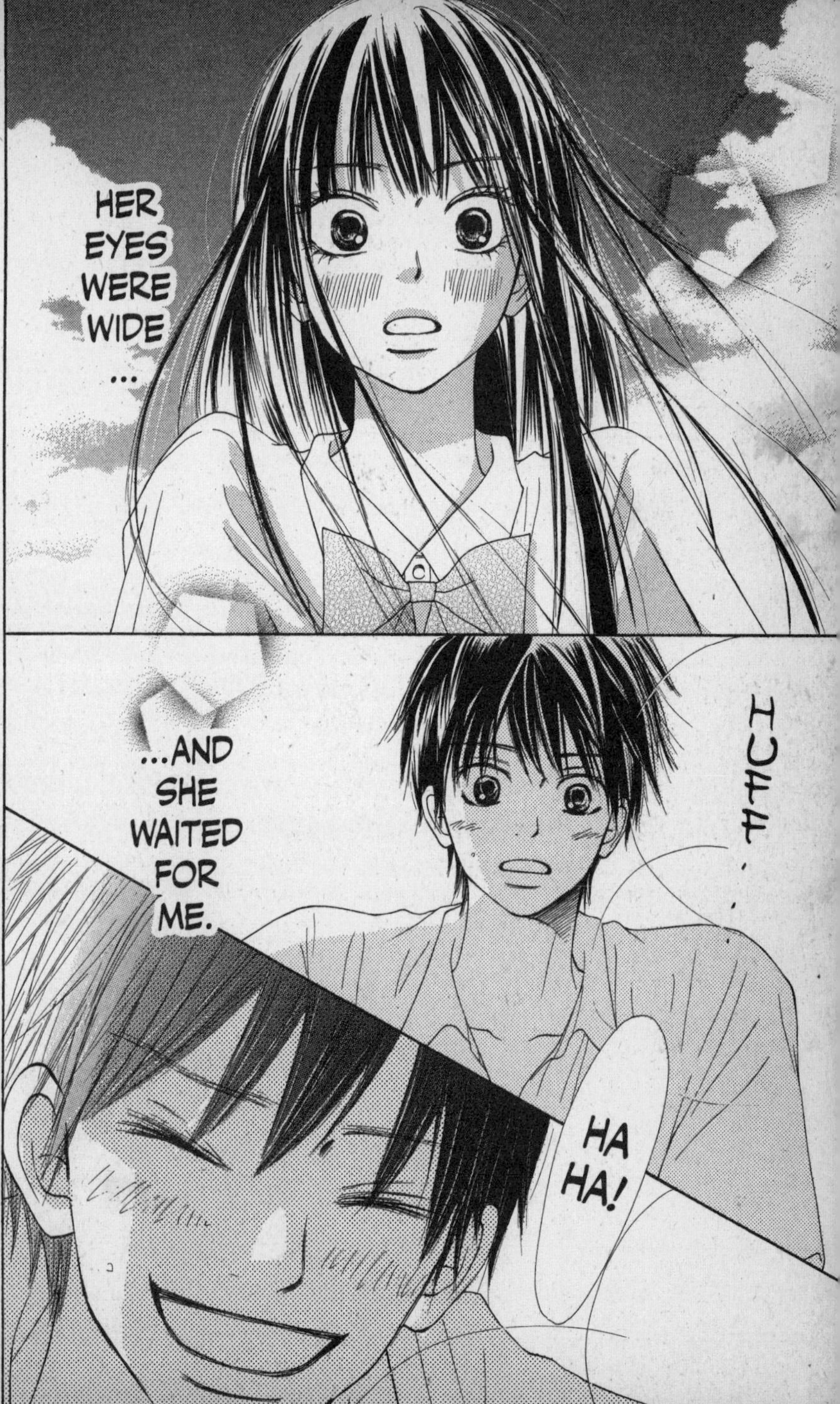
HER EYES WERE WIDE...
HUFF
...AND SHE WAITED FOR ME.
HA HA!

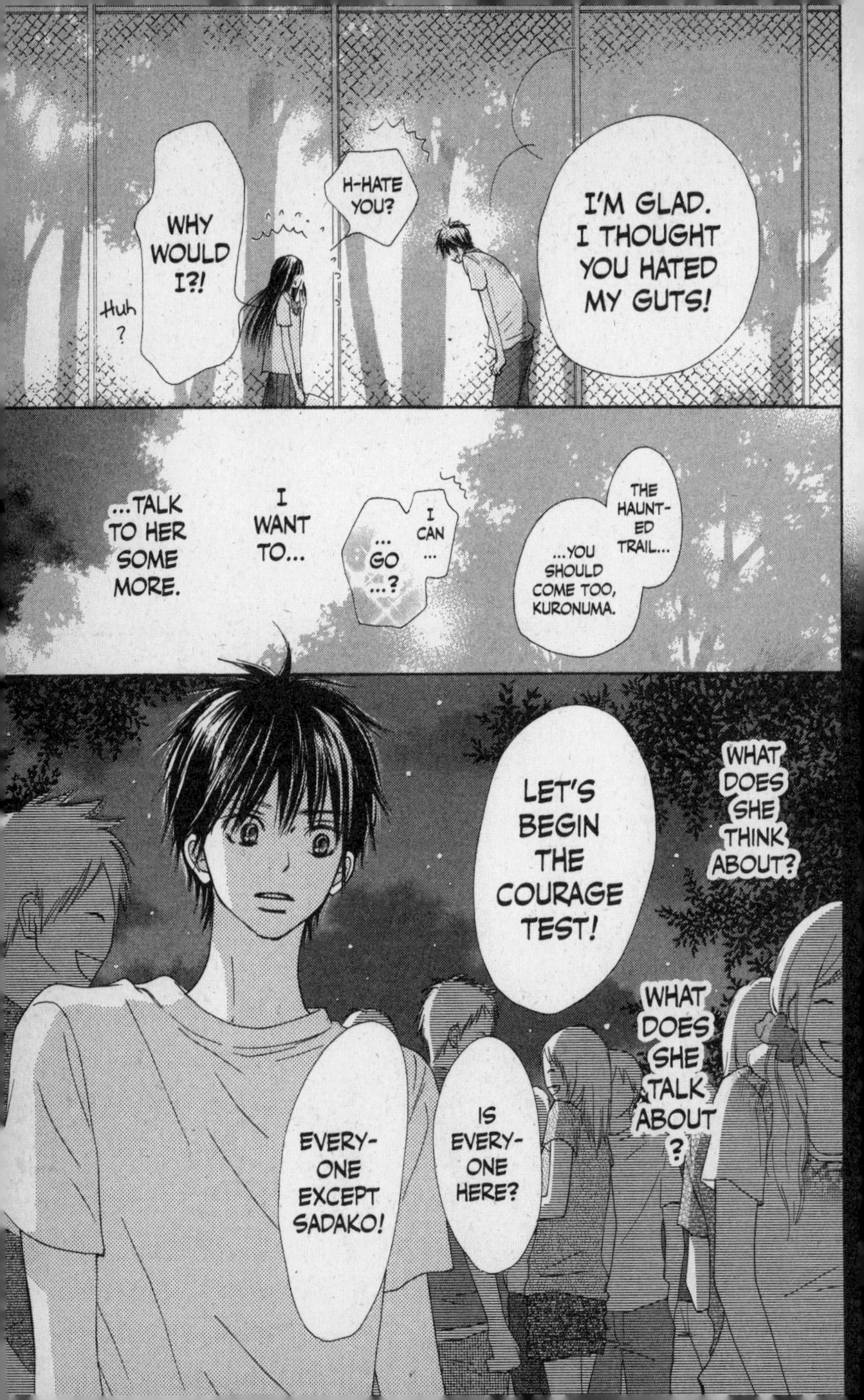
I'M GLAD. I THOUGHT YOU HATED MY GUTS!
H-HATE YOU?
WHY WOULD I?!
Huh ?
THE HAUNTED TRAIL...
...YOU SHOULD COME TOO, KURONUMA.
I CAN ...
... GO ...?
I WANT TO...
...TALK TO HER SOME MORE.
WHAT DOES SHE THINK ABOUT?
LET'S BEGIN THE COURAGE TEST!
WHAT DOES SHE TALK ABOUT?
IS EVERYONE HERE?
EVERYONE EXCEPT SADAKO!

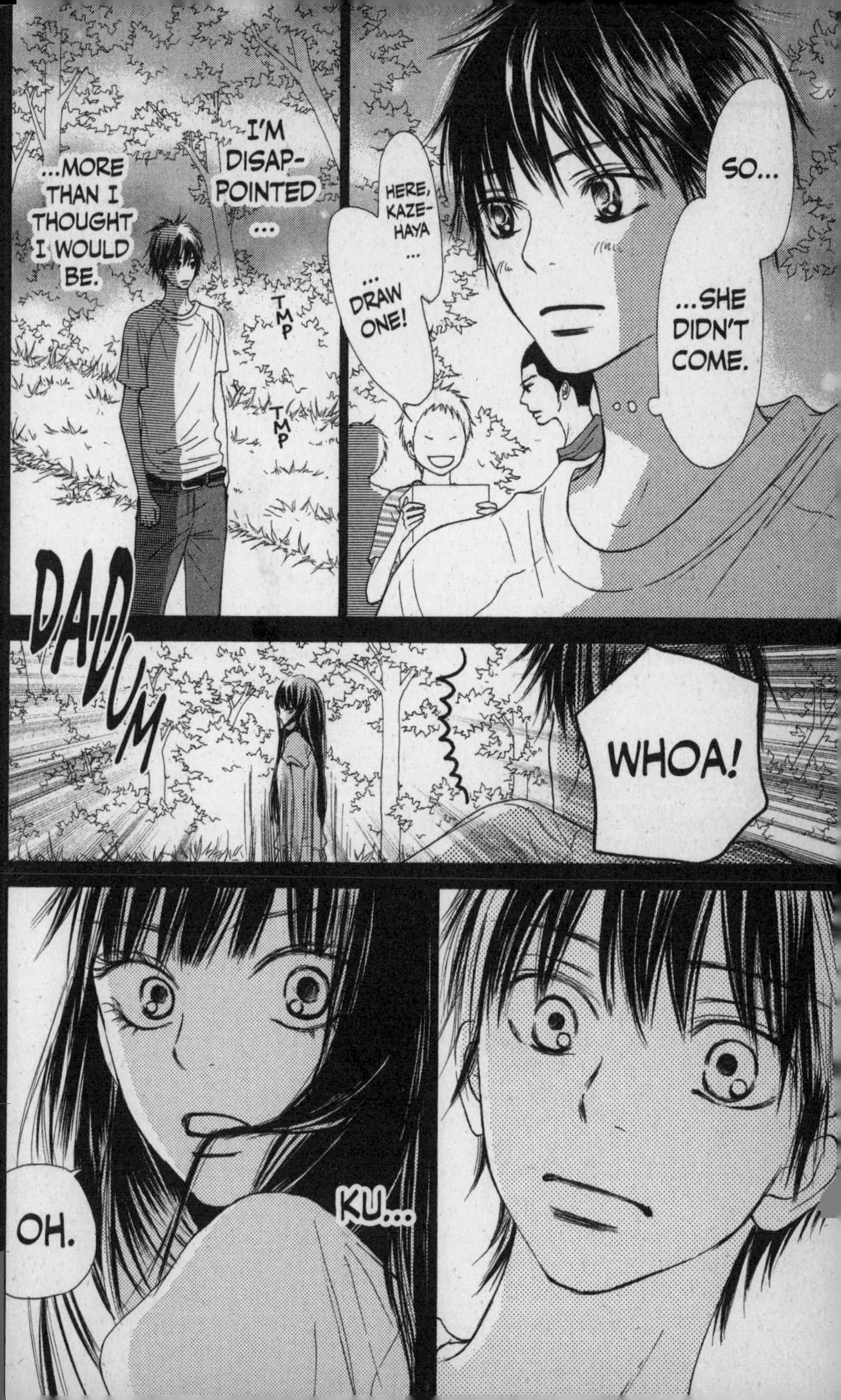
SO...
...SHE DIDN'T COME.
HERE, KAZE-HAYA... ...DRAW ONE!
I'M DISAPPOINTED...
...MORE THAN I THOUGHT I WOULD BE.
TMP TMP
WHOA!
DA-DUM
KU...
OH.

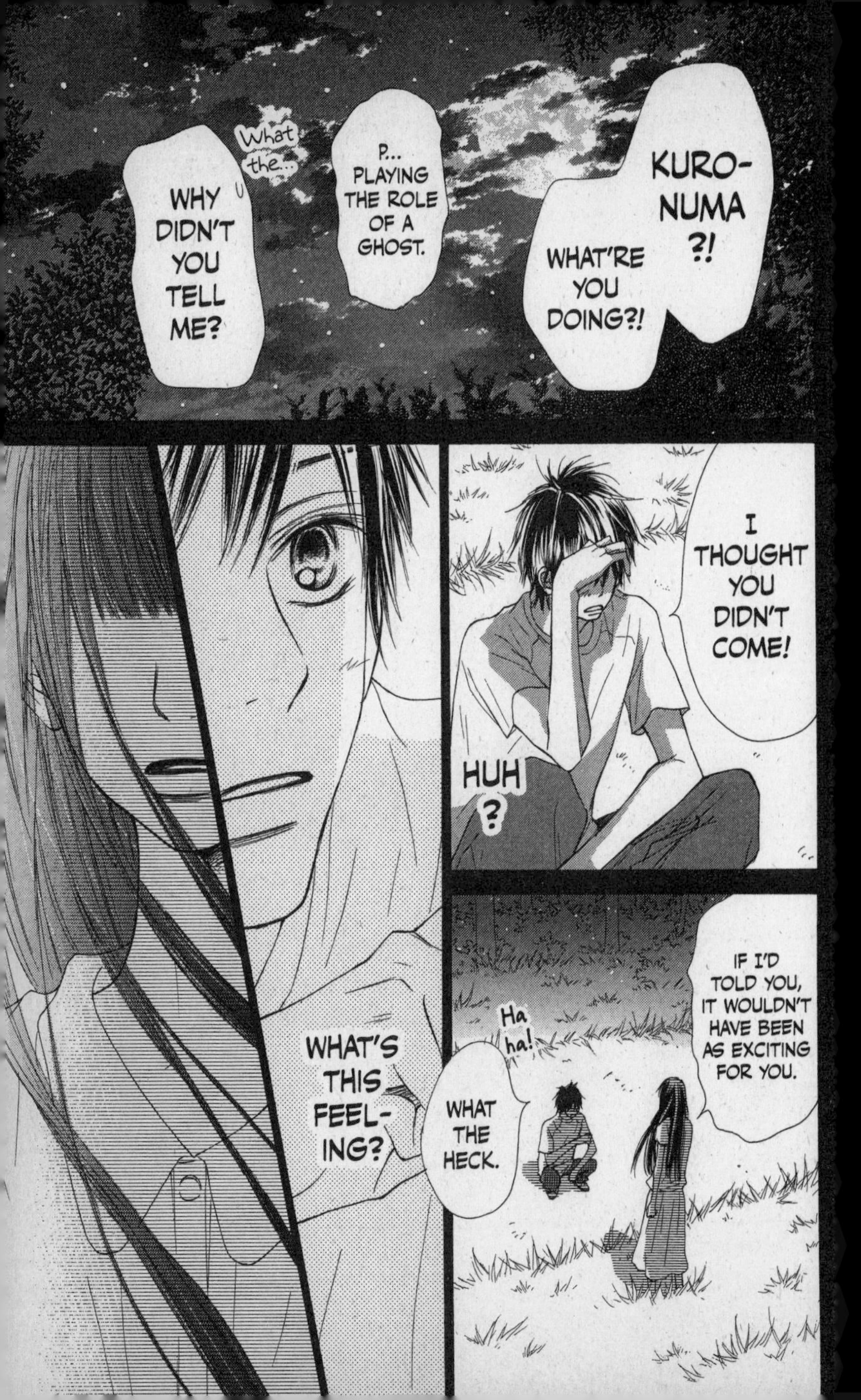
KURO-NUMA?!
WHAT'RE YOU DOING?!
P... PLAYING THE ROLE OF A GHOST.
What the...
WHY DIDN'T YOU TELL ME?
I THOUGHT YOU DIDN'T COME!
HUH?
IF I'D TOLD YOU, IT WOULDN'T HAVE BEEN AS EXCITING FOR YOU.
Ha ha!
WHAT THE HECK.
WHAT'S THIS FEEL-ING?

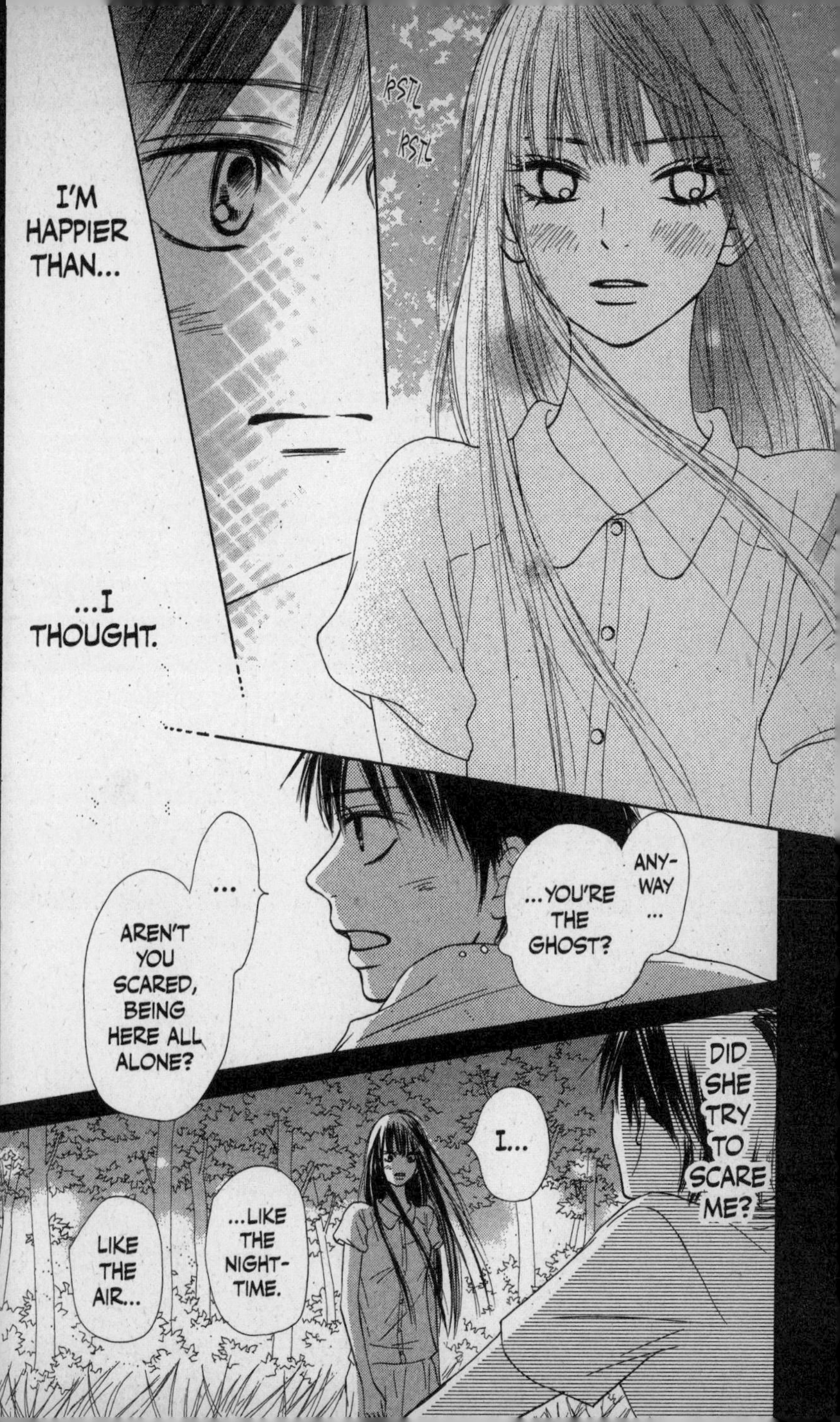
RSTL RSTL
I'M HAPPIER THAN...
...I THOUGHT.
ANY-WAY...
...YOU'RE THE GHOST?
... AREN'T YOU SCARED, BEING HERE ALL ALONE?
DID SHE TRY TO SCARE ME?
I...
...LIKE THE NIGHT-TIME.
LIKE THE AIR...

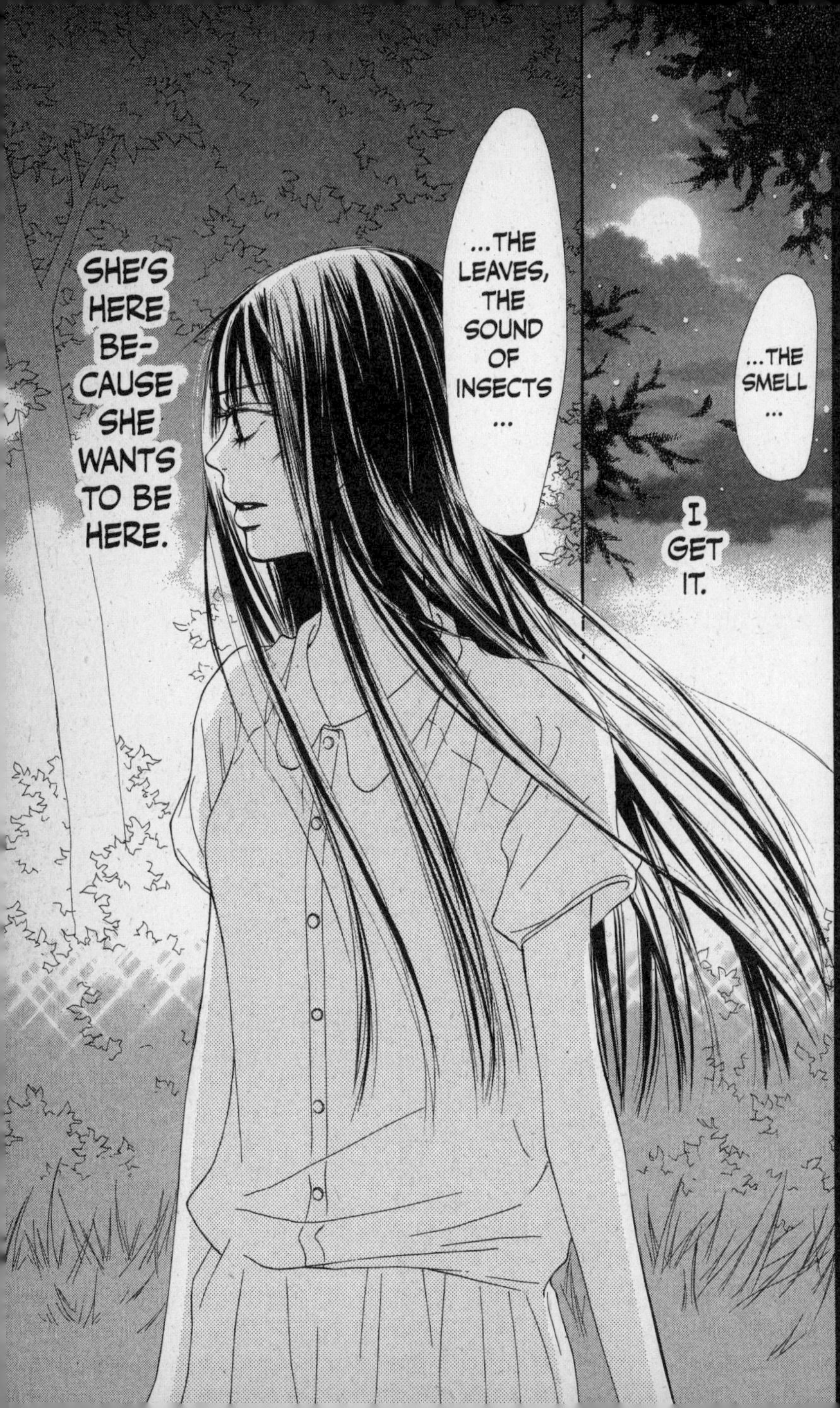
...THE SMELL ...
I GET IT.
...THE LEAVES, THE SOUND OF INSECTS ...
SHE'S HERE BE-CAUSE SHE WANTS TO BE HERE.

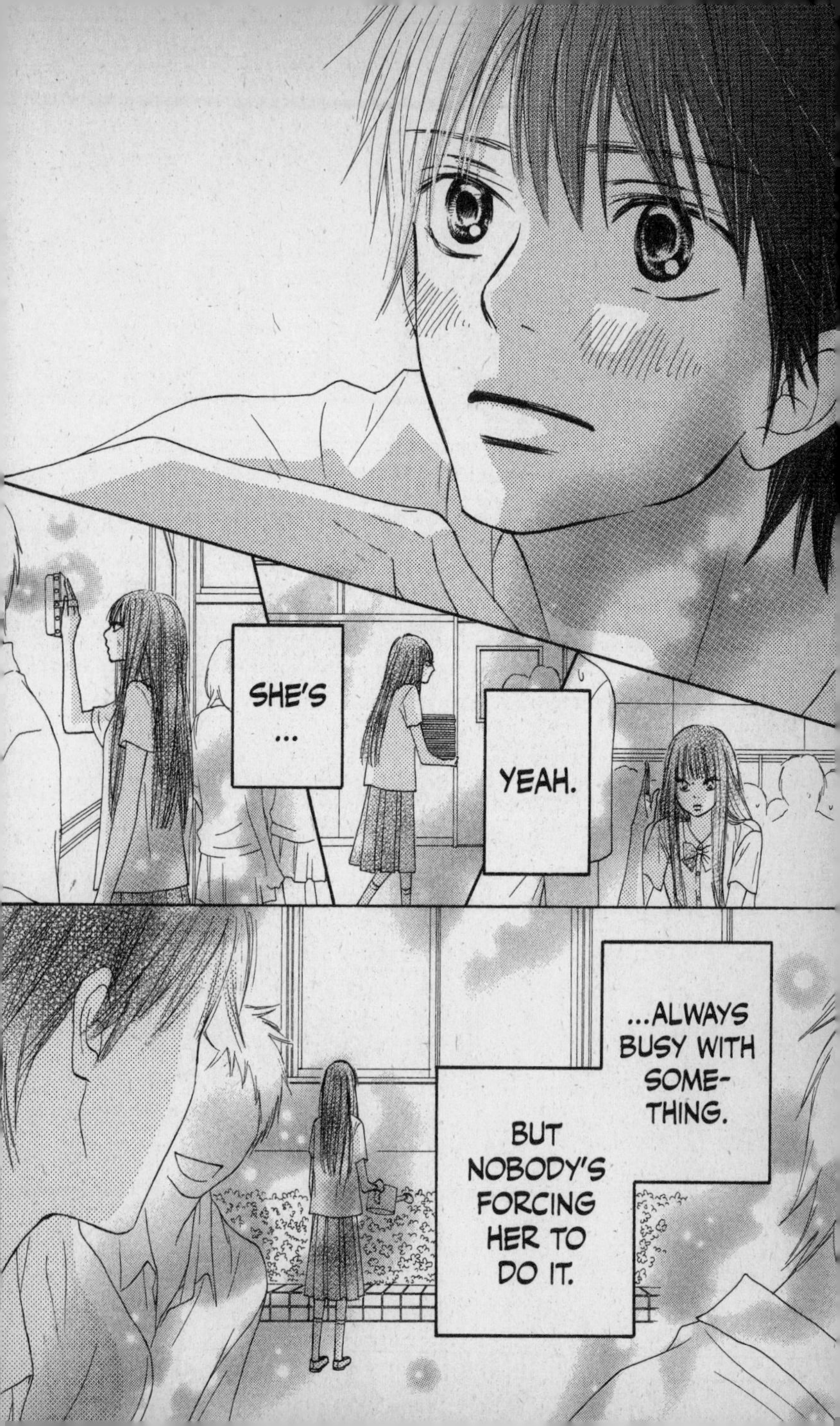
SHE'S ...
YEAH.
...ALWAYS BUSY WITH SOME-THING.
BUT NOBODY'S FORCING HER TO DO IT.

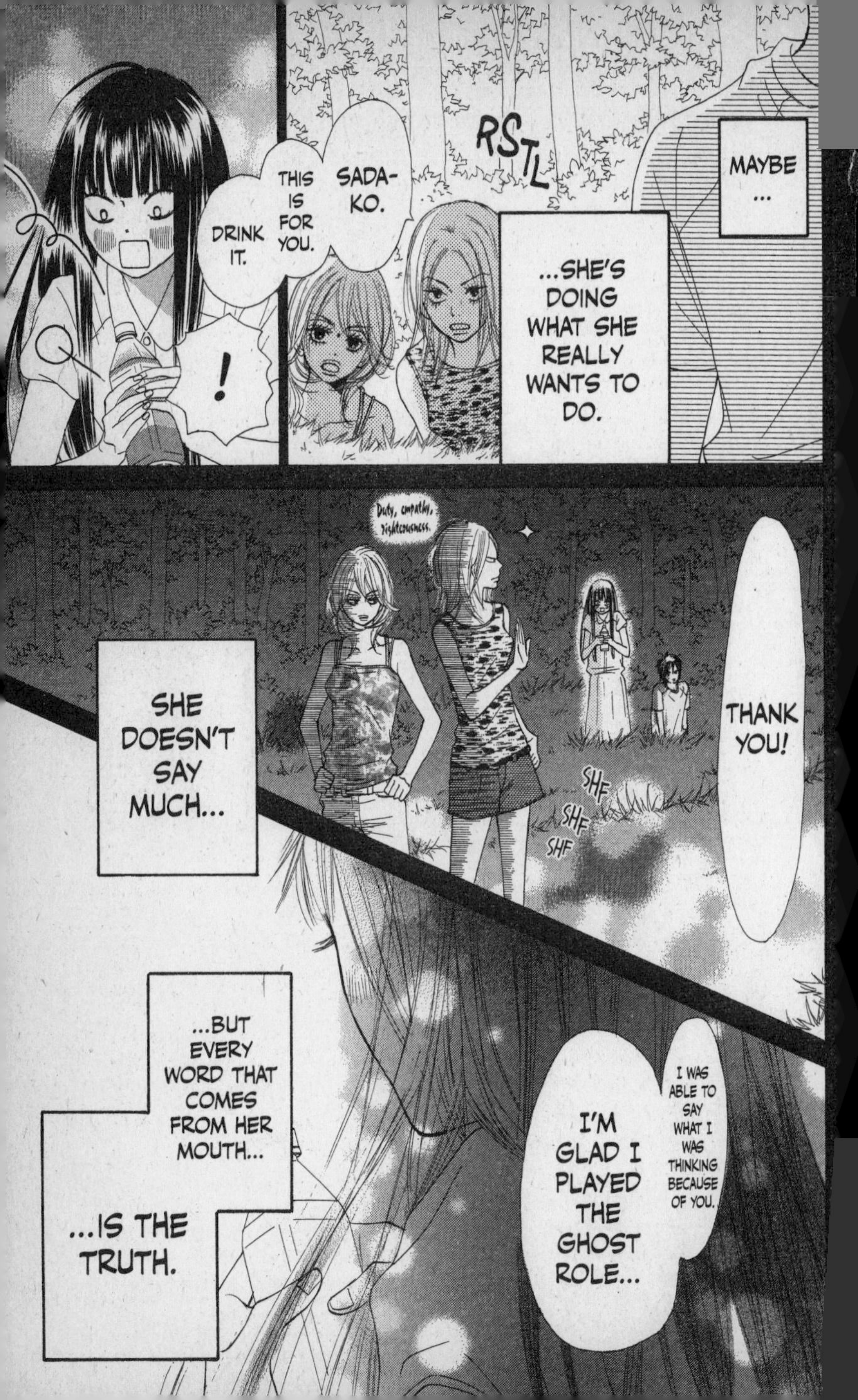
MAYBE ...
...SHE'S DOING WHAT SHE REALLY WANTS TO DO.
RSTL
SADA-KO.
THIS IS FOR YOU.
DRINK IT.
!
THANK YOU!
Duty, empathy, righteousness.
SHF SHF SHF
SHE DOESN'T SAY MUCH...
I WAS ABLE TO SAY WHAT I WAS THINKING BECAUSE OF YOU.
I'M GLAD I PLAYED THE GHOST ROLE...
...BUT EVERY WORD THAT COMES FROM HER MOUTH...
...IS THE TRUTH.

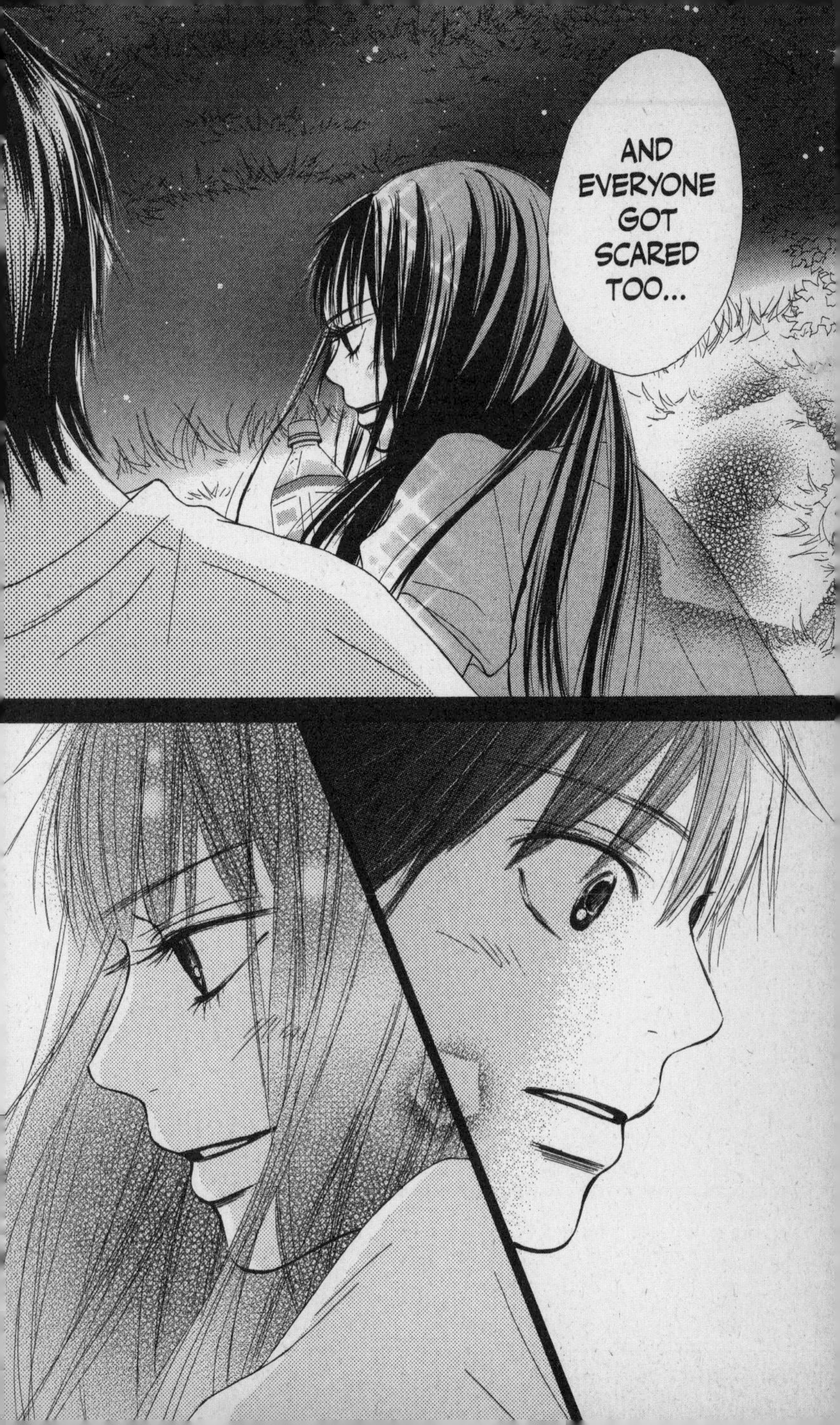
AND EVERYONE GOT SCARED TOO...

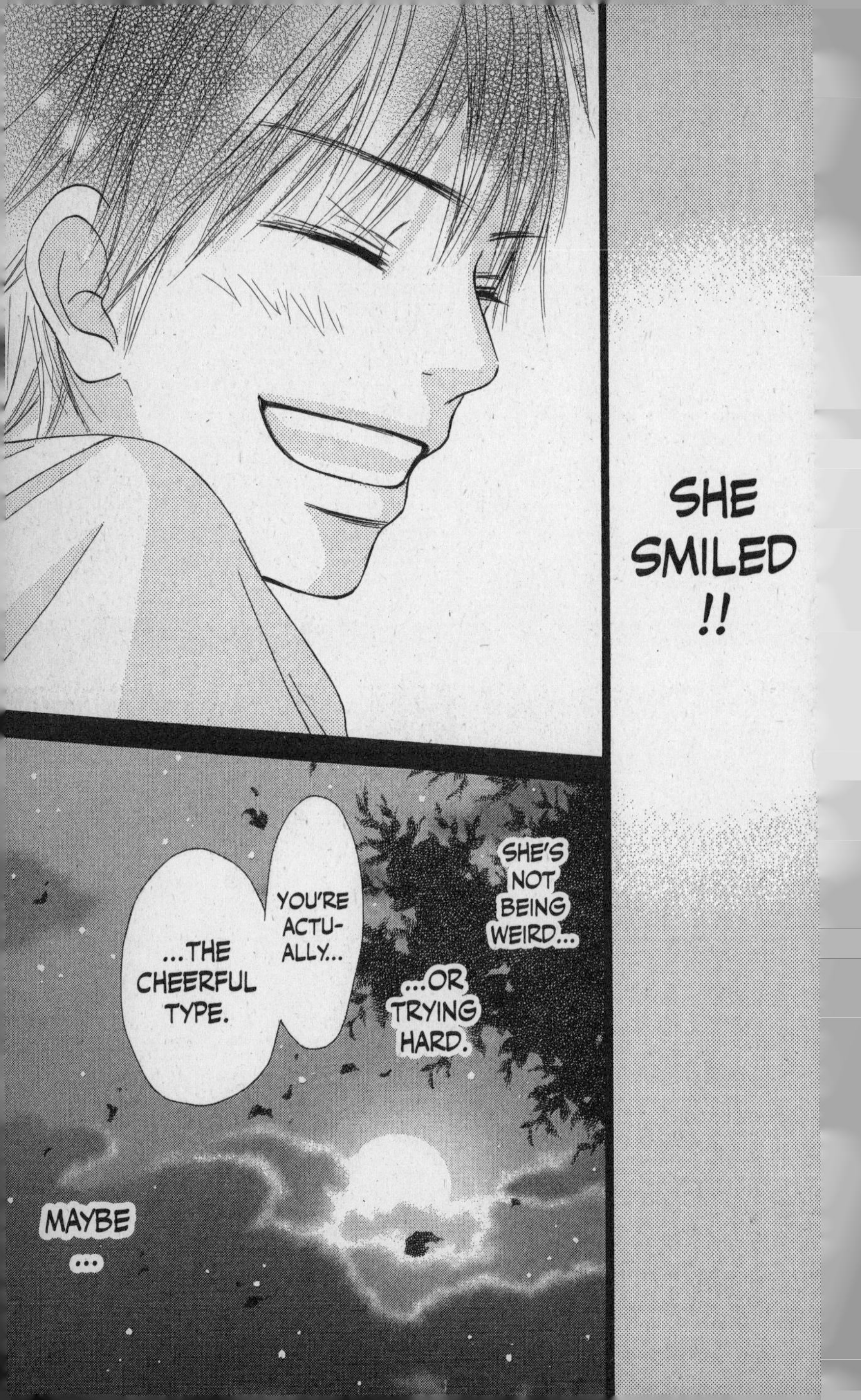
SHE SMILED!!
SHE'S NOT BEING WEIRD...
...OR TRYING HARD.
YOU'RE ACTU-ALLY...
...THE CHEERFUL TYPE.
MAYBE...

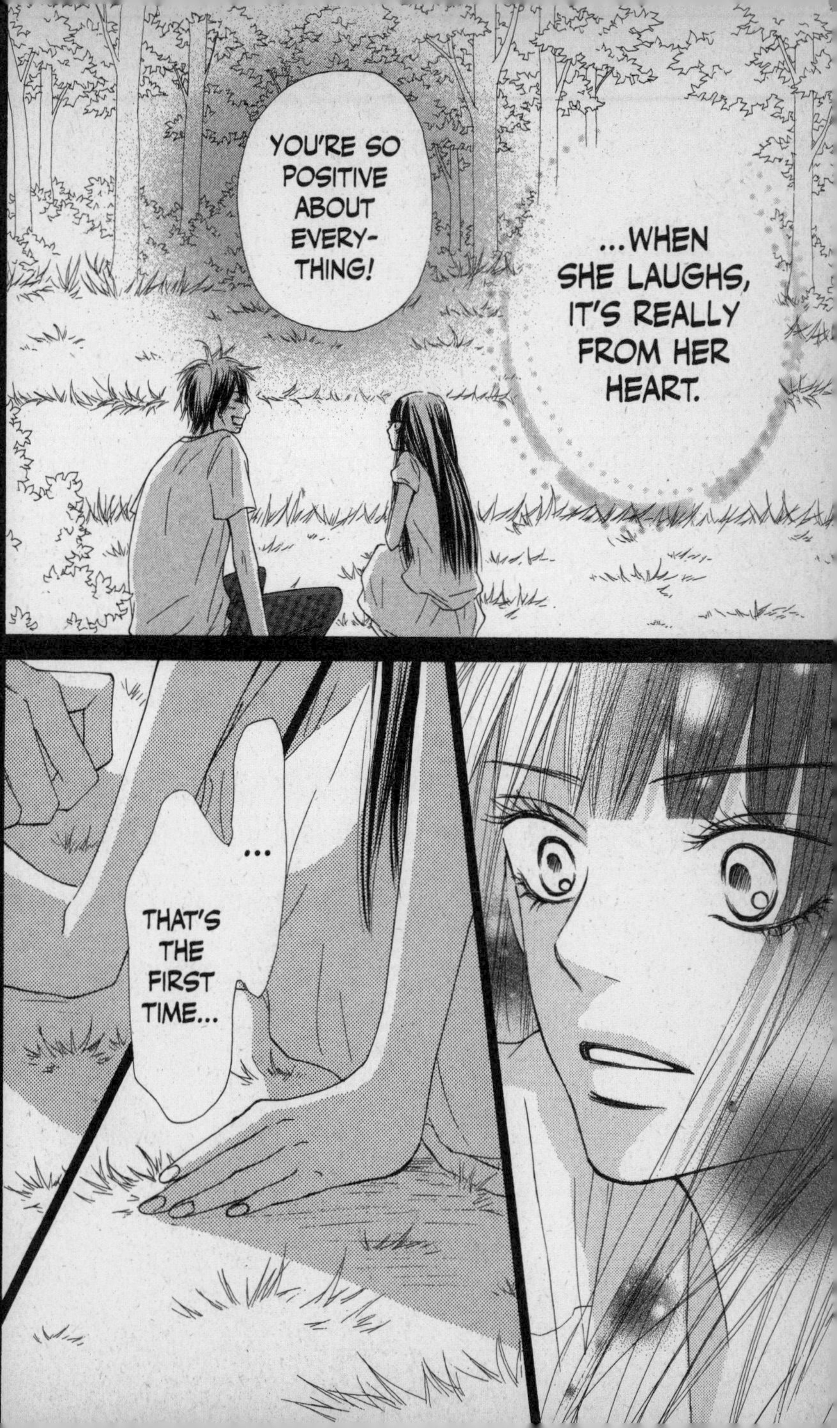
...WHEN SHE LAUGHS, IT'S REALLY FROM HER HEART.
YOU'RE SO POSITIVE ABOUT EVERY-THING!
...
THAT'S THE FIRST TIME...

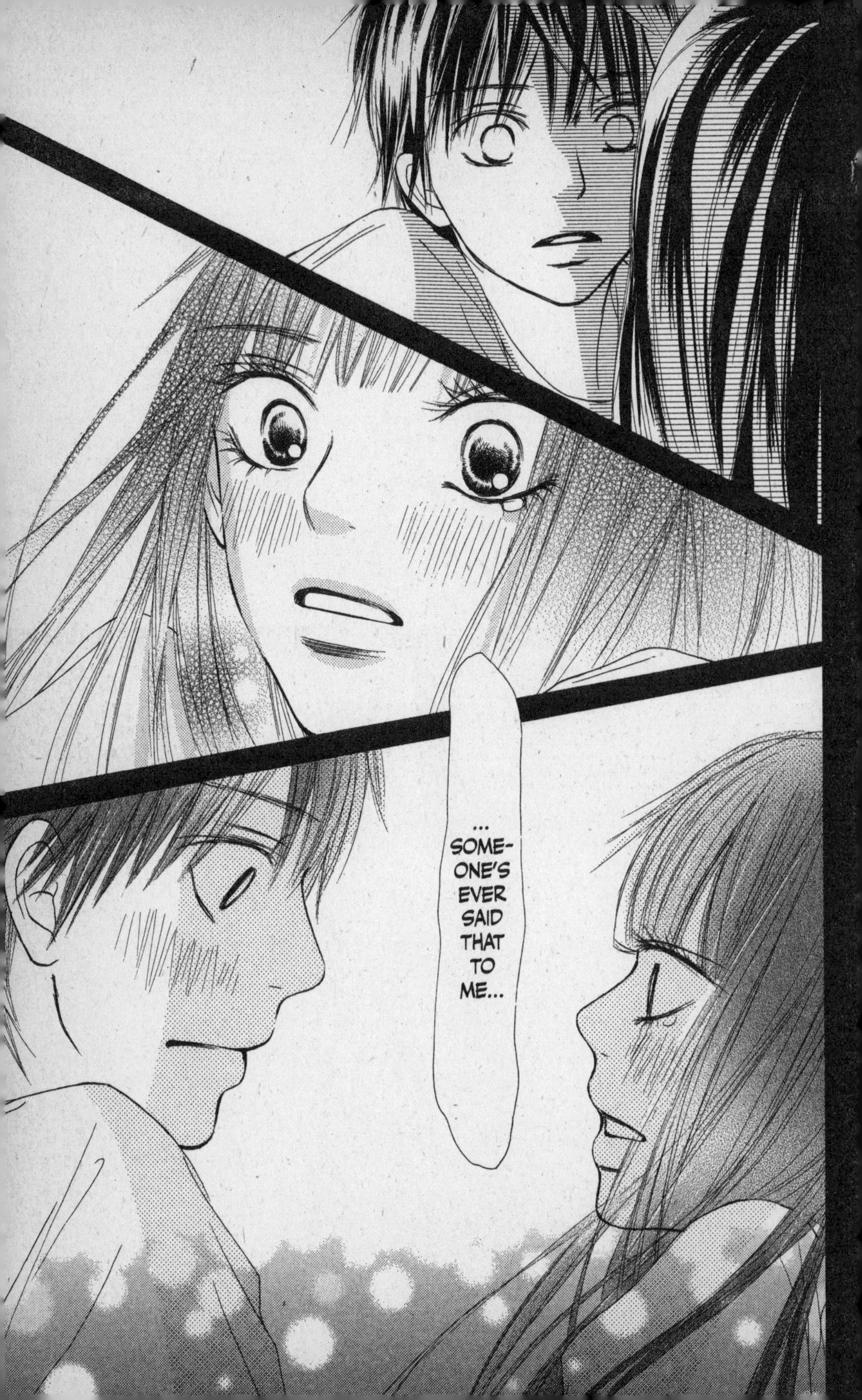
...SOME-ONE'S EVER SAID THAT TO ME...

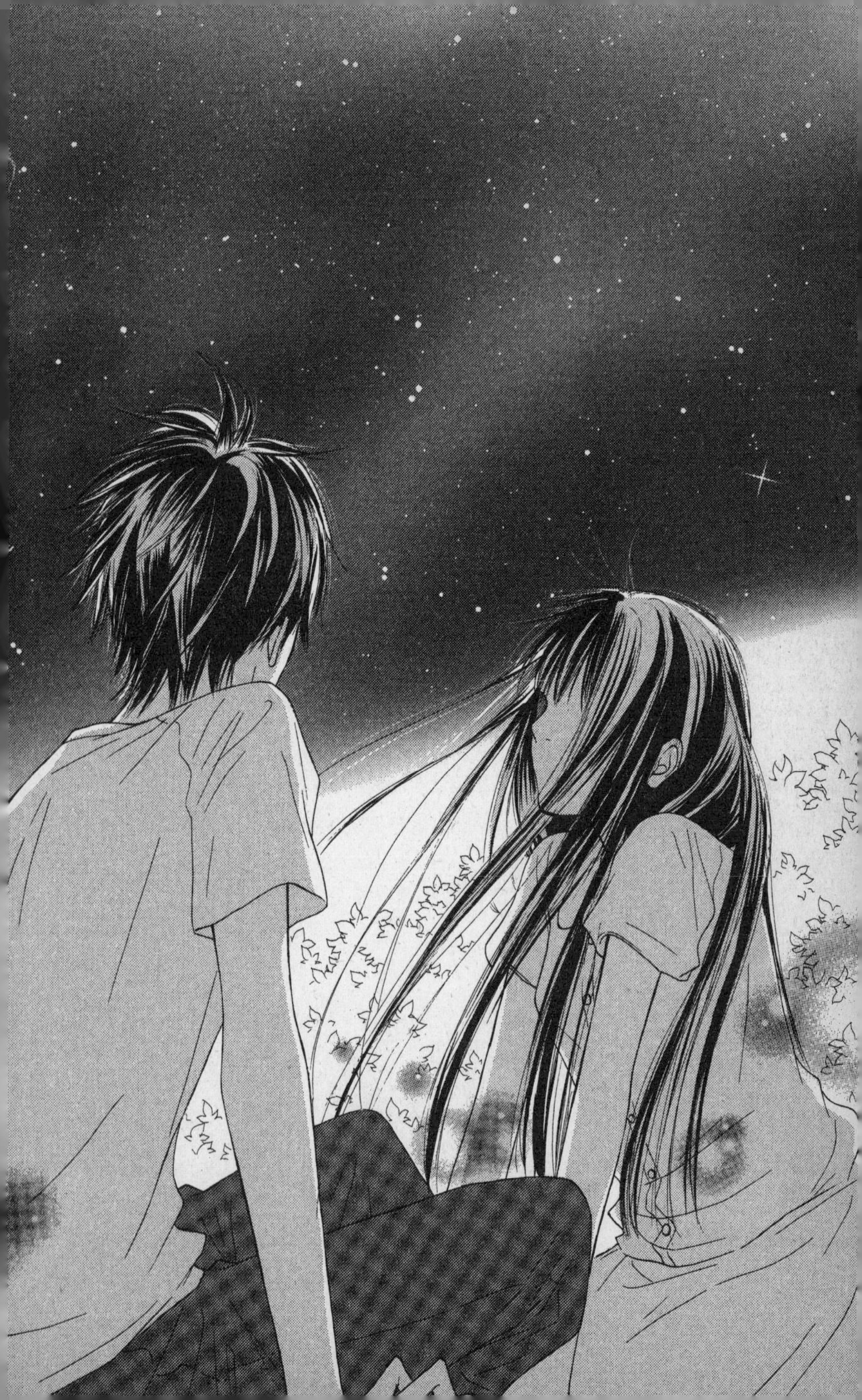

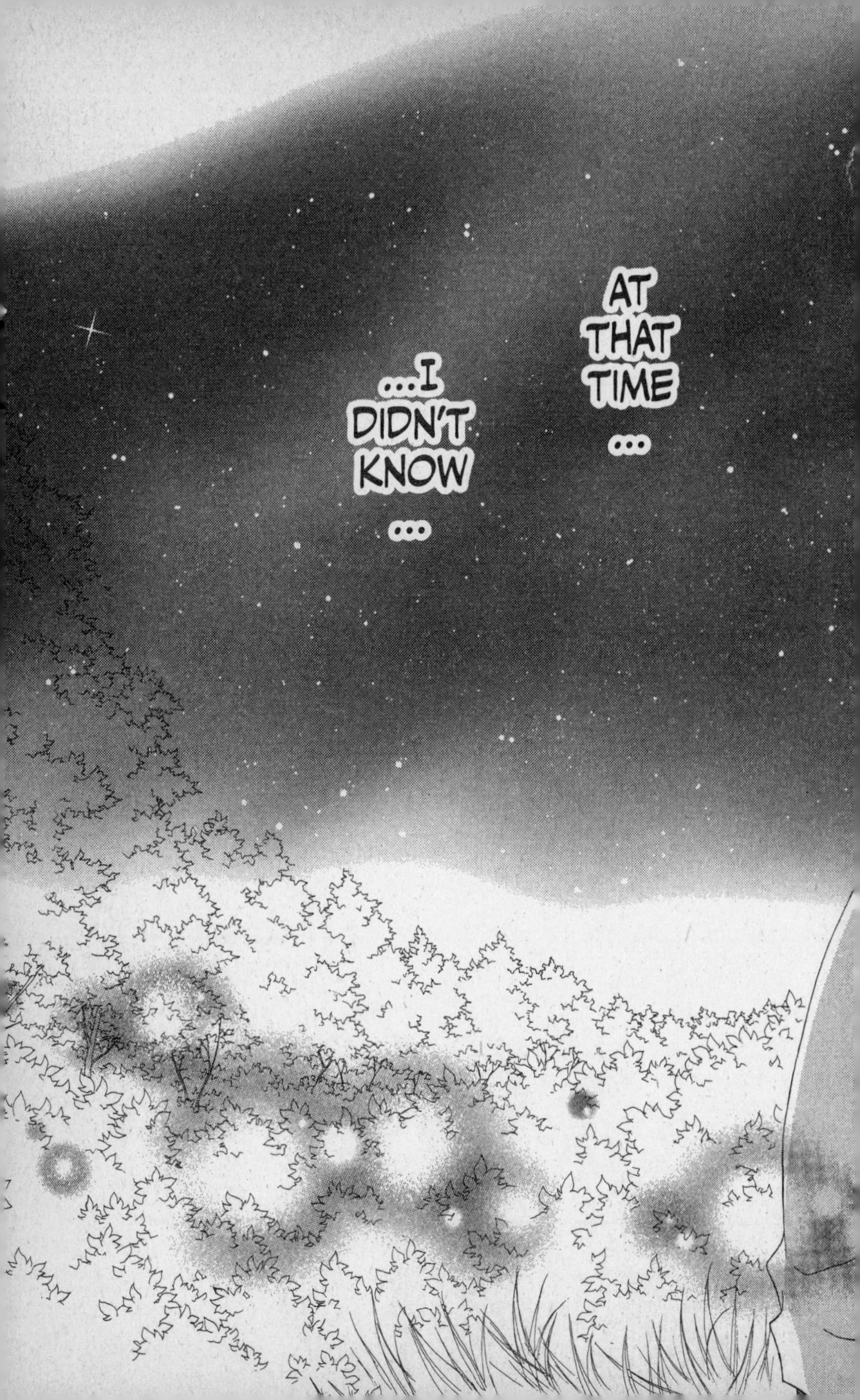
AT THAT TIME...
...I DIDN'T KNOW...

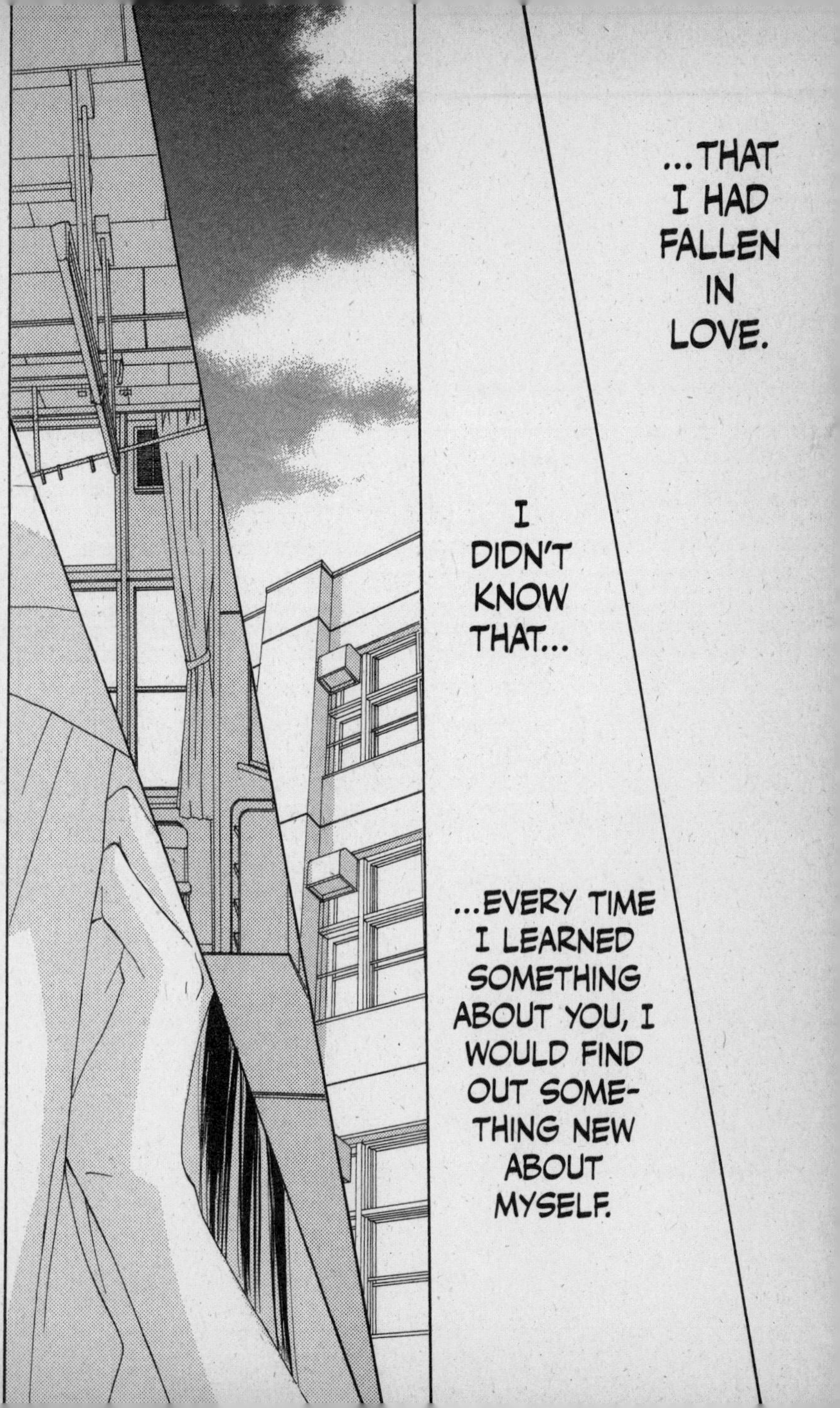
...THAT I HAD FALLEN IN LOVE.
I DIDN'T KNOW THAT...
...EVERY TIME I LEARNED SOMETHING ABOUT YOU, I WOULD FIND OUT SOME-THING NEW ABOUT MYSELF.

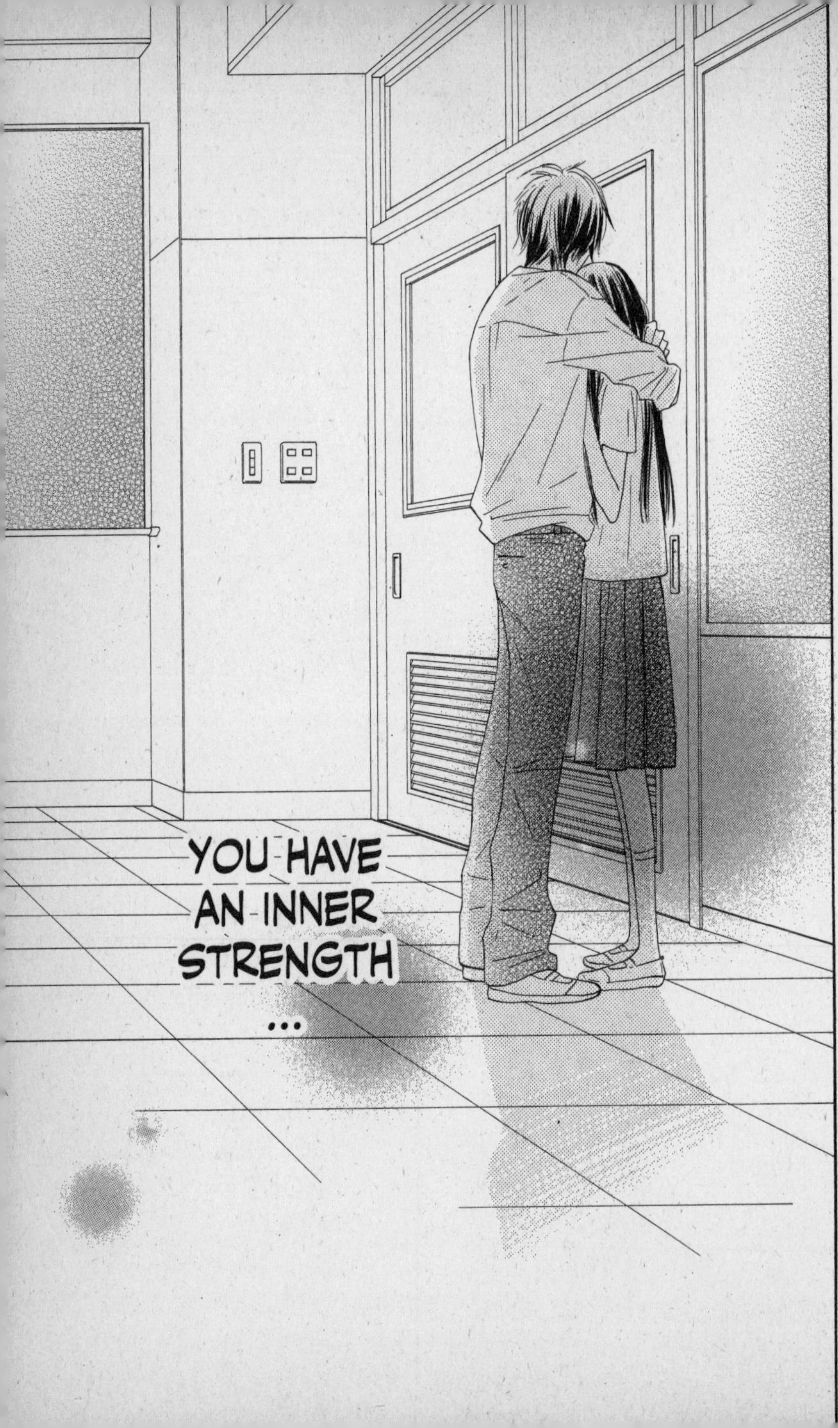
YOU HAVE AN INNER STRENGTH
...

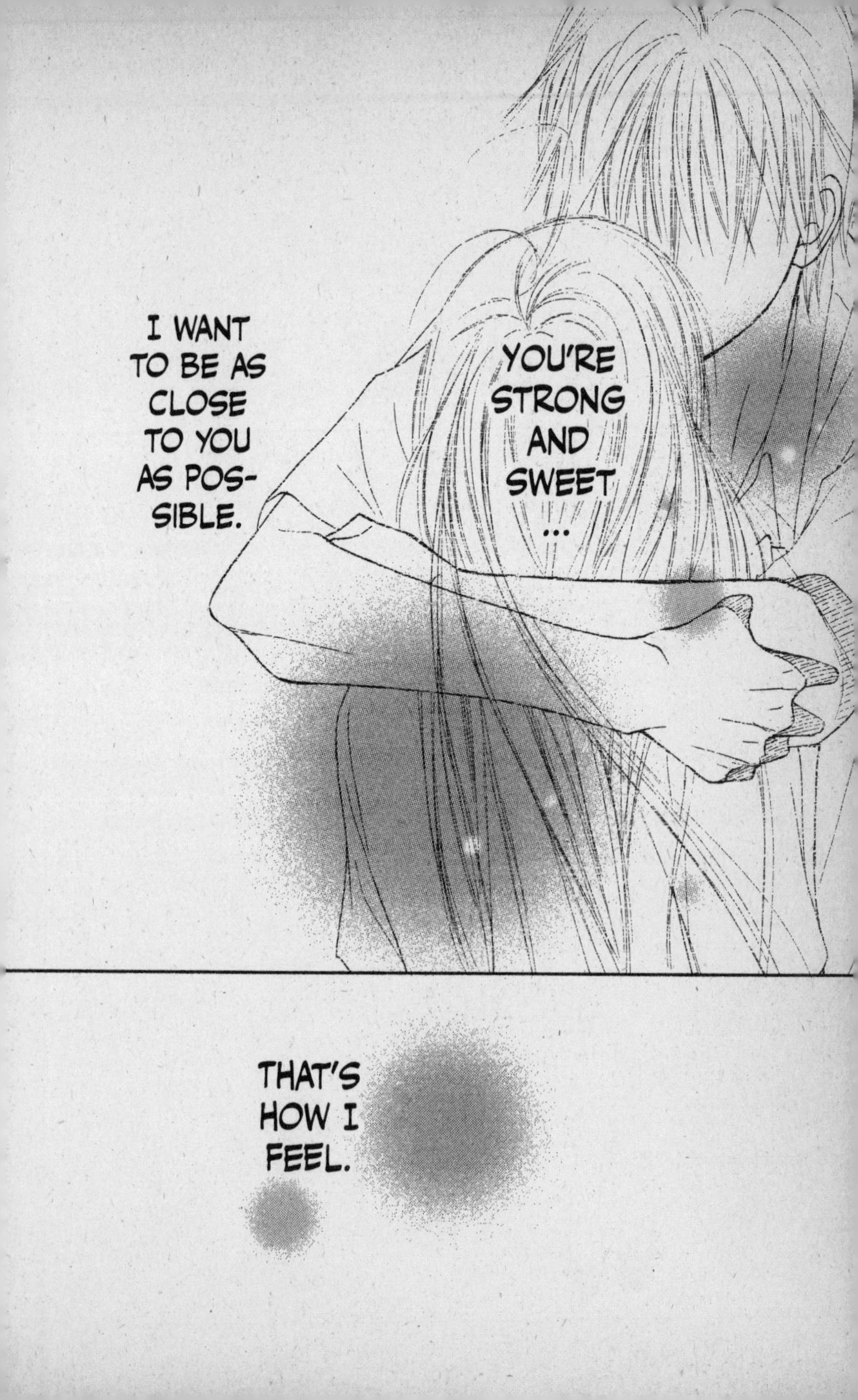
YOU'RE STRONG AND SWEET...
I WANT TO BE AS CLOSE TO YOU AS POS-SIBLE.
THAT'S HOW I FEEL.

Episode 45: Almost Summer Break

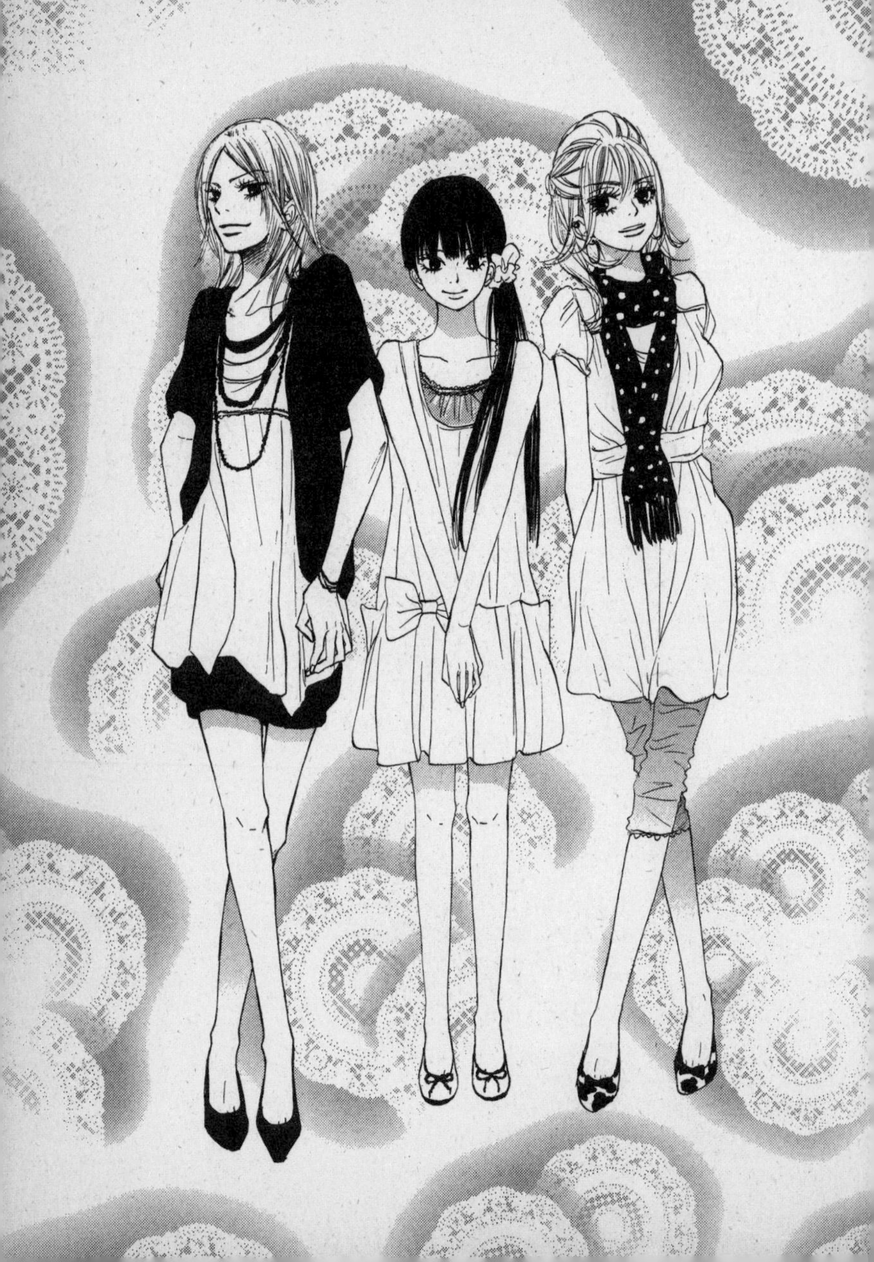

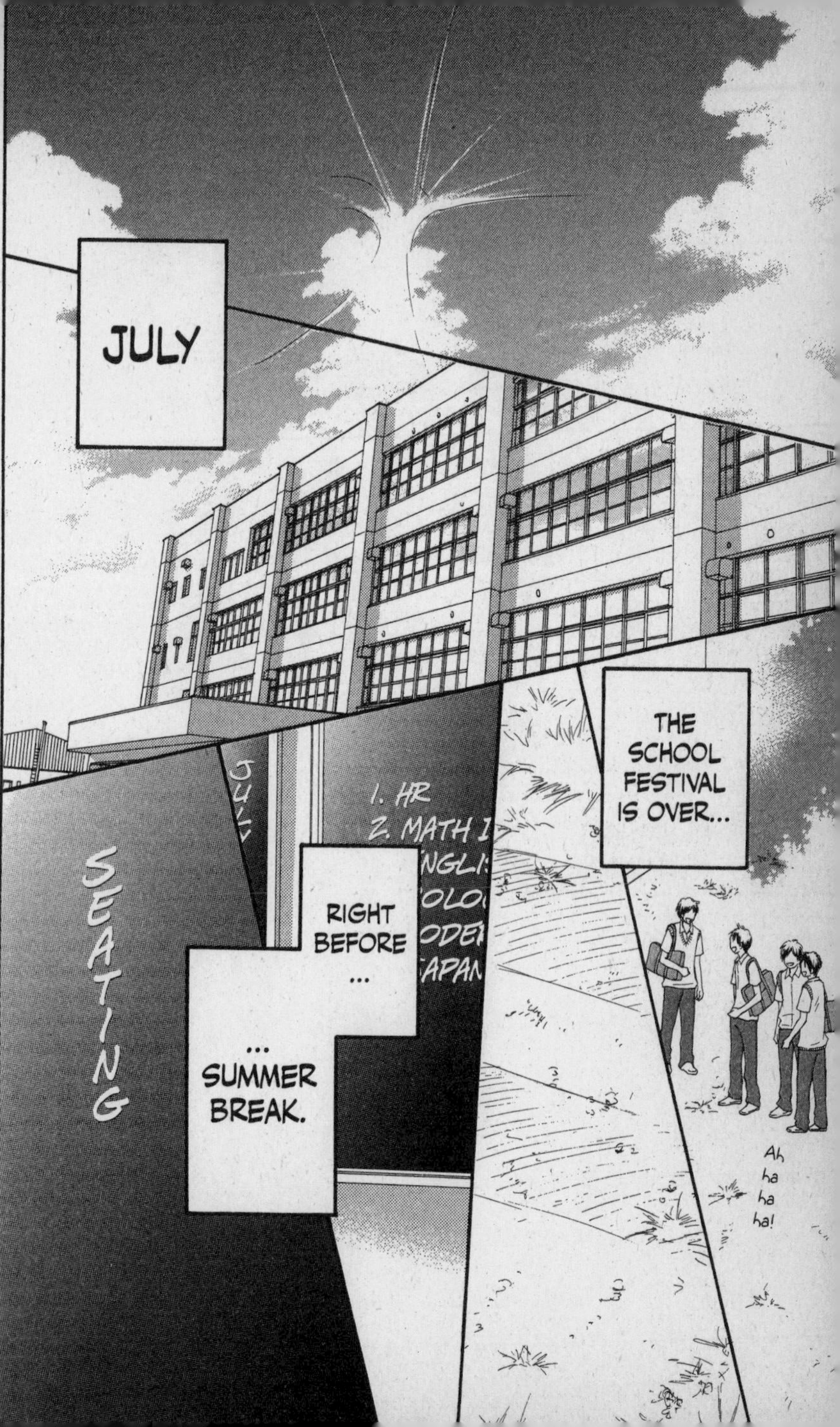
JULY
THE SCHOOL FESTIVAL IS OVER...
Ah ha ha ha!
1. HR
2. MATH I
SEATING
RIGHT BEFORE...
...SUMMER BREAK.

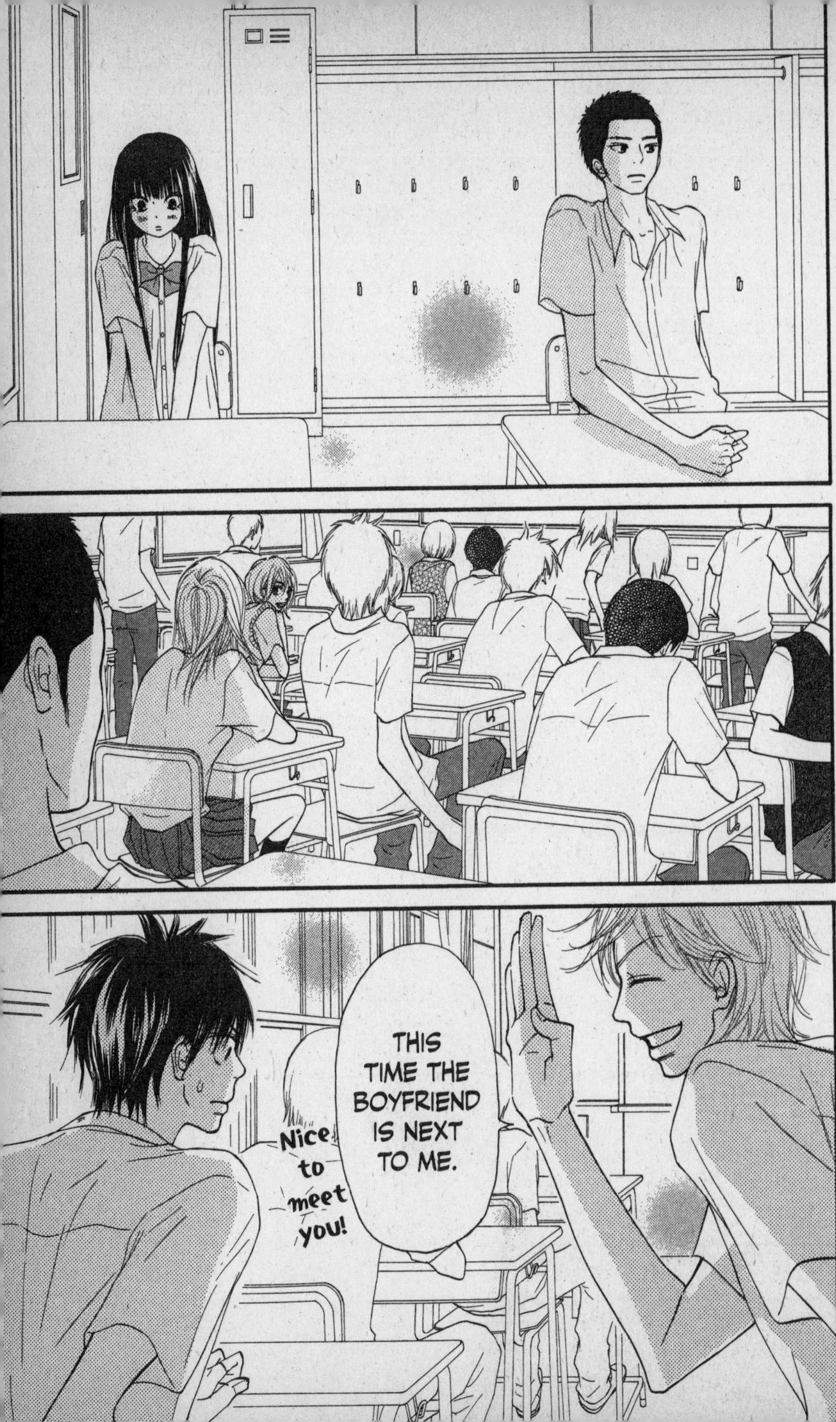
THIS TIME THE BOYFRIEND IS NEXT TO ME.
Nice to meet you!

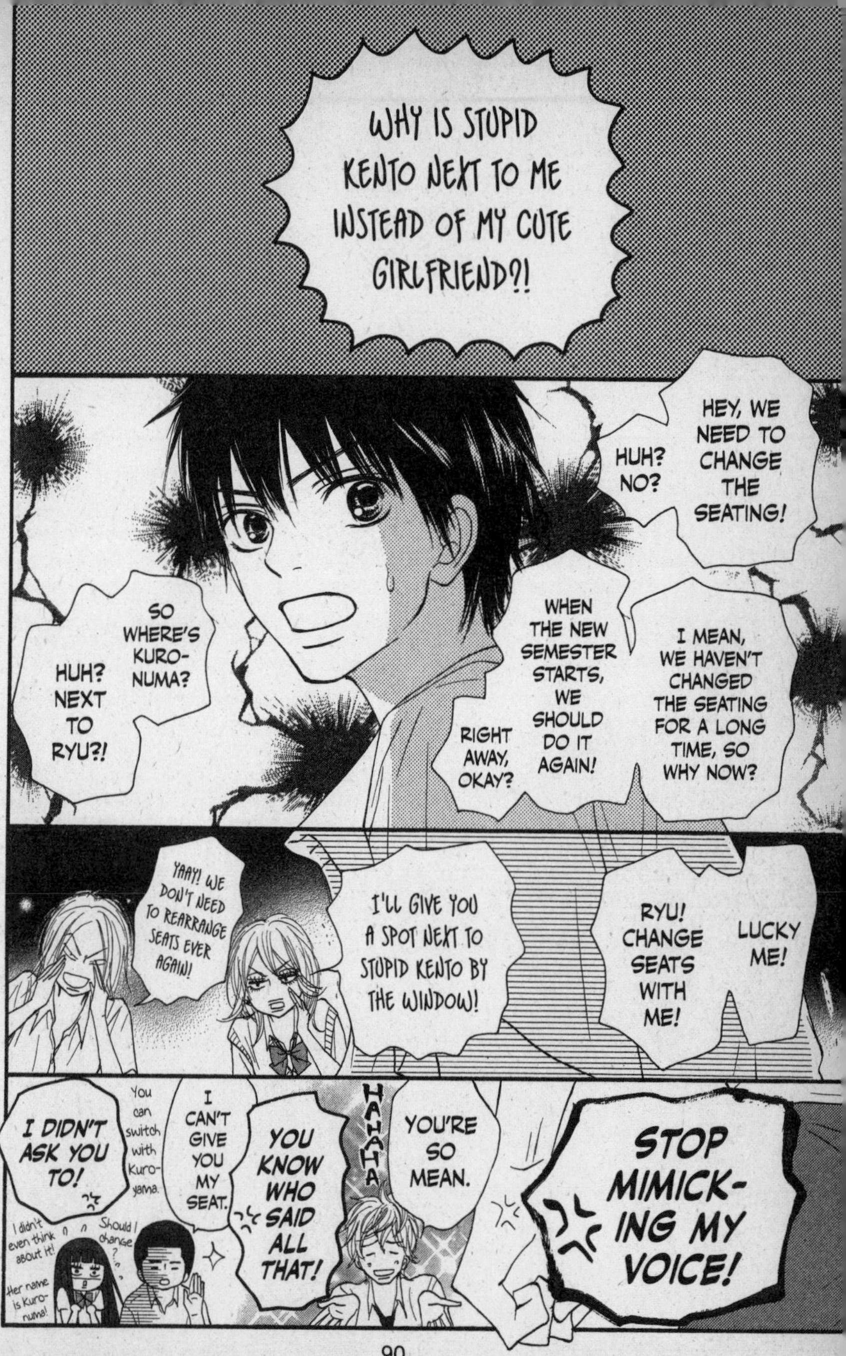
WHY IS STUPID KENTO NEXT TO ME INSTEAD OF MY CUTE GIRLFRIEND?!
HEY, WE NEED TO CHANGE THE SEATING!
HUH? NO?
I MEAN, WE HAVEN'T CHANGED THE SEATING FOR A LONG TIME, SO WHY NOW?
WHEN THE NEW SEMESTER STARTS, WE SHOULD DO IT AGAIN!
RIGHT AWAY, OKAY?
SO WHERE'S KURO-NUMA?
HUH? NEXT TO RYU?!
LUCKY ME!
RYU! CHANGE SEATS WITH ME!
I'LL GIVE YOU A SPOT NEXT TO STUPID KENTO BY THE WINDOW!
YAAY! WE DON'T NEED TO REARRANGE SEATS EVER AGAIN!
STOP MIMICK-ING MY VOICE!
YOU'RE SO MEAN.
HAHAHA
YOU KNOW WHO SAID ALL THAT!
I CAN'T GIVE YOU MY SEAT.
You can switch with Kuro-yama.
I DIDN'T ASK YOU TO!
Should I change?
I didn't even think about it!
Her name is Kuro-numa!

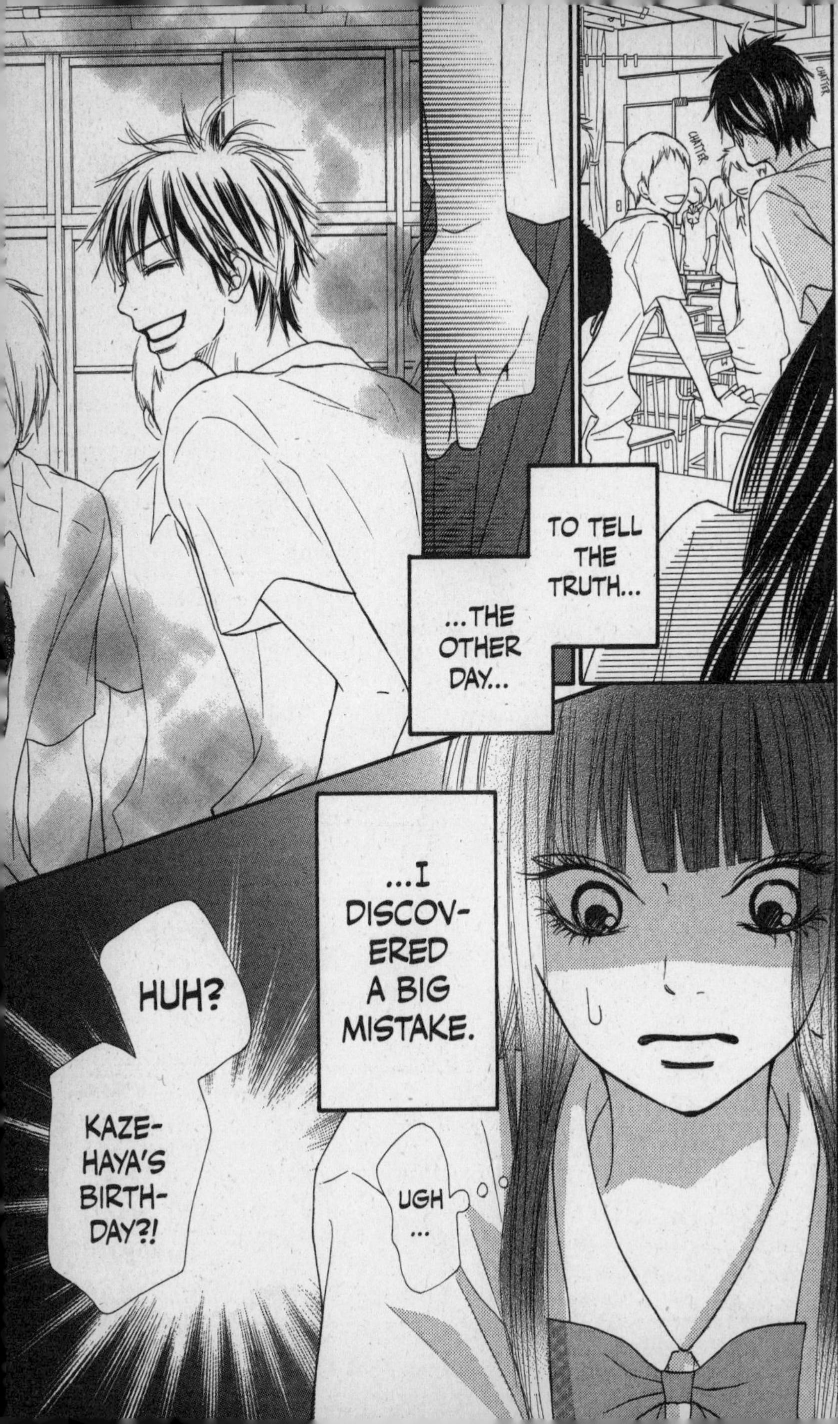
CHATTER
CHATTER
TO TELL THE TRUTH...
...THE OTHER DAY...
...I DISCOVERED A BIG MISTAKE.
UGH ...
HUH?
KAZE-HAYA'S BIRTH-DAY?!

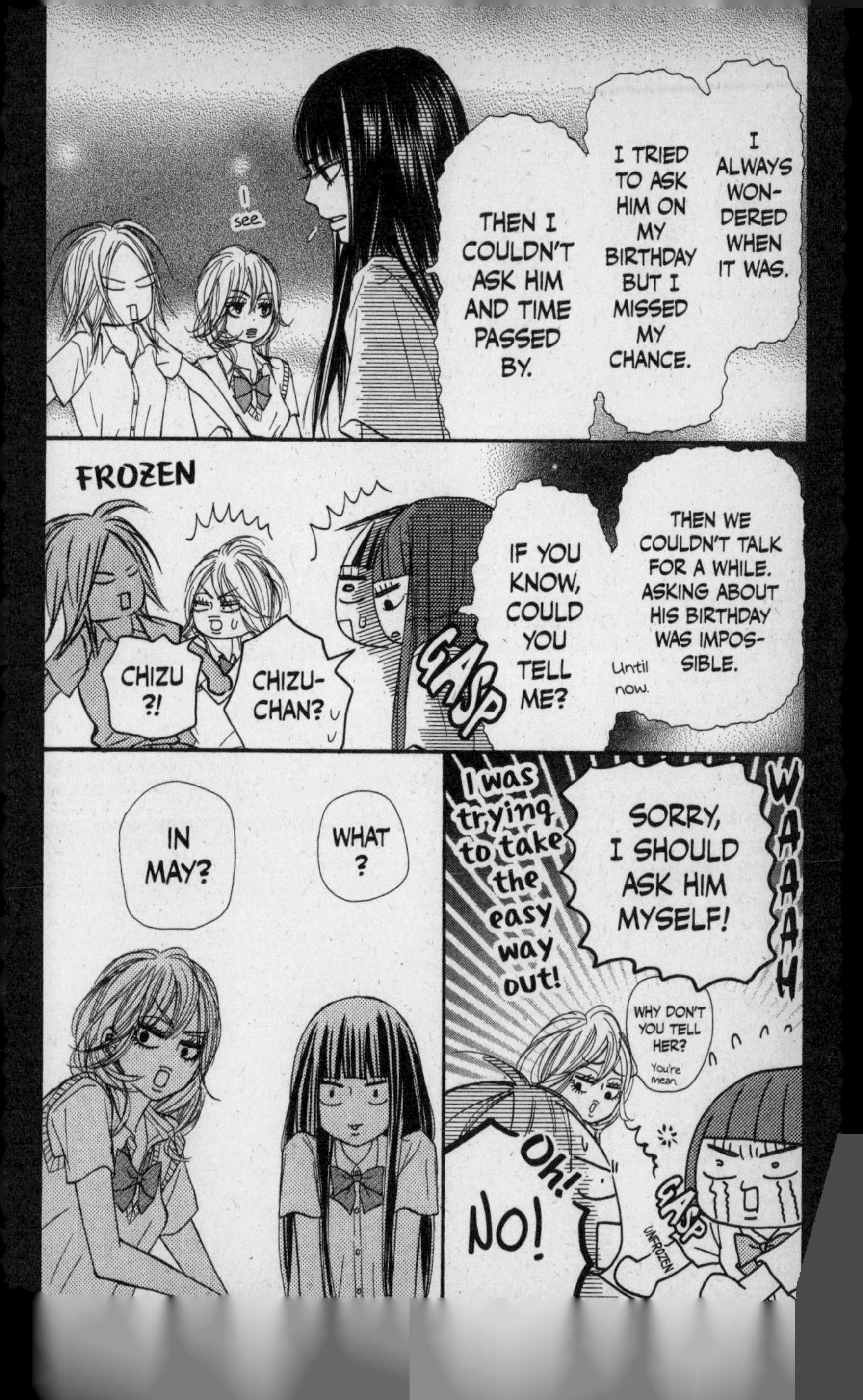
I ALWAYS WONDERED WHEN IT WAS.
I TRIED TO ASK HIM ON MY BIRTHDAY BUT I MISSED MY CHANCE.
THEN I COULDN'T ASK HIM AND TIME PASSED BY.
I see
THEN WE COULDN'T TALK FOR A WHILE. ASKING ABOUT HIS BIRTHDAY WAS IMPOSSIBLE.
Until now.
IF YOU KNOW, COULD YOU TELL ME?
GASP
FROZEN
CHIZU-CHAN?
CHIZU?!
WAAAAH
SORRY, I SHOULD ASK HIM MYSELF!
I was trying to take the easy way out!
WHY DON'T YOU TELL HER?
You're mean.
GASP
UNFROZEN
Oh!
NO!
WHAT?
IN MAY?

KARUPIN on JAPAN 3

Also, I went on a trip to gather ideas for the rest of the series. I will put where I went in the manga later on.

Anyway...

- Photo team:
  - Me
  - Assistants (three)
  - Editor (joined us later)

Because I took my child...

- Baby-sitters:
  - Husband
  - Husband's parents
  - My mother

There were a lot of people!

But nonetheless...

- My daughter got a fever the first day.
- The next day we went to see a doctor.
- I had to breastfeed her since she had no appetite.

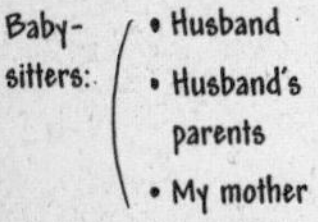

I don't have much milk left.
Sorry

It's hard to travel with a baby!

I broke down after the trip. I had the same symptoms as my daughter had. I made no progress at all on my work.

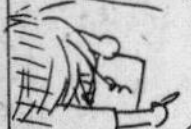

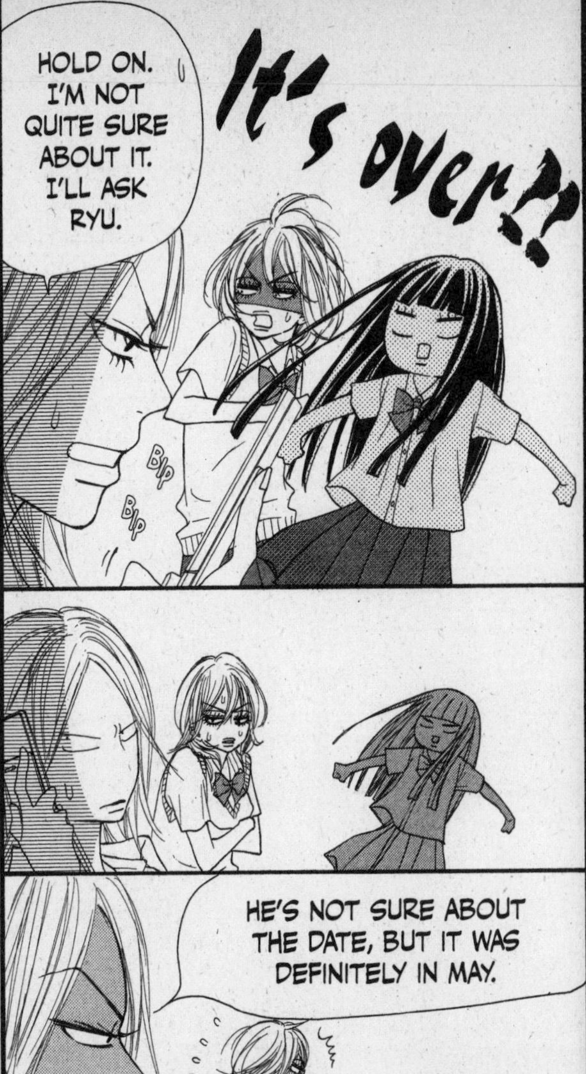

It's over!?
HOLD ON. I'M NOT QUITE SURE ABOUT IT. I'LL ASK RYU.
Bip
Bip
HE'S NOT SURE ABOUT THE DATE, BUT IT WAS DEFINITELY IN MAY.
HEY...
SAWA...
SAWA?!
Are you okay?!

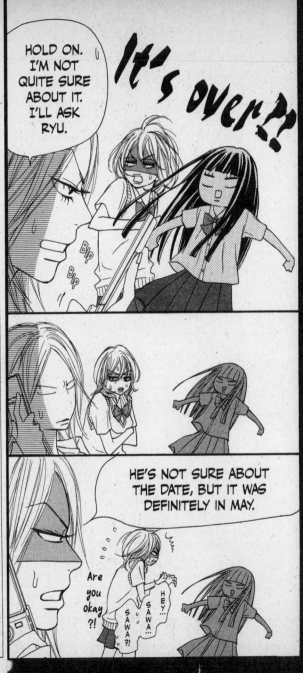

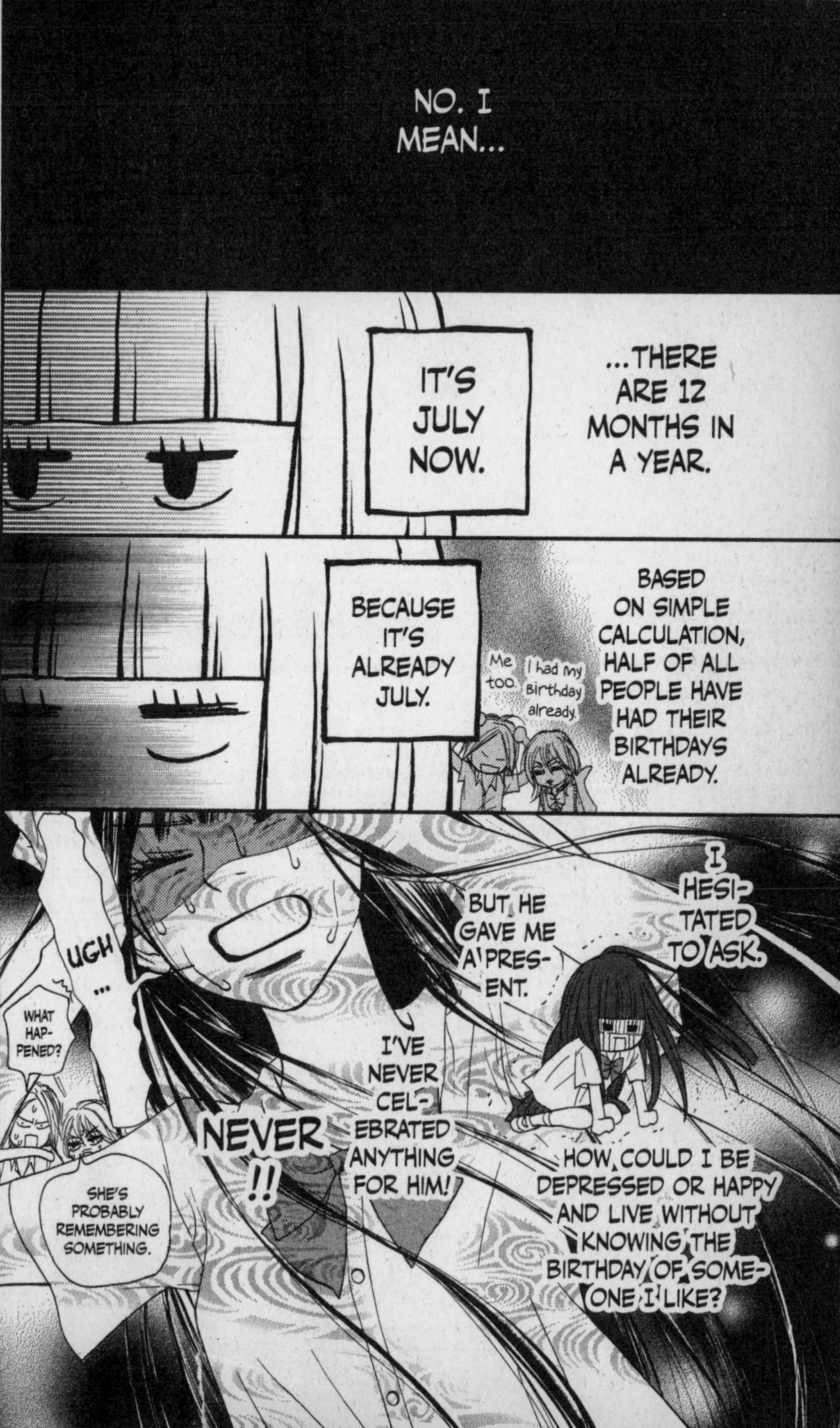
NO. I MEAN...
...THERE ARE 12 MONTHS IN A YEAR.
IT'S JULY NOW.
BASED ON SIMPLE CALCULATION, HALF OF ALL PEOPLE HAVE HAD THEIR BIRTHDAYS ALREADY.
I had my birthday already.
Me too.
BECAUSE IT'S ALREADY JULY.
I HESI-TATED TO ASK.
BUT HE GAVE ME A PRES-ENT.
I'VE NEVER CEL-EBRATED ANYTHING FOR HIM!
NEVER!!
UGH...
WHAT HAP-PENED?
HOW COULD I BE DEPRESSED OR HAPPY AND LIVE WITHOUT KNOWING THE BIRTHDAY OF SOME-ONE I LIKE?
SHE'S PROBABLY REMEMBERING SOMETHING.

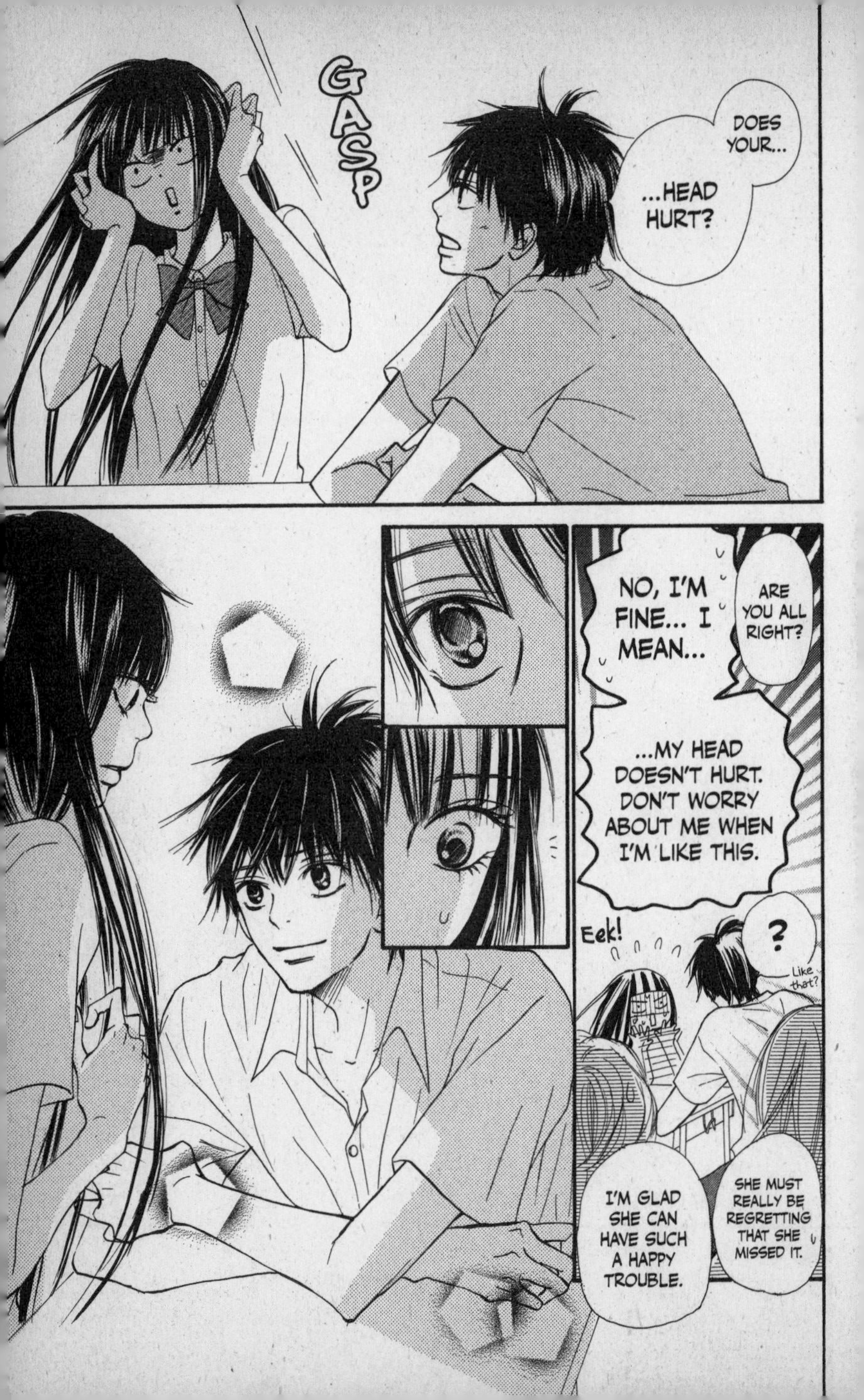
DOES YOUR... ...HEAD HURT?
GASP
ARE YOU ALL RIGHT?
NO, I'M FINE... I MEAN...
...MY HEAD DOESN'T HURT. DON'T WORRY ABOUT ME WHEN I'M LIKE THIS.
?
Like that?
Eek!
SHE MUST REALLY BE REGRETTING THAT SHE MISSED IT.
I'M GLAD SHE CAN HAVE SUCH A HAPPY TROUBLE.

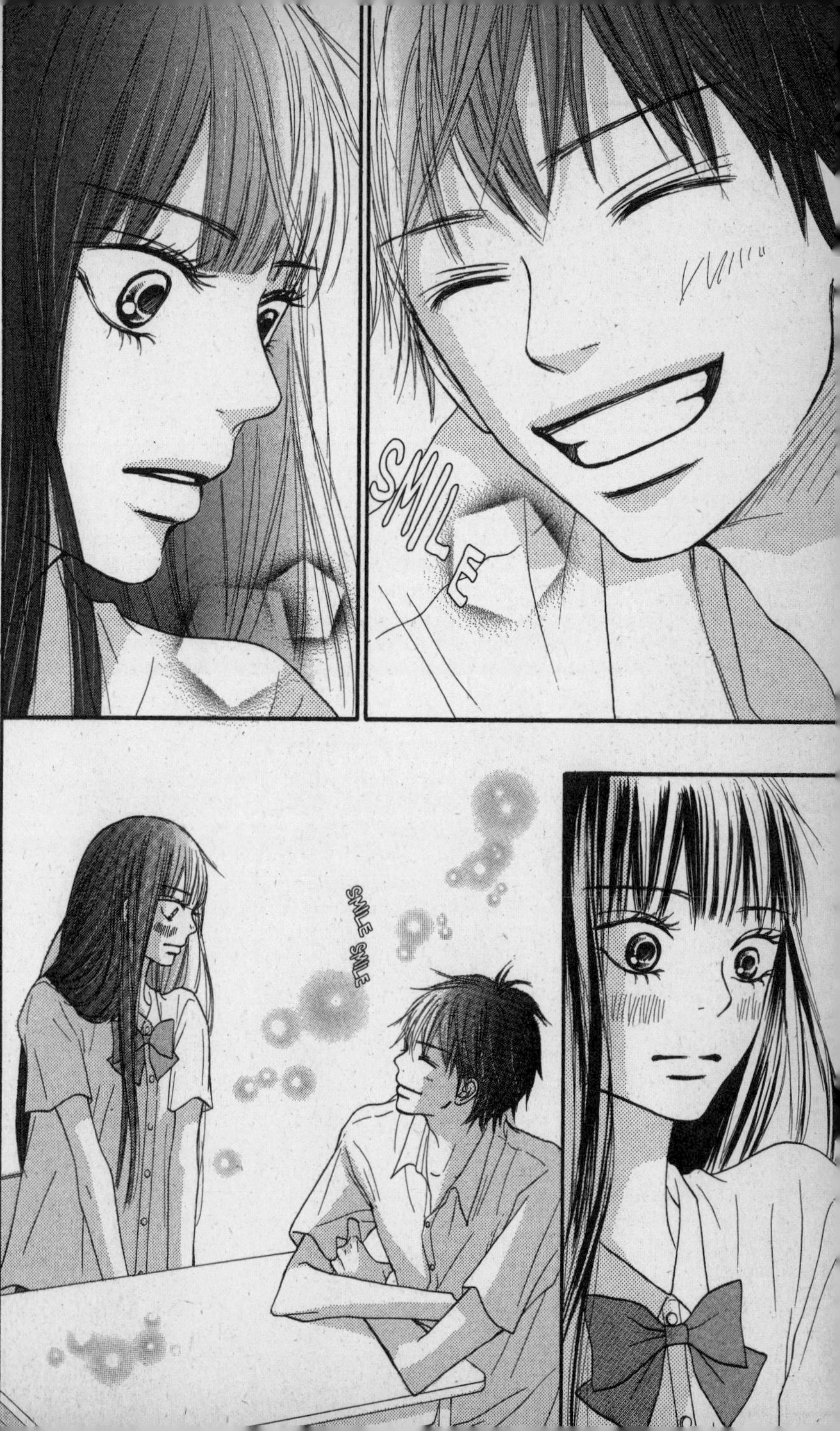
SMILE
SMILE SMILE

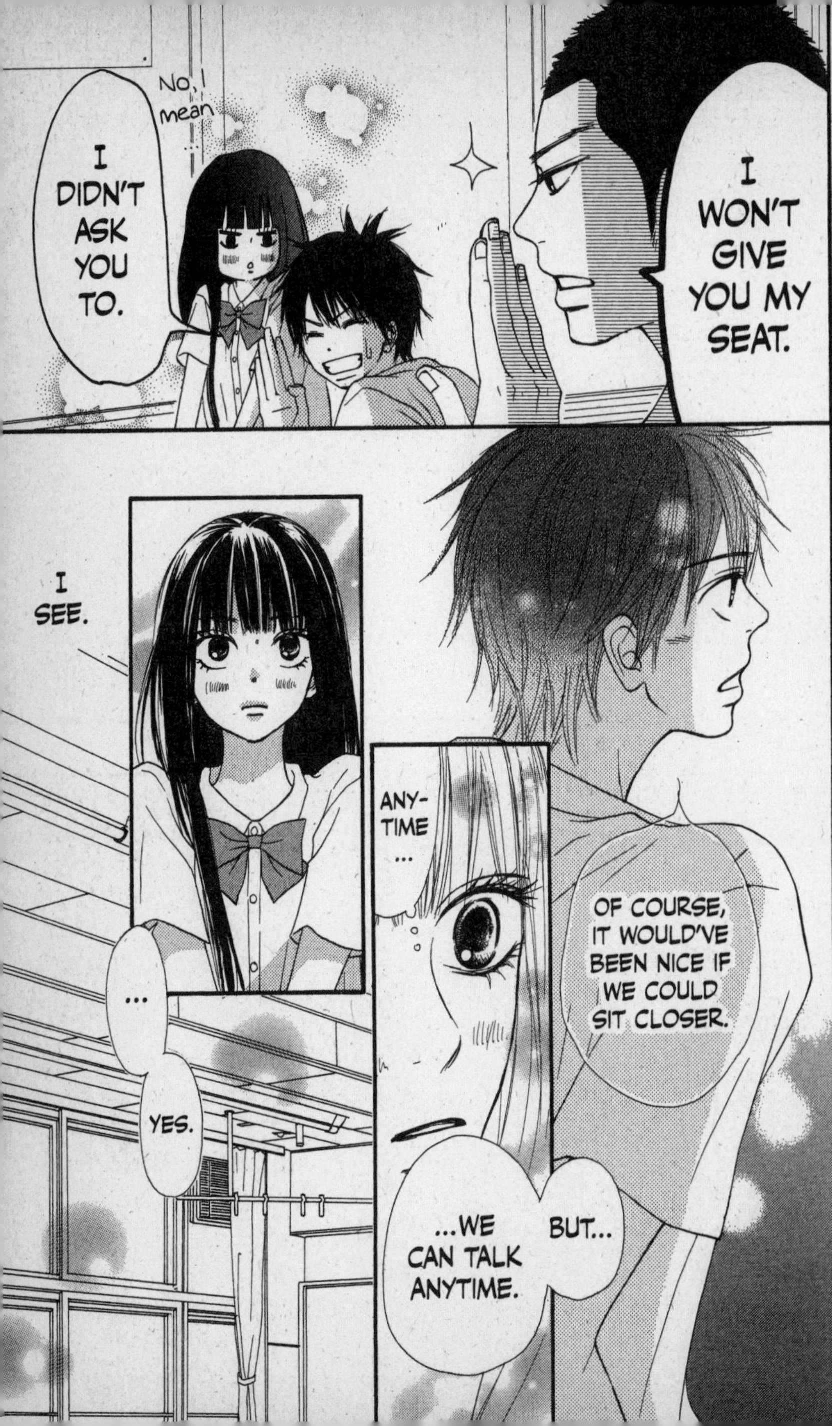
I WON'T GIVE YOU MY SEAT.
No, I mean ...
I DIDN'T ASK YOU TO.
OF COURSE, IT WOULD'VE BEEN NICE IF WE COULD SIT CLOSER.
BUT...
...WE CAN TALK ANYTIME.
ANY-TIME ...
I SEE.
...
YES.

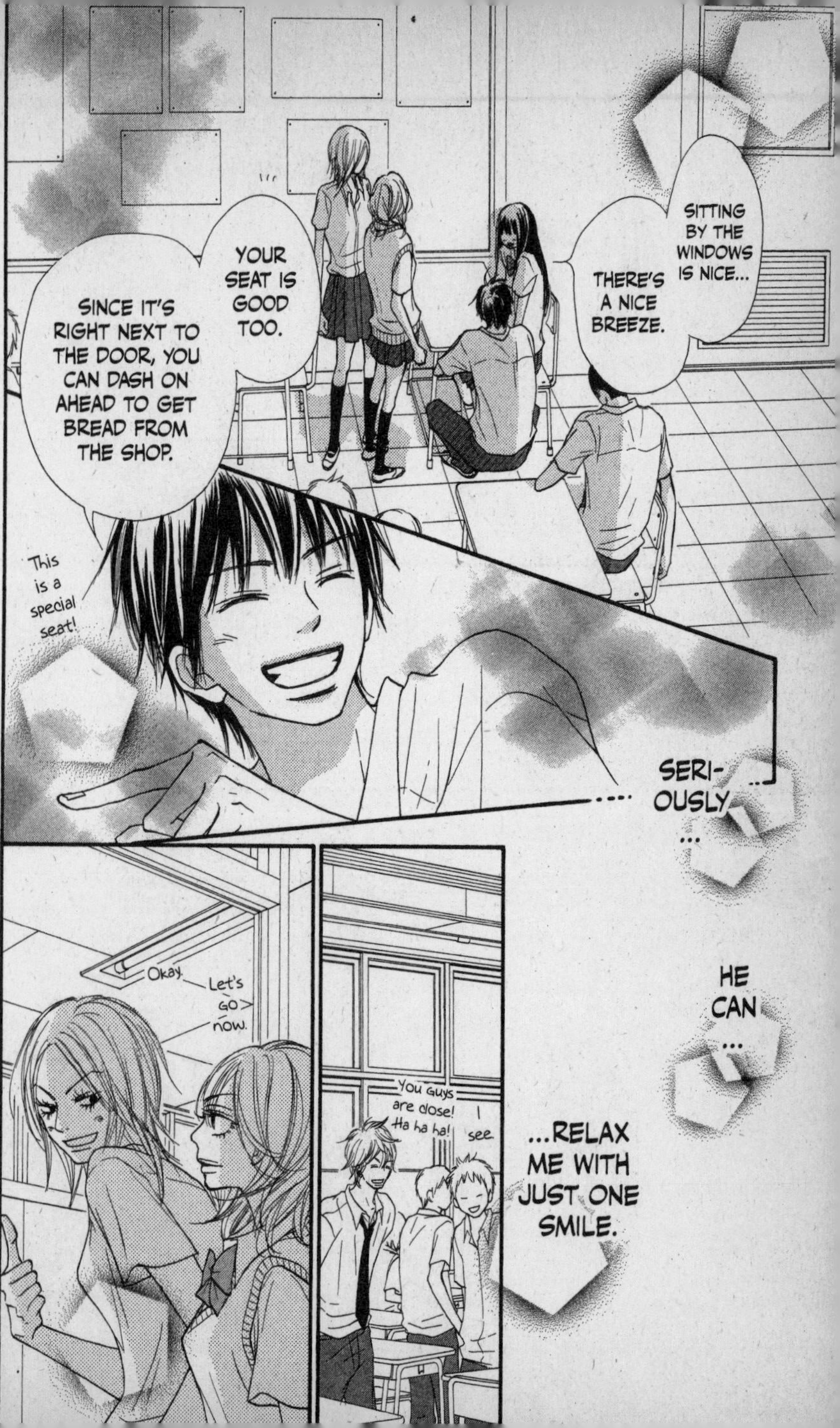
SITTING BY THE WINDOWS IS NICE...
THERE'S A NICE BREEZE.
YOUR SEAT IS GOOD TOO.
SINCE IT'S RIGHT NEXT TO THE DOOR, YOU CAN DASH ON AHEAD TO GET BREAD FROM THE SHOP.
This is a special seat!
SERI-OUSLY...
HE CAN...
...RELAX ME WITH JUST ONE SMILE.
I see.
You guys are close! Ha ha ha!
Okay.
Let's go now.

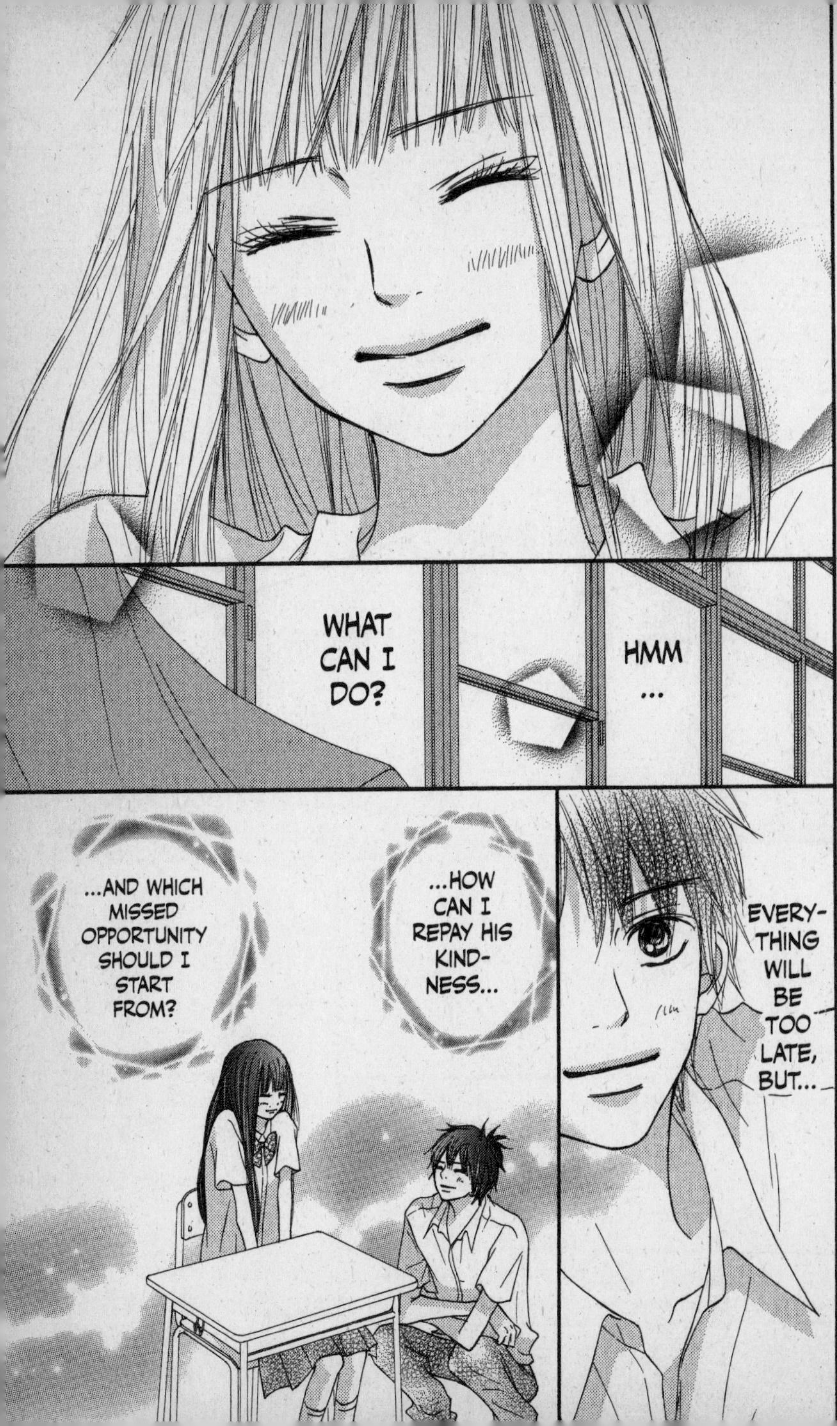
HMM...
WHAT CAN I DO?
EVERYTHING WILL BE TOO LATE, BUT...
...HOW CAN I REPAY HIS KINDNESS...
...AND WHICH MISSED OPPORTUNITY SHOULD I START FROM?

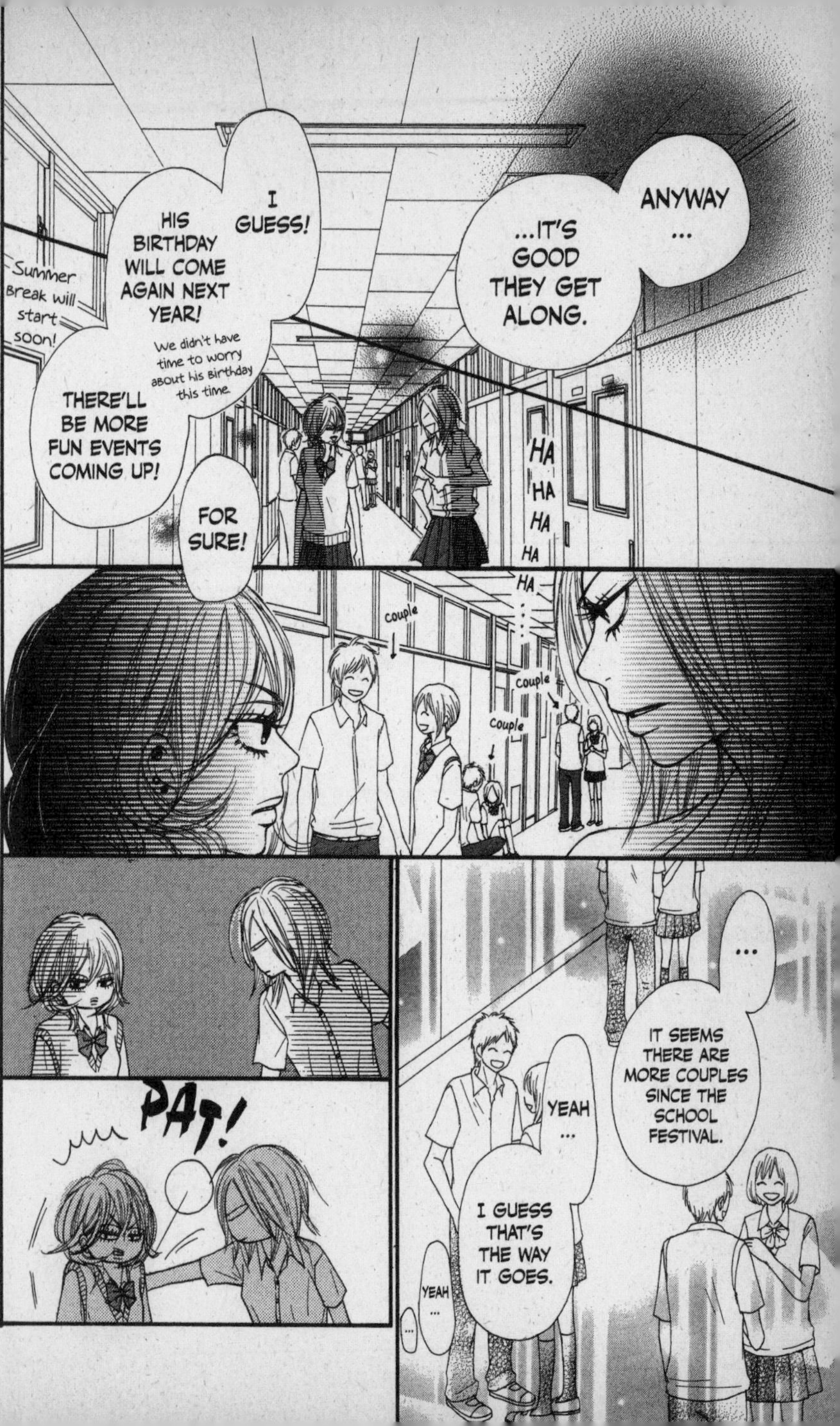
ANYWAY ...
...IT'S GOOD THEY GET ALONG.
HA HA HA HA HA ...
I GUESS!
HIS BIRTHDAY WILL COME AGAIN NEXT YEAR!
We didn't have time to worry about his birthday this time.
Summer Break will start soon!
THERE'LL BE MORE FUN EVENTS COMING UP!
FOR SURE!
couple
couple
couple
...
IT SEEMS THERE ARE MORE COUPLES SINCE THE SCHOOL FESTIVAL.
YEAH ...
I GUESS THAT'S THE WAY IT GOES.
YEAH ...
...
PAT!

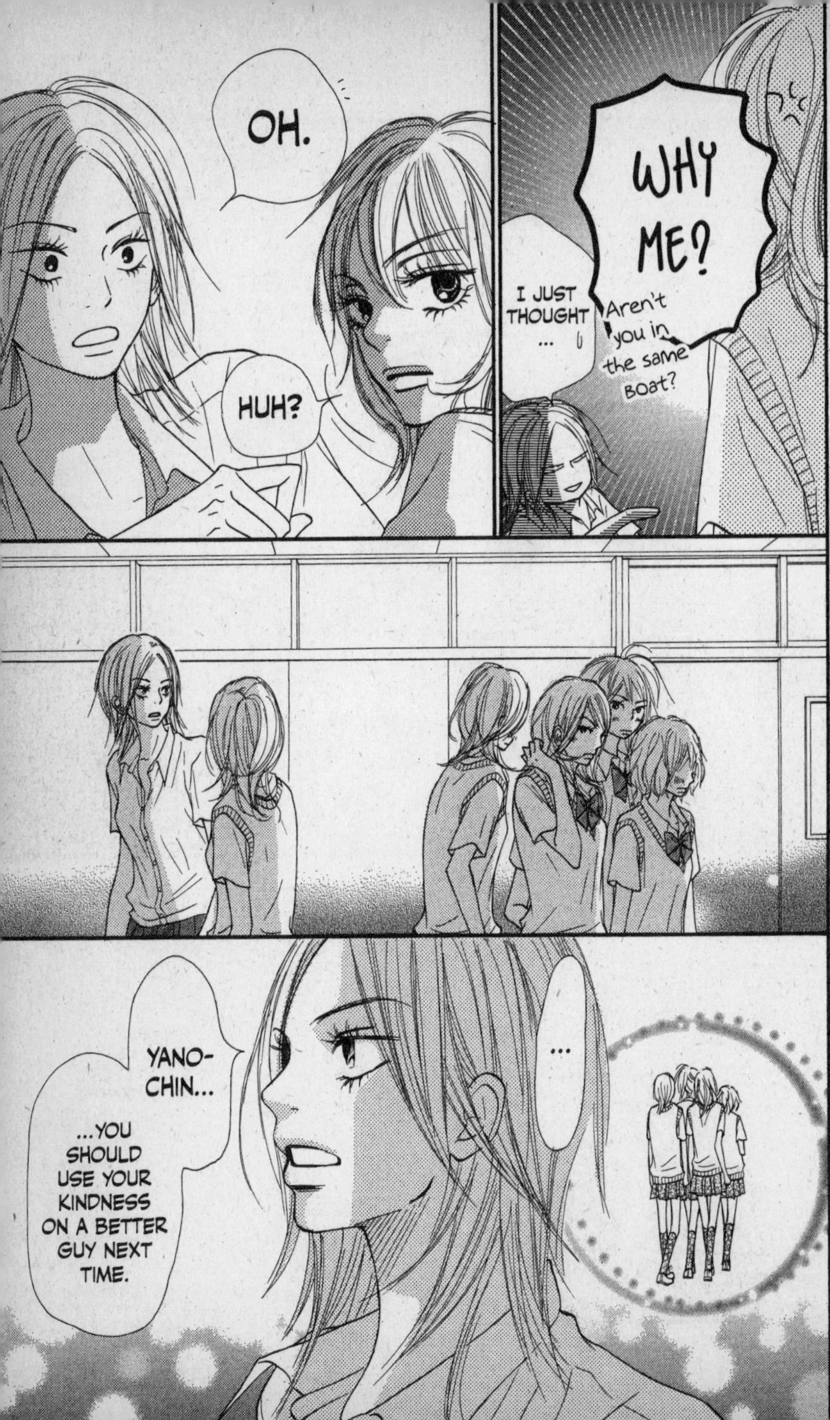
WHY ME?
Aren't you in the same boat?
I JUST THOUGHT...
OH.
HUH?
...
YANO-CHIN...
...YOU SHOULD USE YOUR KINDNESS ON A BETTER GUY NEXT TIME.

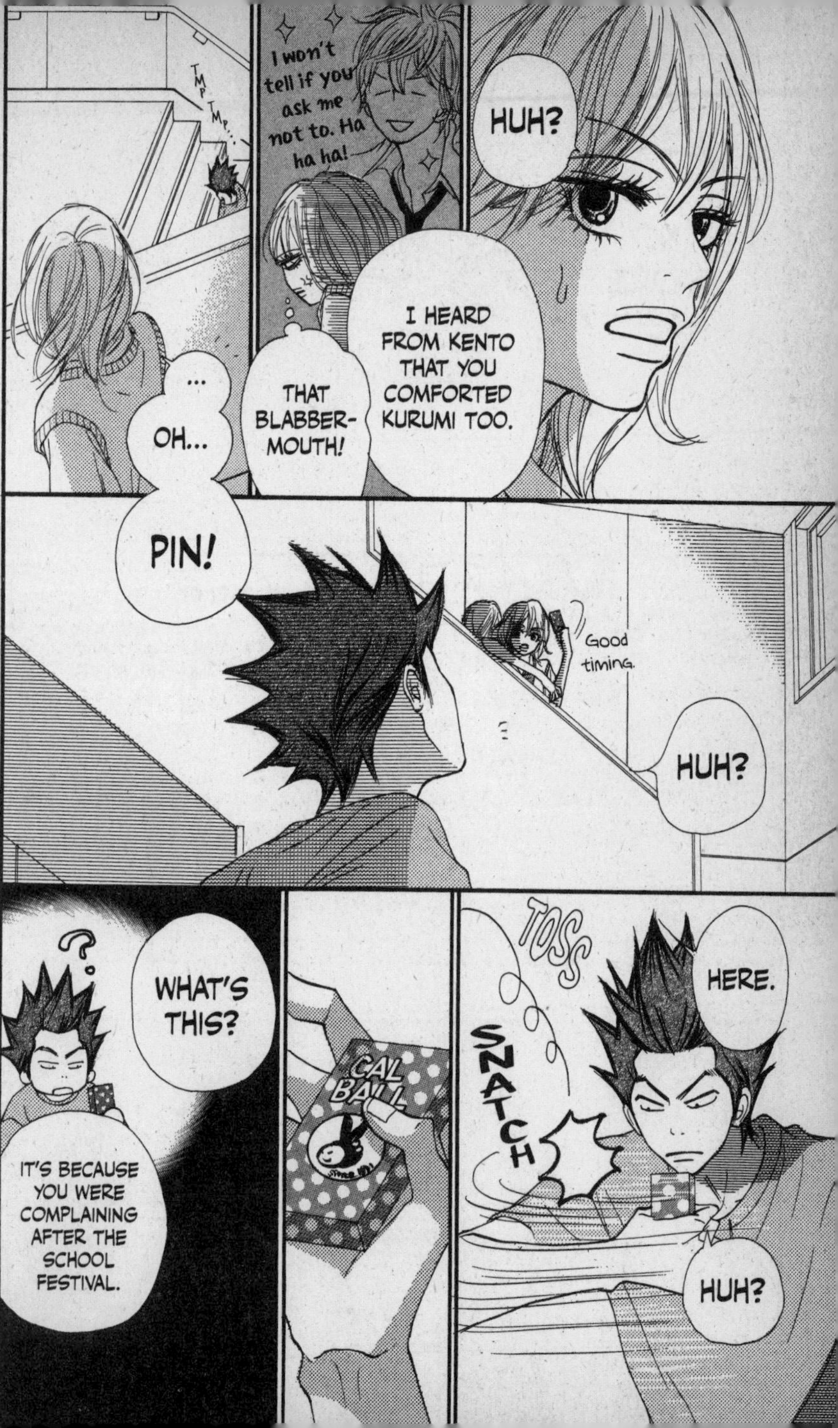
HUH?
I HEARD FROM KENTO THAT YOU COMFORTED KURUMI TOO.
I won't tell if you ask me not to. Ha ha ha!
THAT BLABBER-MOUTH!
TMP TMP...
...
OH...
PIN!
Good timing.
HUH?
TOSS
HERE.
SNATCH
HUH?
CAL BALL
WHAT'S THIS?
IT'S BECAUSE YOU WERE COMPLAINING AFTER THE SCHOOL FESTIVAL.

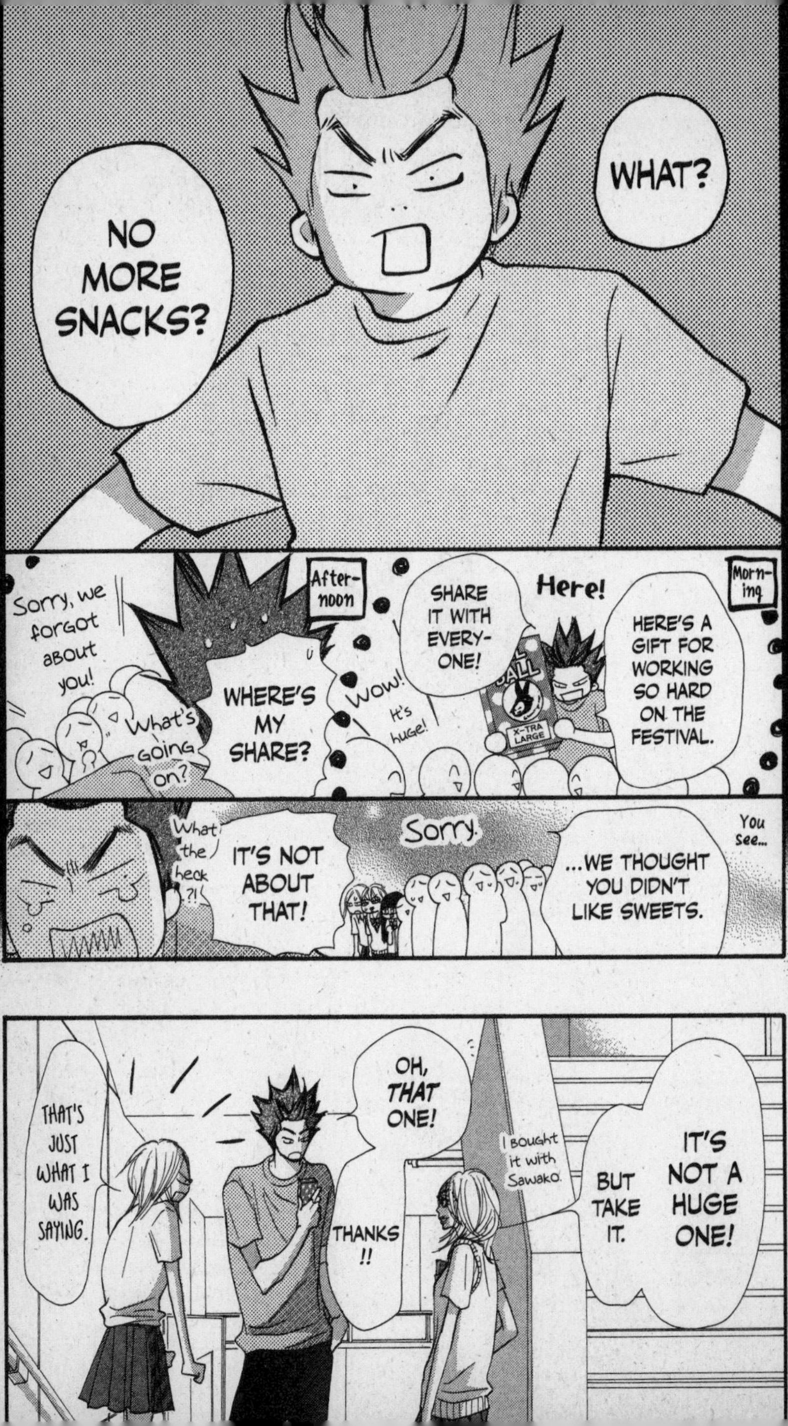
WHAT?
NO MORE SNACKS?
Morning
HERE'S A GIFT FOR WORKING SO HARD ON THE FESTIVAL.
Here!
SHARE IT WITH EVERYONE!
Wow!
It's huge!
X-TRA LARGE
Afternoon
WHERE'S MY SHARE?
What's going on?
Sorry, we forgot about you!
You see...
...WE THOUGHT YOU DIDN'T LIKE SWEETS.
Sorry.
IT'S NOT ABOUT THAT!
What the heck?!
IT'S NOT A HUGE ONE!
BUT TAKE IT.
I bought it with Sawako.
OH, THAT ONE!
THANKS!!
THAT'S JUST WHAT I WAS SAYING.

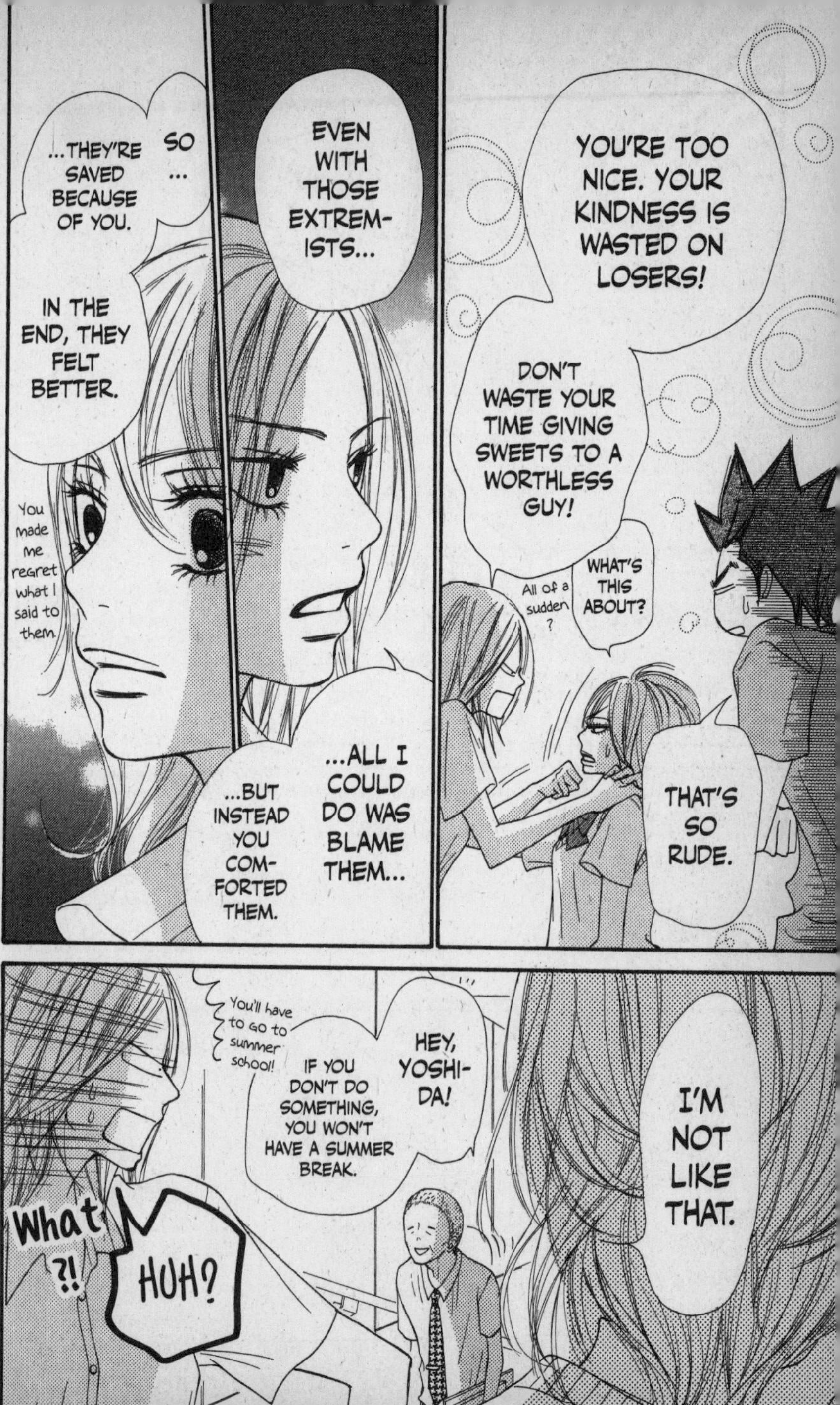
YOU'RE TOO NICE. YOUR KINDNESS IS WASTED ON LOSERS!
DON'T WASTE YOUR TIME GIVING SWEETS TO A WORTHLESS GUY!
WHAT'S THIS ABOUT?
All of a sudden?
THAT'S SO RUDE.
EVEN WITH THOSE EXTREM-ISTS...
...ALL I COULD DO WAS BLAME THEM...
...BUT INSTEAD YOU COM-FORTED THEM.
SO...
...THEY'RE SAVED BECAUSE OF YOU.
IN THE END, THEY FELT BETTER.
You made me regret what I said to them.
I'M NOT LIKE THAT.
HEY, YOSHI-DA!
IF YOU DON'T DO SOMETHING, YOU WON'T HAVE A SUMMER BREAK.
You'll have to go to summer school!
HUH?
What?!

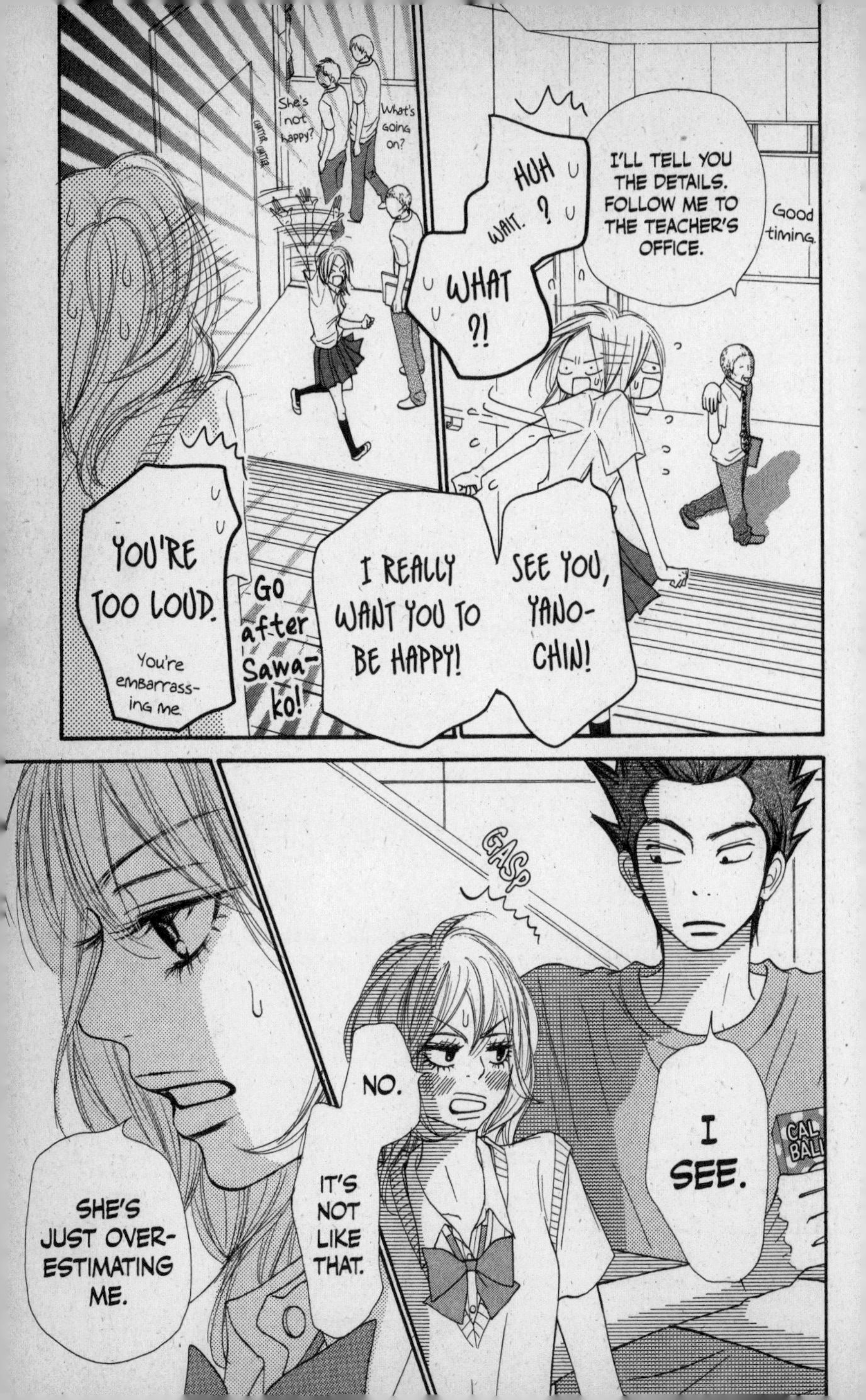
I'LL TELL YOU THE DETAILS. FOLLOW ME TO THE TEACHER'S OFFICE.
Good timing.
HUH? WAIT. WHAT?!
SEE YOU, YANO-CHIN!
I REALLY WANT YOU TO BE HAPPY!
What's going on?
She's not happy?
Go after Sawako!
YOU'RE TOO LOUD.
You're embarrassing me.
GASP
I SEE.
NO.
IT'S NOT LIKE THAT.
SHE'S JUST OVER-ESTIMATING ME.

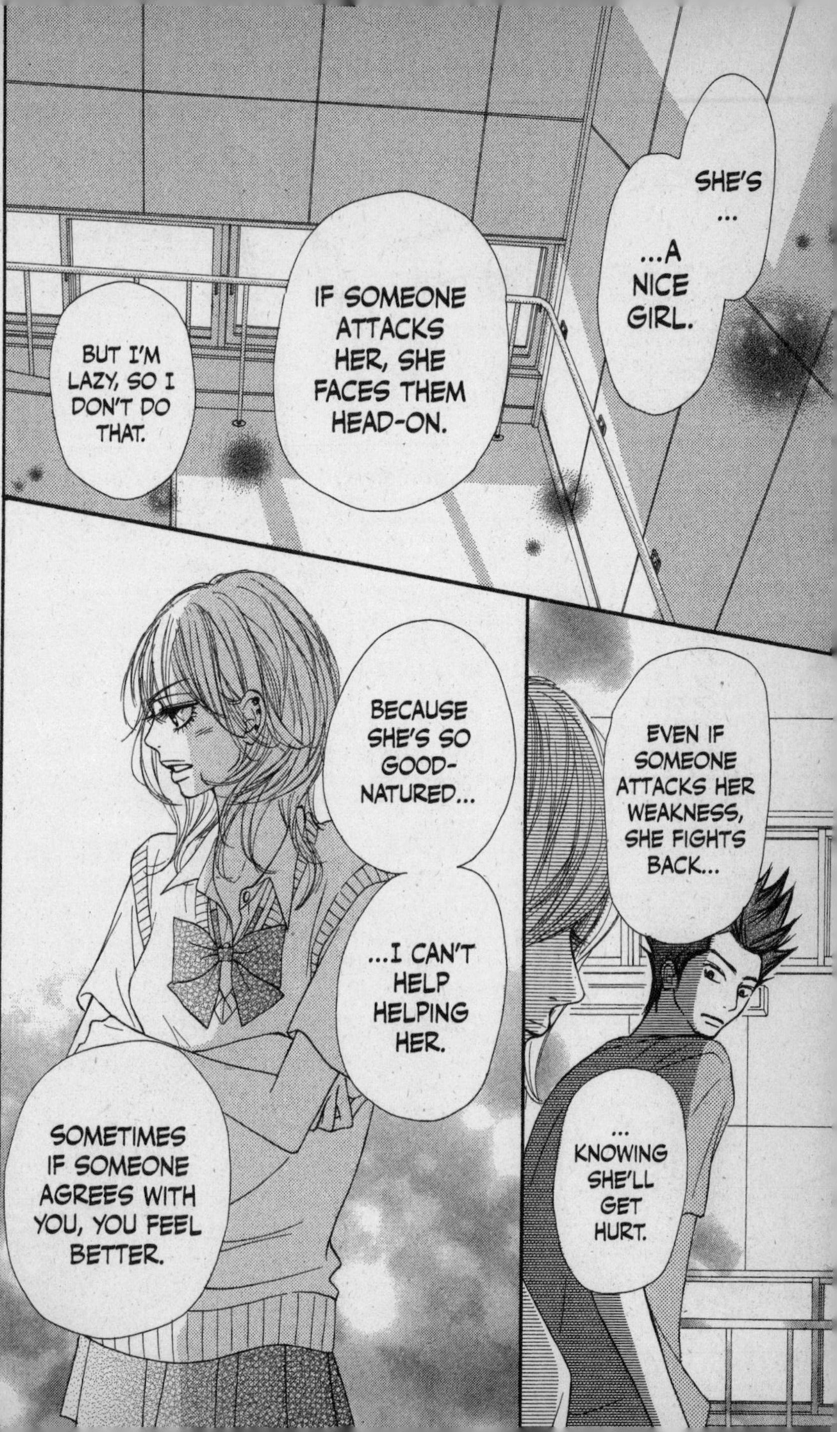
SHE'S ...
...A NICE GIRL.
IF SOMEONE ATTACKS HER, SHE FACES THEM HEAD-ON.
BUT I'M LAZY, SO I DON'T DO THAT.
EVEN IF SOMEONE ATTACKS HER WEAKNESS, SHE FIGHTS BACK...
... KNOWING SHE'LL GET HURT.
BECAUSE SHE'S SO GOOD-NATURED...
...I CAN'T HELP HELPING HER.
SOMETIMES IF SOMEONE AGREES WITH YOU, YOU FEEL BETTER.

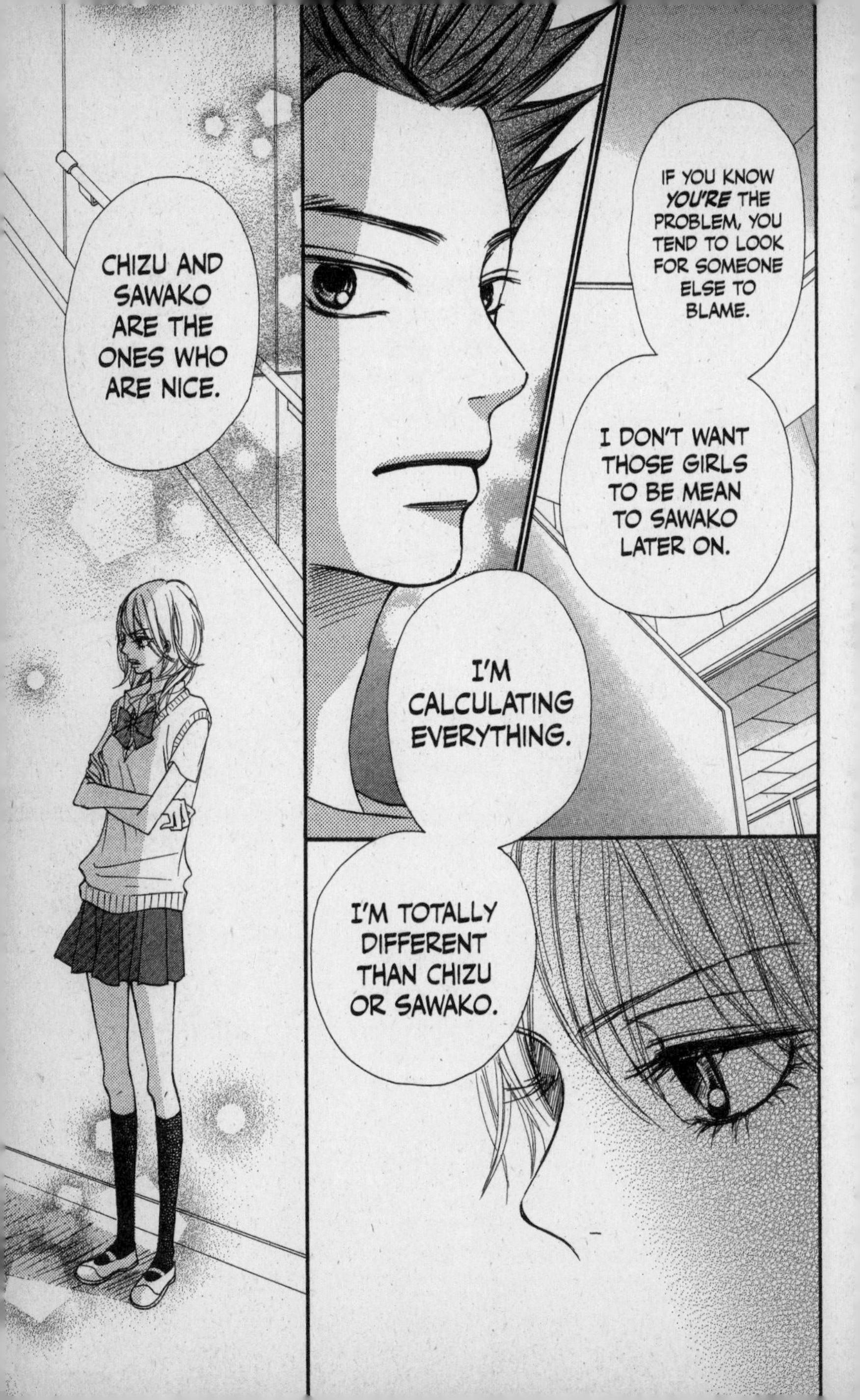
IF YOU KNOW *YOU'RE* THE PROBLEM, YOU TEND TO LOOK FOR SOMEONE ELSE TO BLAME.
I DON'T WANT THOSE GIRLS TO BE MEAN TO SAWAKO LATER ON.
I'M CALCULATING EVERYTHING.
I'M TOTALLY DIFFERENT THAN CHIZU OR SAWAKO.
CHIZU AND SAWAKO ARE THE ONES WHO ARE NICE.

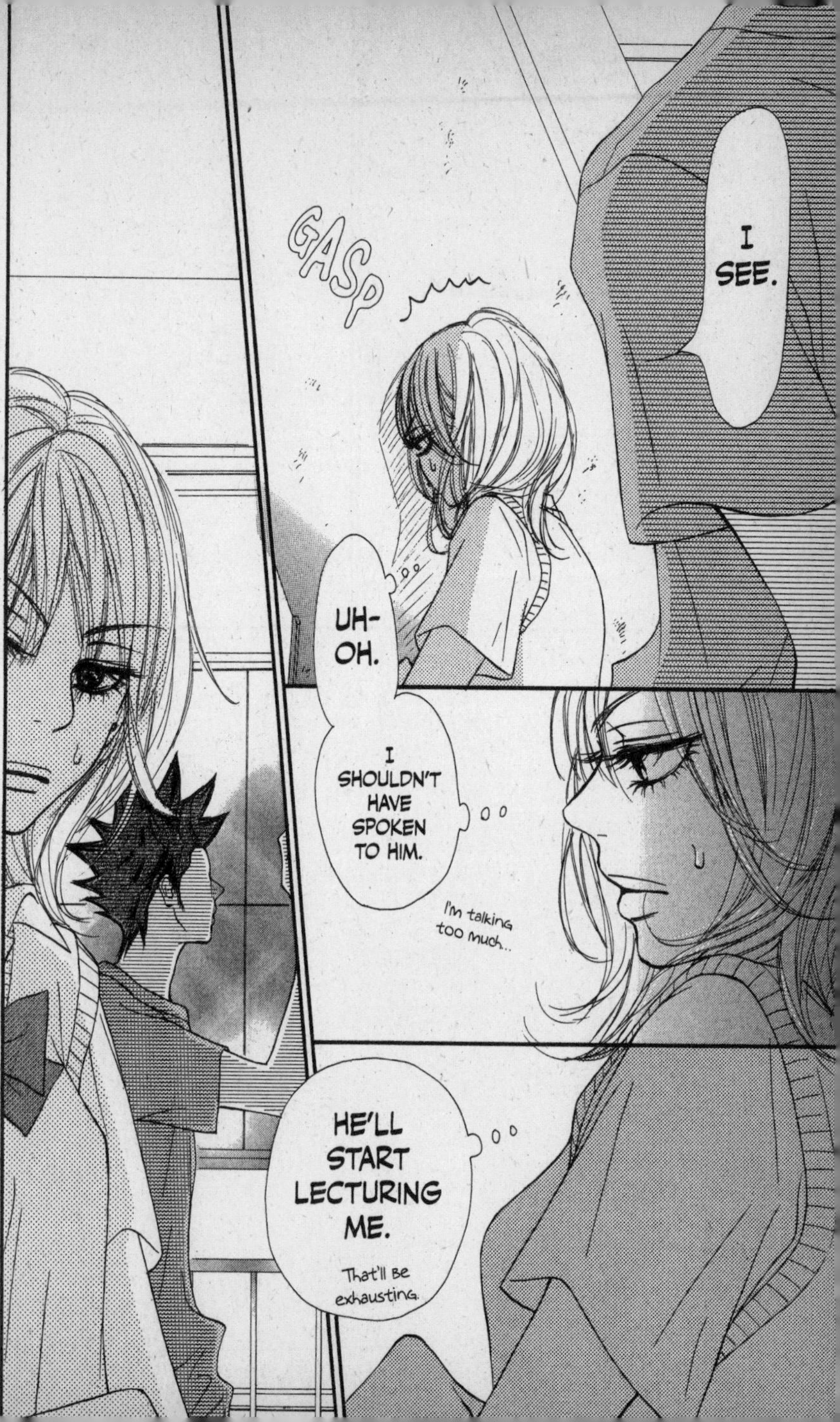
I SEE.
GASP
UH-OH.
I SHOULDN'T HAVE SPOKEN TO HIM.
I'm talking too much...
HE'LL START LECTURING ME.
That'll be exhausting.

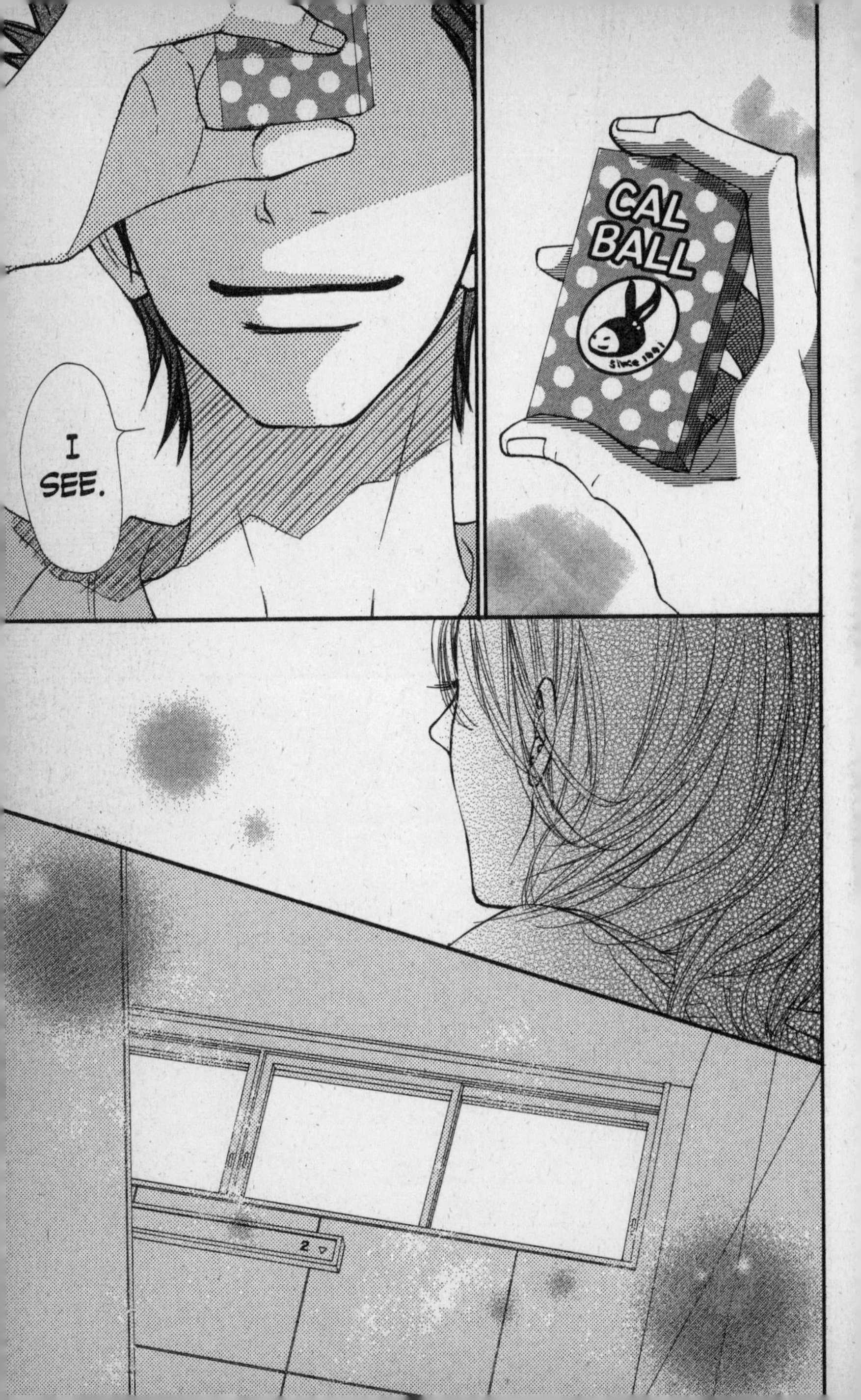
CAL BALL
I SEE.

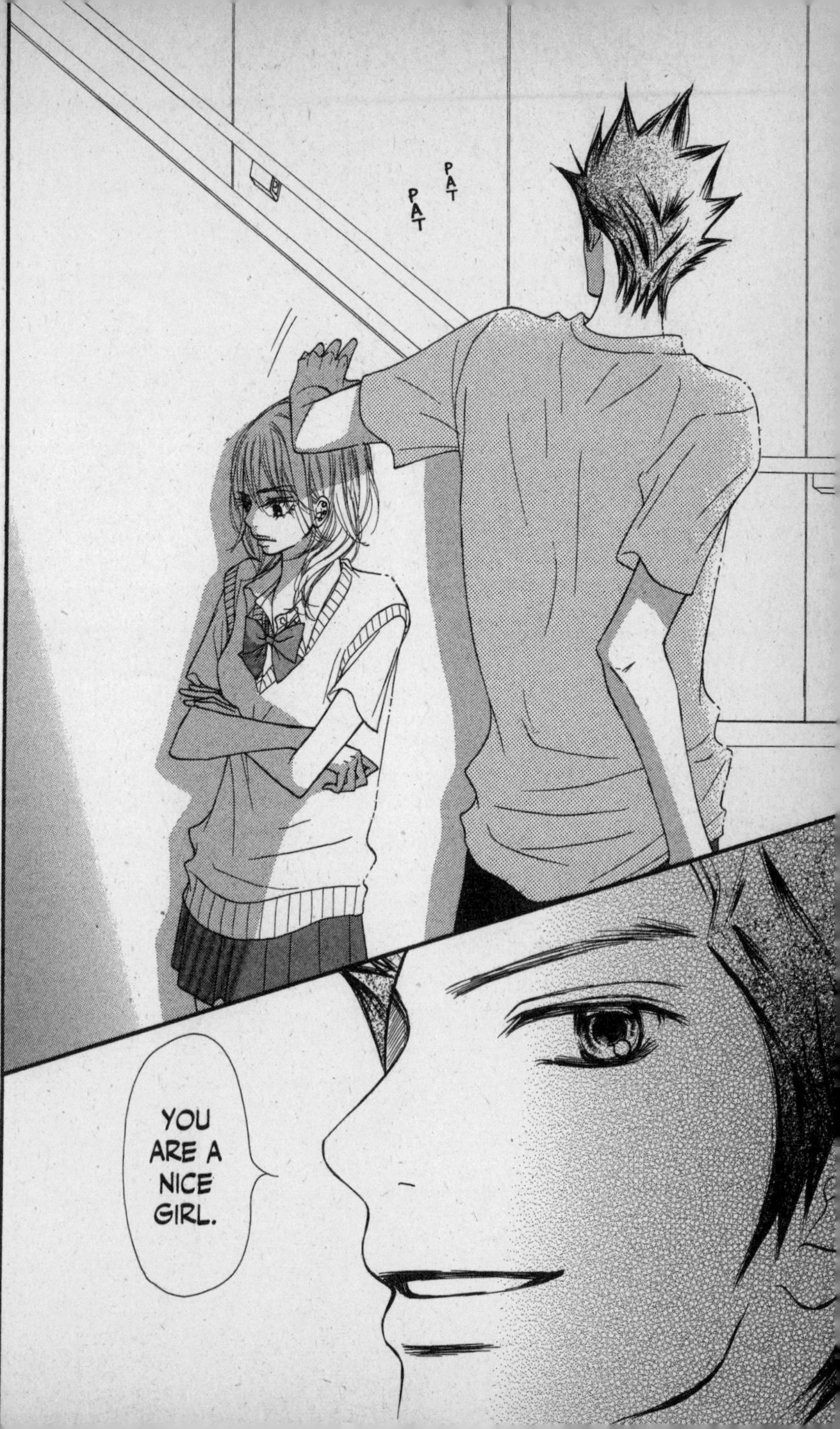
PAT PAT
YOU ARE A NICE GIRL.

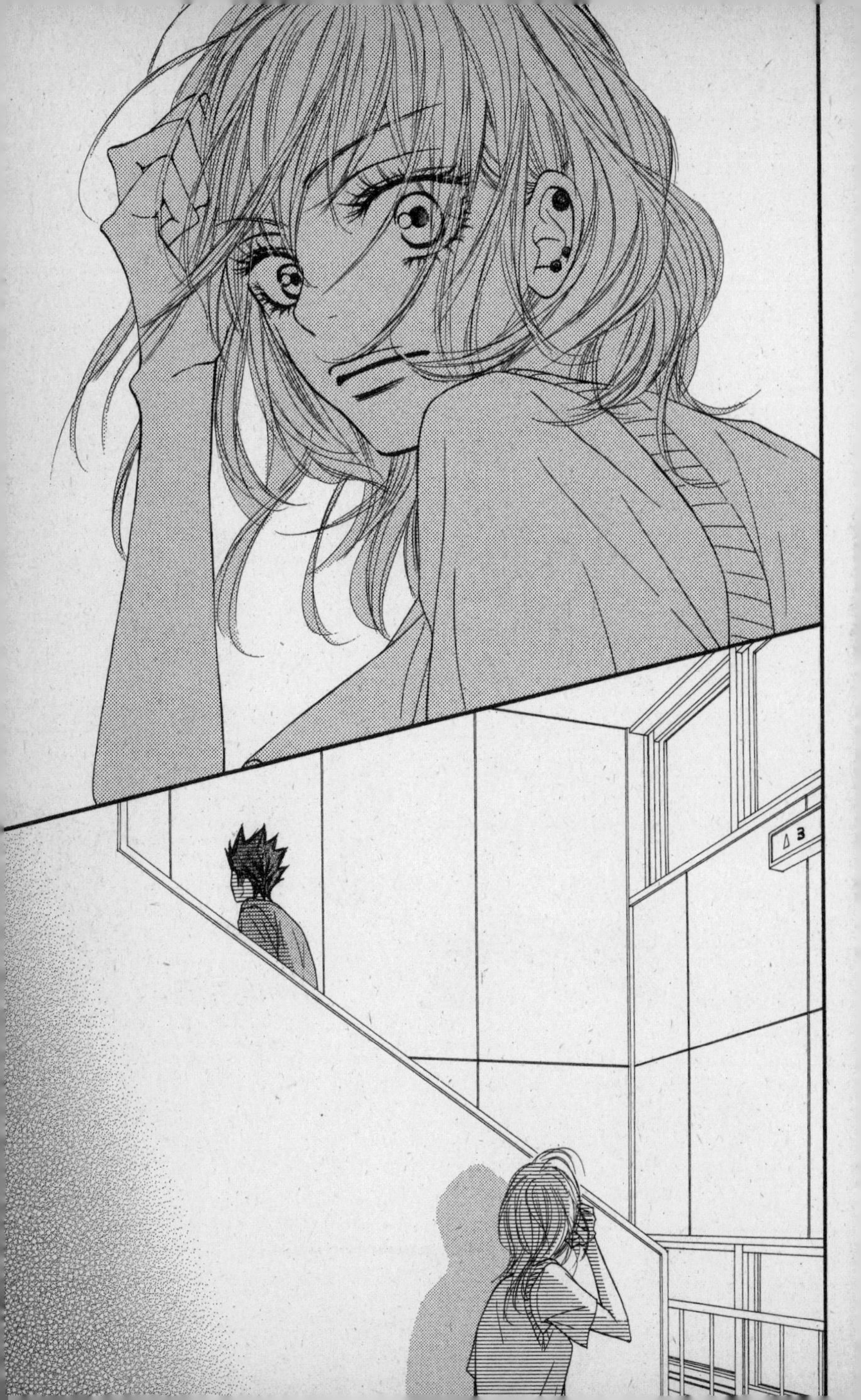
3

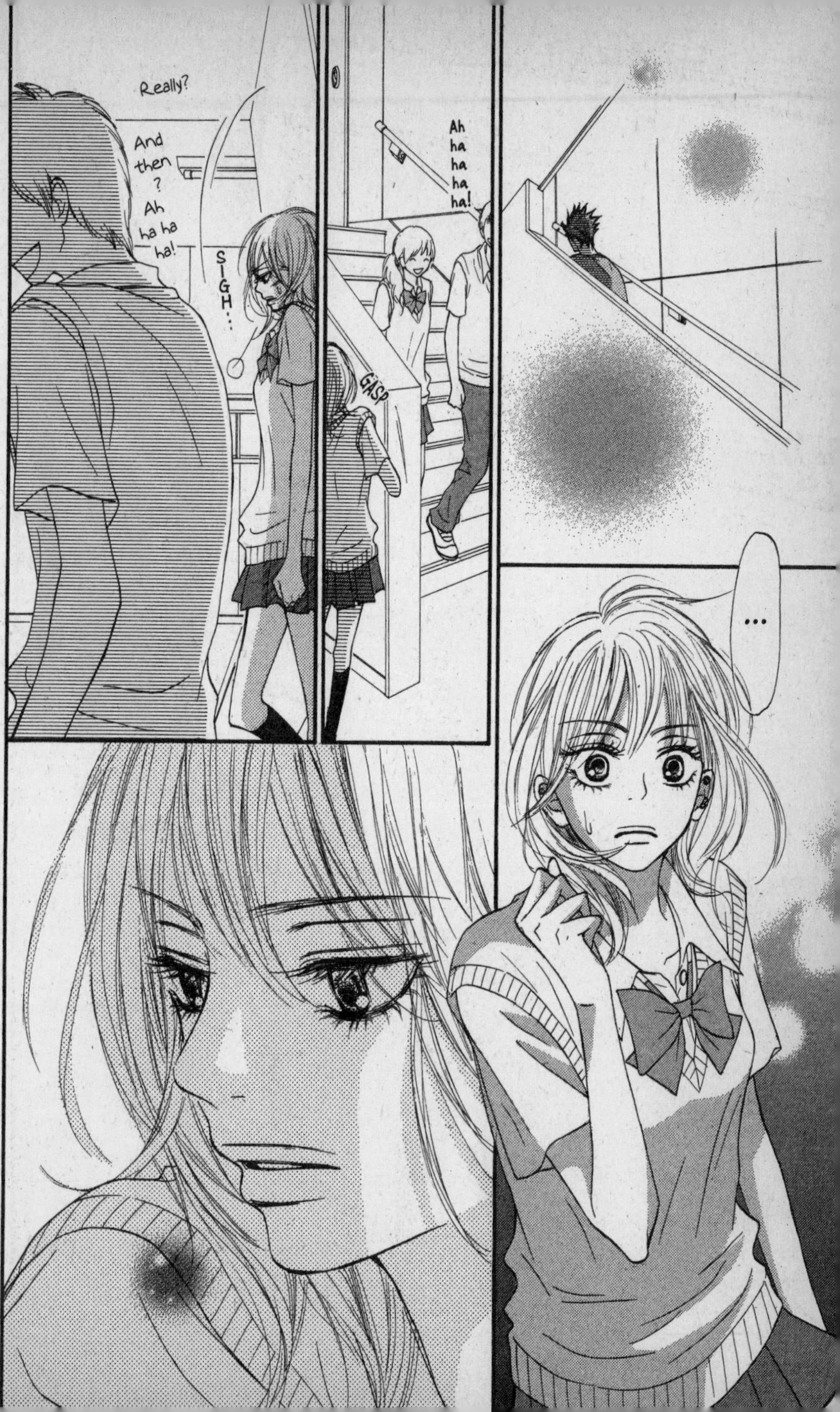
Ah ha ha ha ha!
GASP
Really?
And then?
Ah ha ha ha!
SIGH...
...

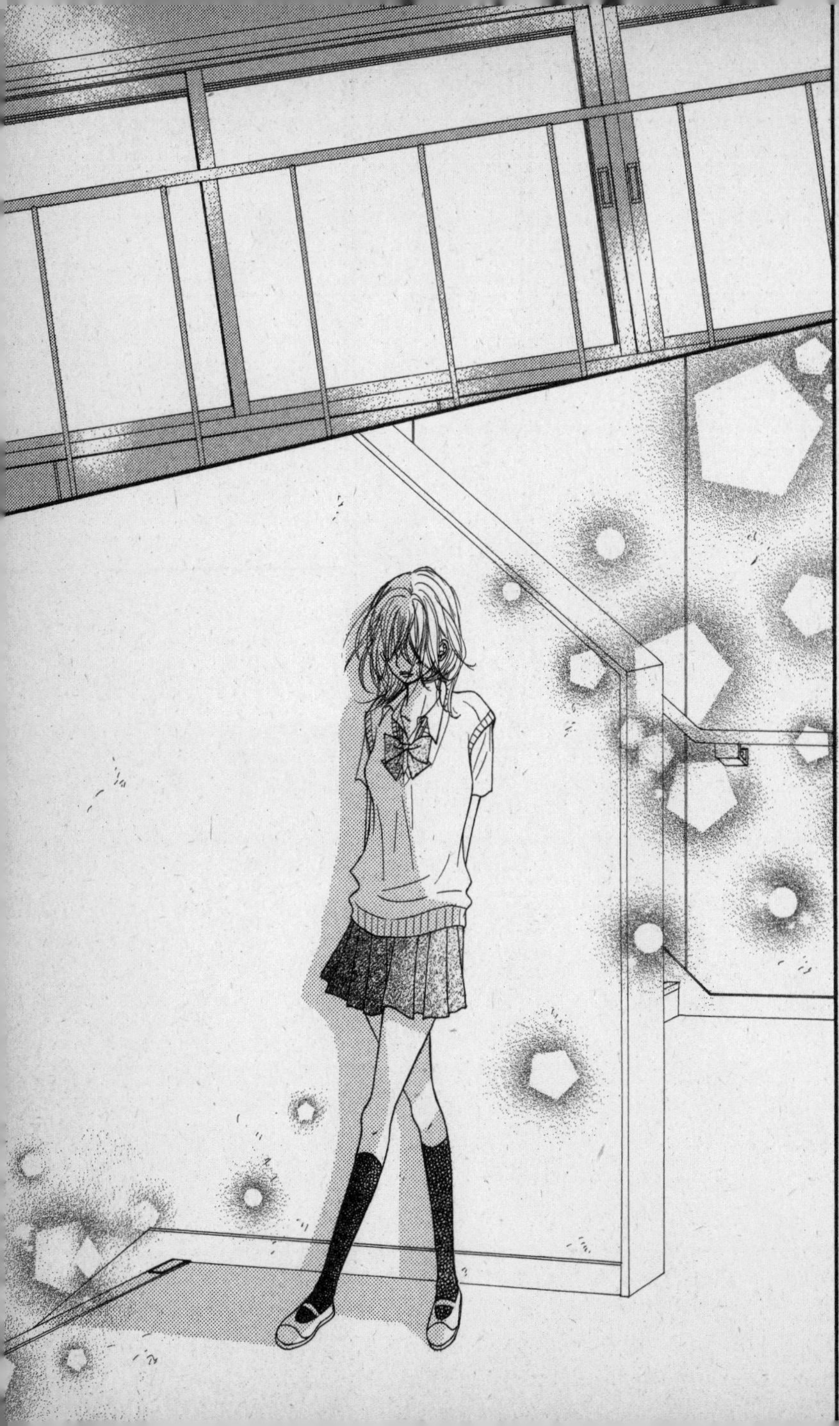

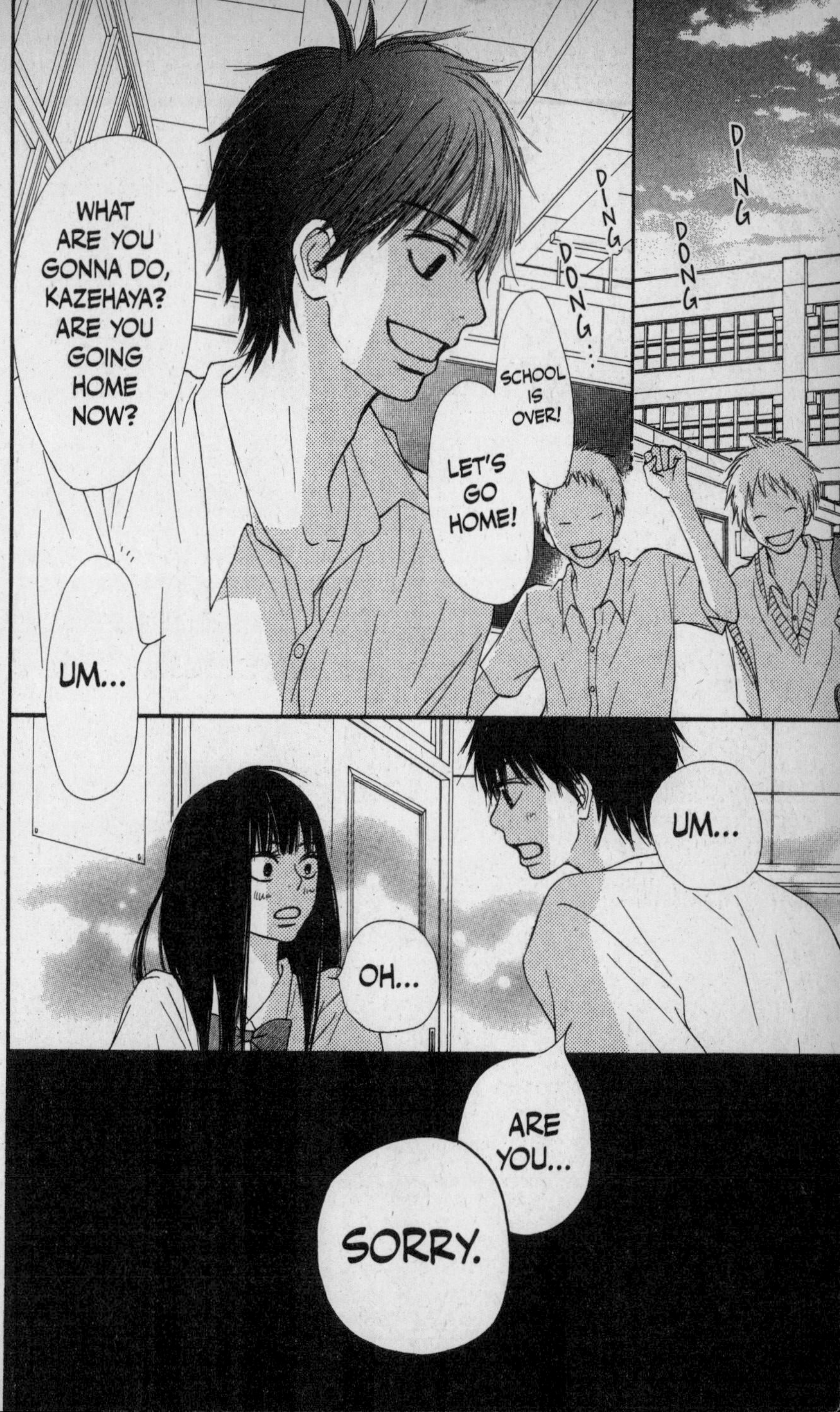
DING DONG
DING DONG...
SCHOOL IS OVER!
LET'S GO HOME!
WHAT ARE YOU GONNA DO, KAZEHAYA? ARE YOU GOING HOME NOW?
UM...
UM...
OH...
ARE YOU...
SORRY.

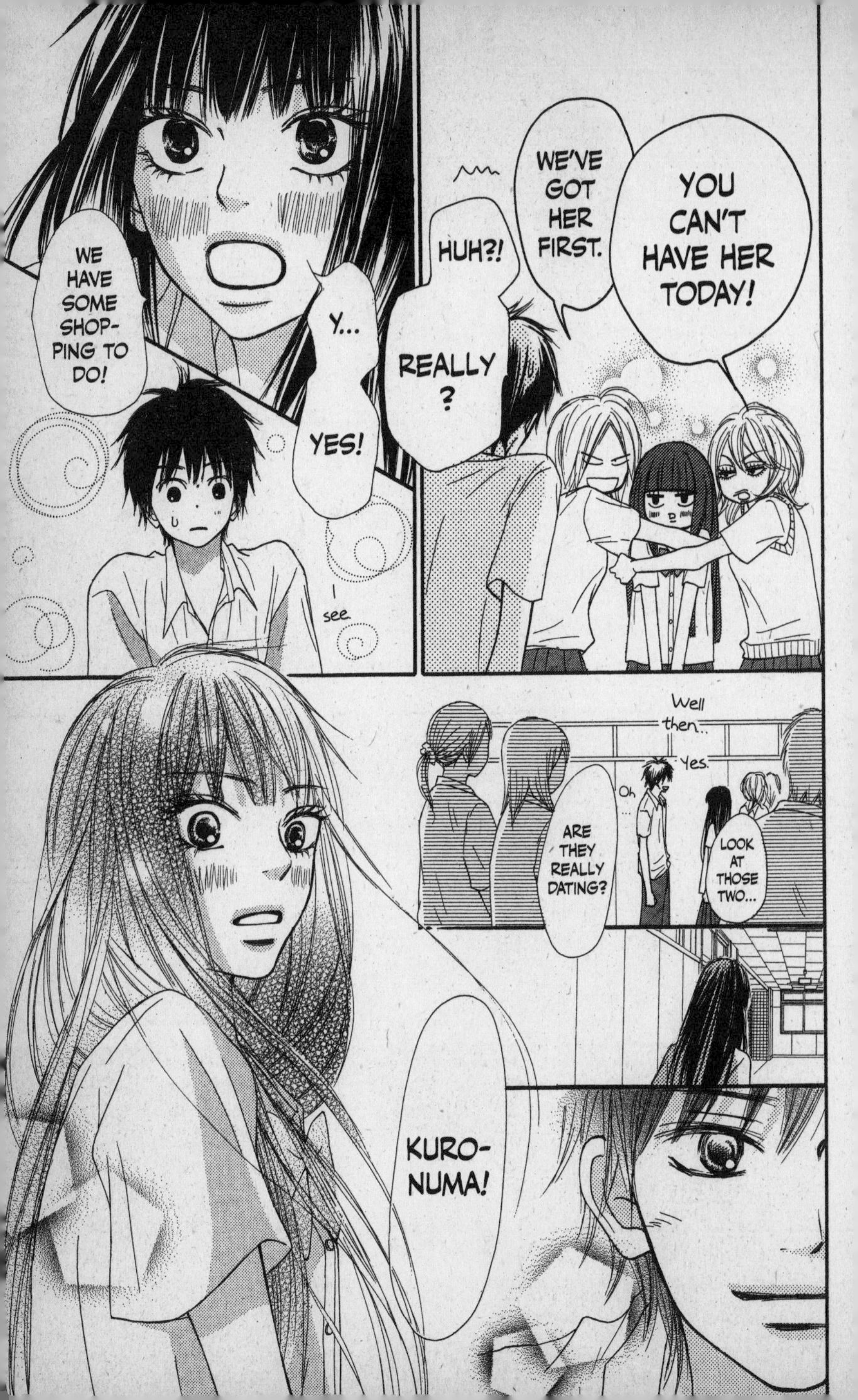
YOU CAN'T HAVE HER TODAY!
WE'VE GOT HER FIRST.
HUH?!
WE HAVE SOME SHOP-PING TO DO!
REALLY?
Y... YES!
I see.
Well then..
Yes.
Oh...
LOOK AT THOSE TWO...
ARE THEY REALLY DATING?
KURO-NUMA!

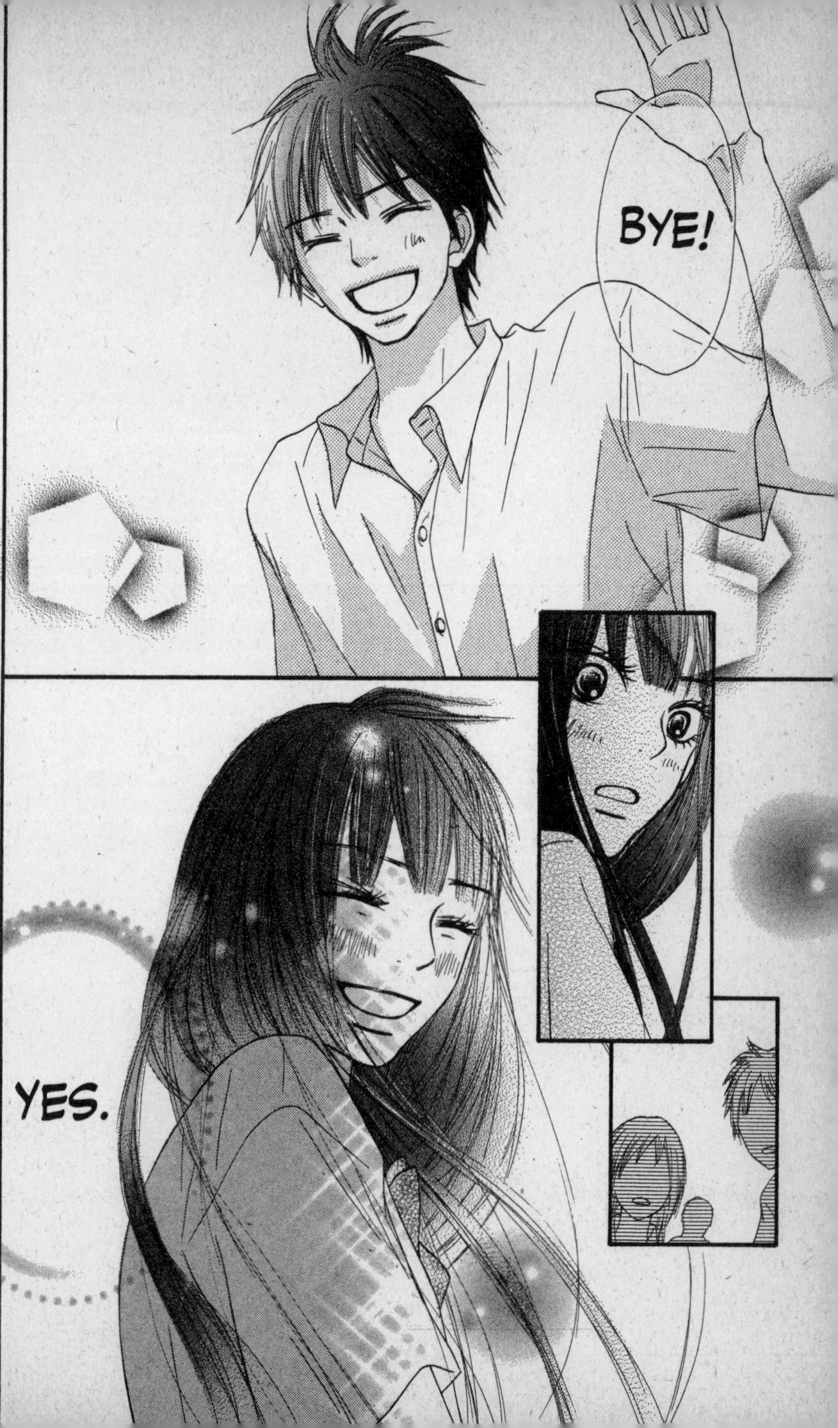
BYE!
YES.

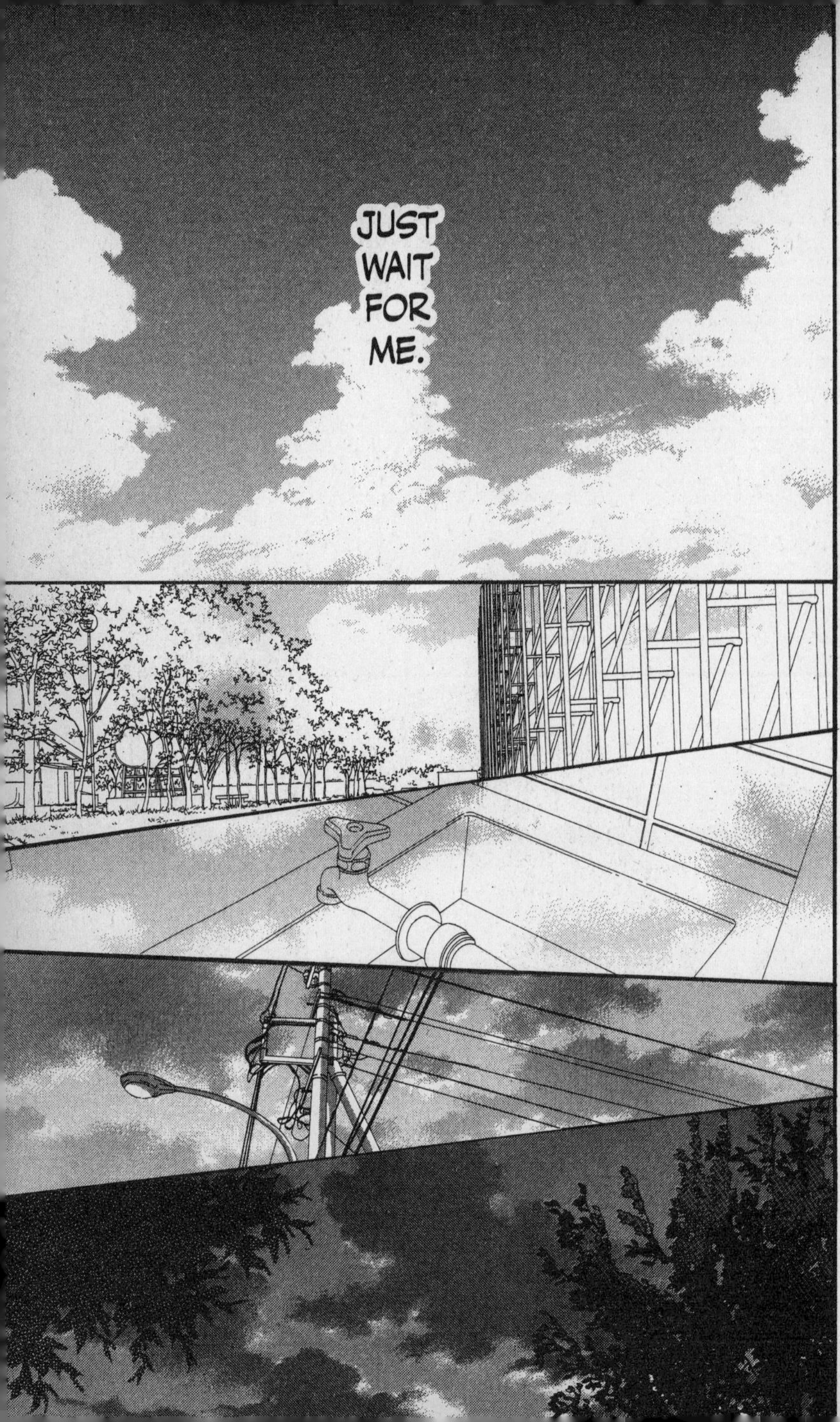
JUST WAIT FOR ME.

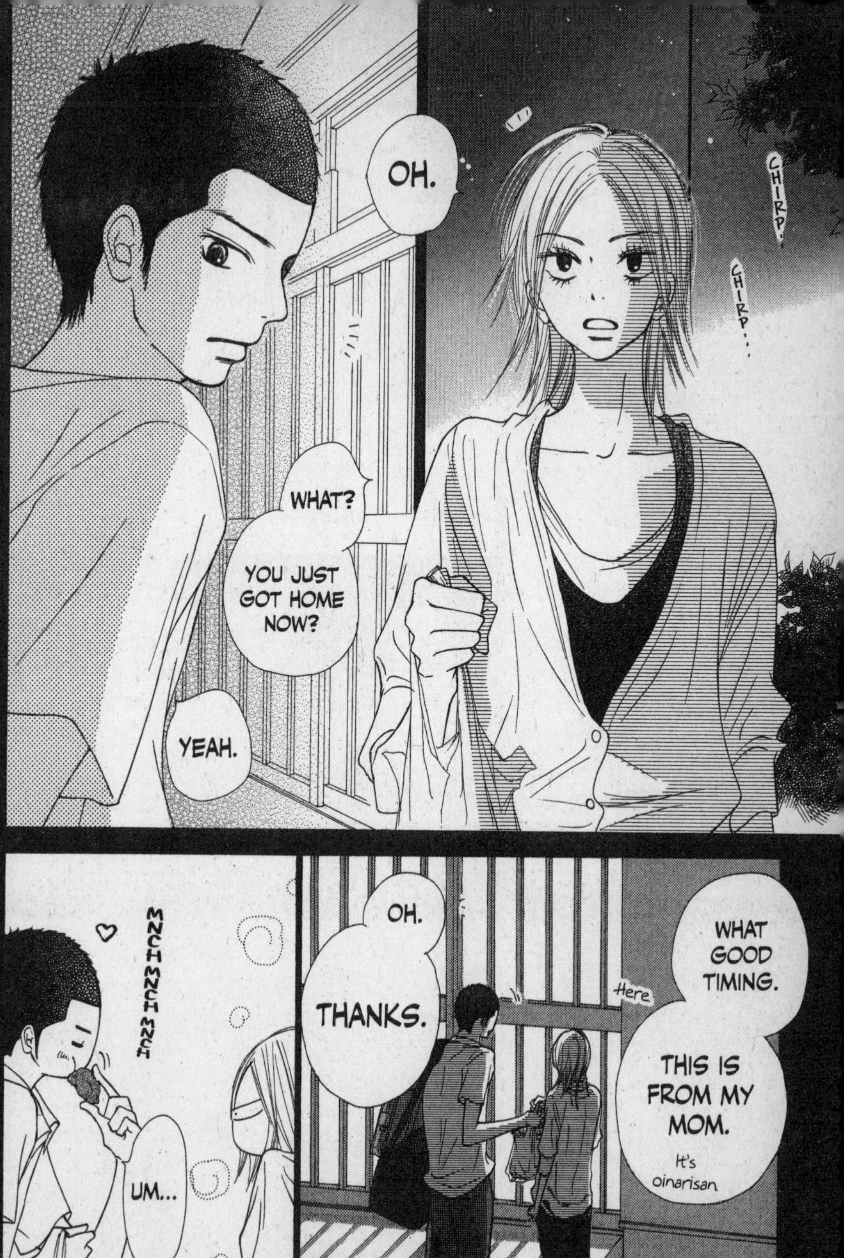
CHIRP.
CHIRP...
OH.
WHAT?
YOU JUST GOT HOME NOW?
YEAH.
Here
WHAT GOOD TIMING.
THIS IS FROM MY MOM.
It's oinarisan
OH.
THANKS.
MNCH MNCH MNCH
UM...

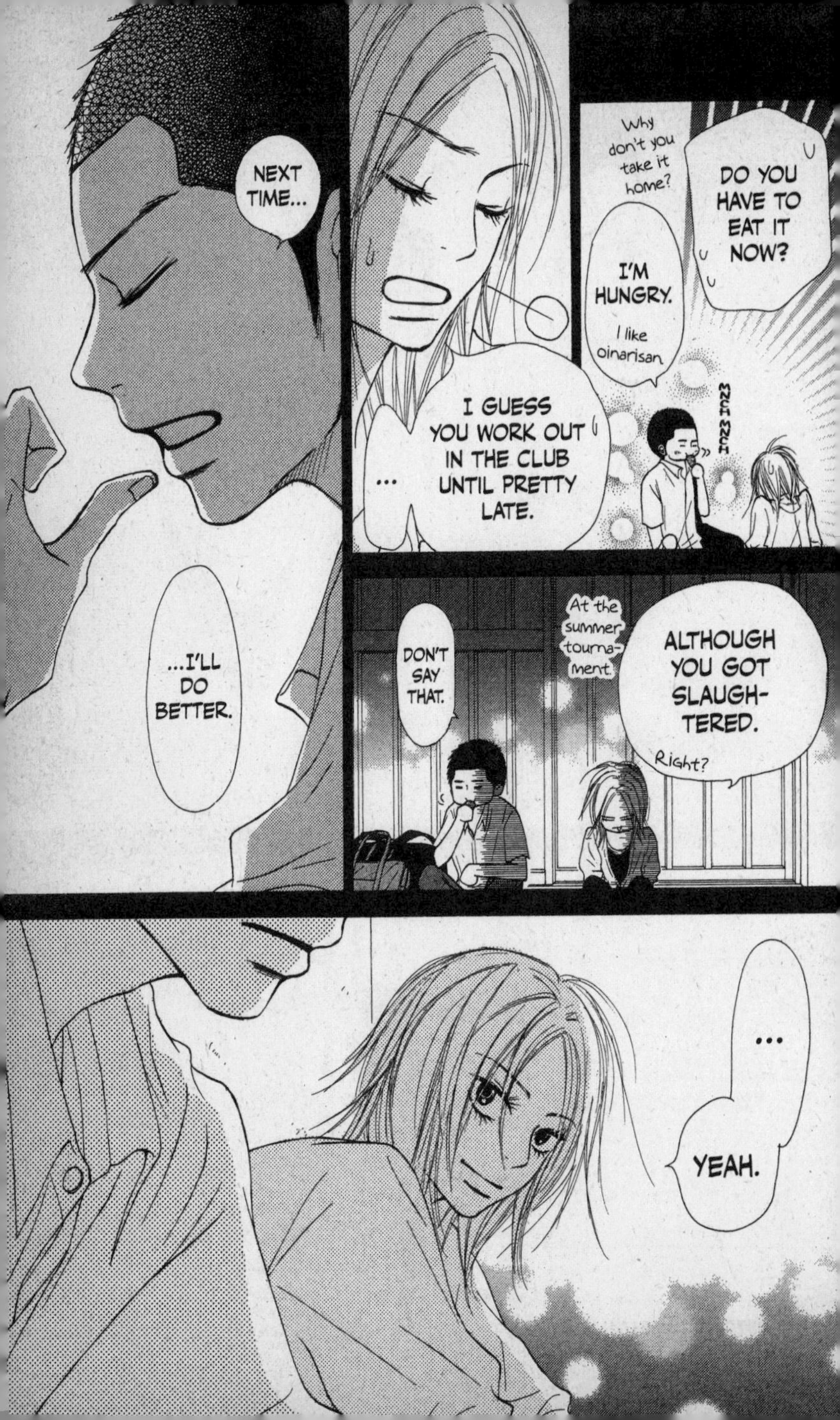

DO YOU HAVE TO EAT IT NOW?
Why don't you take it home?
I'M HUNGRY.
I like oinarisan.
MNCH MNCH
I GUESS YOU WORK OUT IN THE CLUB UNTIL PRETTY LATE.
...
ALTHOUGH YOU GOT SLAUGHTERED.
Right?
At the summer tourna-ment.
DON'T SAY THAT.
NEXT TIME...
...I'LL DO BETTER.
...
YEAH.

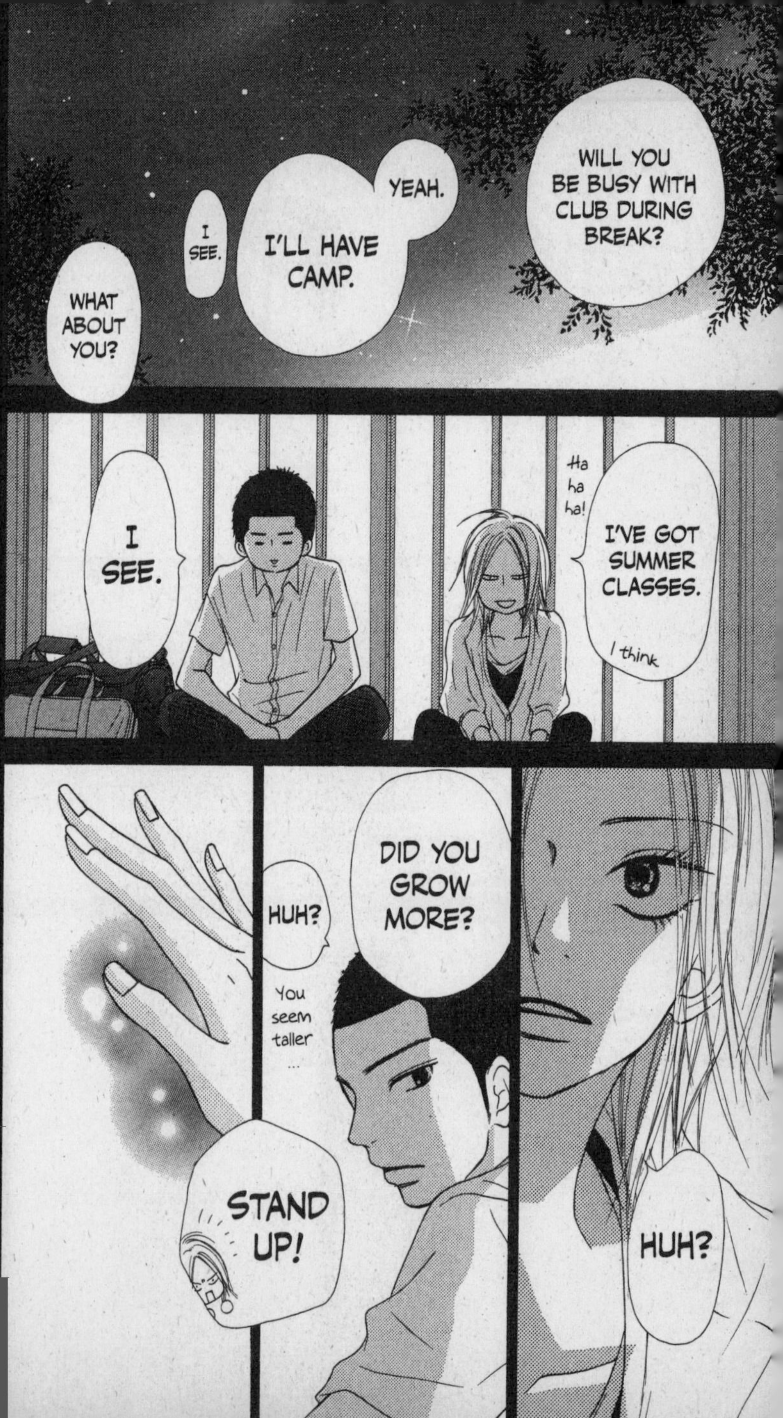
WILL YOU BE BUSY WITH CLUB DURING BREAK?
YEAH.
I'LL HAVE CAMP.
I SEE.
WHAT ABOUT YOU?
Ha ha ha!
I'VE GOT SUMMER CLASSES.
I think
I SEE.
HUH?
DID YOU GROW MORE?
HUH?
You seem taller ...
STAND UP!

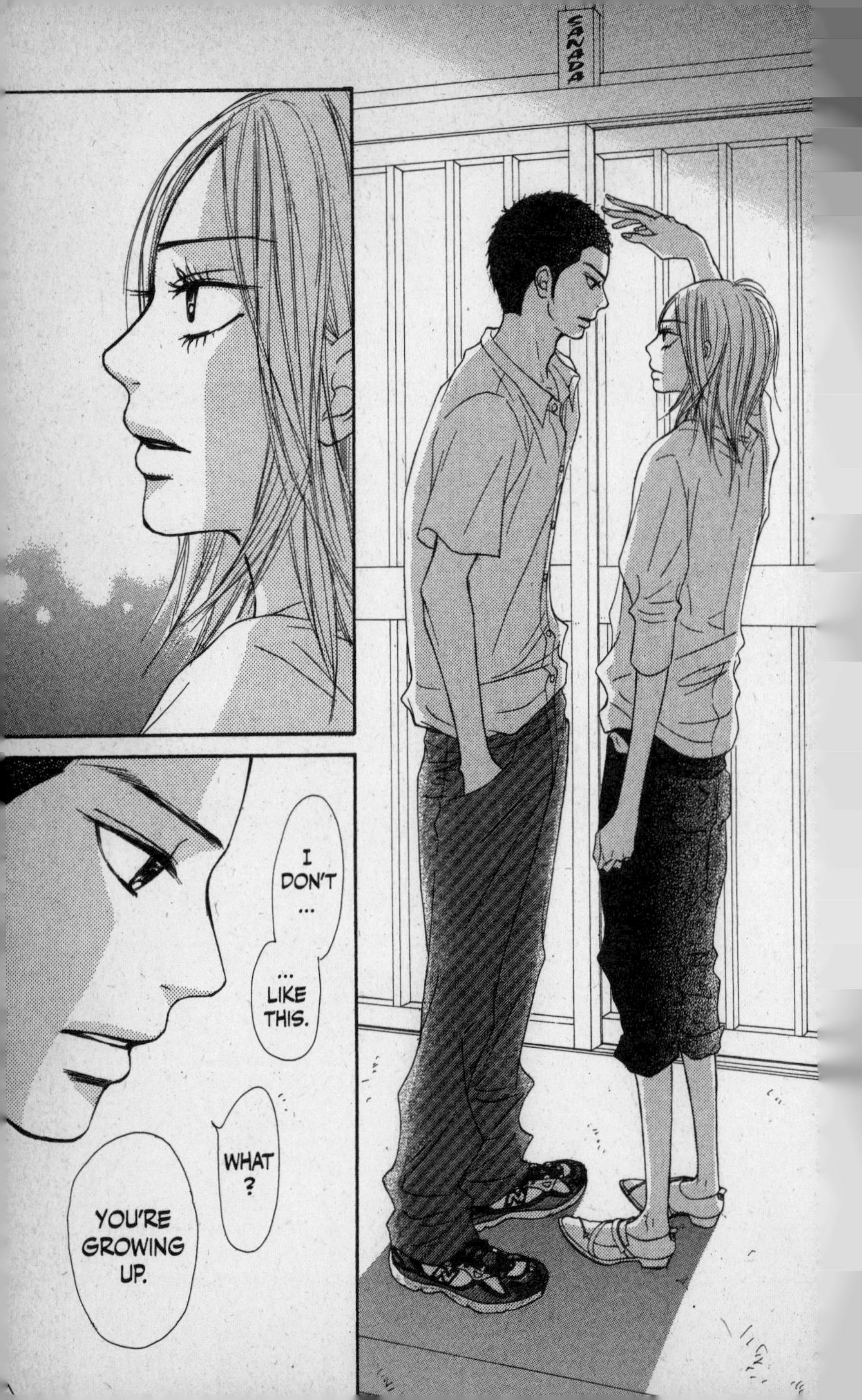
SANADA
I DON'T ...
... LIKE THIS.
WHAT?
YOU'RE GROWING UP.

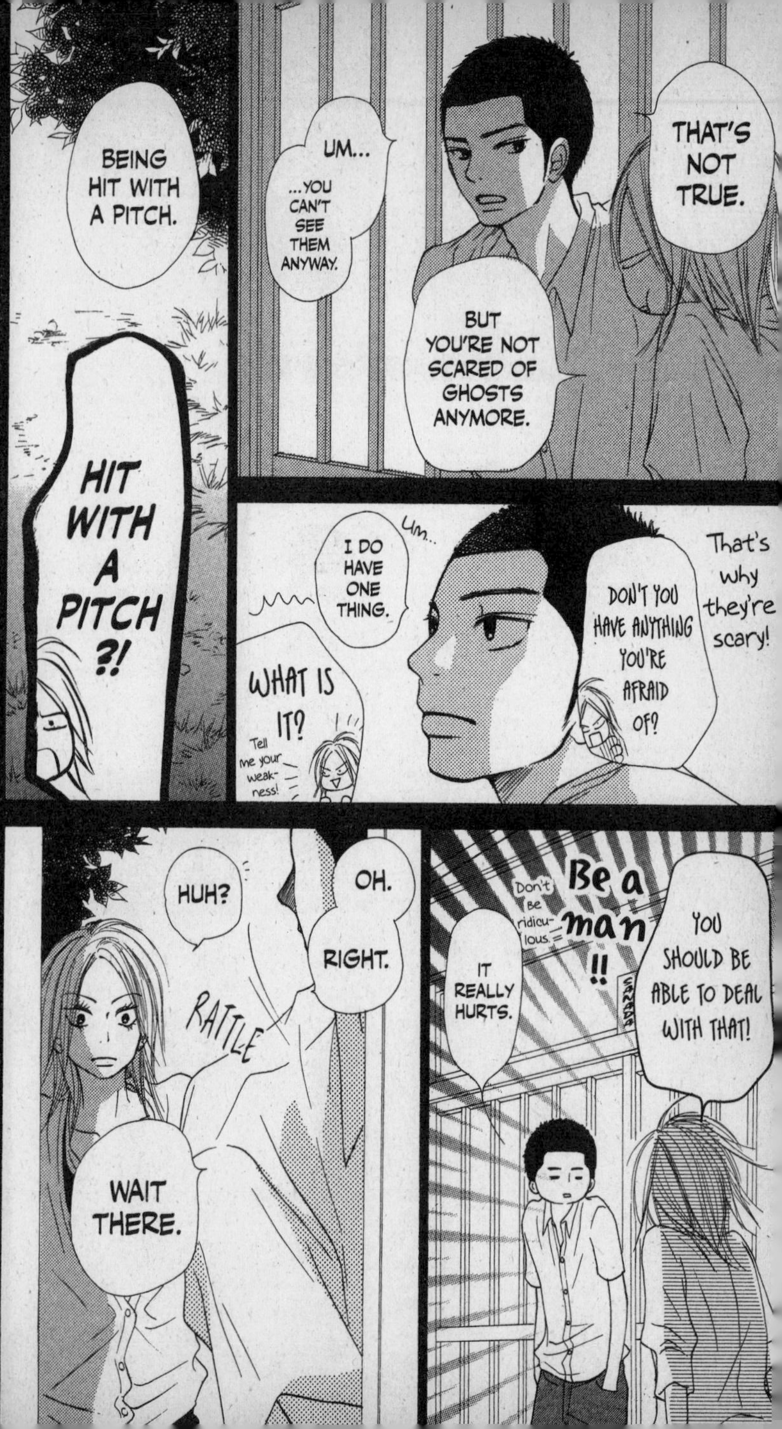
THAT'S NOT TRUE.
BUT YOU'RE NOT SCARED OF GHOSTS ANYMORE.
UM...
...YOU CAN'T SEE THEM ANYWAY.
That's why they're scary!
DON'T YOU HAVE ANYTHING YOU'RE AFRAID OF?
Um...
I DO HAVE ONE THING.
WHAT IS IT?
Tell me your weak-ness!
BEING HIT WITH A PITCH.
HIT WITH A PITCH?!
YOU SHOULD BE ABLE TO DEAL WITH THAT!
Be a man!!
Don't be ridicu-lous.
IT REALLY HURTS.
OH.
RIGHT.
HUH?
RATTLE
WAIT THERE.

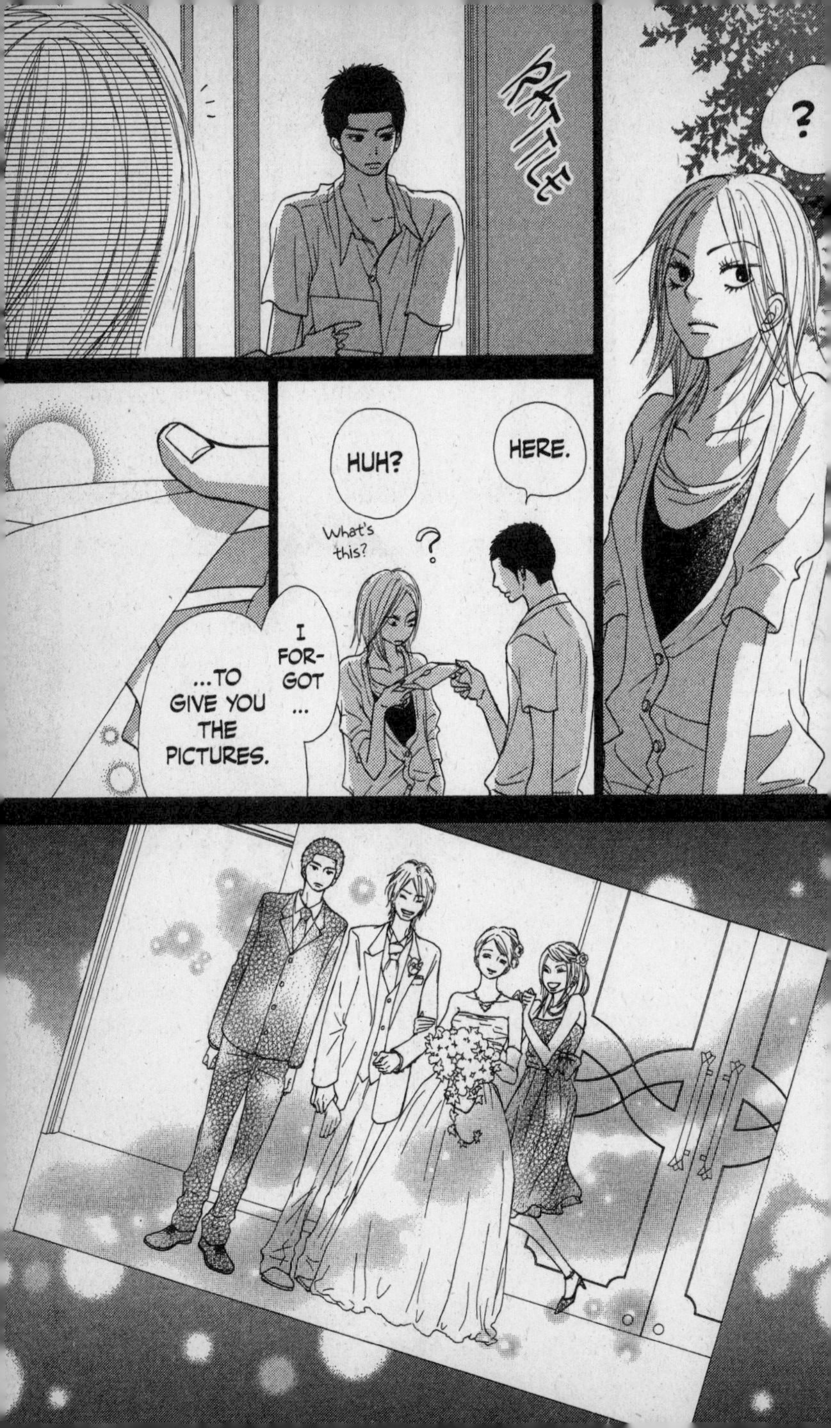
?
RATTLE
HERE.
HUH?
What's this?
?
I FORGOT...
...TO GIVE YOU THE PICTURES.

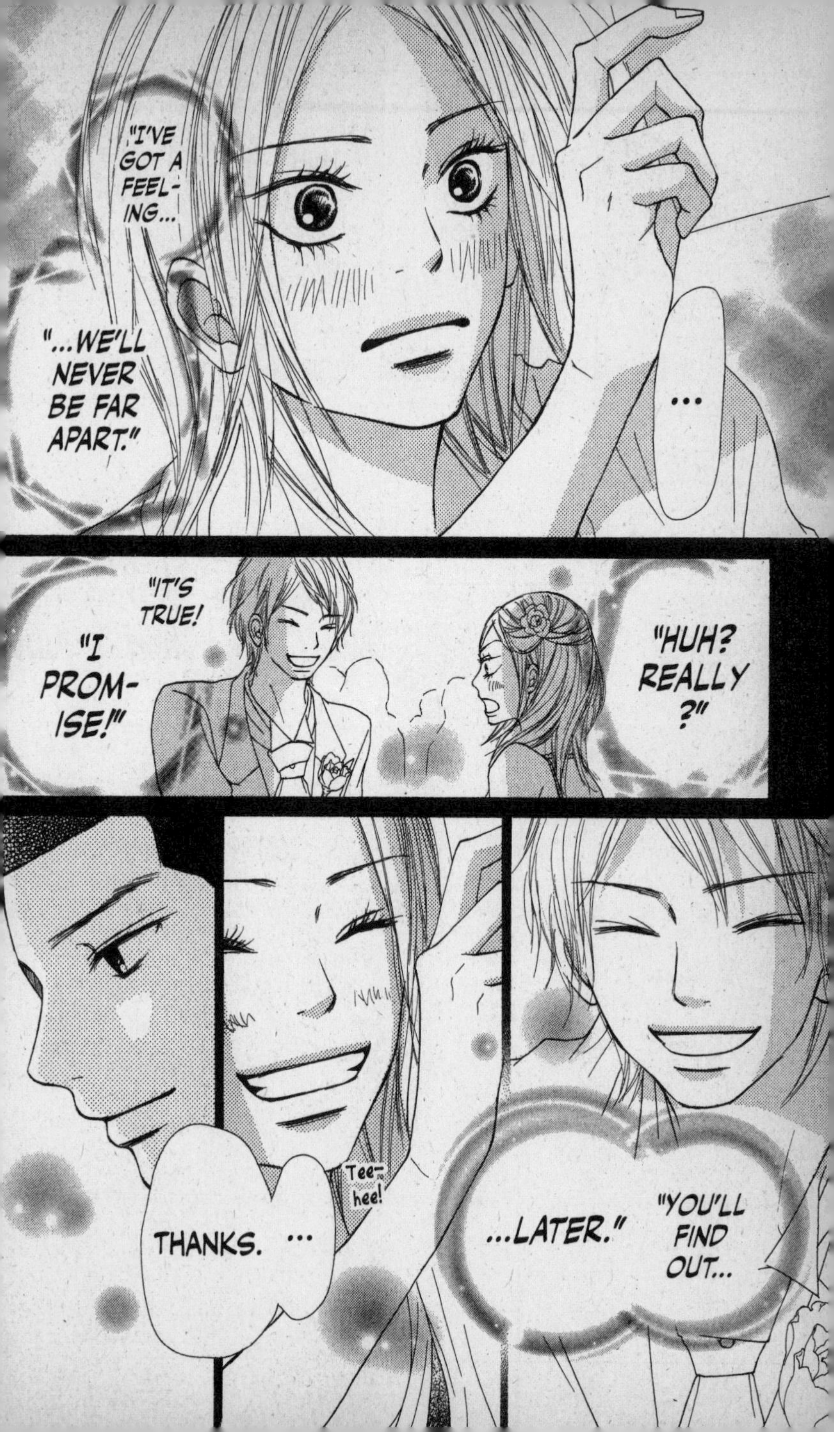
"I'VE GOT A FEELING...
"...WE'LL NEVER BE FAR APART."
...
"HUH? REALLY?"
"IT'S TRUE!
"I PROMISE!"
"YOU'LL FIND OUT...
...LATER."
Tee-hee!
THANKS. ...

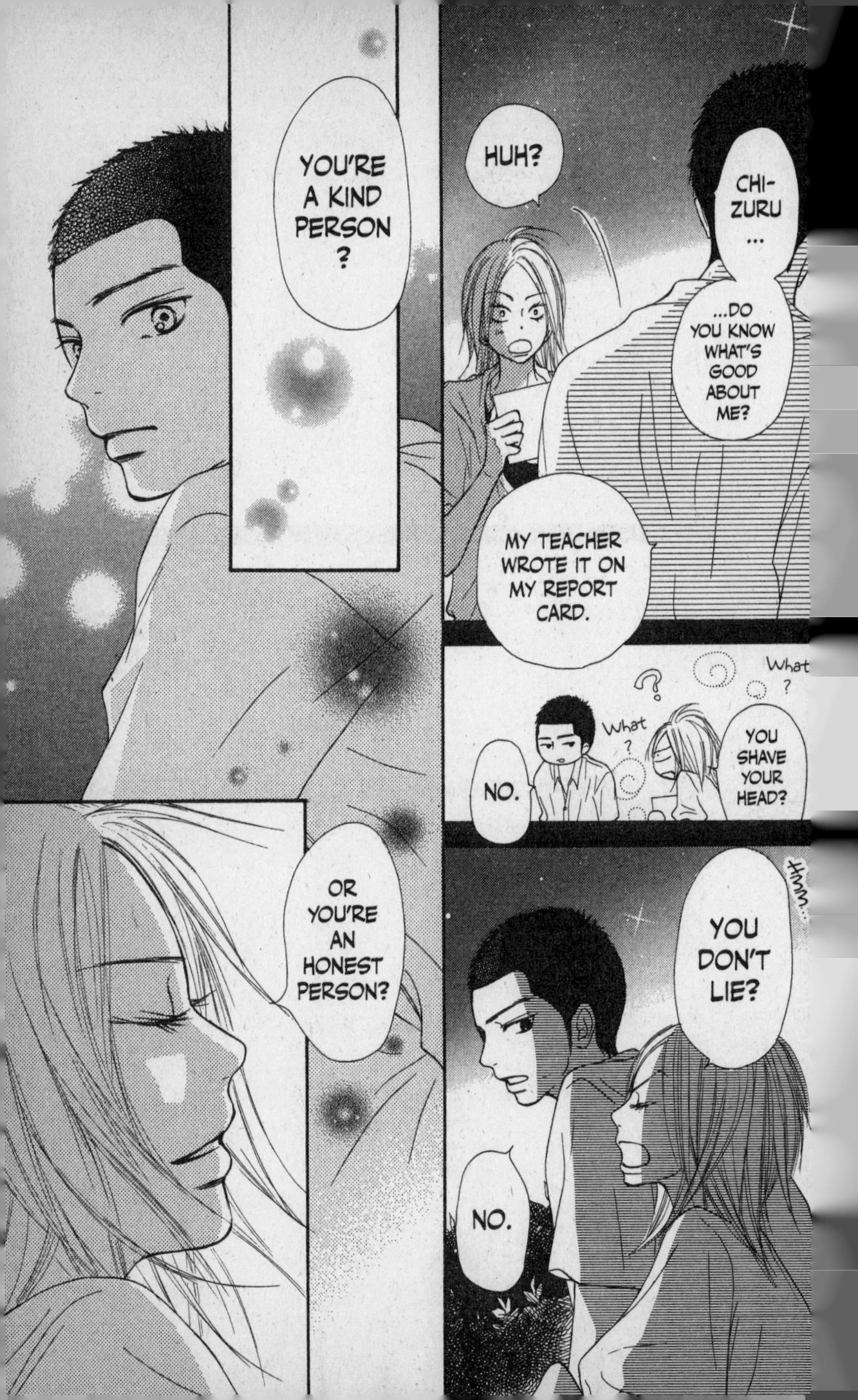
CHI-ZURU...
...DO YOU KNOW WHAT'S GOOD ABOUT ME?
HUH?
MY TEACHER WROTE IT ON MY REPORT CARD.
What ?
YOU SHAVE YOUR HEAD?
What ?
NO.
YOU DON'T LIE?
NO.
YOU'RE A KIND PERSON ?
OR YOU'RE AN HONEST PERSON?

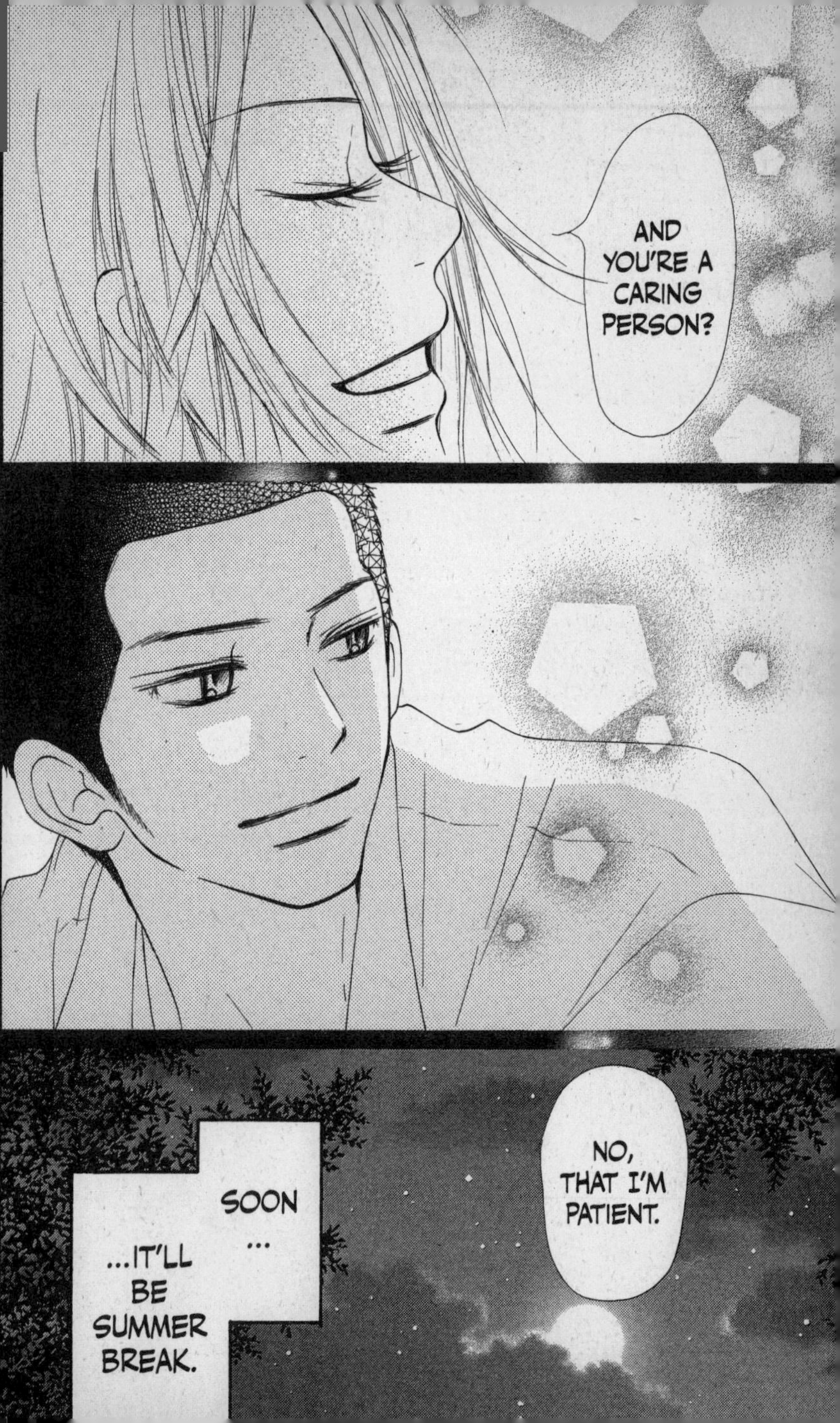
AND YOU'RE A CARING PERSON?
NO, THAT I'M PATIENT.
SOON ...
...IT'LL BE SUMMER BREAK.

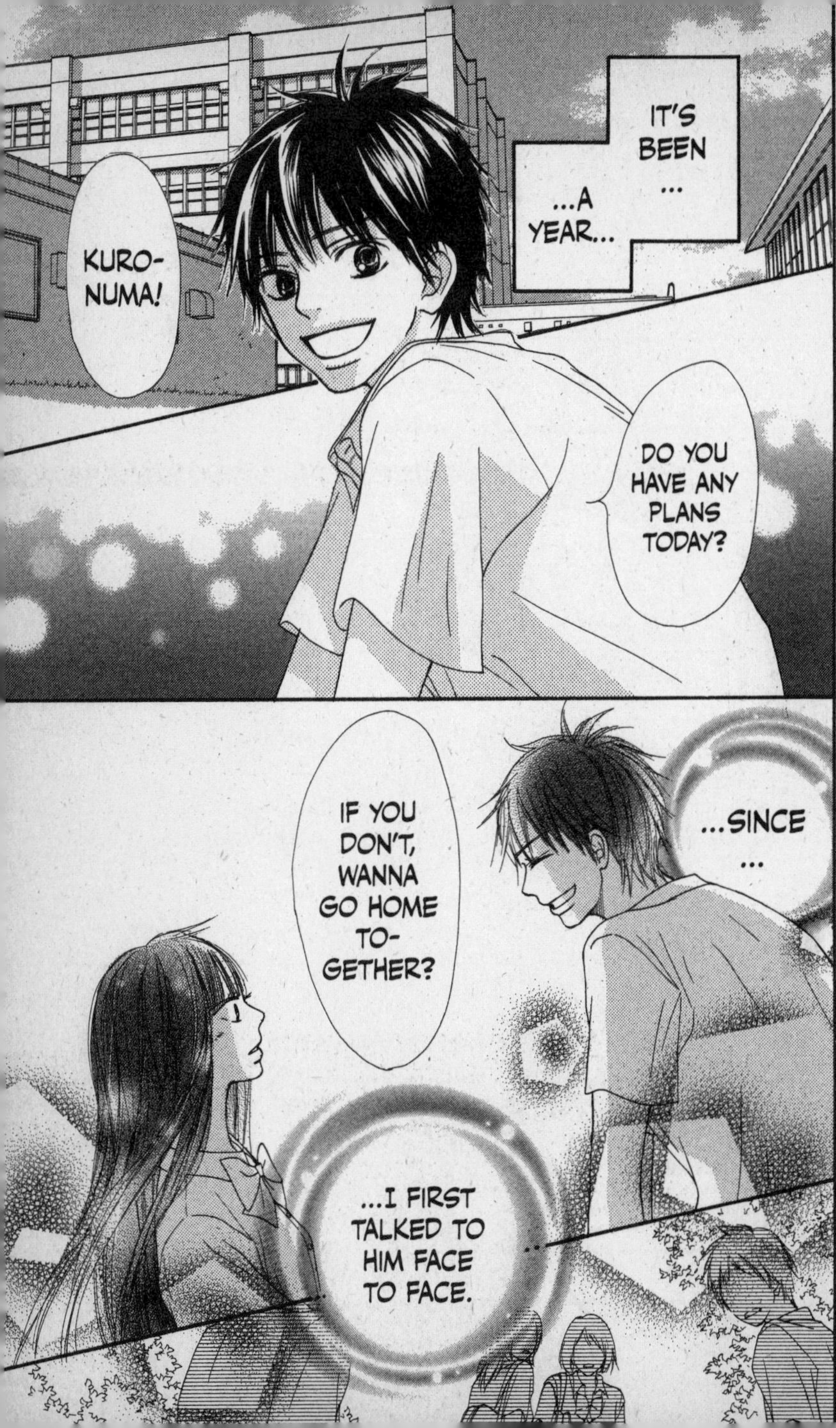
IT'S BEEN ... ...A YEAR...
KURO-NUMA!
DO YOU HAVE ANY PLANS TODAY?
...SINCE ...
IF YOU DON'T, WANNA GO HOME TO-GETHER?
...I FIRST TALKED TO HIM FACE TO FACE.

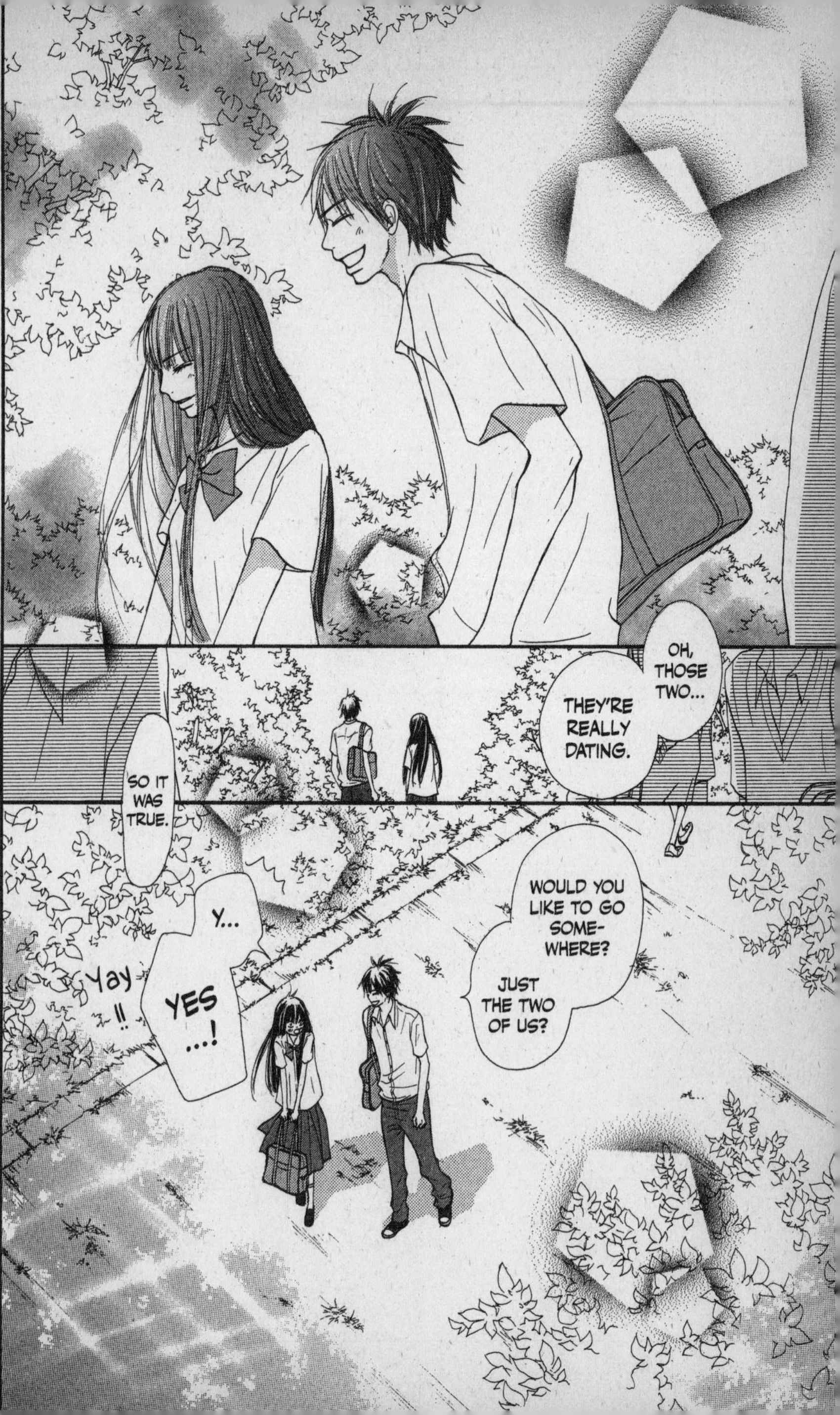
OH, THOSE TWO...
THEY'RE REALLY DATING.
SO IT WAS TRUE.
WOULD YOU LIKE TO GO SOME-WHERE?
JUST THE TWO OF US?
Y...
YES ...!
Yay !!

Episode 46: Date

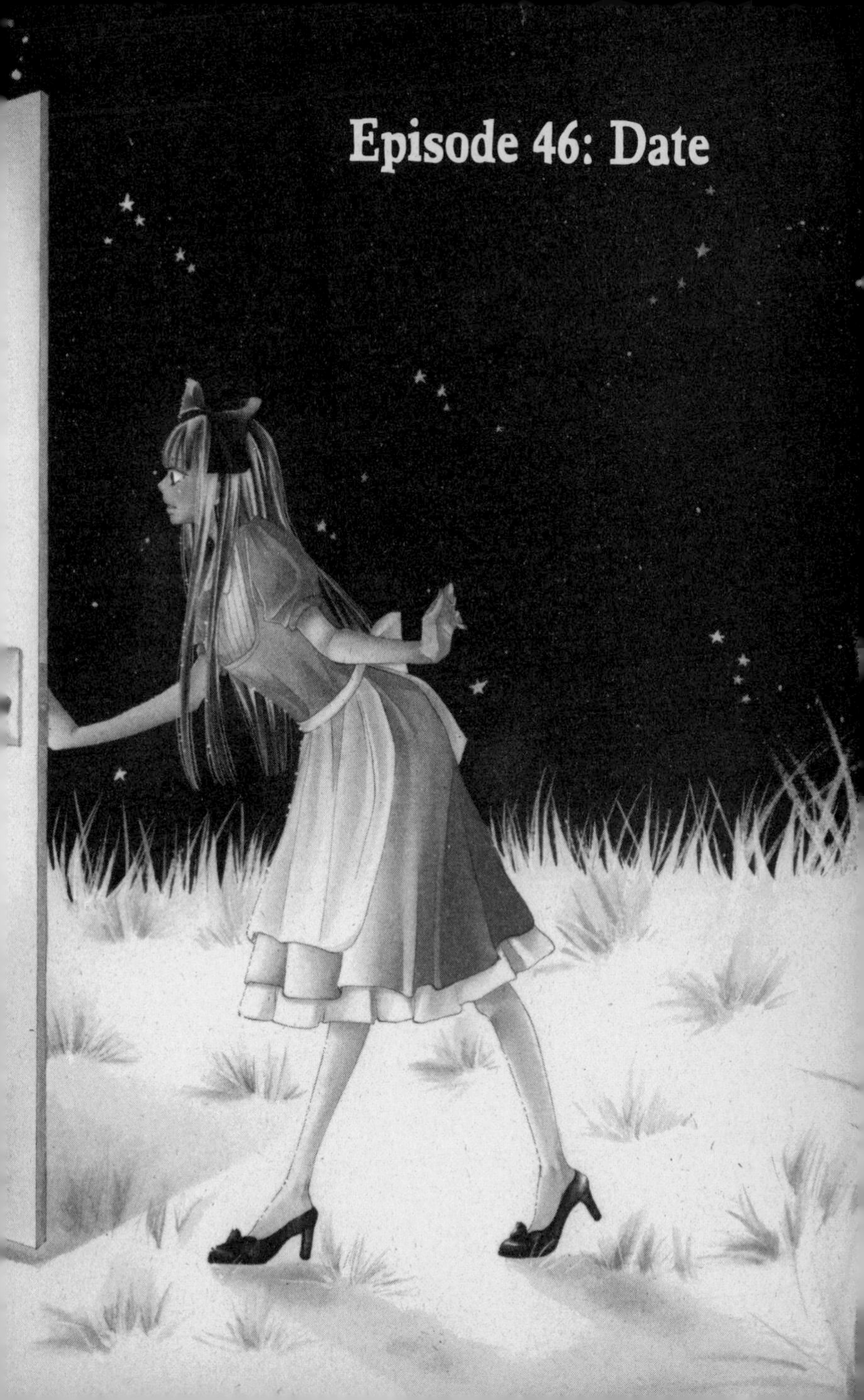

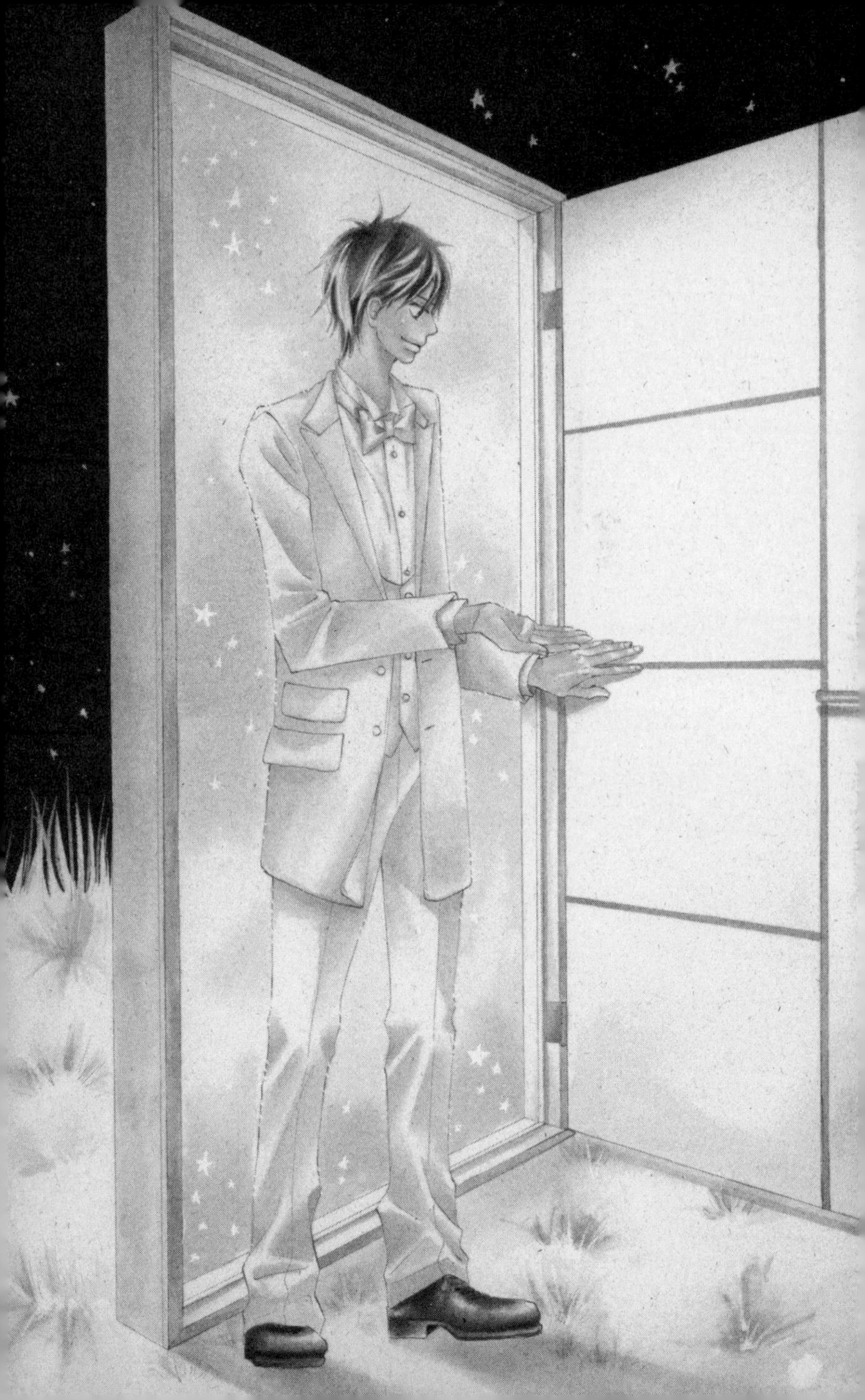

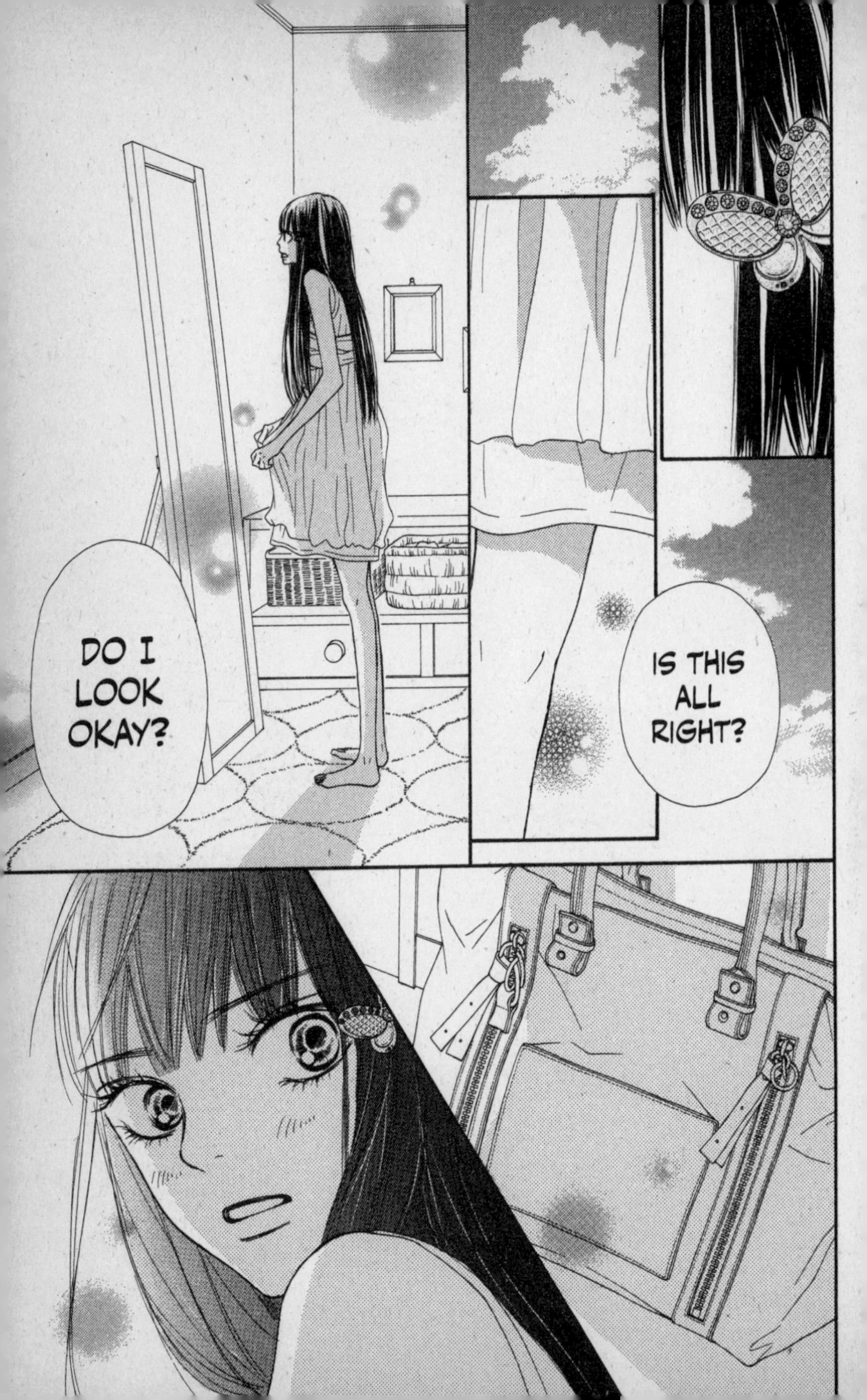
IS THIS ALL RIGHT?
DO I LOOK OKAY?

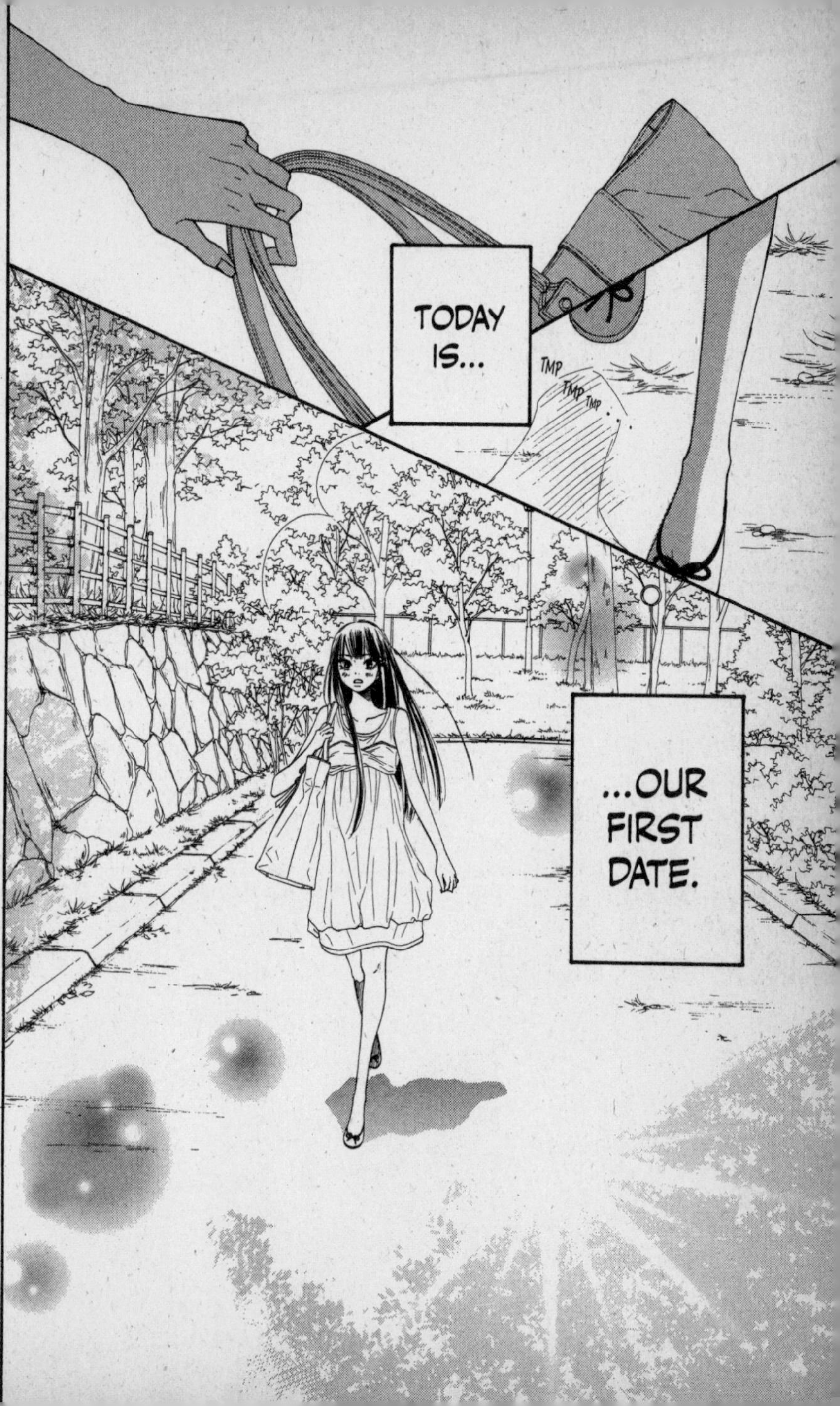
TODAY IS...
TMP TMP TMP
...OUR FIRST DATE.

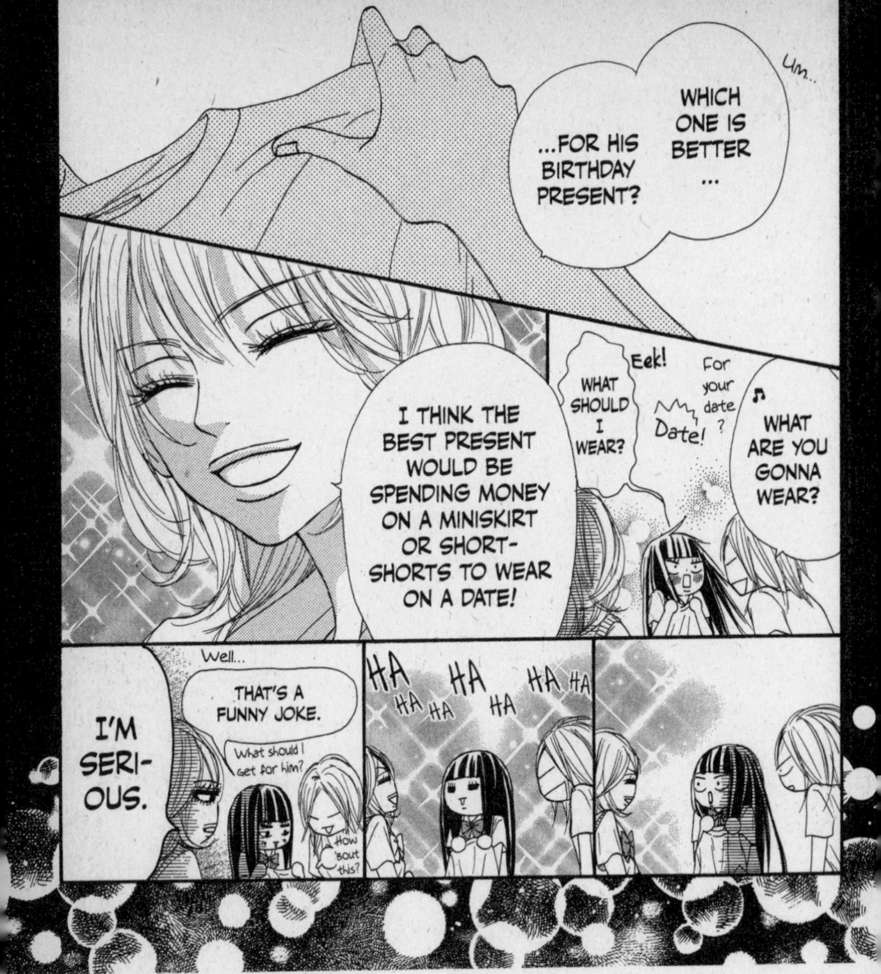
Um...
WHICH ONE IS BETTER ...
...FOR HIS BIRTHDAY PRESENT?
WHAT ARE YOU GONNA WEAR?
For your date?
Date!
Eek!
WHAT SHOULD I WEAR?
I THINK THE BEST PRESENT WOULD BE SPENDING MONEY ON A MINISKIRT OR SHORT-SHORTS TO WEAR ON A DATE!
HA HA HA HA HA HA HA
Well...
THAT'S A FUNNY JOKE.
What should I get for him?
How 'bout this?
I'M SERIOUS.

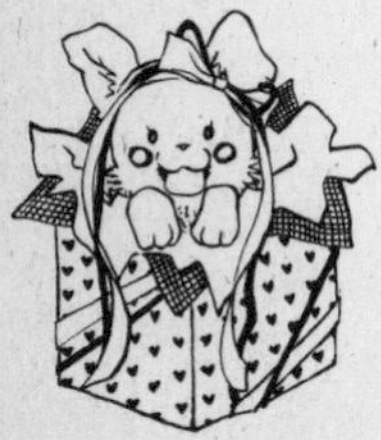

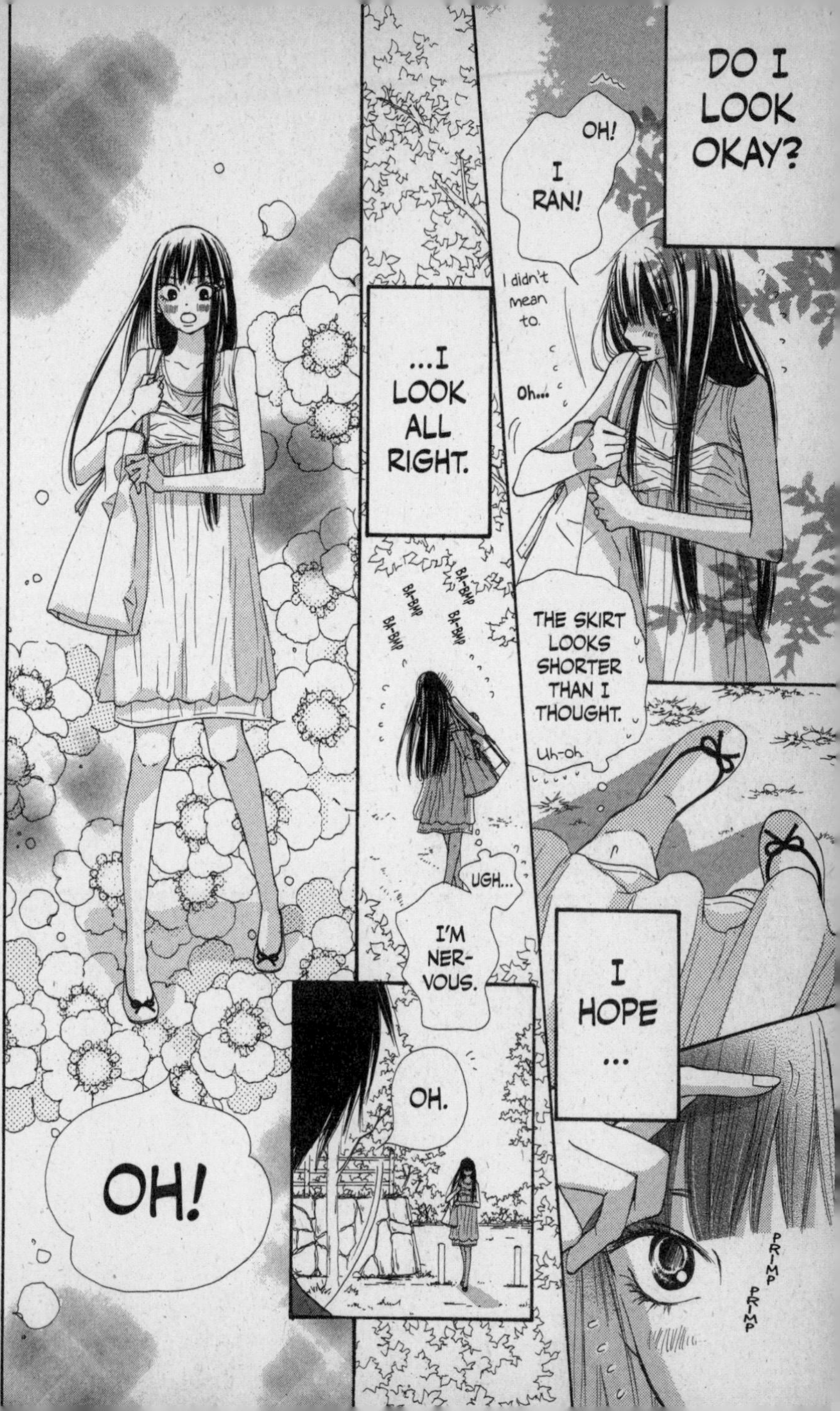
DO I LOOK OKAY?
OH! I RAN!
I didn't mean to.
Oh...
THE SKIRT LOOKS SHORTER THAN I THOUGHT.
Uh-oh.
I HOPE ...
PRIMP PRIMP
...I LOOK ALL RIGHT.
BA-BMP BA-BMP BA-BMP BA-BMP
UGH... I'M NER-VOUS.
OH.
OH!

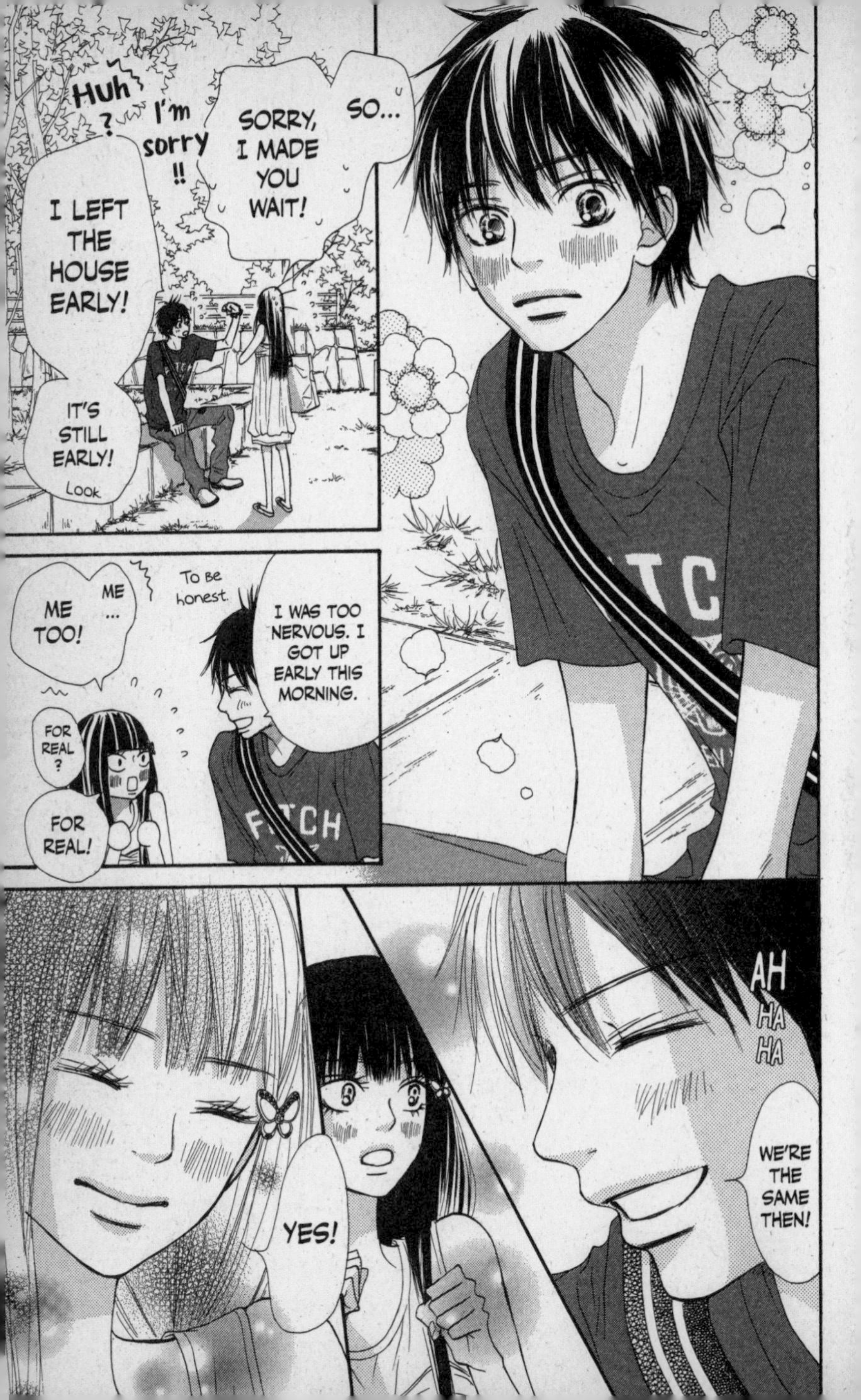
SO...
SORRY, I MADE YOU WAIT!
I'm sorry!!
Huh?
I LEFT THE HOUSE EARLY!
IT'S STILL EARLY!
Look
I WAS TOO NERVOUS. I GOT UP EARLY THIS MORNING.
To be honest.
ME ... ME TOO!
FOR REAL?
FOR REAL!
AH HA HA
WE'RE THE SAME THEN!
YES!

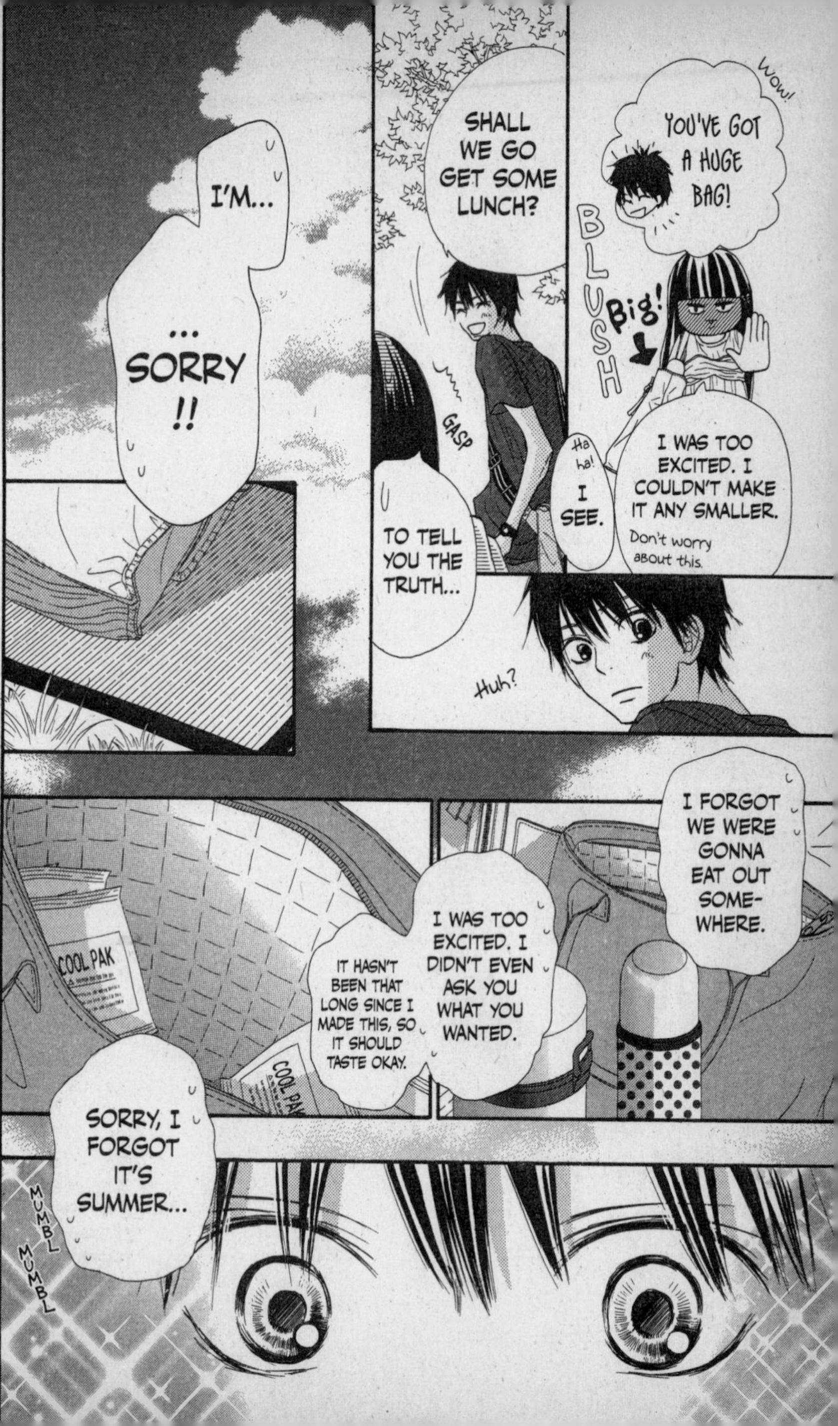
Wow!
YOU'VE GOT A HUGE BAG!
BLUSH
Big!
I WAS TOO EXCITED. I COULDN'T MAKE IT ANY SMALLER.
Don't worry about this.
Ha ha!
I SEE.
SHALL WE GO GET SOME LUNCH?
GASP
TO TELL YOU THE TRUTH...
Huh?
I'M...
... SORRY !!
I FORGOT WE WERE GONNA EAT OUT SOME-WHERE.
I WAS TOO EXCITED. I DIDN'T EVEN ASK YOU WHAT YOU WANTED.
IT HASN'T BEEN THAT LONG SINCE I MADE THIS, SO IT SHOULD TASTE OKAY.
COOL PAK
COOL PAK
SORRY, I FORGOT IT'S SUMMER...
MUMBL MUMBL

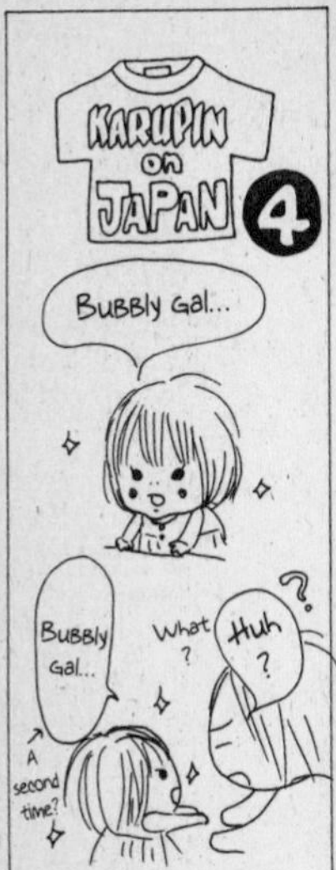
KARUPIN on JAPAN 4
Bubbly Gal...
Bubbly Gal...
What ?
Huh ?
A second time?

My daughter, who used to talk like that, is now 1 year old and walking around.

She always says, "Burira, burira."

What's "burira"?

She can also mimic animal sounds!

This sounds like a diary! Sorry, I have to take down memos so I don't forget!

I wonder if the next graphic novel will come out around the fall? Until then, please "burira, burira." And then at that time please "burira, burira." For those of you who will see me at the autograph signing, please "burira, burira"!

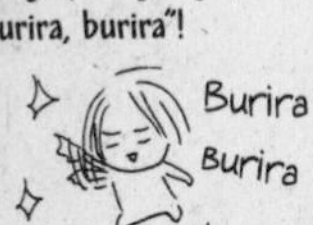
Burira
Burira

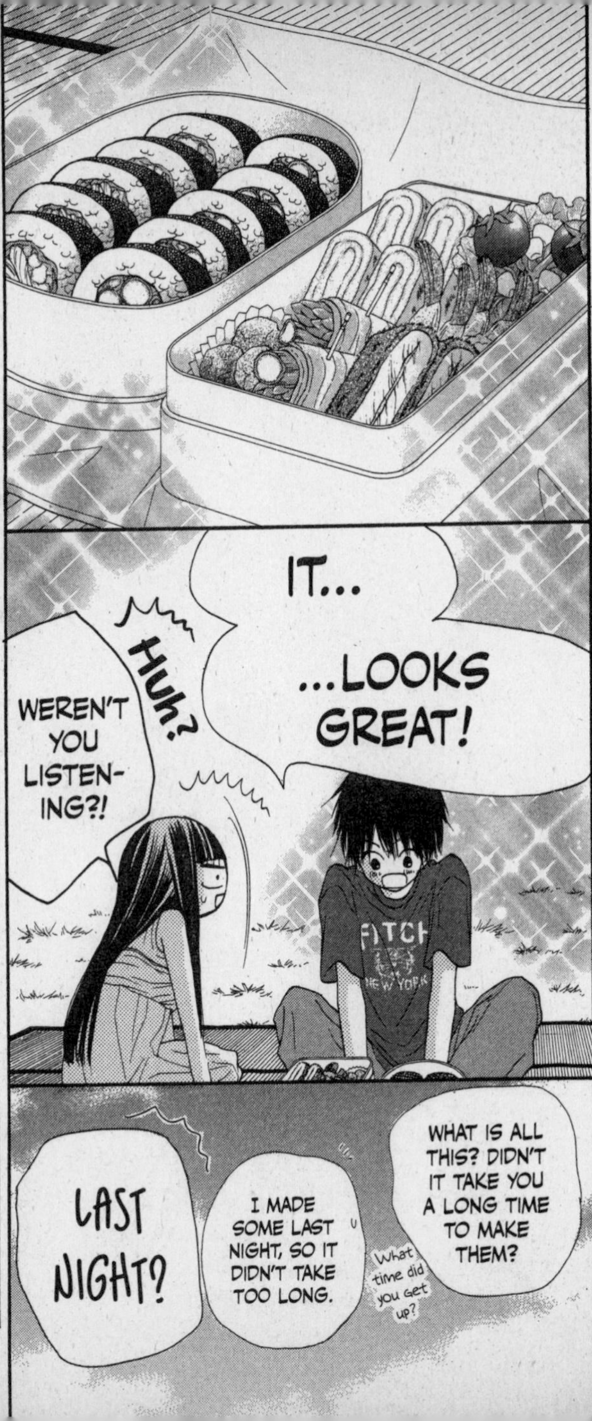
IT... ...LOOKS GREAT!
Huh?
WEREN'T YOU LISTENING?!
WHAT IS ALL THIS? DIDN'T IT TAKE YOU A LONG TIME TO MAKE THEM?
What time did you get up?
I MADE SOME LAST NIGHT, SO IT DIDN'T TAKE TOO LONG.
LAST NIGHT?

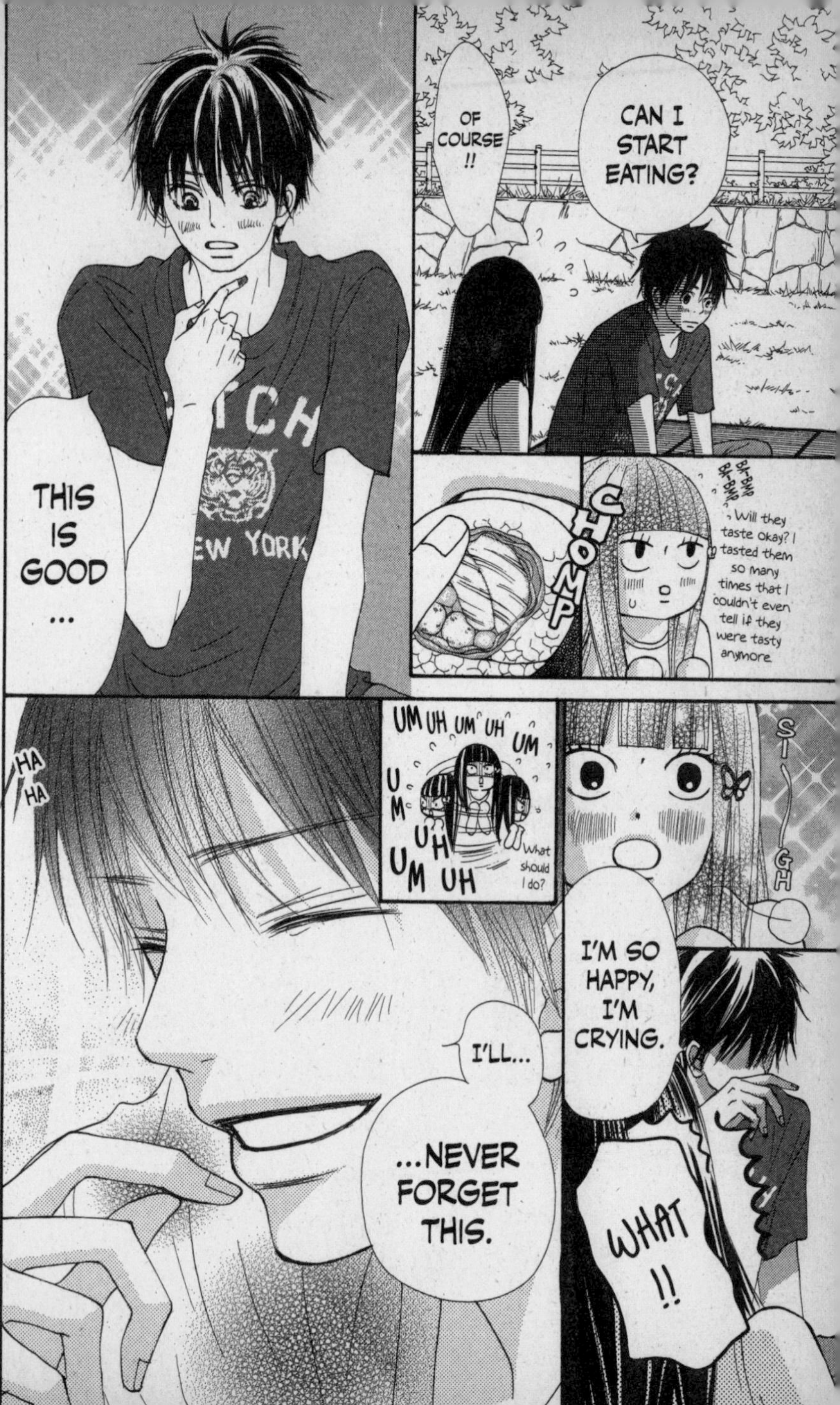
CAN I START EATING?
OF COURSE!!
BA-BMP BA-BMP
CHOMP
Will they taste okay? I tasted them so many times that I couldn't even tell if they were tasty anymore
THIS IS GOOD...
SI-I-GH
UM UH UM UH UM
UM UH UM UH
What should I do?
HA HA
I'LL...
...NEVER FORGET THIS.
I'M SO HAPPY, I'M CRYING.
WHAT!!

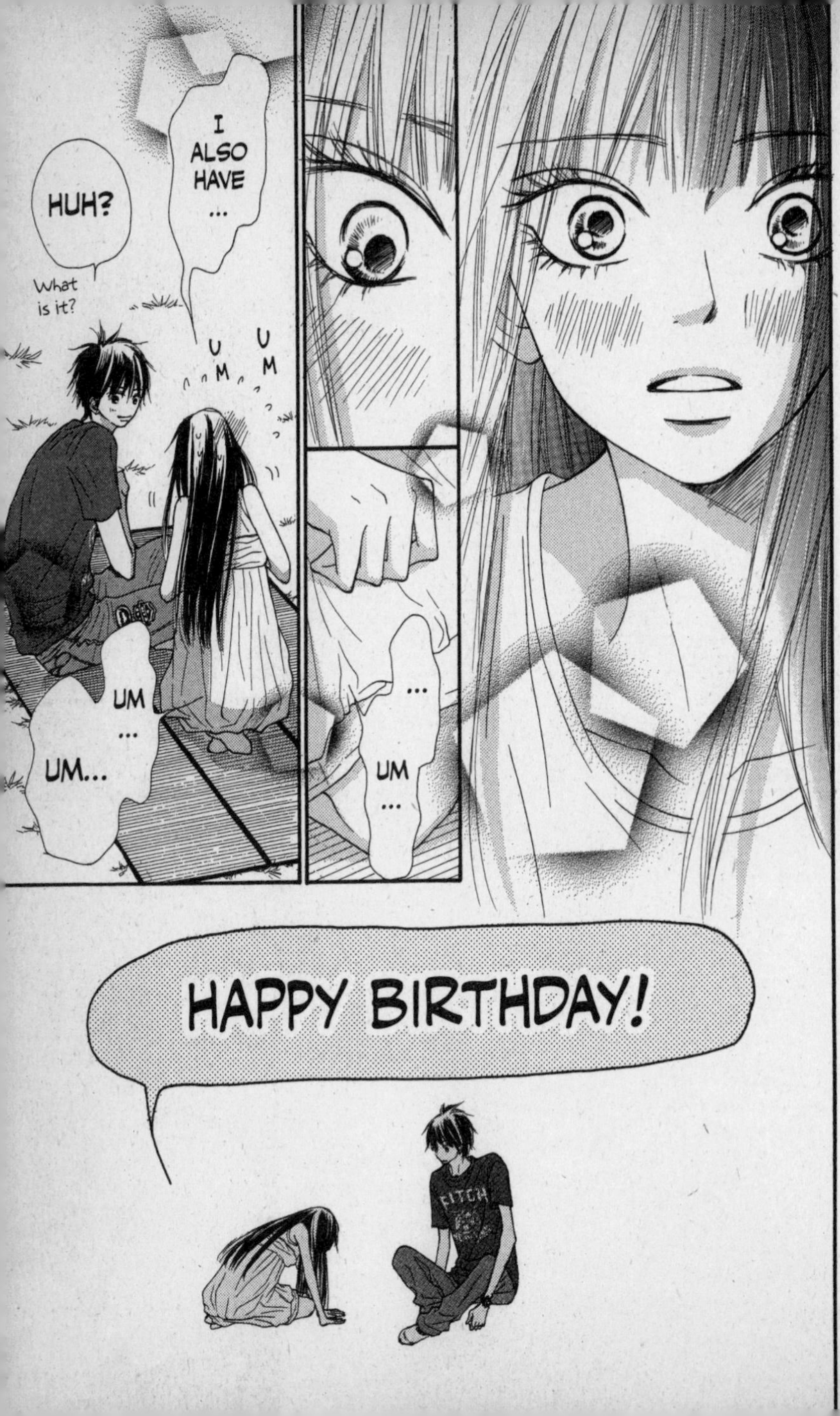
... UM ...
I ALSO HAVE ...
HUH?
What is it?
UM UM
UM ... UM...
HAPPY BIRTHDAY!

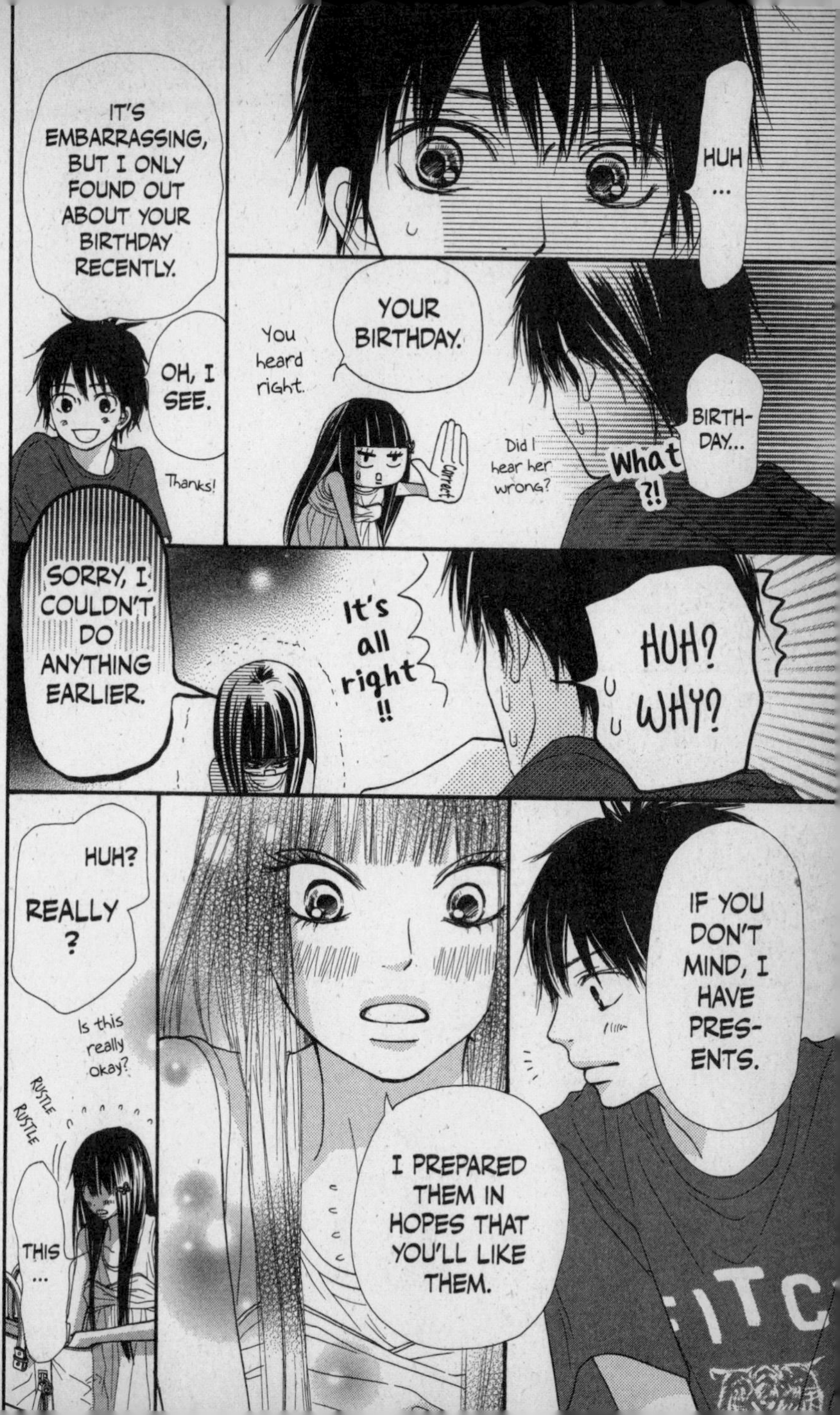
HUH ...
BIRTH-DAY...
What ?!
Did I hear her wrong?
YOUR BIRTHDAY.
You heard right.
Correct
IT'S EMBARRASSING, BUT I ONLY FOUND OUT ABOUT YOUR BIRTHDAY RECENTLY.
OH, I SEE.
Thanks!
HUH? WHY?
It's all right !!
SORRY, I COULDN'T DO ANYTHING EARLIER.
IF YOU DON'T MIND, I HAVE PRES-ENTS.
I PREPARED THEM IN HOPES THAT YOU'LL LIKE THEM.
HUH? REALLY ?
Is this really okay?
RUSTLE RUSTLE
THIS ...

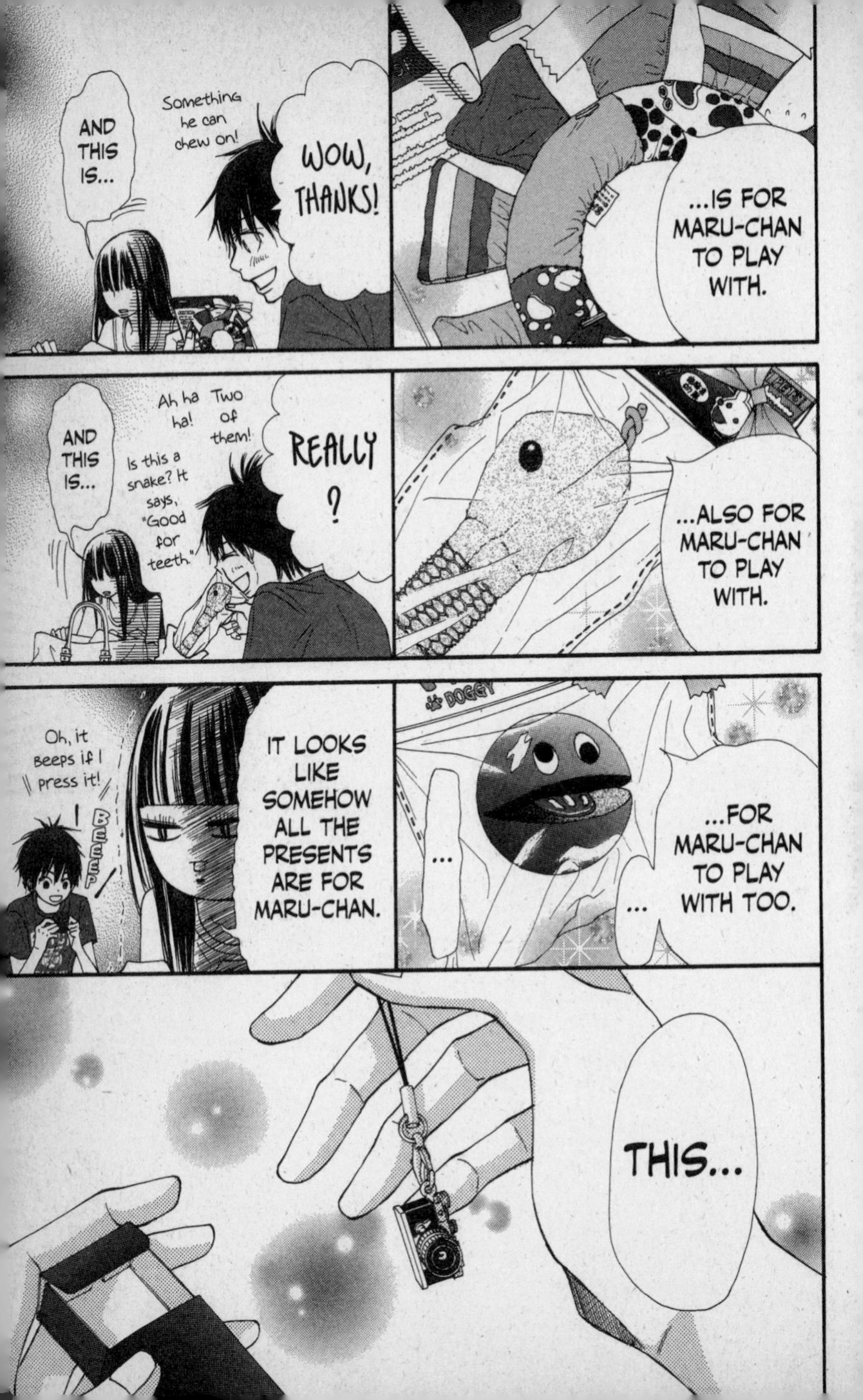
...IS FOR MARU-CHAN TO PLAY WITH.
WOW, THANKS!
Something he can chew on!
AND THIS IS...
...ALSO FOR MARU-CHAN TO PLAY WITH.
REALLY?
Ah ha ha! Two of them!
Is this a snake? It says, "Good for teeth."
AND THIS IS...
DOGGY
...FOR MARU-CHAN TO PLAY WITH TOO.
...
...
IT LOOKS LIKE SOMEHOW ALL THE PRESENTS ARE FOR MARU-CHAN.
Oh, it beeps if I press it!
!
BEEEP
THIS...

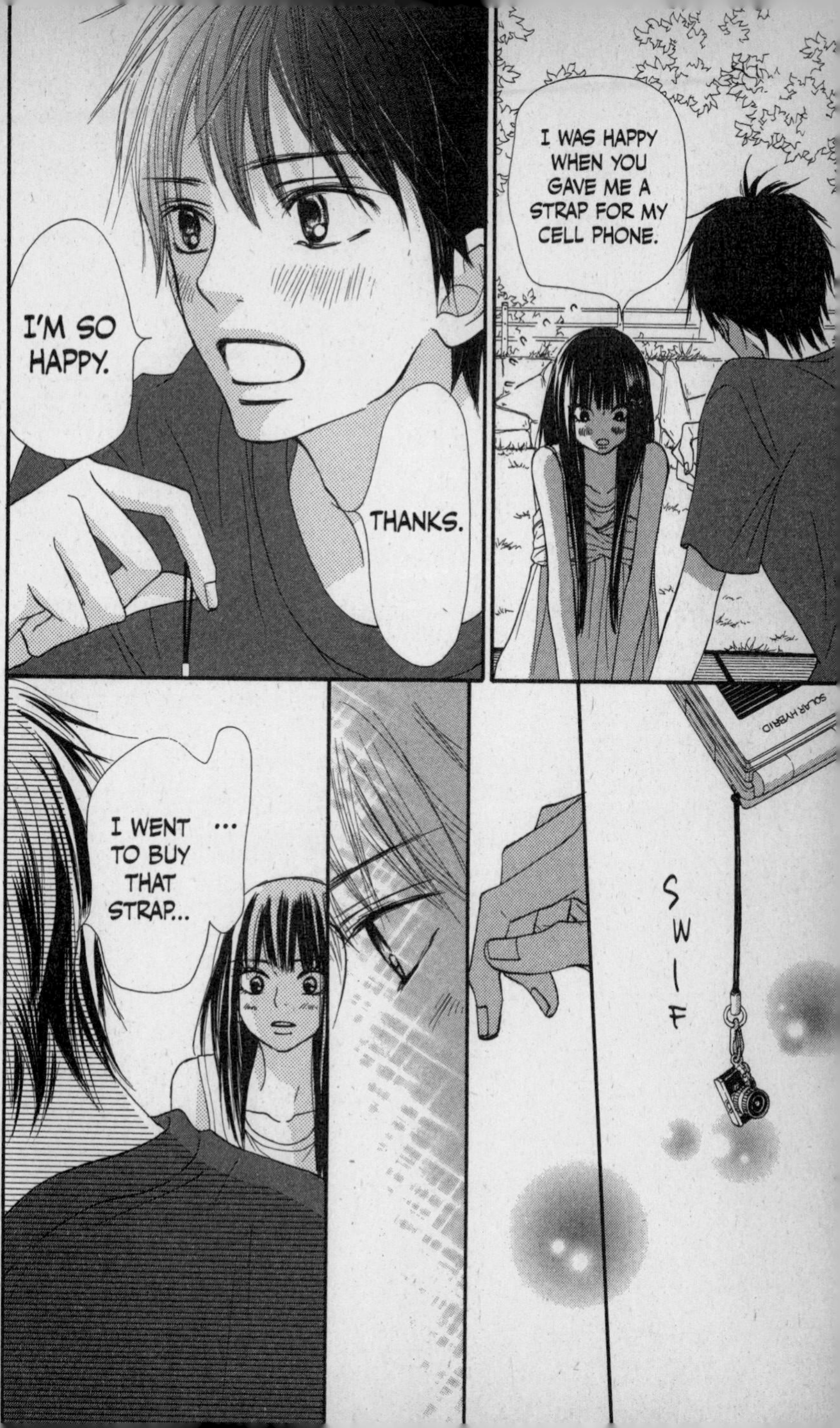
I WAS HAPPY WHEN YOU GAVE ME A STRAP FOR MY CELL PHONE.
I'M SO HAPPY.
THANKS.
SOLAR HYBRID
SWIF
I WENT TO BUY THAT STRAP...
...

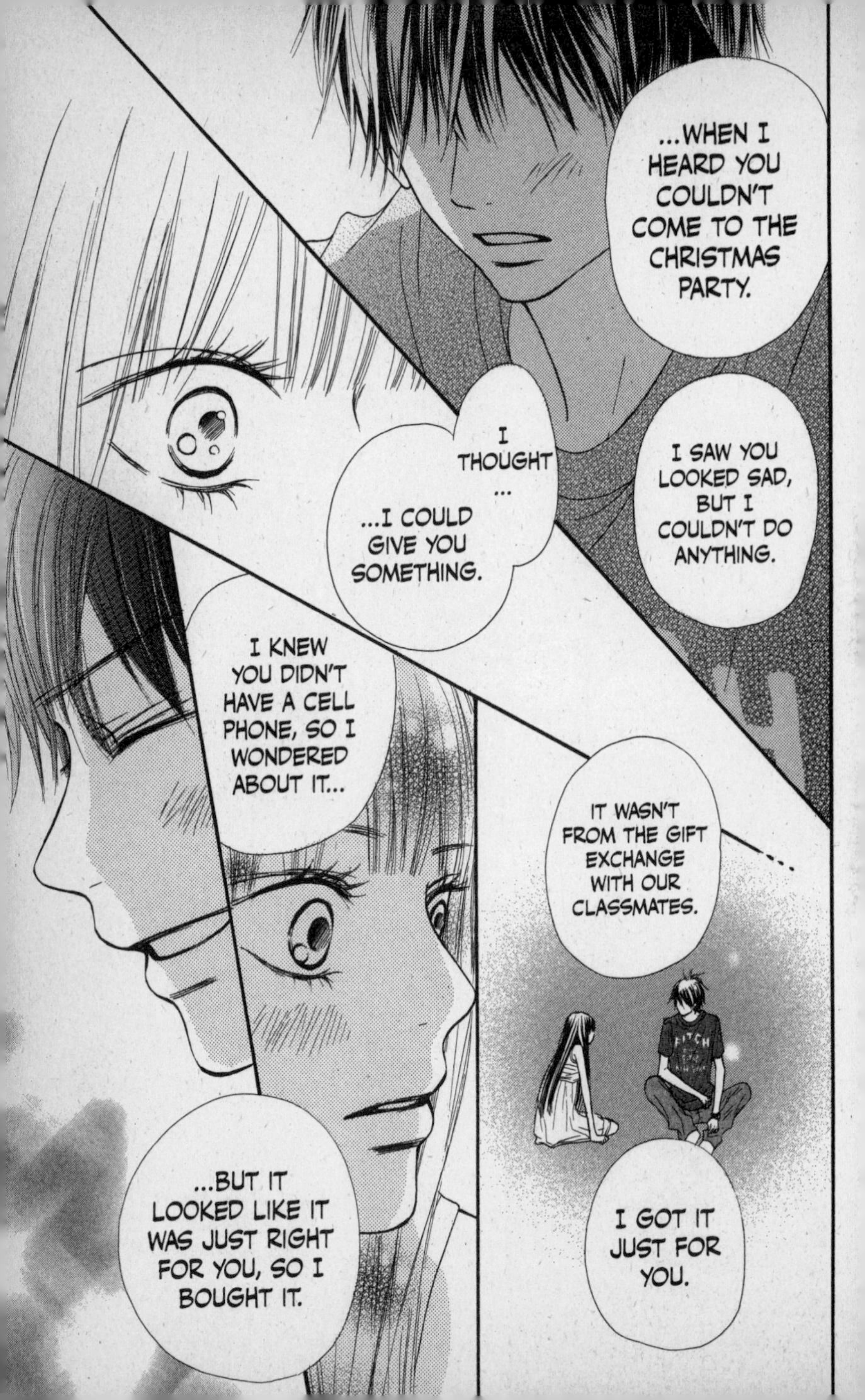
...WHEN I HEARD YOU COULDN'T COME TO THE CHRISTMAS PARTY.
I SAW YOU LOOKED SAD, BUT I COULDN'T DO ANYTHING.
I THOUGHT...
...I COULD GIVE YOU SOMETHING.
I KNEW YOU DIDN'T HAVE A CELL PHONE, SO I WONDERED ABOUT IT...
...BUT IT LOOKED LIKE IT WAS JUST RIGHT FOR YOU, SO I BOUGHT IT.
IT WASN'T FROM THE GIFT EXCHANGE WITH OUR CLASSMATES.
I GOT IT JUST FOR YOU.

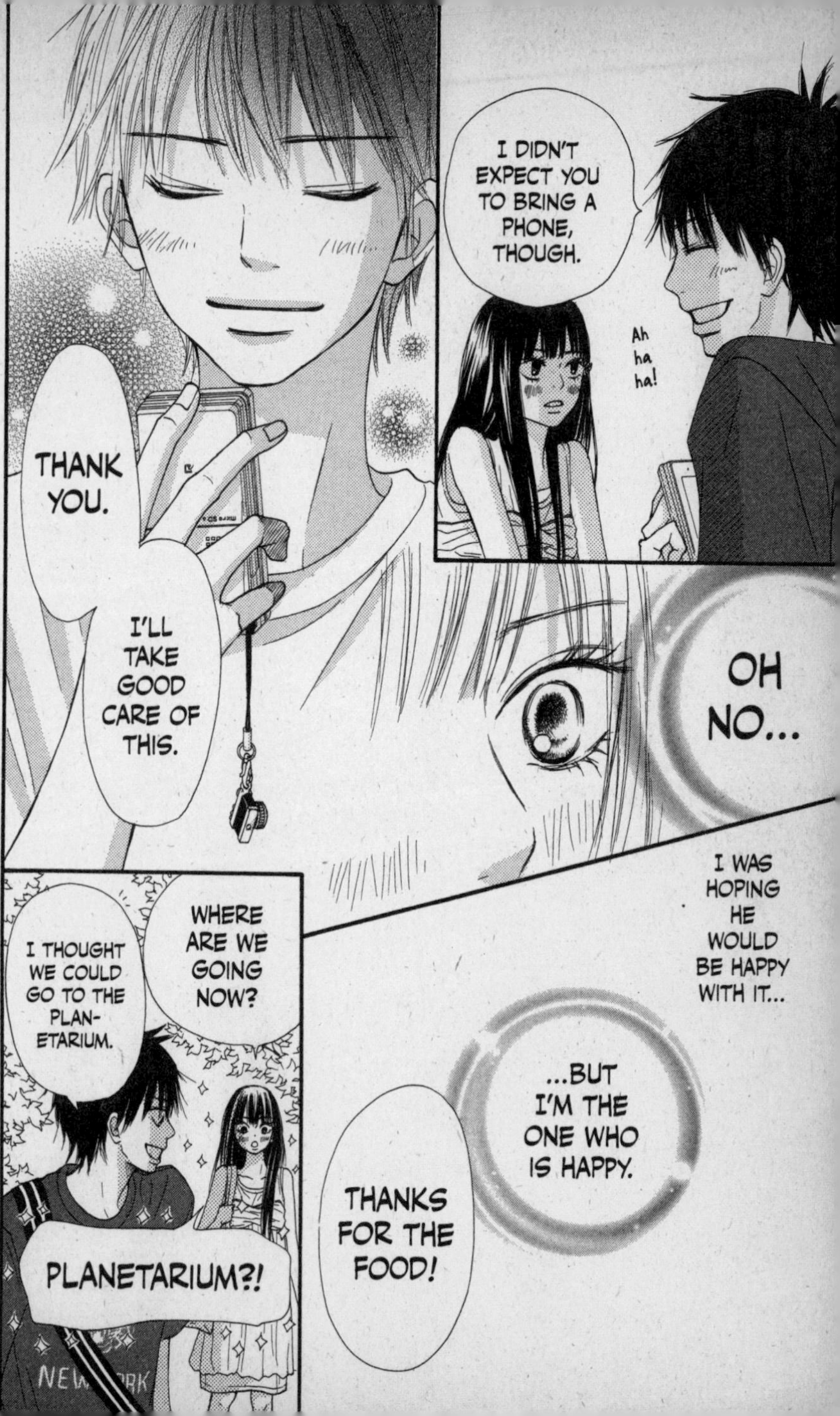
I DIDN'T EXPECT YOU TO BRING A PHONE, THOUGH.
Ah ha ha!
OH NO...
THANK YOU.
I'LL TAKE GOOD CARE OF THIS.
I WAS HOPING HE WOULD BE HAPPY WITH IT...
...BUT I'M THE ONE WHO IS HAPPY.
THANKS FOR THE FOOD!
WHERE ARE WE GOING NOW?
I THOUGHT WE COULD GO TO THE PLAN-ETARIUM.
PLANETARIUM?!
NEW YORK

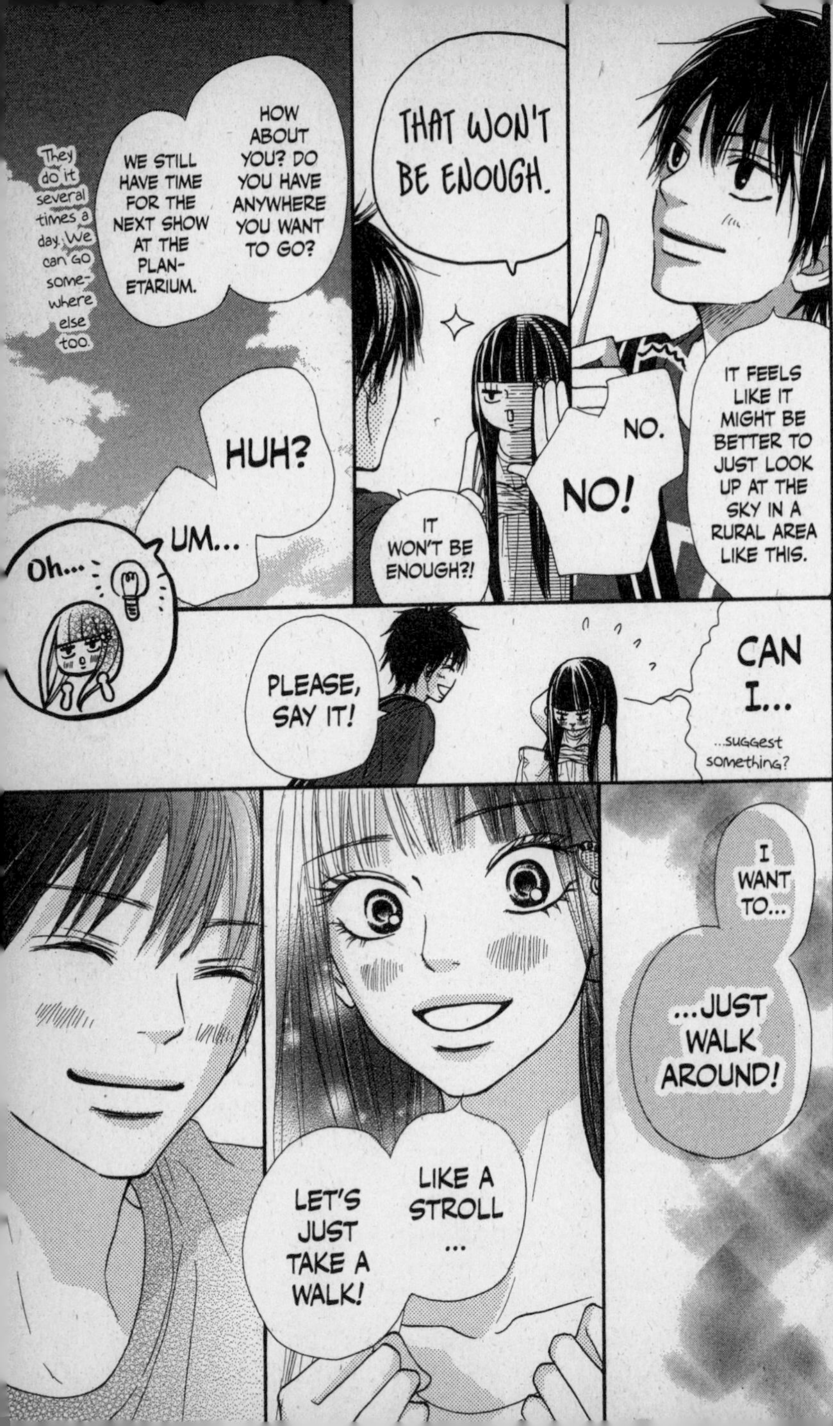
IT FEELS LIKE IT MIGHT BE BETTER TO JUST LOOK UP AT THE SKY IN A RURAL AREA LIKE THIS.
NO.
NO!
THAT WON'T BE ENOUGH.
IT WON'T BE ENOUGH?!
HOW ABOUT YOU? DO YOU HAVE ANYWHERE YOU WANT TO GO?
WE STILL HAVE TIME FOR THE NEXT SHOW AT THE PLAN-ETARIUM.
They do it several times a day. We can go some-where else too.
HUH?
UM...
CAN I...
...suggest something?
PLEASE, SAY IT!
Oh...
I WANT TO...
...JUST WALK AROUND!
LIKE A STROLL ...
LET'S JUST TAKE A WALK!

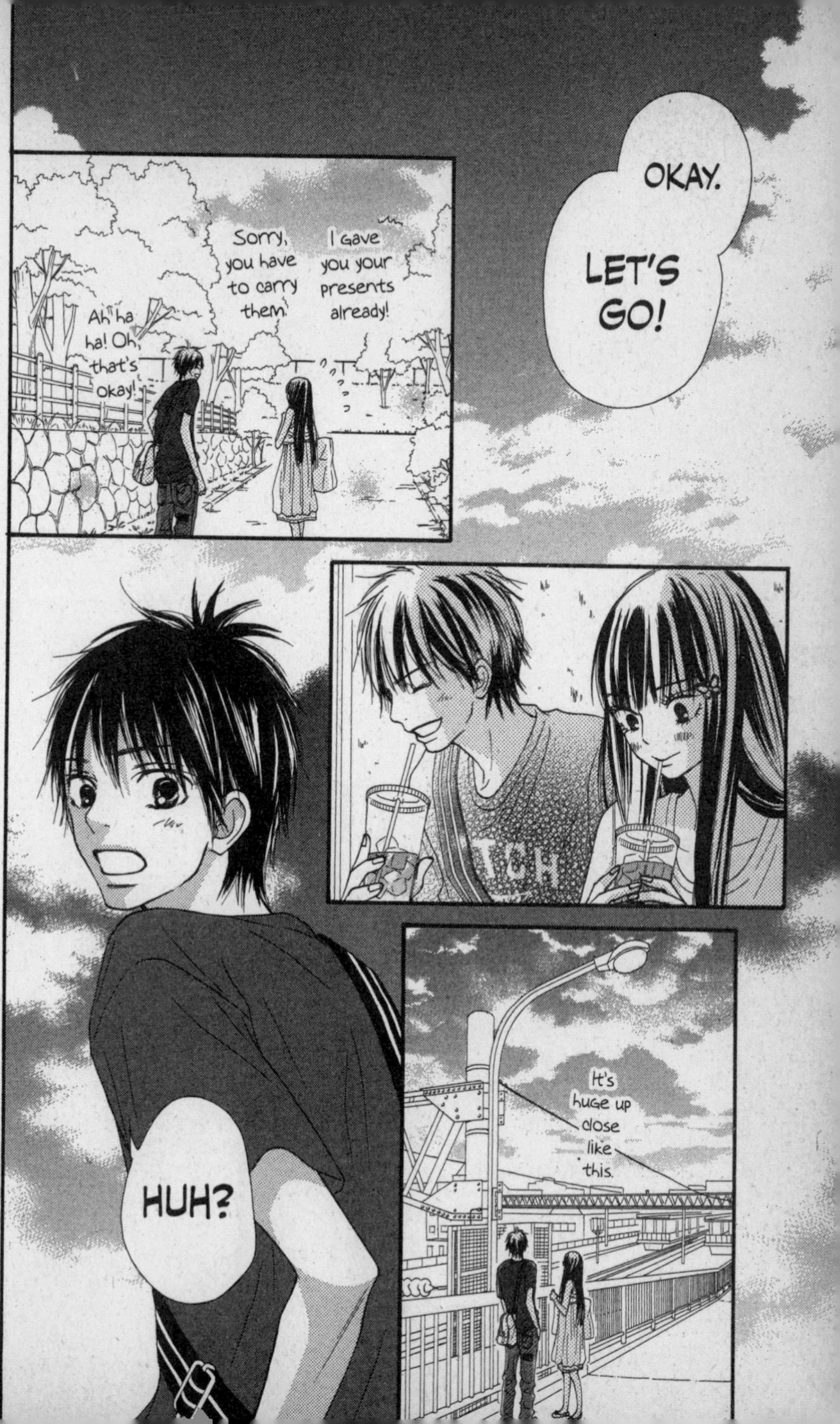
OKAY. LET'S GO!
I gave you your presents already!
Sorry, you have to carry them.
Ah ha ha! Oh, that's okay!
It's huge up close like this.
HUH?

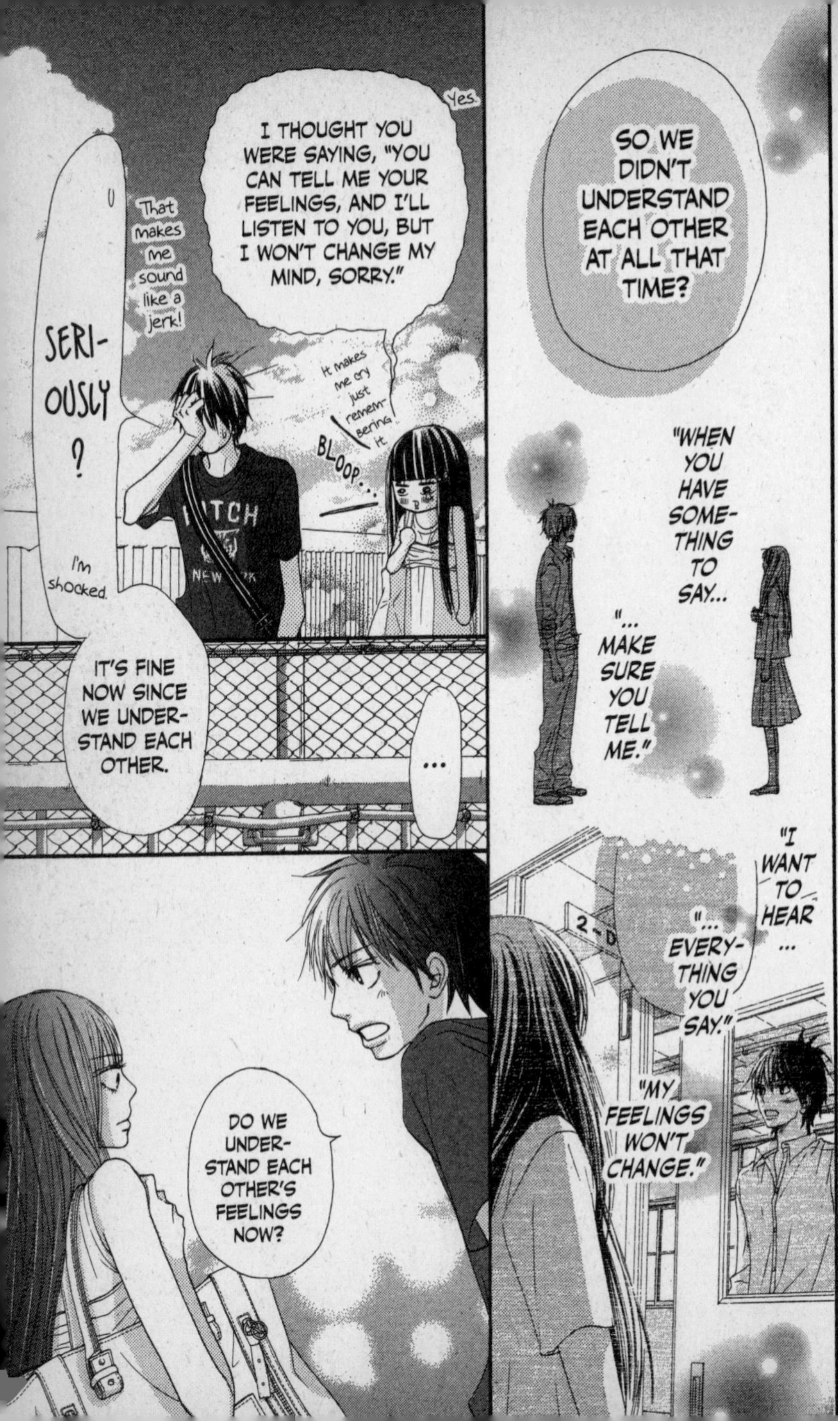
SO WE DIDN'T UNDERSTAND EACH OTHER AT ALL THAT TIME?
"WHEN YOU HAVE SOMETHING TO SAY...
"... MAKE SURE YOU TELL ME."
"I WANT TO HEAR...
"... EVERYTHING YOU SAY."
2-D
"MY FEELINGS WON'T CHANGE."
Yes.
I THOUGHT YOU WERE SAYING, "YOU CAN TELL ME YOUR FEELINGS, AND I'LL LISTEN TO YOU, BUT I WON'T CHANGE MY MIND, SORRY."
It makes me cry just remembering it.
BLOOP...
That makes me sound like a jerk!
SERIOUSLY?
I'm shocked.
IT'S FINE NOW SINCE WE UNDERSTAND EACH OTHER.
...
DO WE UNDERSTAND EACH OTHER'S FEELINGS NOW?

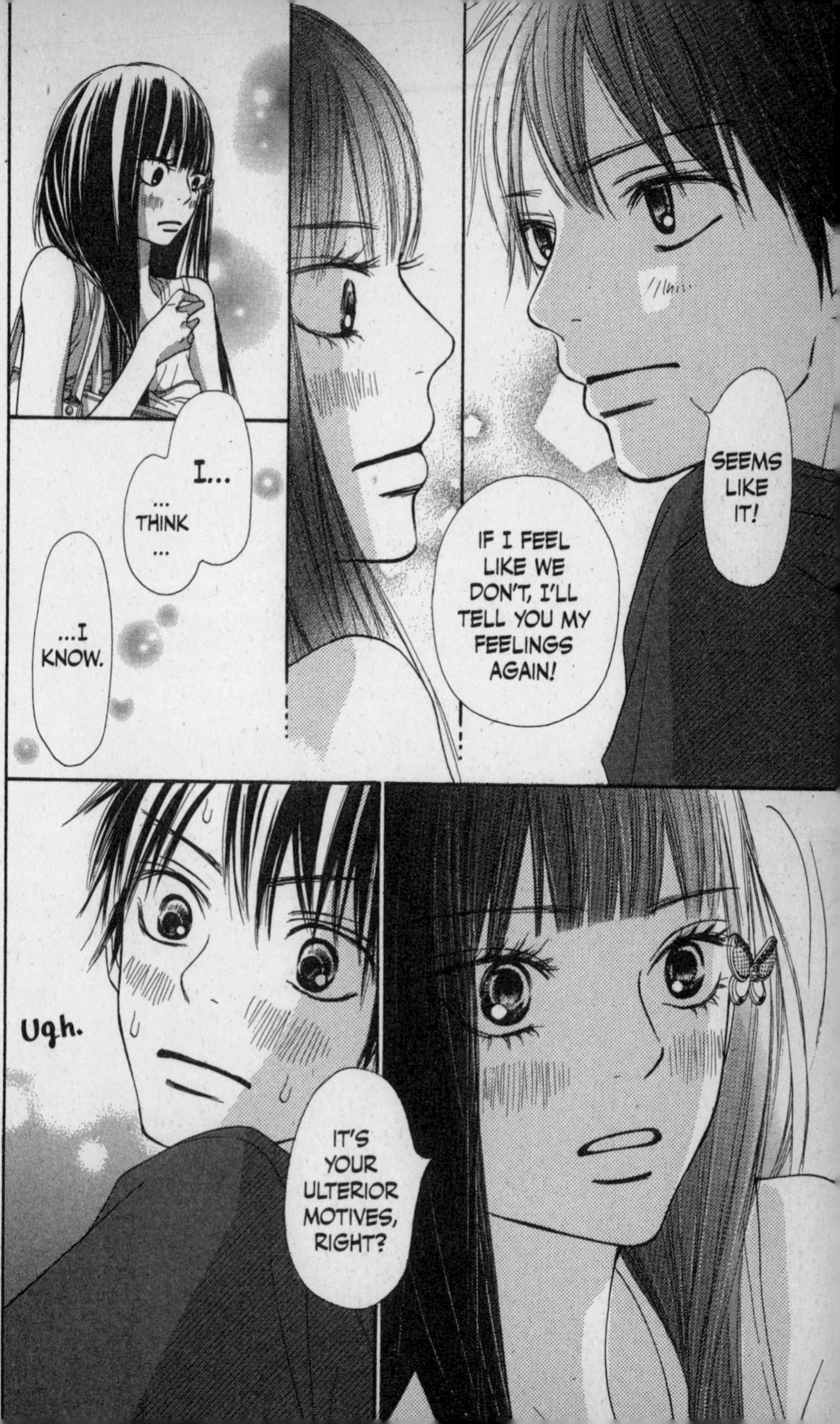
SEEMS LIKE IT!
IF I FEEL LIKE WE DON'T, I'LL TELL YOU MY FEELINGS AGAIN!
I... ... THINK ...
...I KNOW.
IT'S YOUR ULTERIOR MOTIVES, RIGHT?
Ugh.

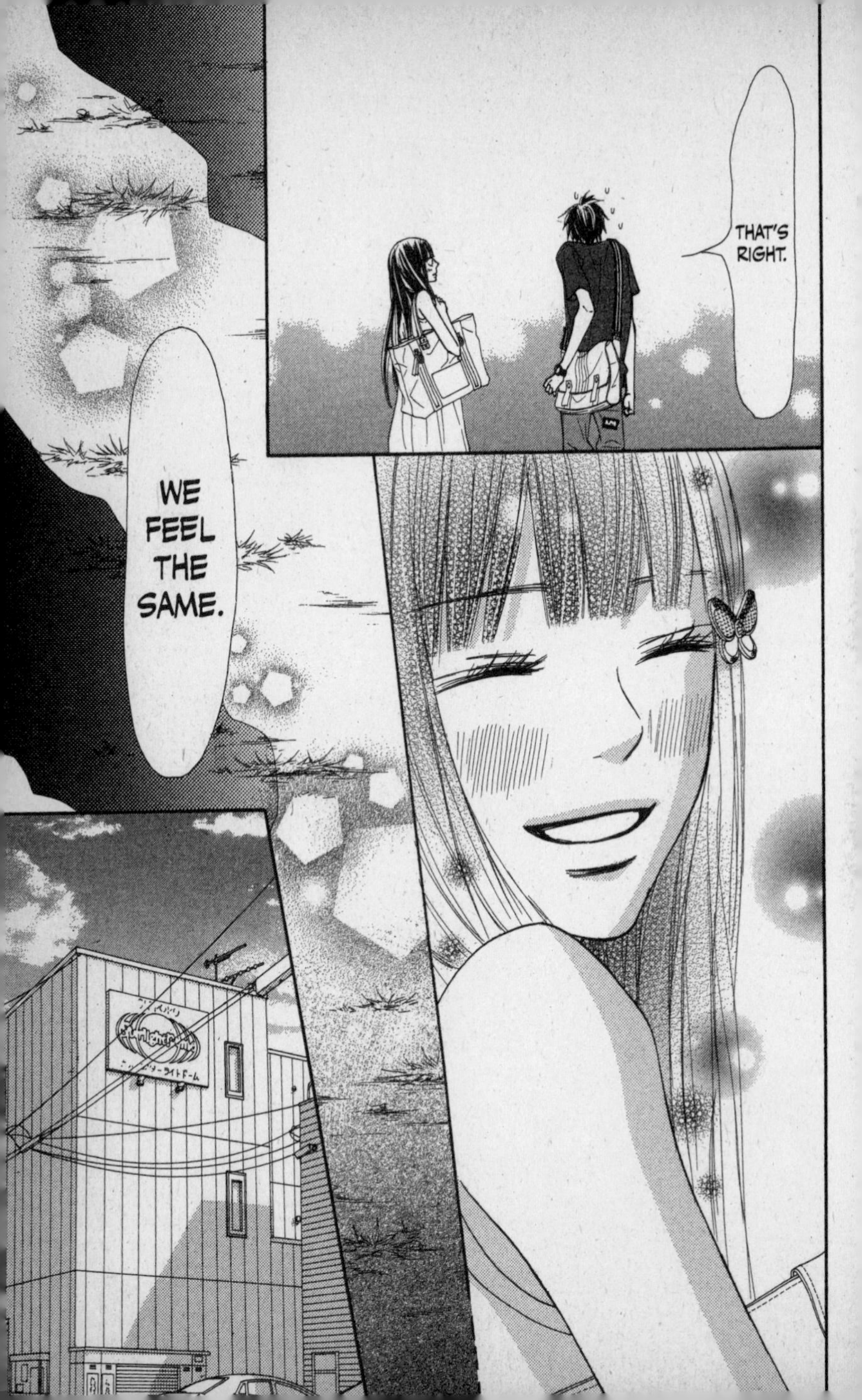
THAT'S RIGHT.
WE FEEL THE SAME.

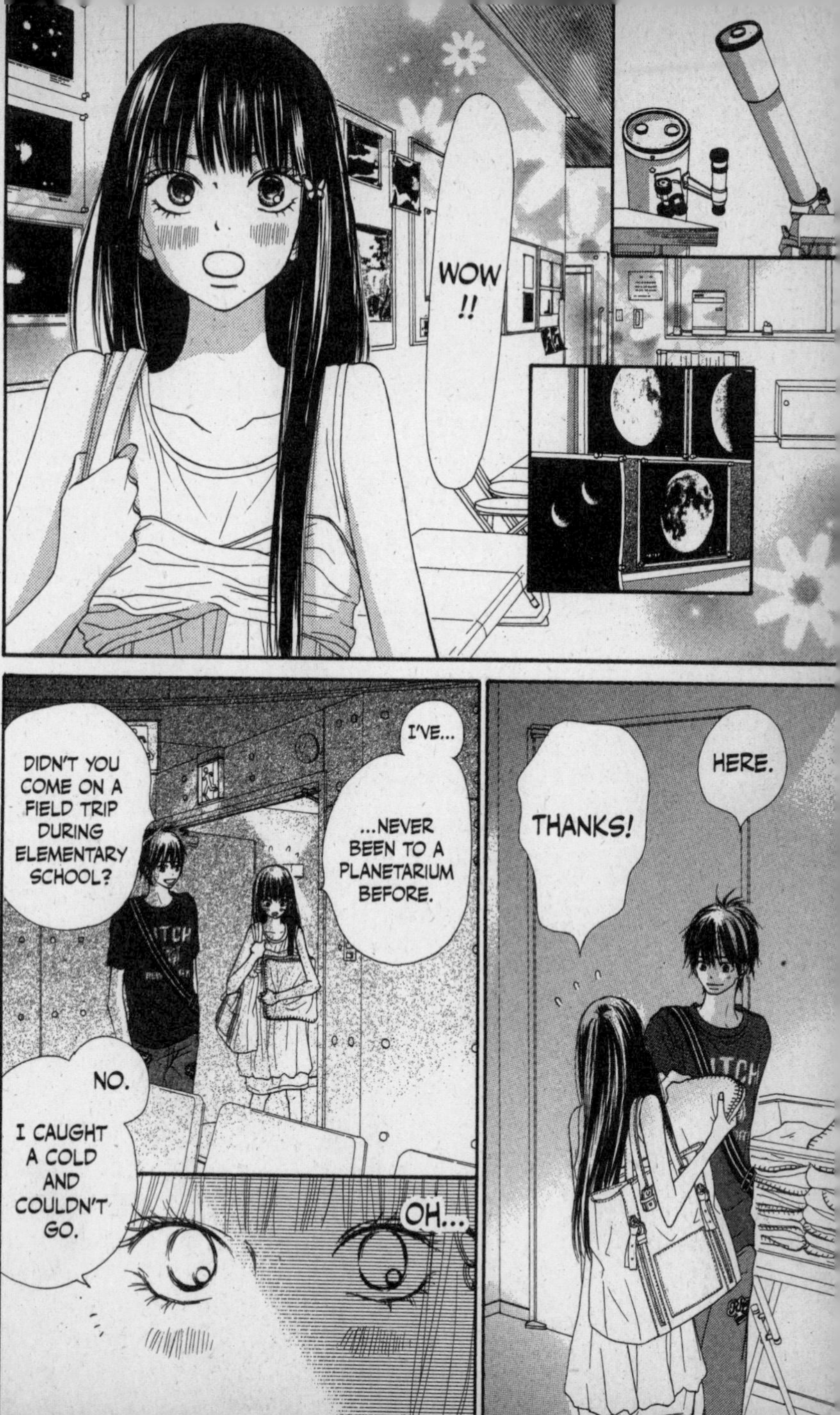
WOW !!
HERE.
THANKS!
I'VE...
...NEVER BEEN TO A PLANETARIUM BEFORE.
DIDN'T YOU COME ON A FIELD TRIP DURING ELEMENTARY SCHOOL?
NO.
I CAUGHT A COLD AND COULDN'T GO.
OH...

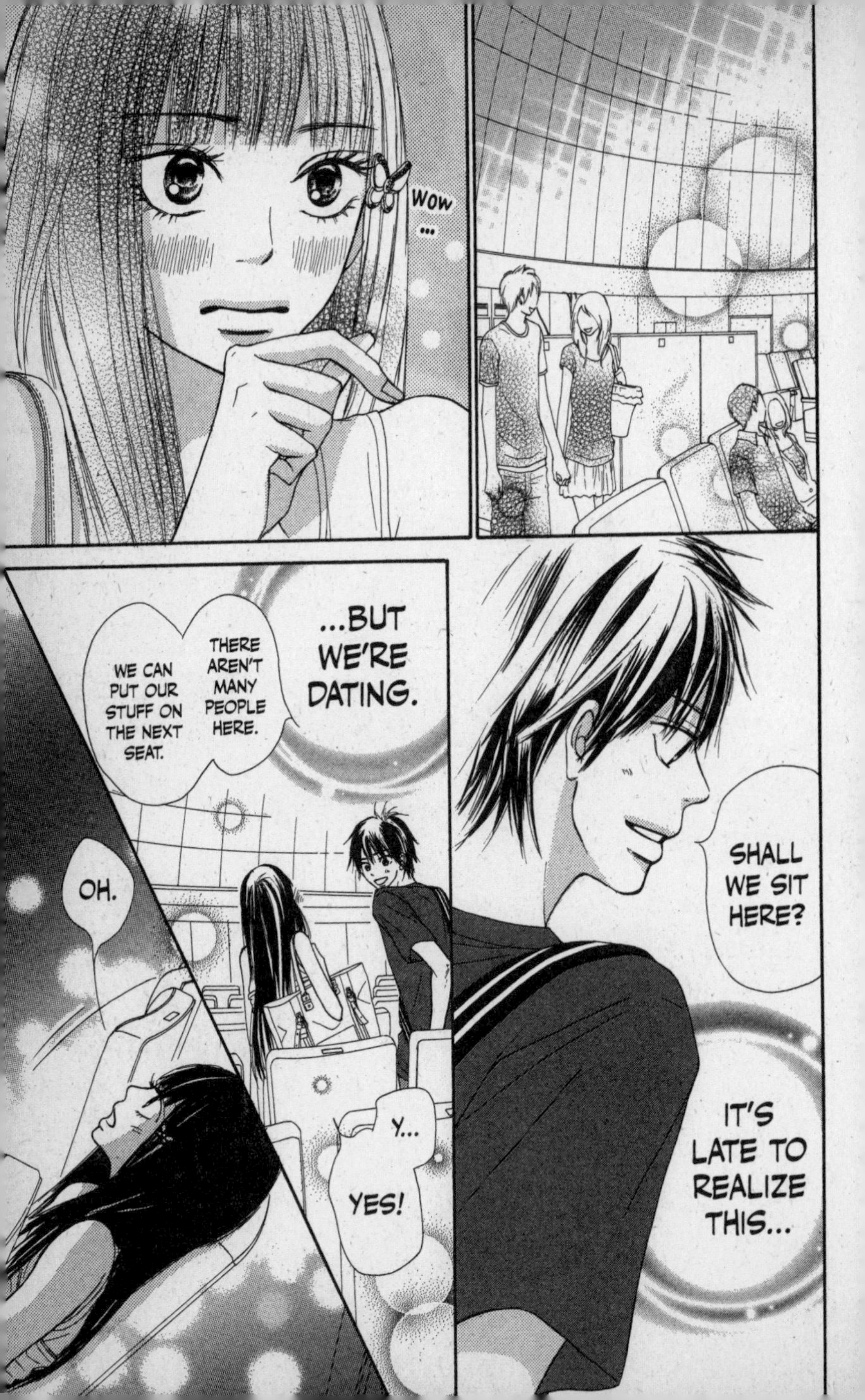
WOW ...
SHALL WE SIT HERE?
IT'S LATE TO REALIZE THIS...
...BUT WE'RE DATING.
THERE AREN'T MANY PEOPLE HERE.
WE CAN PUT OUR STUFF ON THE NEXT SEAT.
OH.
Y...
YES!

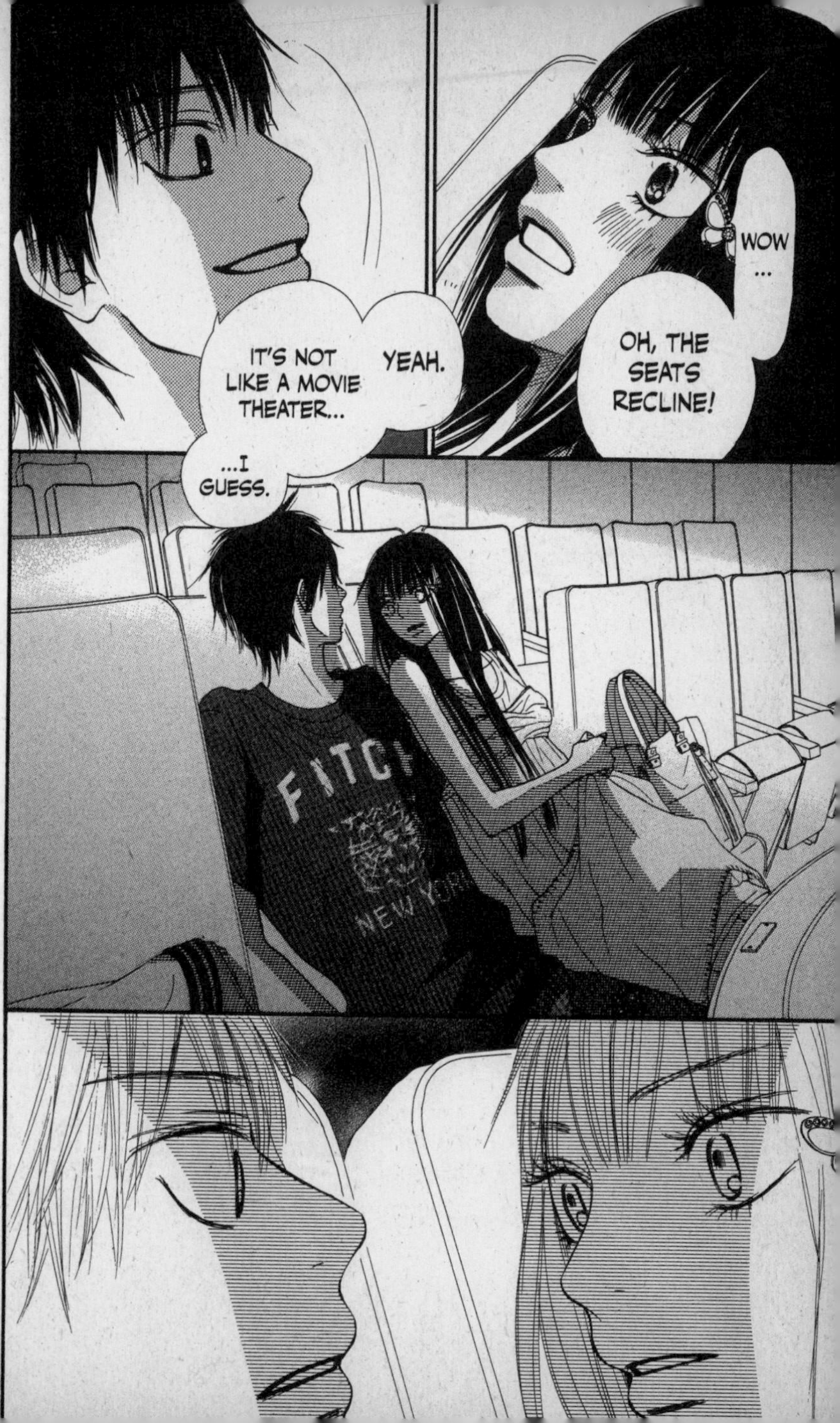
WOW ...
OH, THE SEATS RECLINE!
YEAH.
IT'S NOT LIKE A MOVIE THEATER...
...I GUESS.

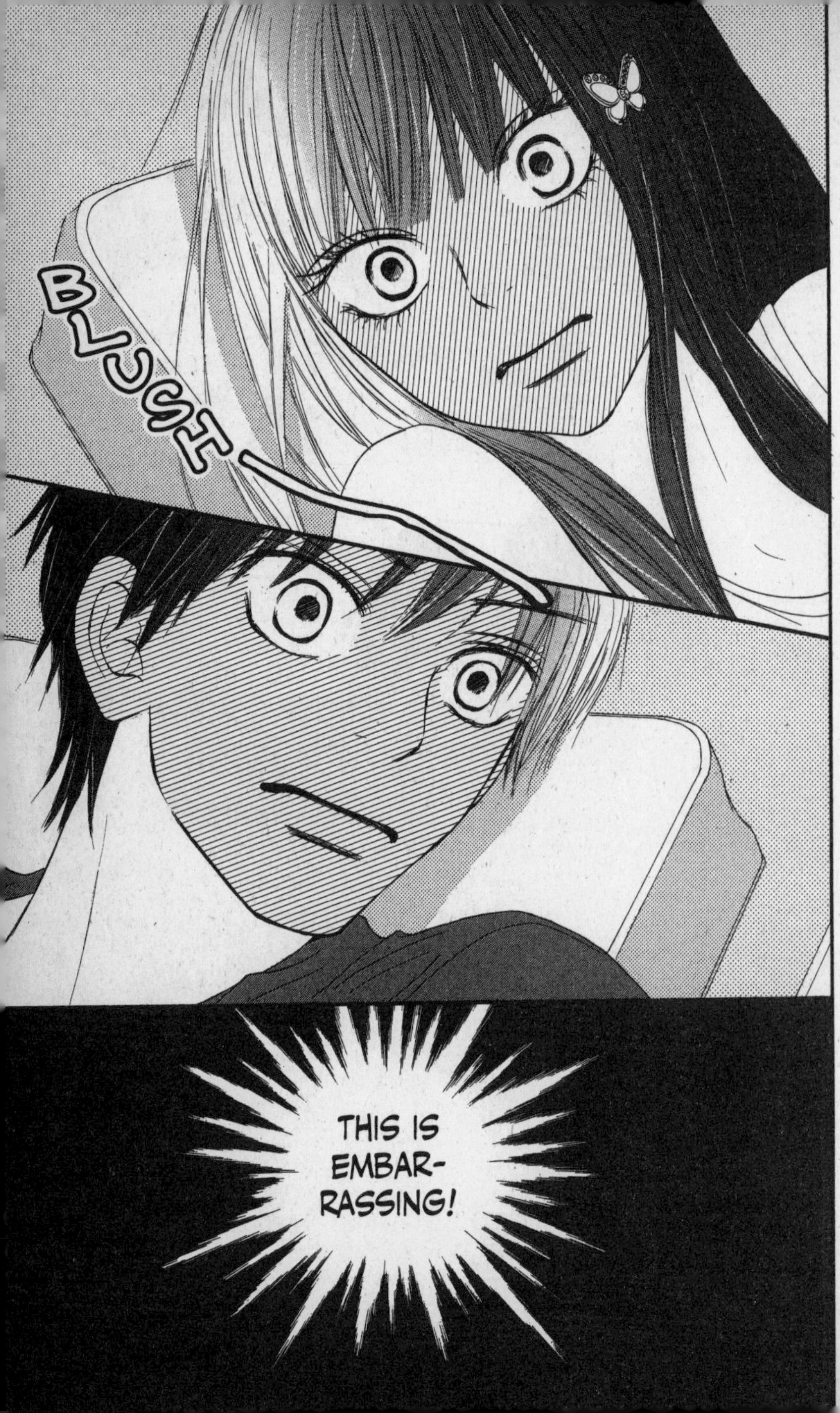
BLUSH
THIS IS EMBAR-RASSING!

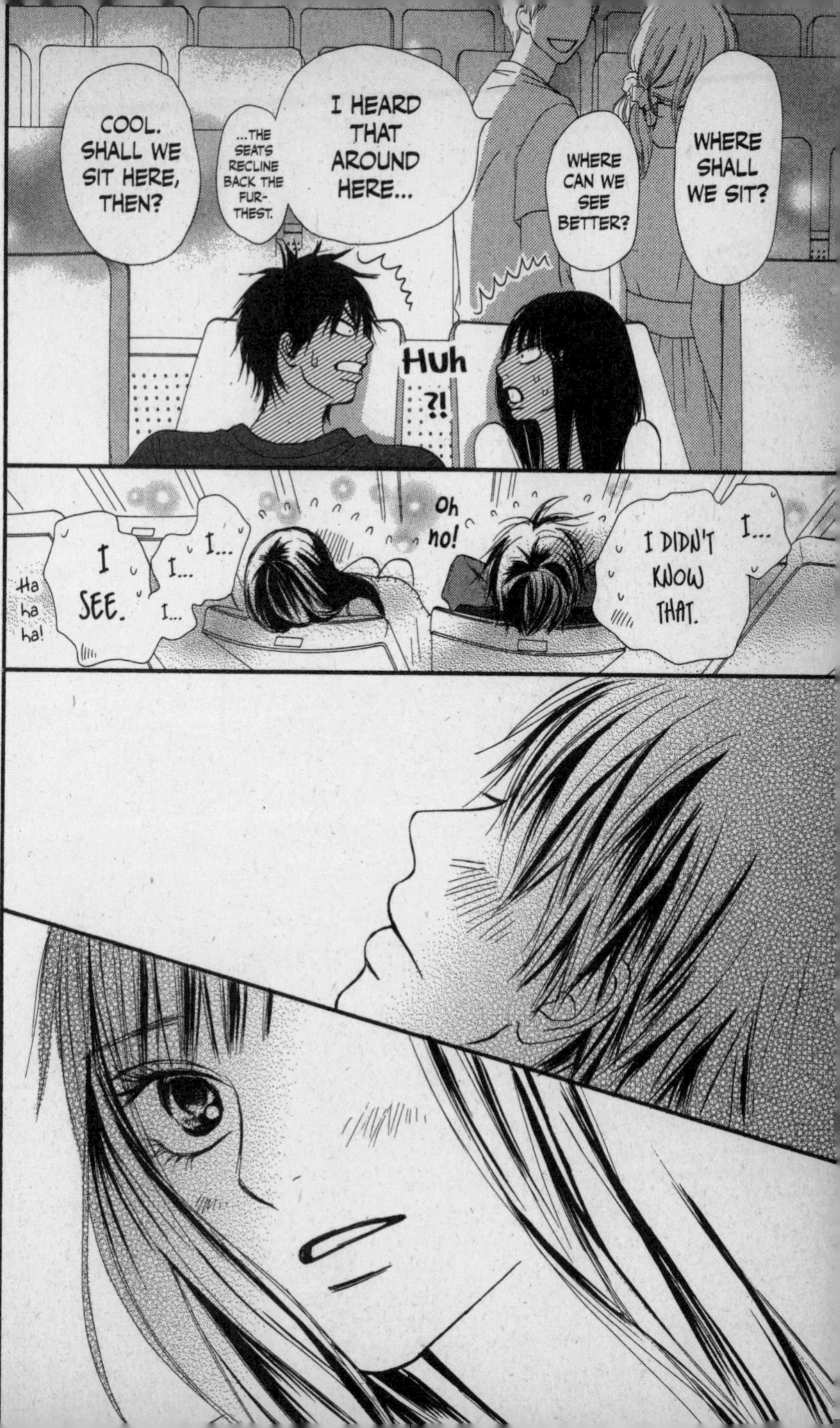
WHERE SHALL WE SIT?
WHERE CAN WE SEE BETTER?
I HEARD THAT AROUND HERE...
...THE SEATS RECLINE BACK THE FUR-THEST.
COOL. SHALL WE SIT HERE, THEN?
Huh ?!
I...
I DIDN'T KNOW THAT.
Oh no!
I... I... I...
I SEE.
Ha ha ha!

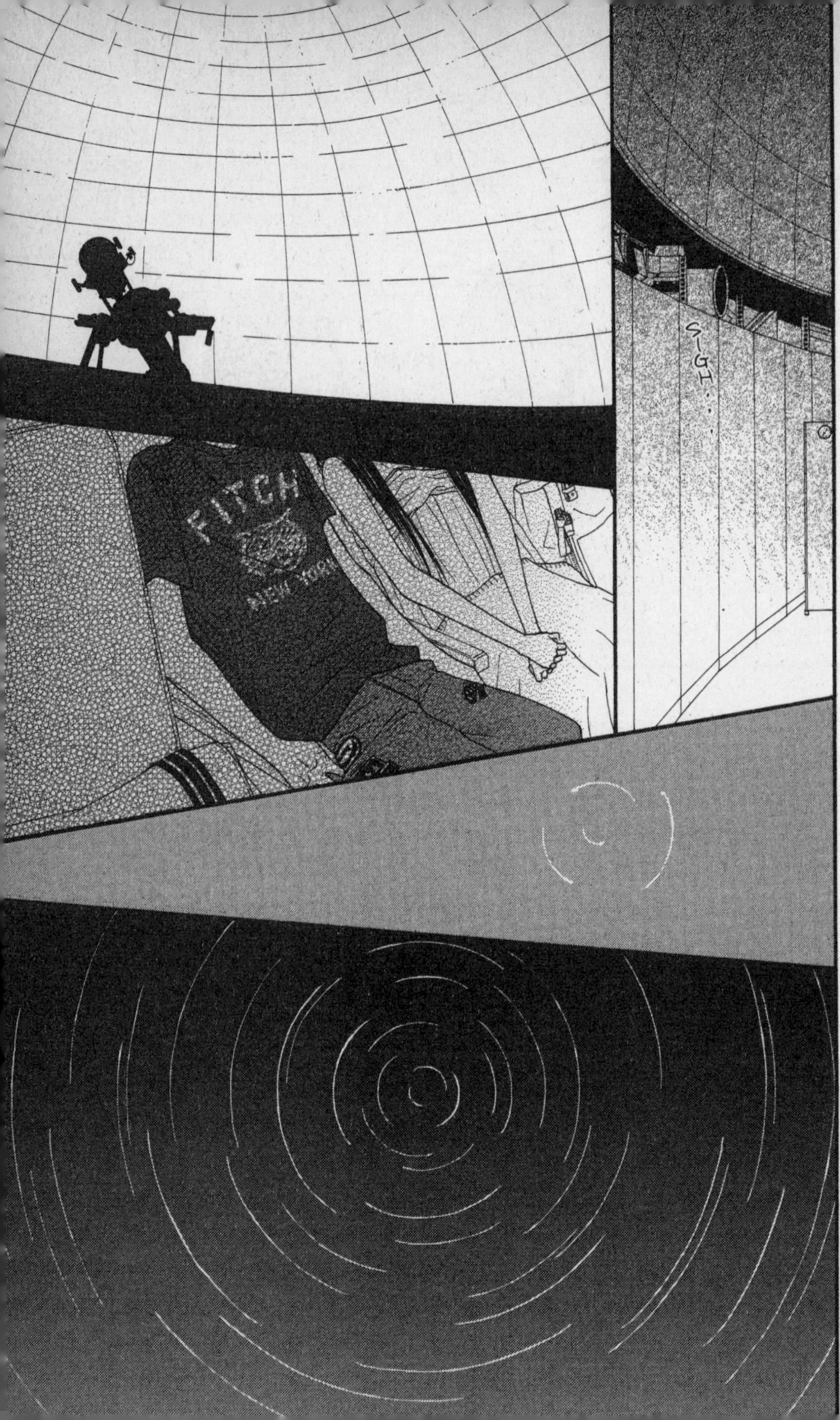
SIGH...
FITCH
NEW YORK

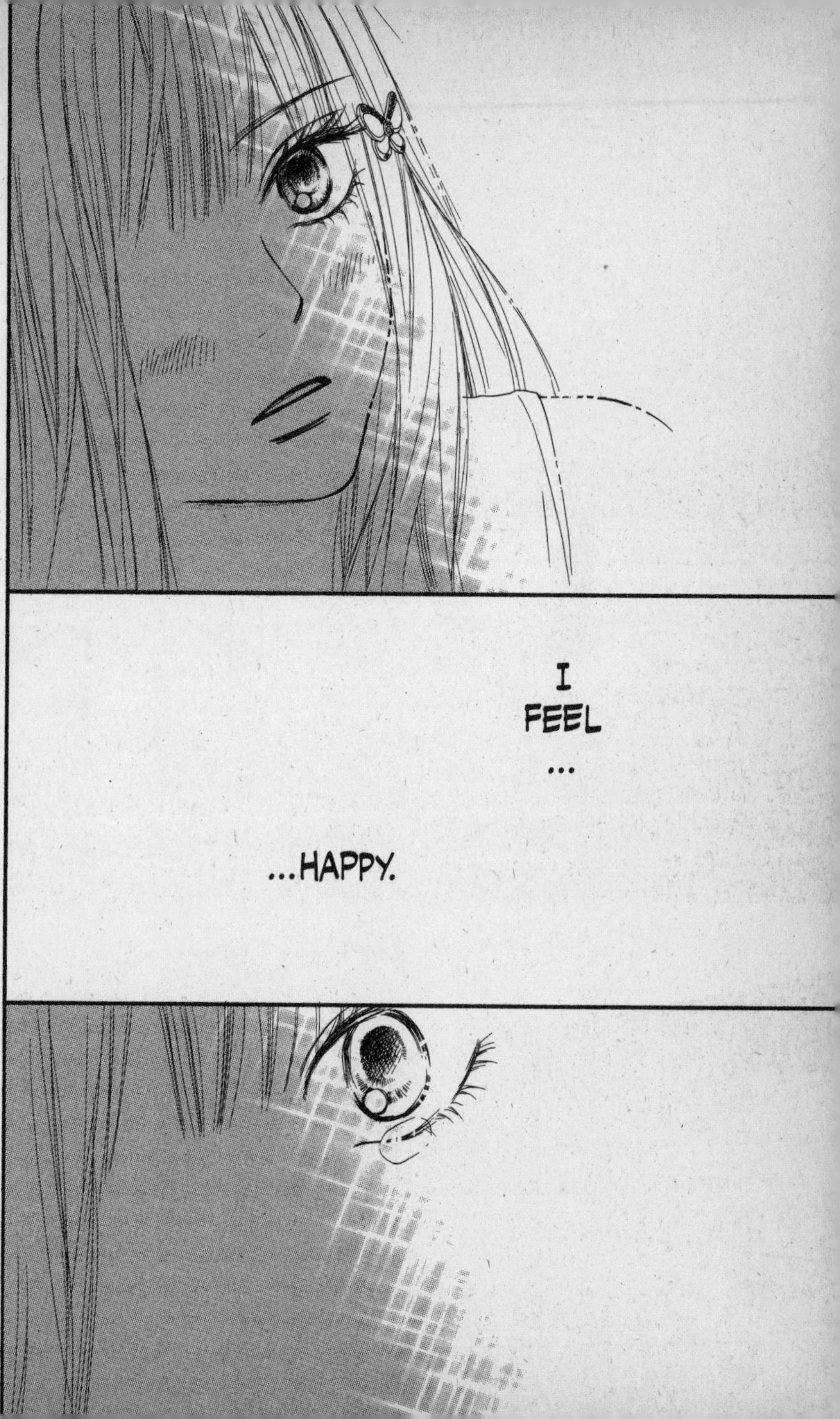
I FEEL ...
...HAPPY.

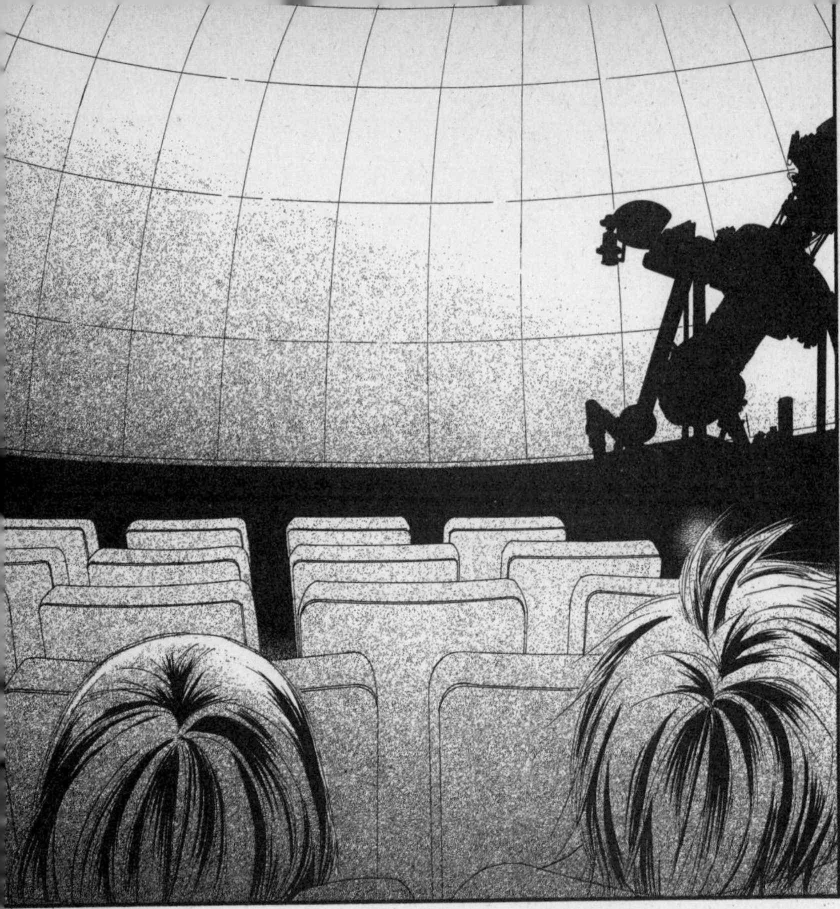
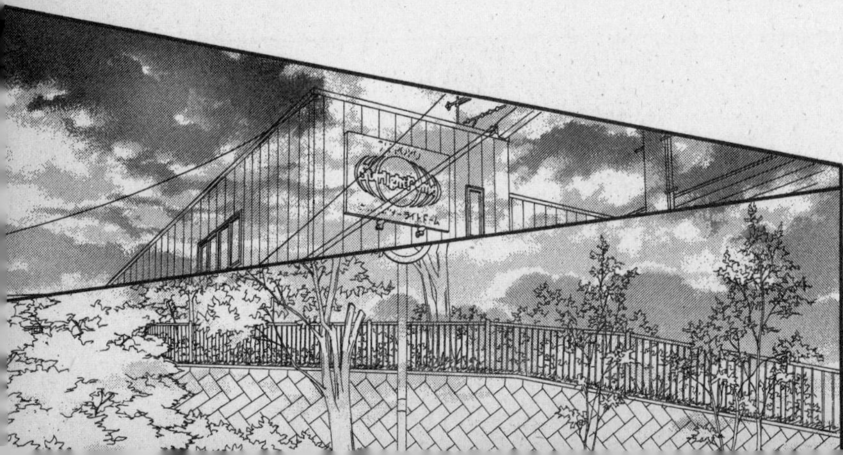

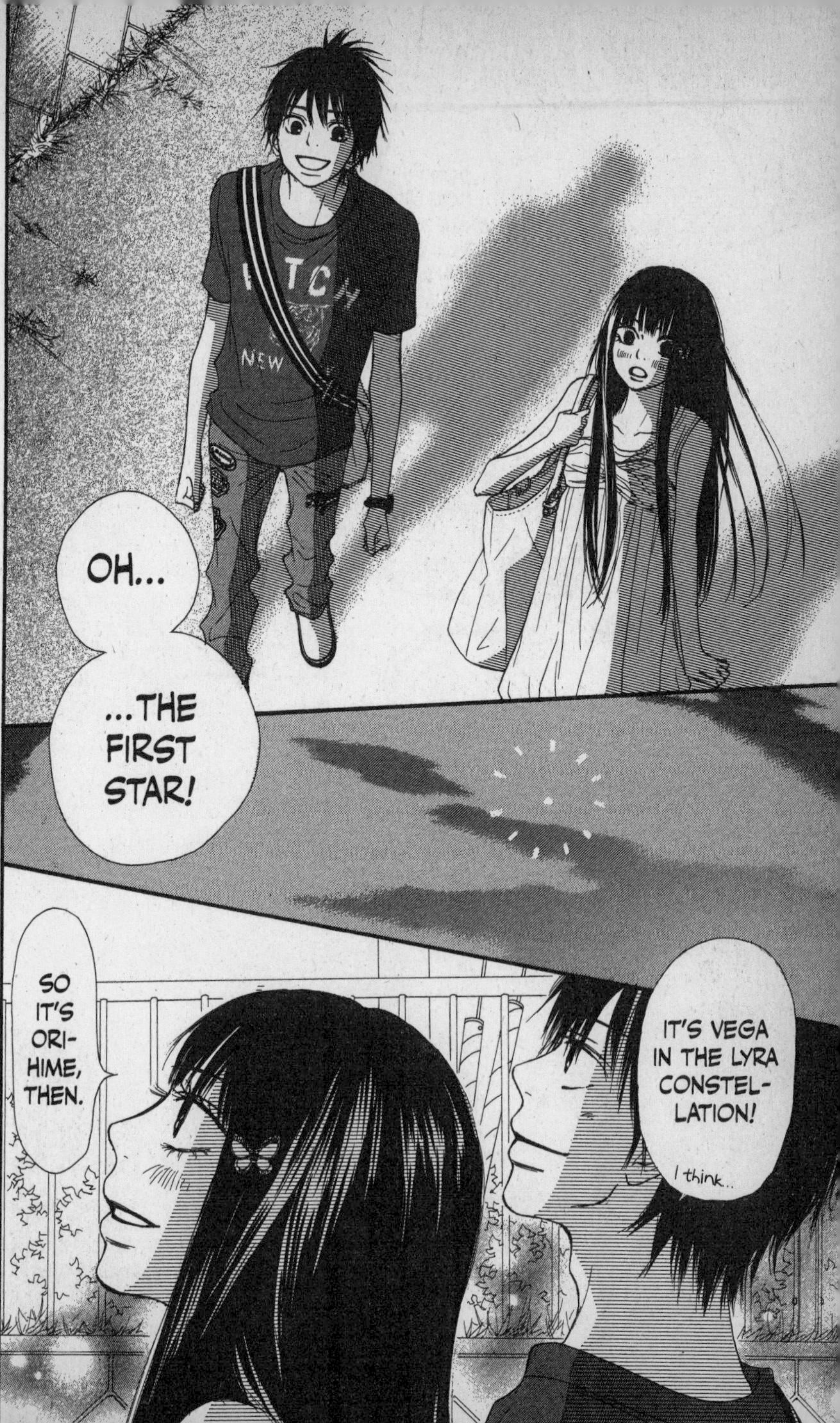
OH...
...THE FIRST STAR!
IT'S VEGA IN THE LYRA CONSTELLATION!
I think...
SO IT'S ORIHIME, THEN.

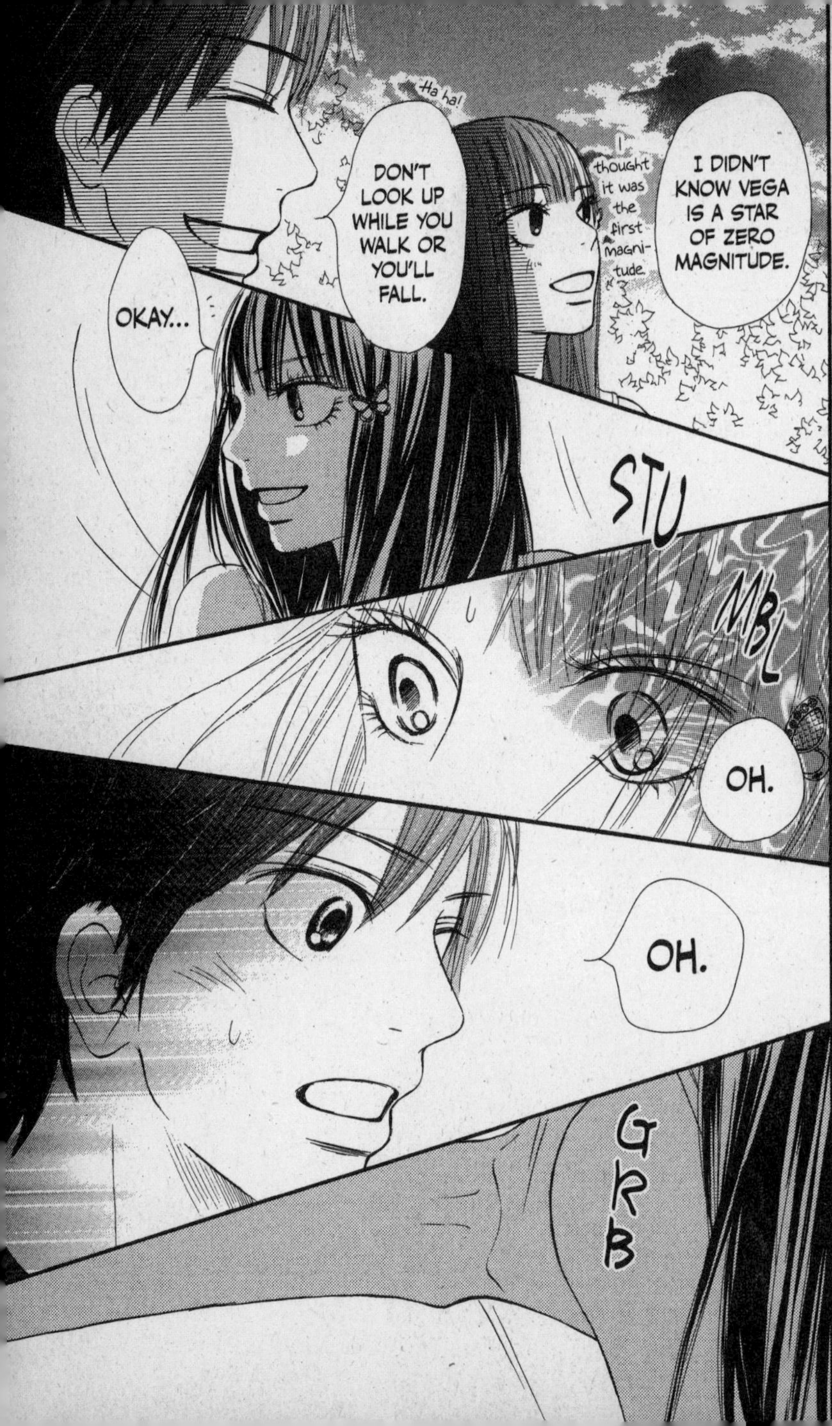
I DIDN'T KNOW VEGA IS A STAR OF ZERO MAGNITUDE.
I thought it was the first magnitude.
Ha ha!
DON'T LOOK UP WHILE YOU WALK OR YOU'LL FALL.
OKAY...
STU
MBL
OH.
OH.
GRB

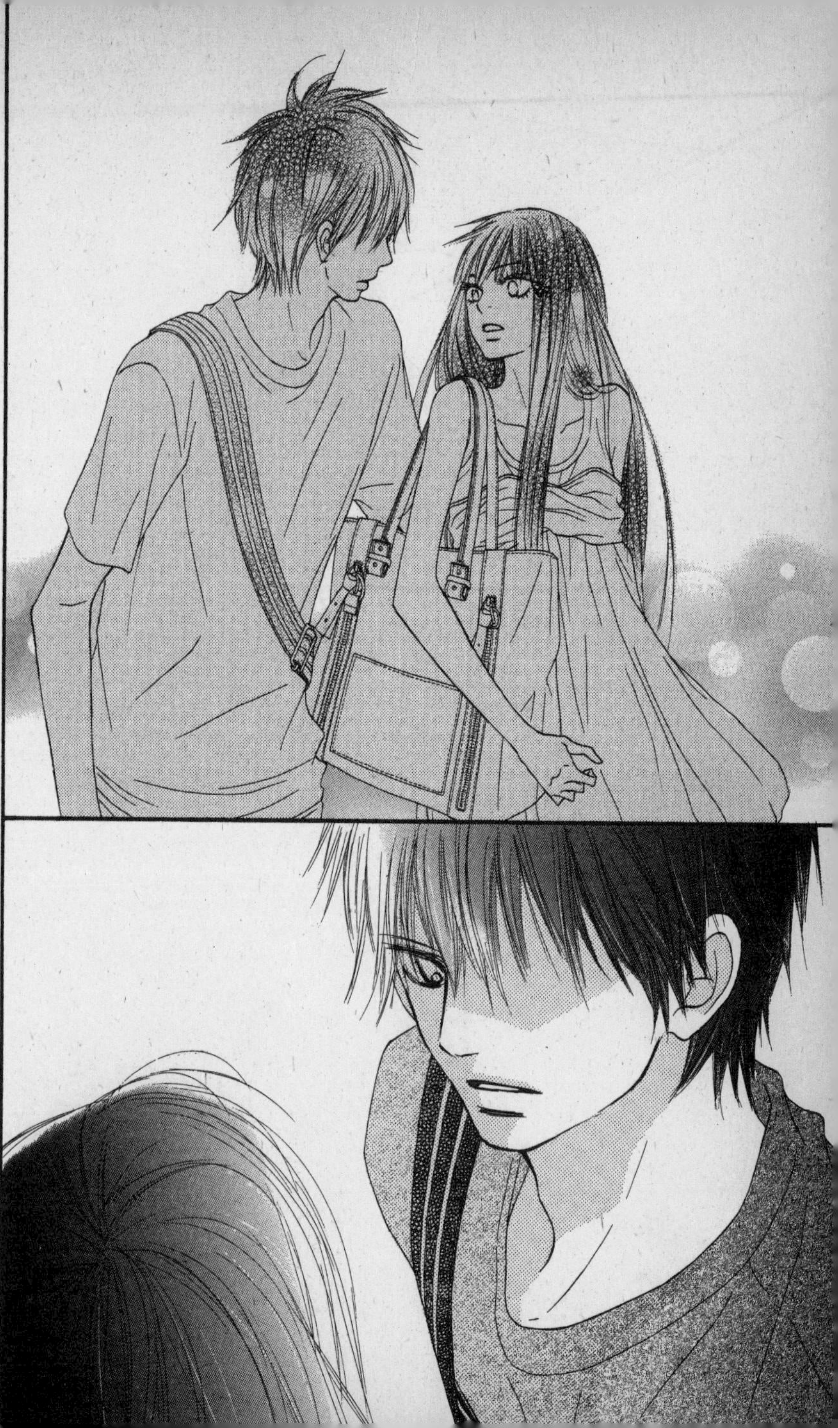

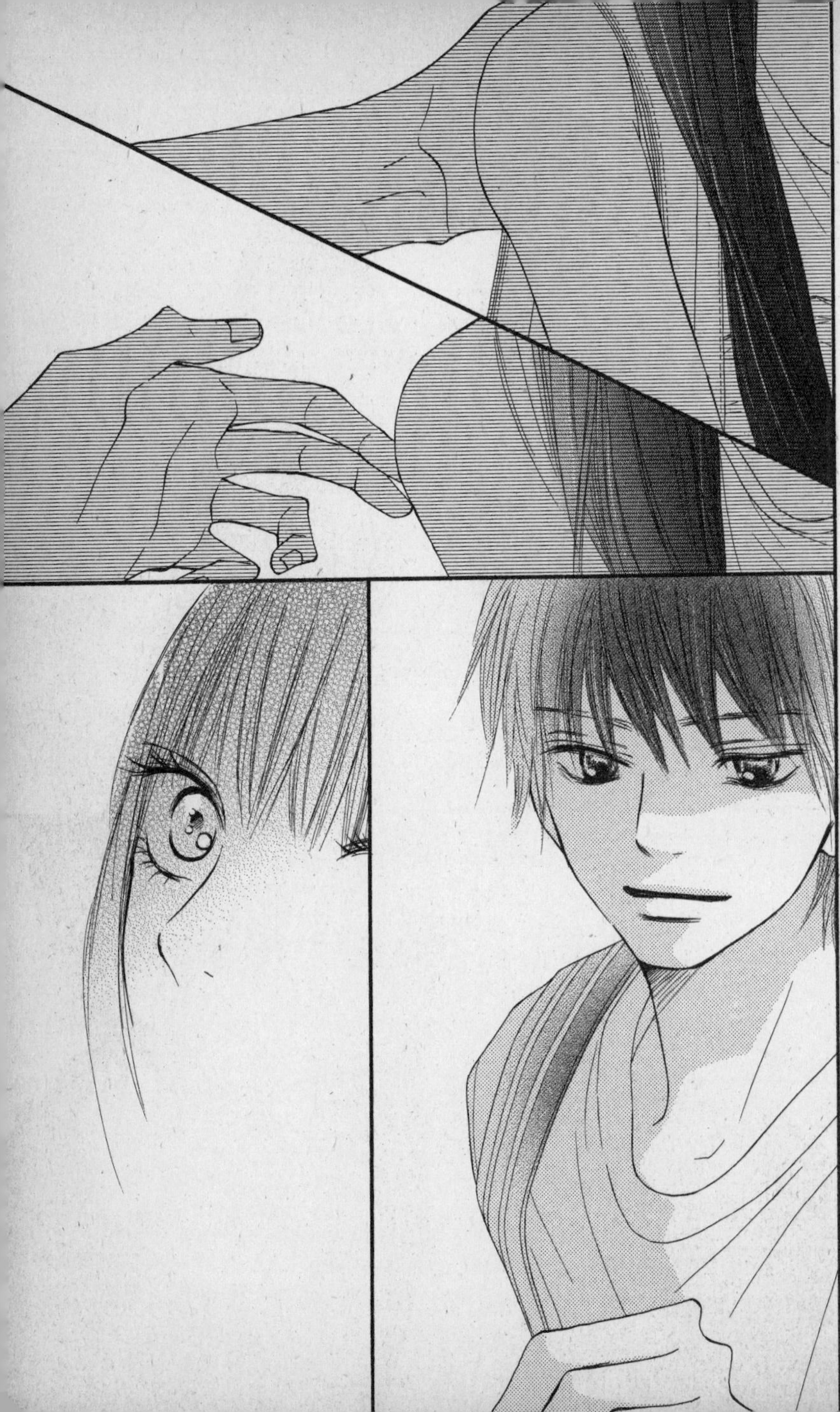

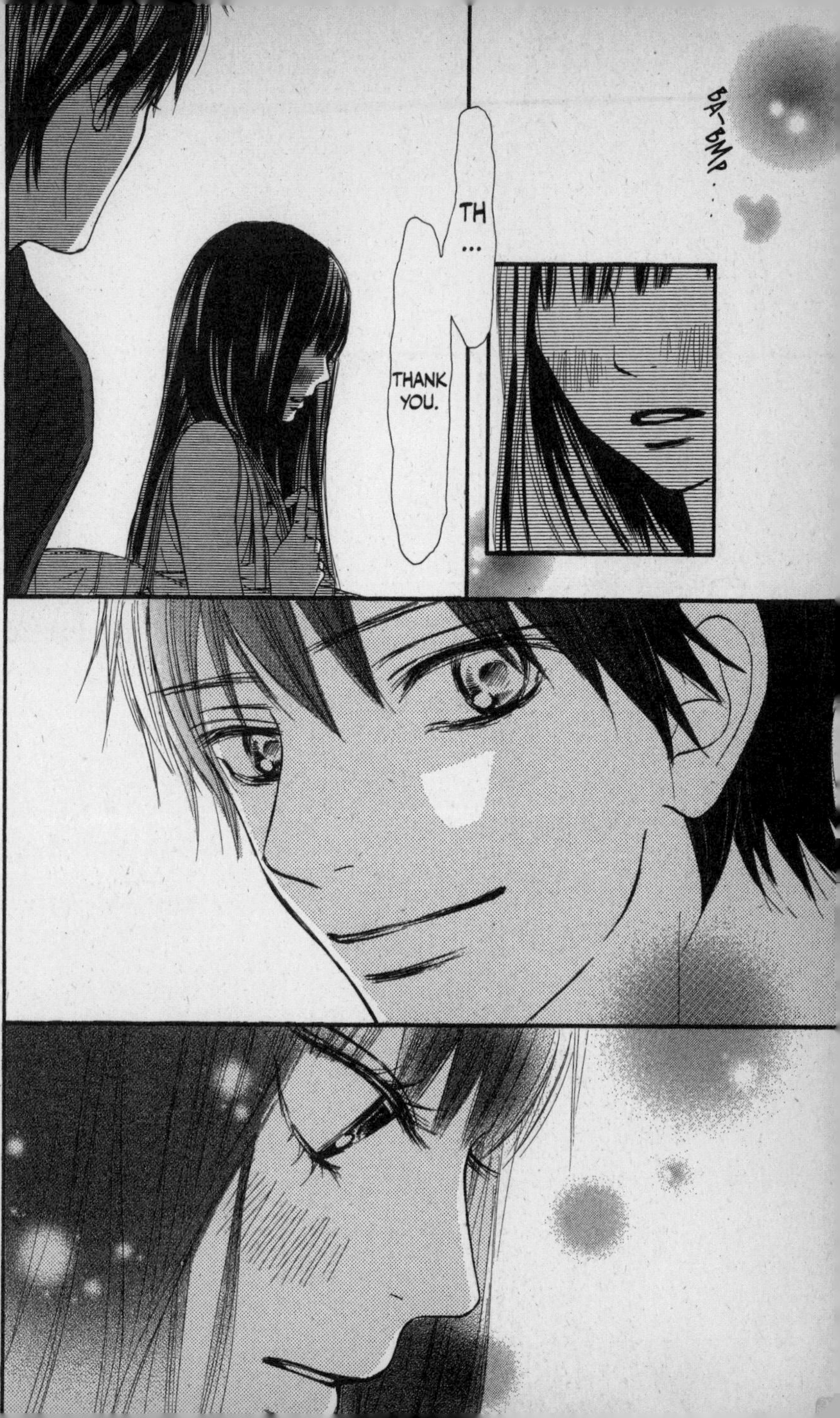
BA-BMP . .
TH ...
THANK YOU.

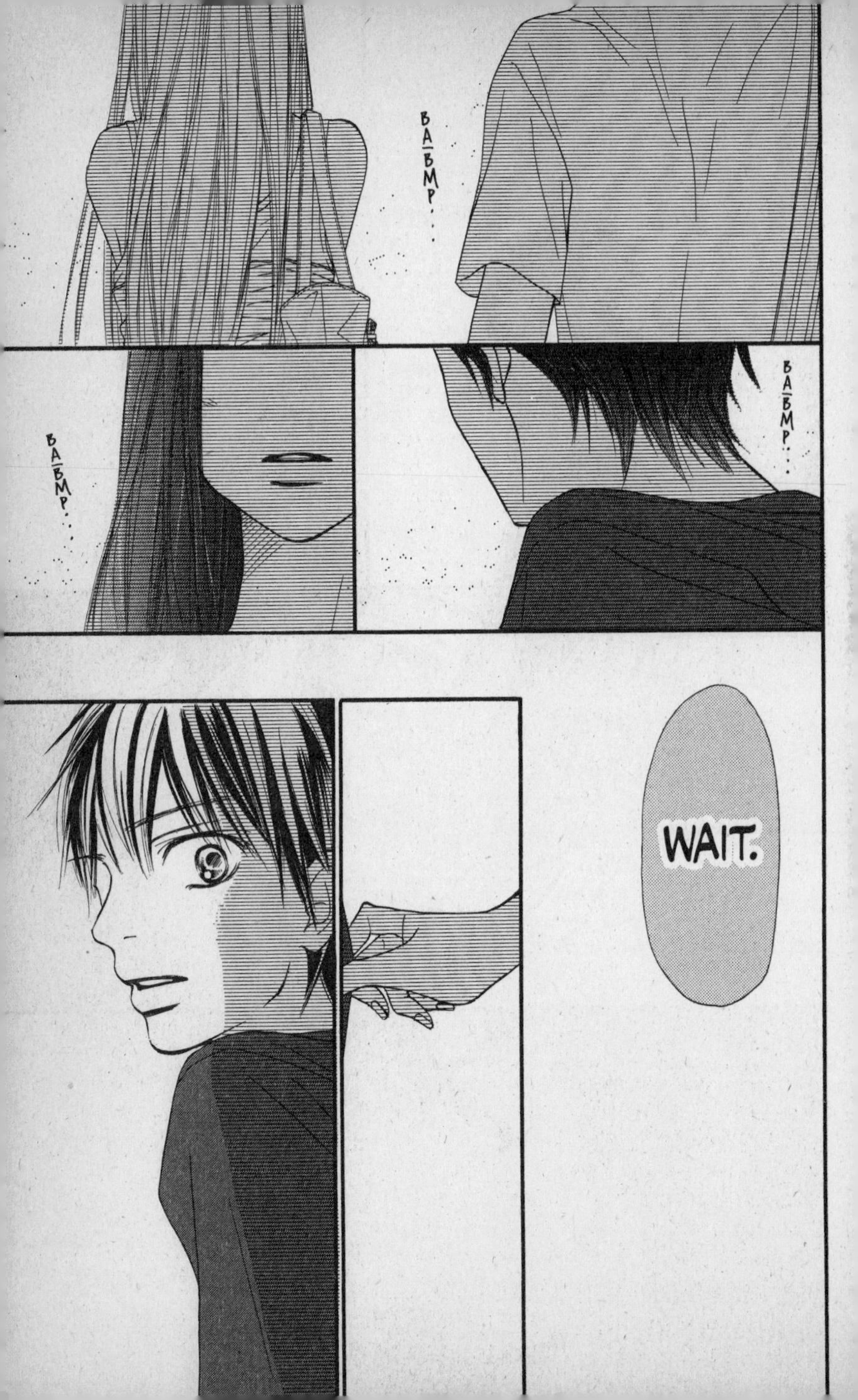

BA-BMP..
BA-BMP..
BA-BMP..
WAIT.

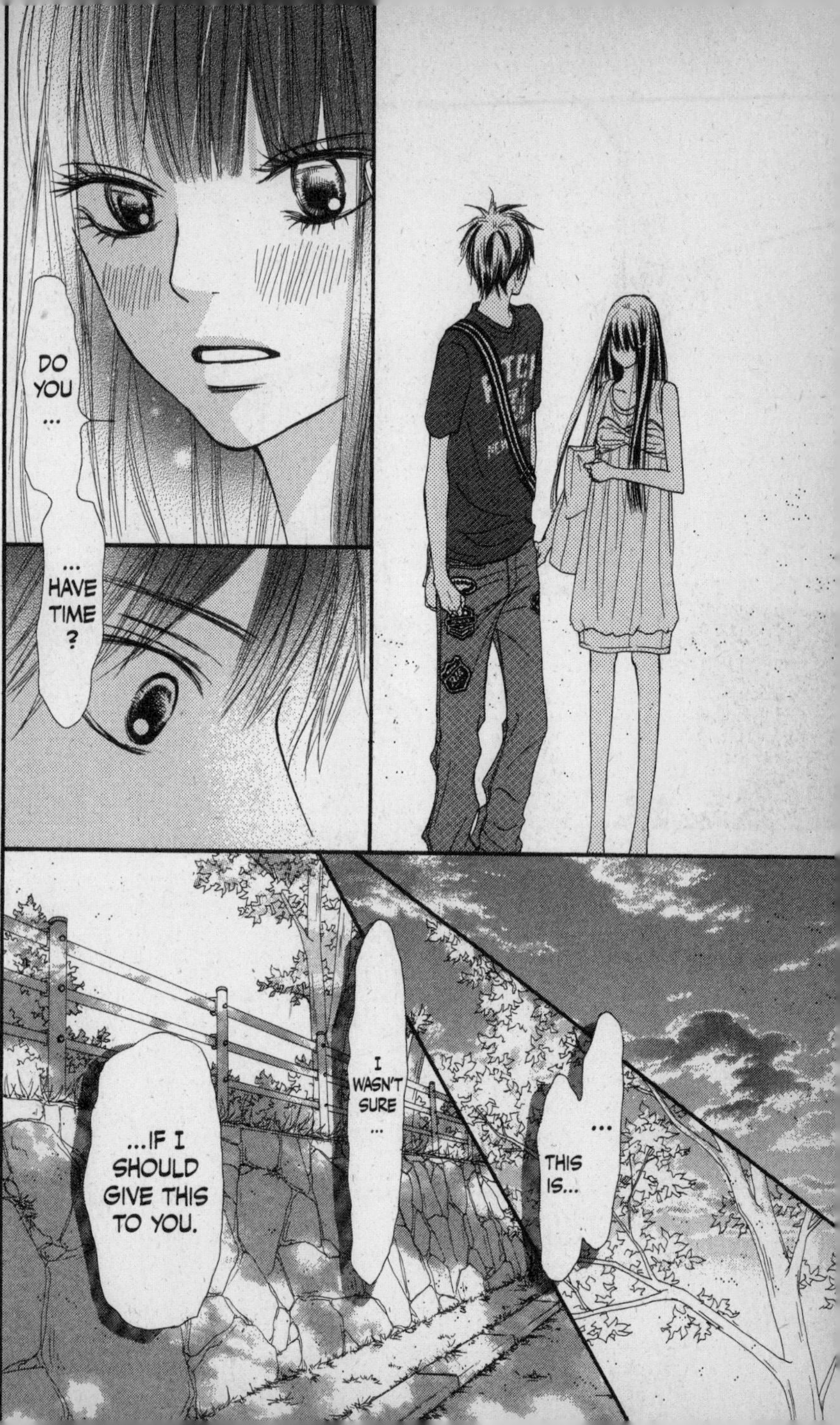
DO YOU ... ... HAVE TIME ?
... THIS IS...
I WASN'T SURE ...
...IF I SHOULD GIVE THIS TO YOU.

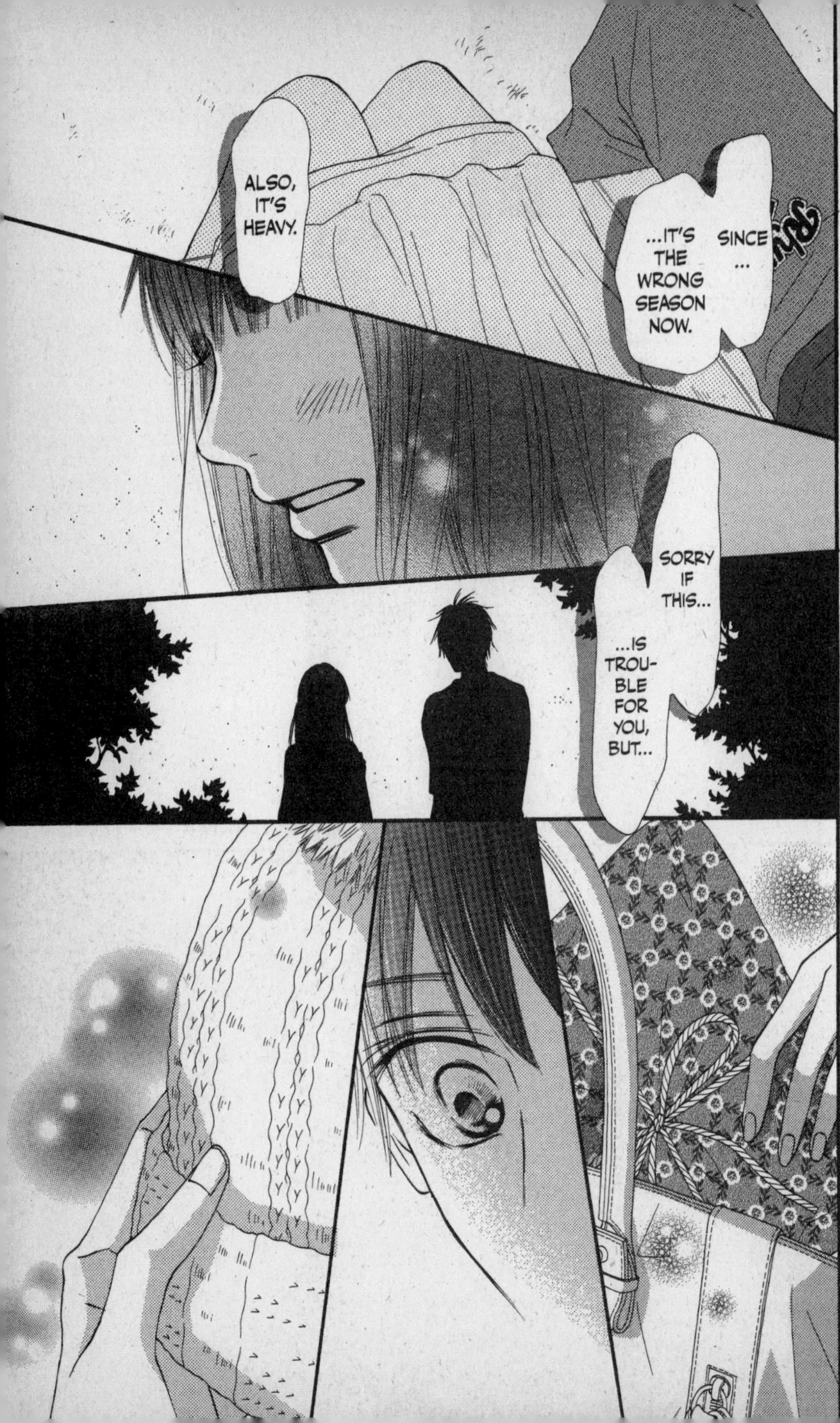
SINCE...
...IT'S THE WRONG SEASON NOW.
ALSO, IT'S HEAVY.
SORRY IF THIS...
...IS TROUBLE FOR YOU, BUT...

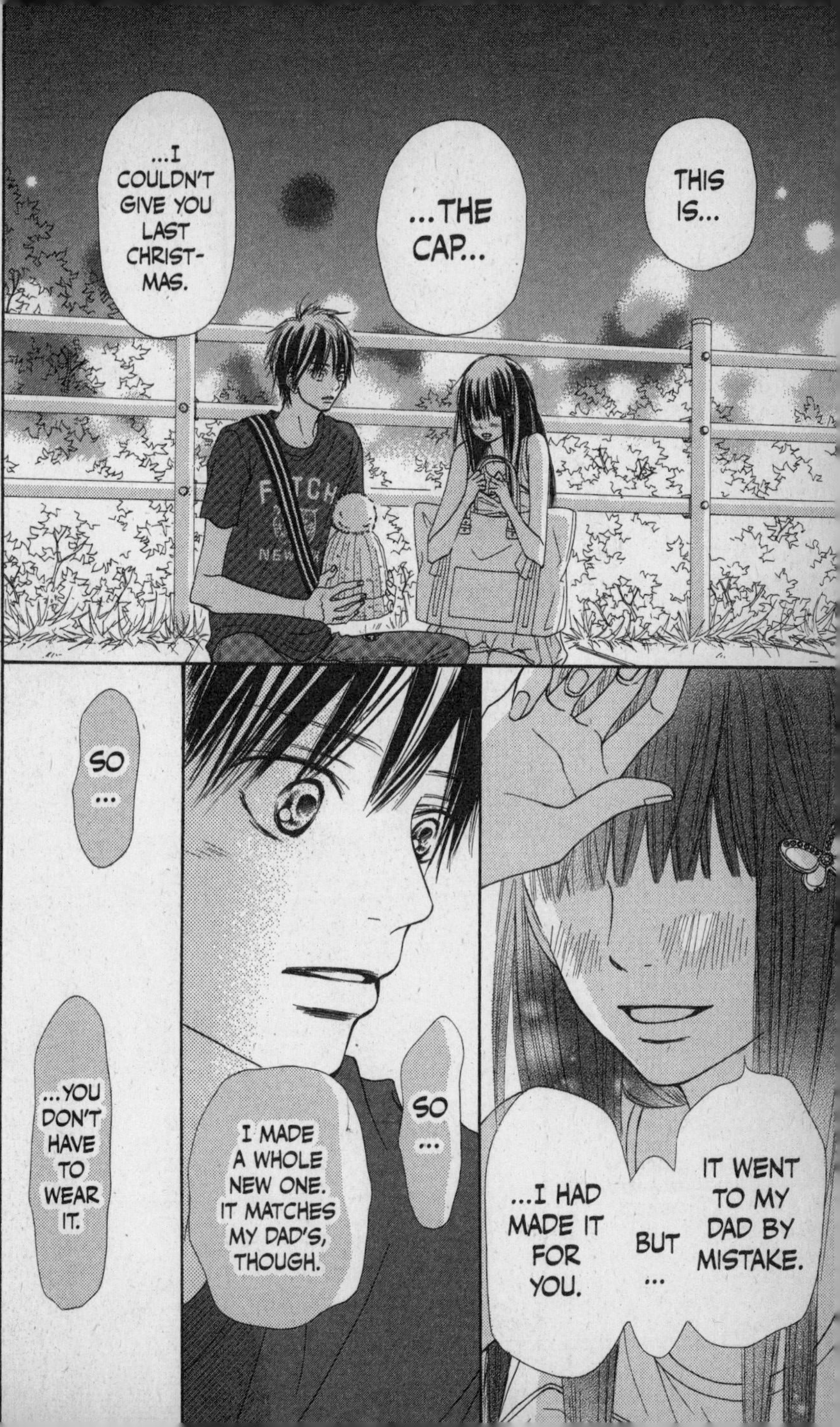
THIS IS...
...THE CAP...
...I COULDN'T GIVE YOU LAST CHRIST-MAS.
IT WENT TO MY DAD BY MISTAKE.
BUT ...
...I HAD MADE IT FOR YOU.
SO ...
I MADE A WHOLE NEW ONE. IT MATCHES MY DAD'S, THOUGH.
SO ...
...YOU DON'T HAVE TO WEAR IT.

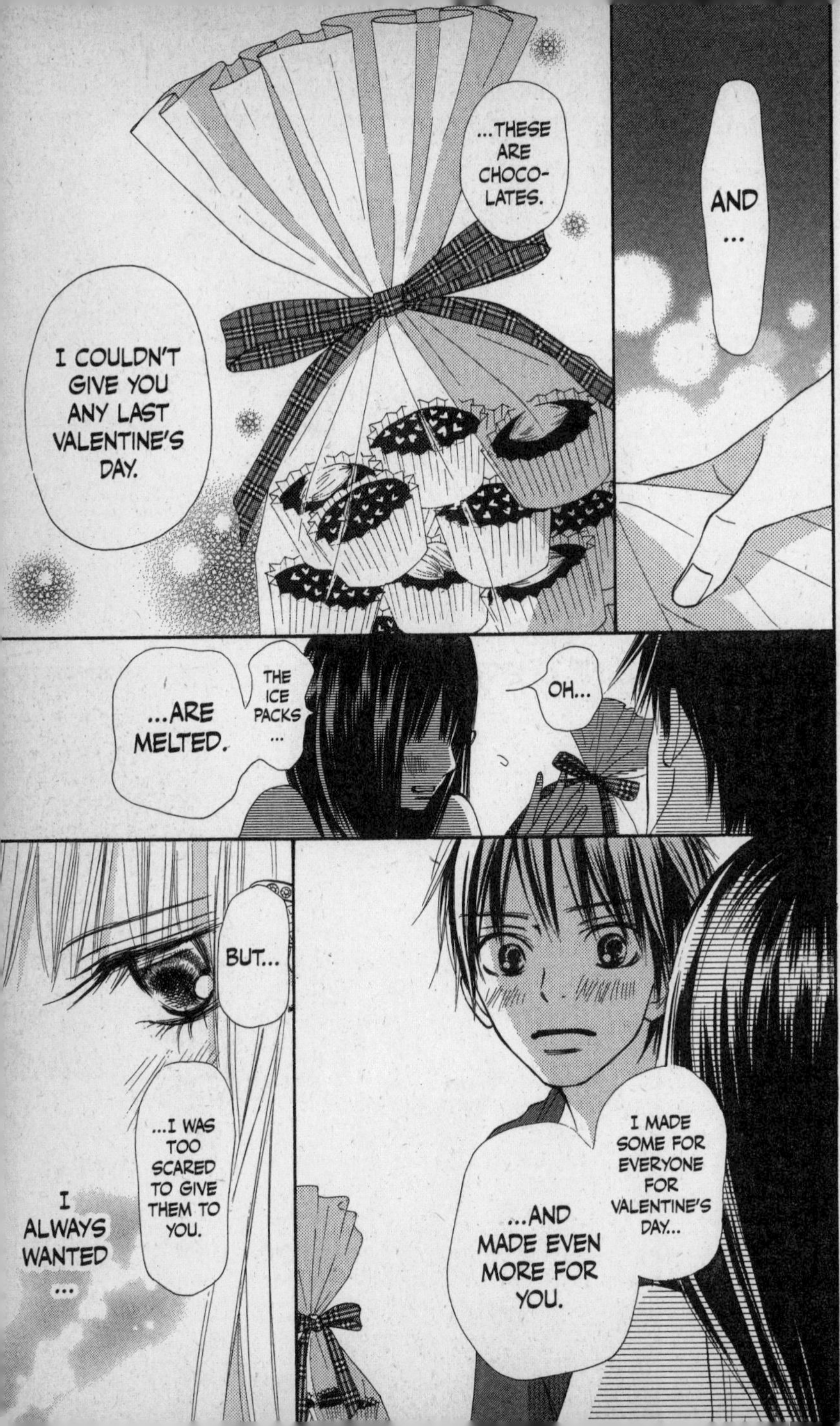
AND ...
...THESE ARE CHOCO-LATES.
I COULDN'T GIVE YOU ANY LAST VALENTINE'S DAY.
OH...
THE ICE PACKS ...
...ARE MELTED.
I MADE SOME FOR EVERYONE FOR VALENTINE'S DAY...
...AND MADE EVEN MORE FOR YOU.
BUT...
...I WAS TOO SCARED TO GIVE THEM TO YOU.
I ALWAYS WANTED ...

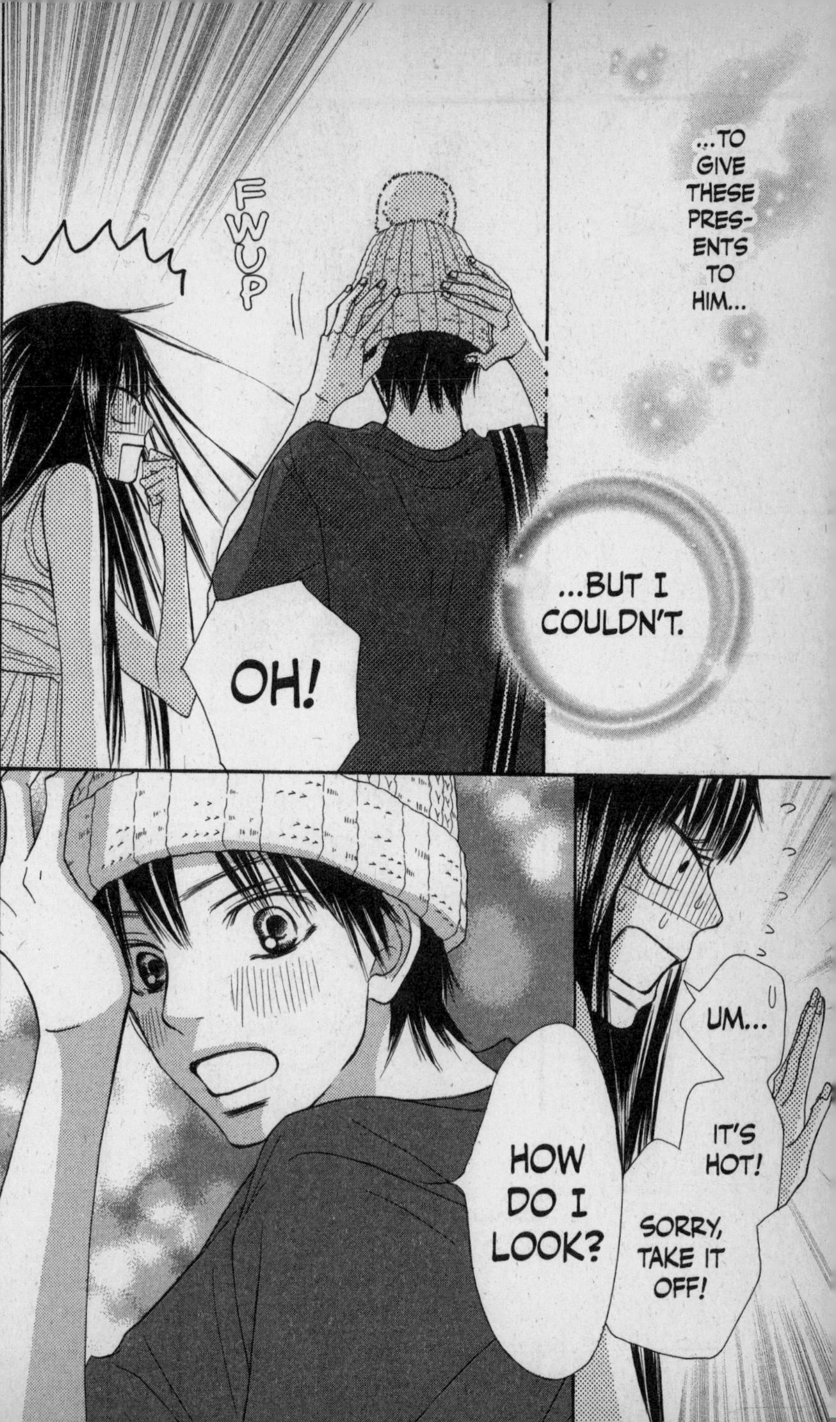
...TO GIVE THESE PRES- ENTS TO HIM...
...BUT I COULDN'T.
FWUP
OH!
UM...
IT'S HOT!
SORRY, TAKE IT OFF!
HOW DO I LOOK?

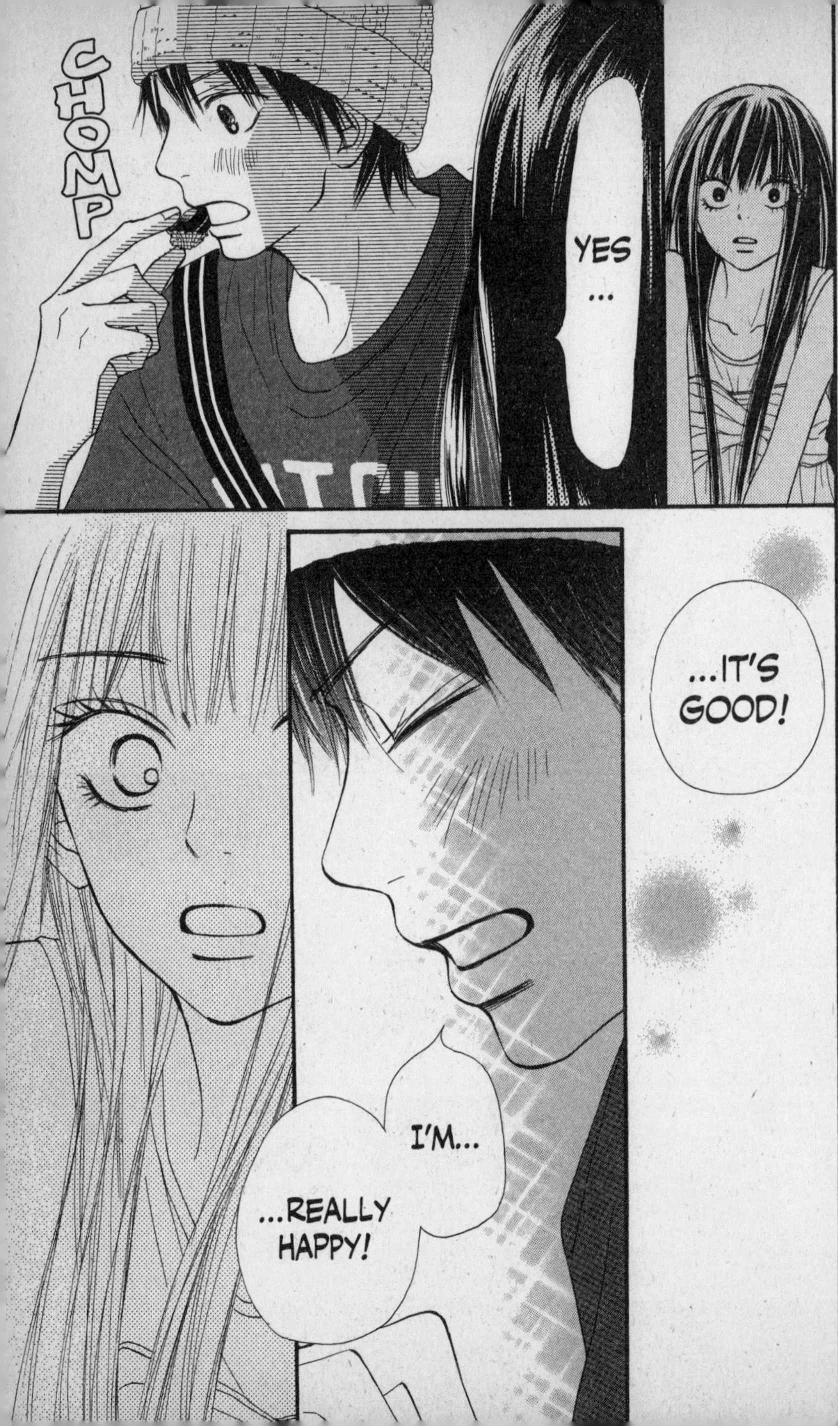
YES...
CHOMP
...IT'S GOOD!
I'M...
...REALLY HAPPY!

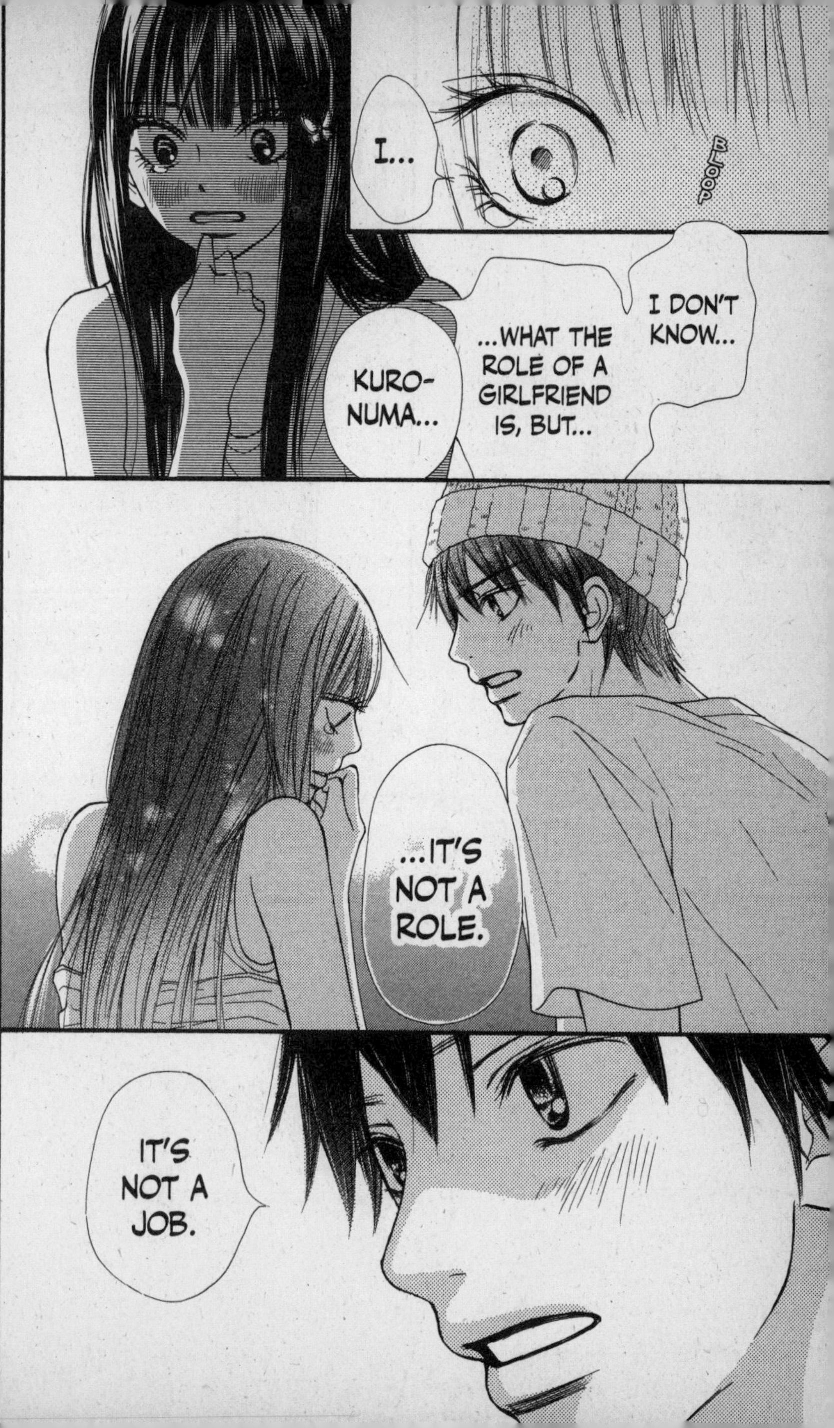
BLOOP
I...
I DON'T KNOW...
...WHAT THE ROLE OF A GIRLFRIEND IS, BUT...
KURO-NUMA...
...IT'S NOT A ROLE.
IT'S NOT A JOB.

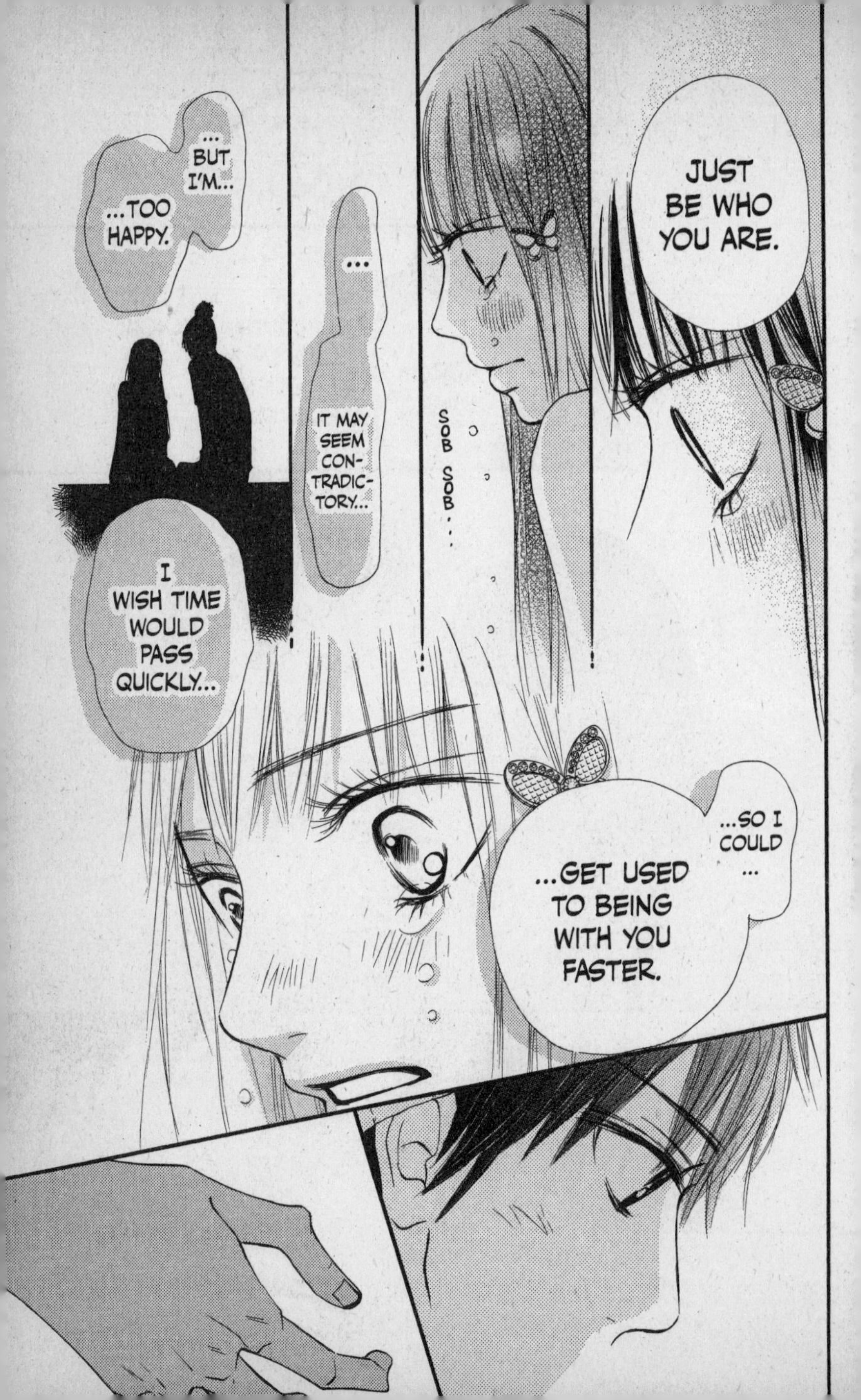
JUST BE WHO YOU ARE.
SOB SOB...
...
IT MAY SEEM CON-TRADIC-TORY...
...BUT I'M...
...TOO HAPPY.
I WISH TIME WOULD PASS QUICKLY...
...SO I COULD...
...GET USED TO BEING WITH YOU FASTER.

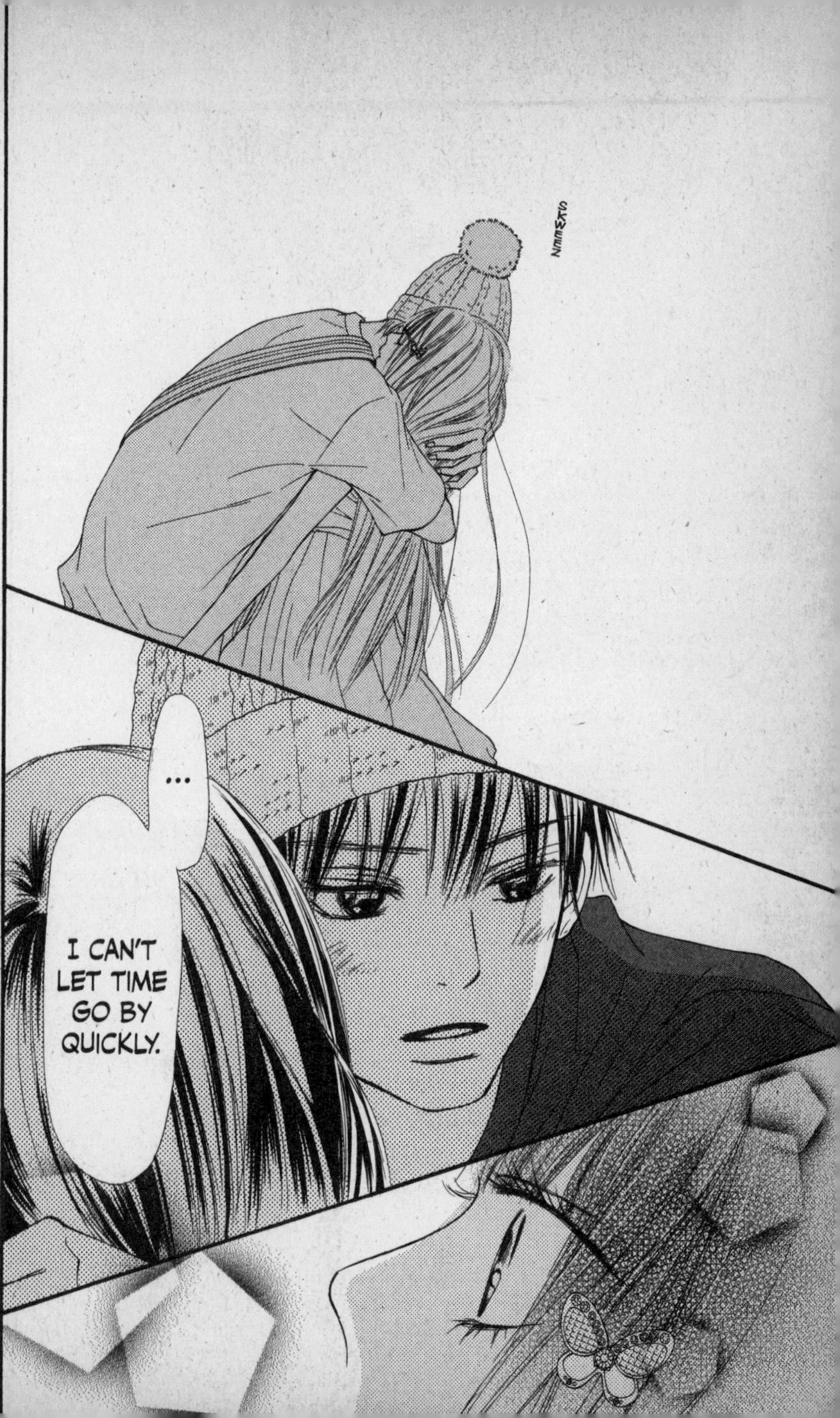
SKWEEN
...
I CAN'T LET TIME GO BY QUICKLY.

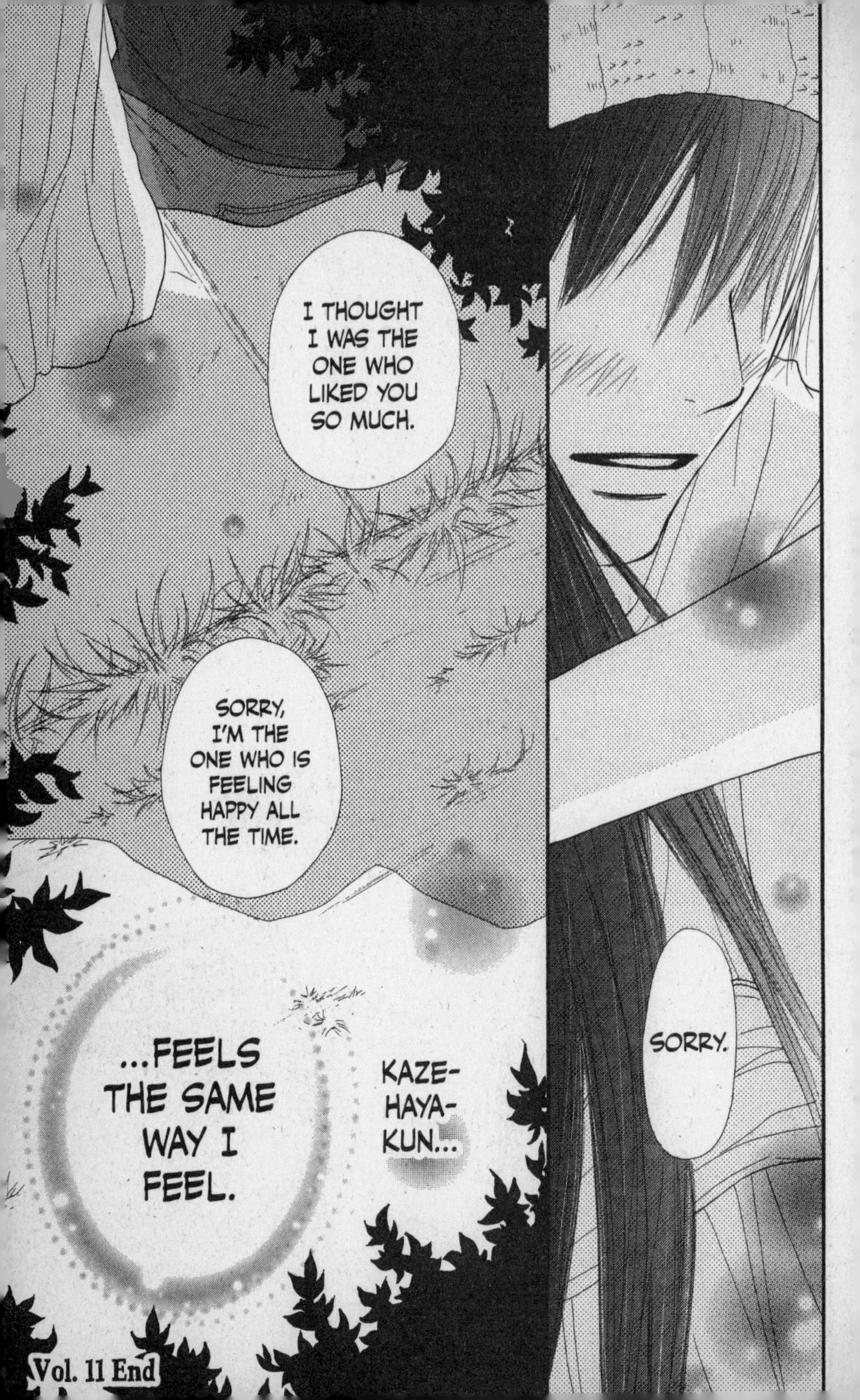
SORRY.
I THOUGHT I WAS THE ONE WHO LIKED YOU SO MUCH.
SORRY, I'M THE ONE WHO IS FEELING HAPPY ALL THE TIME.
KAZE-HAYA-KUN...
...FEELS THE SAME WAY I FEEL.
Vol. 11 End

From me (the editor) to you (the reader).

Here are some Japanese culture explanations that will help you better understand the references in the *Kimi ni Todoke* world.

Honorifics:
When saying someone's name in Japanese, a suffix is often attached to indicate how familiar the speaker is with the person. Some are more polite and respectful, while others are endearing. Calling someone by just their first name is the most informal.
-*kun* is used for young men or boys, usually someone you are familiar with.
-*chan* is used for young women, girls or young children and can be used as a term of endearment.
-*san* is used for someone you respect or are not close to, or to be polite.

Page 17, Golden Week:
One of Japan's busiest holiday seasons, with four national holidays within the seven-day period of April 29 to May 5.

Page 17, Mikako Tabe-chan and Haruma Miura-kun:
Mikako Tabe and Haruma Miura play Sawako and Kazehaya in the live-action film *Kimi ni Todoke*, which came out in Japan in 2010.

Page 55, fan book:
The *Kimi ni Todoke Fan Book* and volume 11 came out in June 2010 in Japan.

Page 62, haunted trail event:
In Japan, this type of spooky courage test game is called *kimodameshi*.

Page 118, oinarisan:
Also called *inarizushi*, *oinarisan* is sushi rice mixed with ingredients such as carrots and shiitake mushrooms, stuffed in a sweet, deep-fried tofu pouch.

Page 160, Orihime:
The Star Festival, on July 7, celebrates the meeting of Orihime (the star Vega) and Hikoboshi (the star Altair), lovers who are allowed to meet only once a year on this night. The rest of the year they are said to be separated by the Milky Way.

Right now, while I'm writing these comments, filming for the *Kimi ni Todoke* movie is underway. Unfortunately, I can't go watch, but my editor sends me photographs and tells me about the cast—and it all sounds cute and fun. Although I'm looking forward to the movie's opening, I'm going to be sad when it's all over. However, there's another fun plan in the works, so please look forward to it.

--Karuho Shiina

Karuho Shiina was born and raised in Hokkaido, Japan. Though *Kimi ni Todoke* is only her second series following many one-shot stories, it has already racked up accolades from various "Best Manga of the Year" lists. Winner of the 2008 Kodansha Manga Award for the shojo category, *Kimi ni Todoke* also placed fifth in the first-ever Manga Taisho (Cartoon Grand Prize) contest in 2008. In Japan, an animated TV series debuted in October 2009, and a live-action film was released in 2010.

Kimi ni Todoke
VOL. 11

Shojo Beat Edition

STORY AND ART BY
KARUHO SHIINA

Translation/Ari Yasuda, HC Language Solutions, Inc.
Touch-up Art & Lettering/Vanessa Satone
Design/Nozomi Akashi
Editor/Carrie Shepherd

KIMI NI TODOKE © 2005 by Karuho Shiina
All rights reserved. First published in Japan in 2005 by SHUEISHA Inc.,
Tokyo. English translation rights arranged by SHUEISHA Inc.

Printed in Canada

Published by VIZ Media, LLC
P.O. Box 77010
San Francisco, CA 94107

10 9 8 7 6 5 4 3 2 1
First printing, November 2011

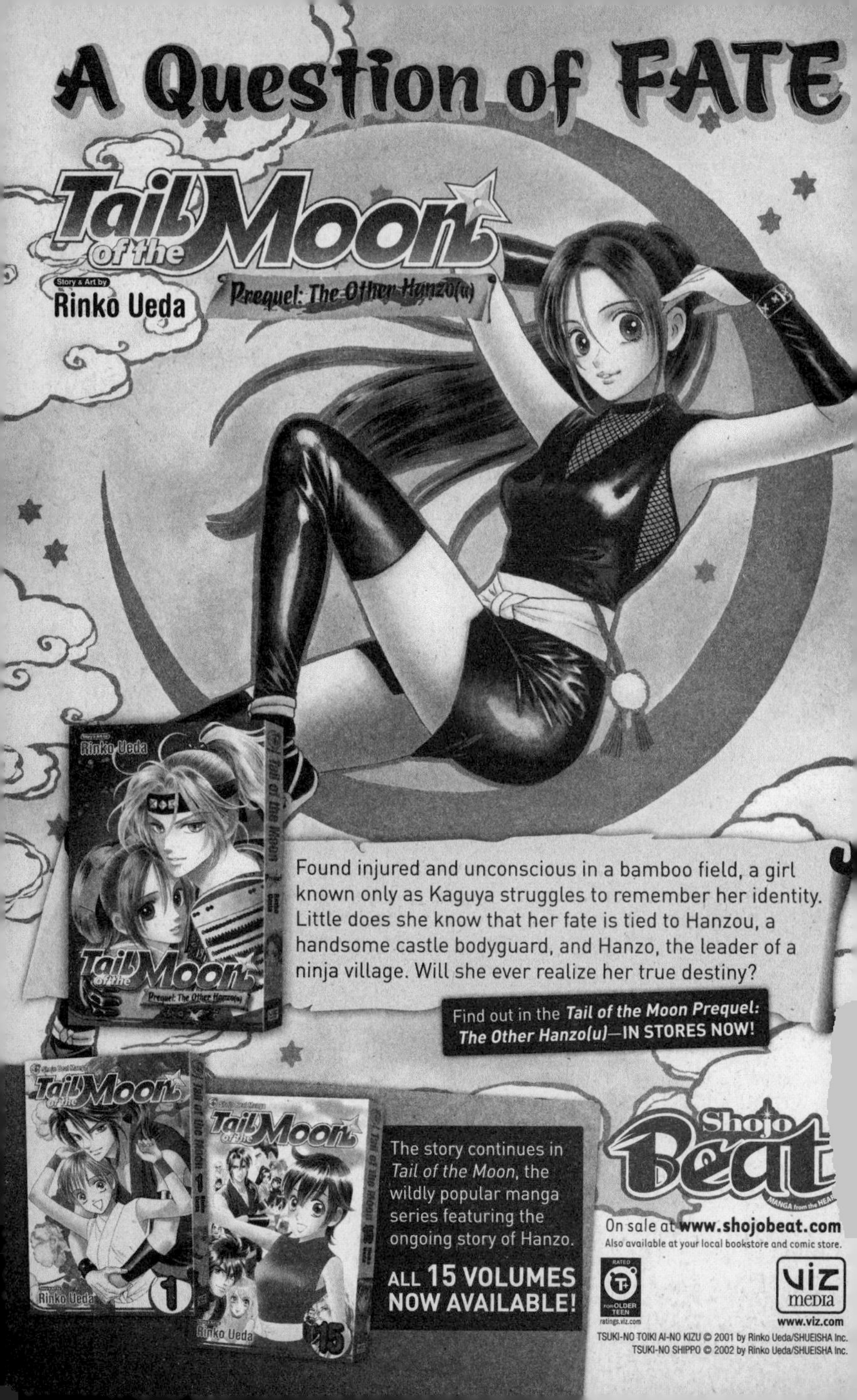
A Question of FATE
Tail of the Moon
Story & Art by
Rinko Ueda
Prequel: The Other Hanzo(u)
Found injured and unconscious in a bamboo field, a girl known only as Kaguya struggles to remember her identity. Little does she know that her fate is tied to Hanzou, a handsome castle bodyguard, and Hanzo, the leader of a ninja village. Will she ever realize her true destiny?
Find out in the Tail of the Moon Prequel: The Other Hanzo(u)—IN STORES NOW!
The story continues in Tail of the Moon, the wildly popular manga series featuring the ongoing story of Hanzo.
ALL 15 VOLUMES NOW AVAILABLE!
Shojo Beat
MANGA from the HEART
On sale at www.shojobeat.com
Also available at your local bookstore and comic store.
RATED T+ FOR OLDER TEEN
ratings.viz.com
viz media
www.viz.com
TSUKI-NO TOIKI AI-NO KIZU © 2001 by Rinko Ueda/SHUEISHA Inc.
TSUKI-NO SHIPPO © 2002 by Rinko Ueda/SHUEISHA Inc.

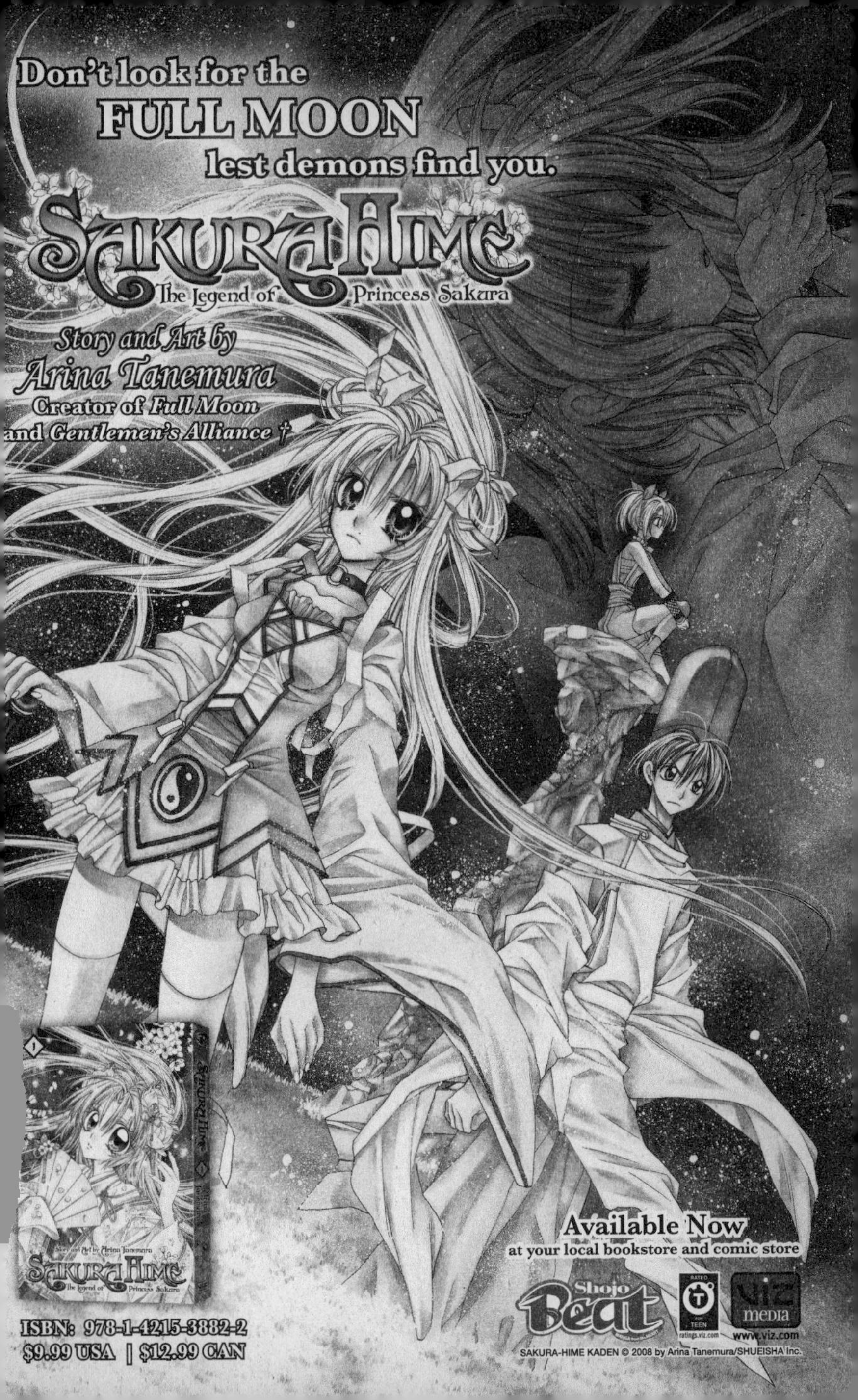
Don't look for the
FULL MOON
lest demons find you.
SAKURA HIME
The Legend of Princess Sakura
Story and Art by
Arina Tanemura
Creator of Full Moon
and Gentlemen's Alliance †
ISBN: 978-1-4215-3882-2
$9.99 USA | $12.99 CAN
Available Now
at your local bookstore and comic store
Shojo Beat
RATED T FOR TEEN
ratings.viz.com
VIZ media
www.viz.com
SAKURA-HIME KADEN © 2008 by Arina Tanemura/SHUEISHA Inc.